STYLISTIC VIRTUE AND VIC'

What is style, and why does it matter? This book answers these questions by recovering the concept of "stylistic virtue," once foundational to rhetoric and aesthetics but largely forgotten today. Stylistic virtues like "ease" and "grace" are distinguishing properties that help realize a text's essential character. First described by Aristotle, they were integral to the development of formalist methods and modern literary criticism. The first half of the book excavates the theory of stylistic virtue during its period of greatest ascendance, in the late eighteenth and nineteenth centuries, when belletristic rhetoric shaped how the art of literary style and "the aesthetic" were understood. The second half offers new readings of Thackeray, Trollope, and Meredith to show how stylistic virtue changes our understanding of style in the novel and challenges conventional approaches to interpreting the ethics of art.

MATTHEW SUSSMAN is a lecturer in the Department of English at the University of Sydney.

CAMBRIDGE STUDIES IN NINETEENTH-CENTURY LITERATURE AND CULTURE

Nineteenth-century literature and culture have proved a rich field for interdisciplinary studies. Since 1994, books in this series have tracked the intersections and tensions between Victorian literature and the visual arts, politics, gender and sexuality, race, social organisation, economic life, technical innovations, scientific thought – in short, culture in its broadest sense. Many of our books are now classics in a field which since the series' inception has seen powerful engagements with Marxism, feminism, visual studies, post-colonialism, critical race studies, new historicism, new formalism, transnationalism, queer studies, human rights and liberalism, disability studies, and global studies. Theoretical challenges and historiographical shifts continue to unsettle scholarship on the nineteenth century in productive ways. New work on the body and the senses, the environment and climate, race and the decolonisation of literary studies, biopolitics and materiality, the animal and the human, the local and the global, politics and form, queerness and gender identities, and intersectional theory is re-animating the field. This series aims to accommodate and promote the most interesting work being undertaken on the frontiers of nineteenth-century literary studies, connecting the field with the urgent critical questions that are being asked today. We seek to publish work from a diverse range of authors, and stand for anti-racism, anti-colonialism and against discrimination in all forms.

A complete list of titles published will be found at the end of the book.

STYLISTIC VIRTUE AND VICTORIAN FICTION

Form, Ethics, and the Novel

MATTHEW SUSSMAN
The University of Sydney

CAMBRIDGE
UNIVERSITY PRESS

CAMBRIDGE
UNIVERSITY PRESS

Shaftesbury Road, Cambridge CB2 8EA, United Kingdom

One Liberty Plaza, 20th Floor, New York, NY 10006, USA

477 Williamstown Road, Port Melbourne, VIC 3207, Australia

314–321, 3rd Floor, Plot 3, Splendor Forum, Jasola District Centre, New Delhi – 110025, India

103 Penang Road, #05–06/07, Visioncrest Commercial, Singapore 238467

Cambridge University Press is part of Cambridge University Press & Assessment, a department of the University of Cambridge.

We share the University's mission to contribute to society through the pursuit of education, learning and research at the highest international levels of excellence.

www.cambridge.org
Information on this title: www.cambridge.org/9781108965903

DOI: 10.1017/9781108966436

First published 2021
First paperback edition 2024

A catalogue record for this publication is available from the British Library

Library of Congress Cataloging-in-Publication data
NAMES: Sussman, Matthew, author.
TITLE: Stylistic virtue and Victorian fiction : form, ethics and the novel / Matthew Sussman.
DESCRIPTION: Cambridge, United Kingdom ; New York, NY : Cambridge University Press, 2021. | Series: Cambridge studies in nineteenth-century literature and culture | Includes bibliographical references and index.
IDENTIFIERS: LCCN 2021000598 (print) | LCCN 2021000599 (ebook) | ISBN 9781108832946 (hardback) | ISBN 9781108965903 (paperback) | ISBN 9781108966436 (ebook)
SUBJECTS: LCSH: English fiction – 19th century – History and criticism. | English language – Style. | English language – Rhetoric. | England – Intellectual life – 19th century. | BISAC: LITERARY CRITICISM / European / English, Irish, Scottish, Welsh | LITERARY CRITICISM / European / English, Irish, Scottish, Welsh
CLASSIFICATION: LCC PR878.S78 S87 2021 (print) | LCC PR878.S78 (ebook) | DDC 823/.80934–dc23
LC record available at https://lccn.loc.gov/2021000598
LC ebook record available at https://lccn.loc.gov/2021000599

ISBN 978-1-108-83294-6 Hardback
ISBN 978-1-108-96590-3 Paperback

Contents

Illustrations

Acknowledgments

This book could not have been written without the support of numerous people and institutions. At Harvard, I am profoundly grateful for the unwavering beneficence of Helen Vendler and the generous mentorship of Philip Fisher, Marjorie Garber, and Leah Price. Whatever virtues I possess as a scholar I owe to this formidable team, whose critical excellence sets the lasting standard for my own. For other insight and encouragement, I thank Amanda Claybaugh, Jim Engell, Luke Menand, Elaine Scarry, and James Simpson, and, for workshopping early drafts, members of the British Literature Colloquium, the Mahindra Humanities Center, and the American Academy of Arts and Sciences, especially Patricia Meyer Spacks.

Warm and supportive colleagues have made the University of Sydney a propitious environment for research. I am deeply grateful to John Frow, whose indispensable guidance rescued this project from paralysis and spurred it toward completion, and Helen Small, from Oxford, whose assiduous feedback and editing substantially improved the manuscript. I owe a large debt to Bruce Gardiner, Sean Pryor, and Vanessa Smith for their helpful comments (among other kind words) on the completed draft. For their interest and inspiration, I also thank Mark Byron, Anthony Cordingley, Paul Giles, Sarah Gleeson-White, Margaret Harris, Martijn Konings, David Larkin, Peter Marks, Olivia Murphy, Nicola Parsons, Liam Semler, and Elisabeth Valiente-Riedl.

Along the way, this project has benefited enormously from the input of energetic colleagues. For their love of style, and the style of their scholarship, I thank Jonathan Farina and Daniel Tyler. For helpful advice and other contributions, I thank Joseph Bristow, Ella Dzelzainis, Lauren Goodlad, Benjy Kahan, J. Hillis Miller, Catherine Robson, Jason Rudy, David Russell, Jonah Siegel, and Nikki Skillman. I was lucky enough to benefit from the first-rate research assistance of Alix Beeston, now thriving in her own academic career, as well as an engaging network of fellow scholars in the Interdisciplinary Nineteenth-Century Study Group at the University of Sydney. At Cambridge University Press, Bethany Thomas, Katie Idle, and Victoria Parrin have shepherded this project with a happy combination of kindness and efficiency.

No manner of flourishing would be possible without the support of a loving family. I wish to thank my parents, Fern and Jackie, for teaching me to savor the pleasures of imagination and analysis in equal measure; my sister Jillian and her family, who always knew when (and when not) to ask about "the book"; and my grandparents, now dearly missed. To my wife, Lili, I am most indebted, for love, courage, intellectual comradery, and joy. I dedicate this book to her.

—

Portions of Chapter 2 were originally published as "Stylistic Virtue in Nineteenth-Century Criticism," *Victorian Studies* 56.2 (Winter 2014): 225–49. Portions of Chapter 5 were originally published as "Trollope's Honesty," *Studies in English Literature 1500–1900* 53.4 (Autumn 2013): 877–95. I am grateful for permission to reprint.

INTRODUCTION

What Is Stylistic Virtue?

One of the more estranging features of Victorian literary criticism is the widespread use of a virtue-based vocabulary for the description and interpretation of texts. At best, words such as "manly," "delicate," "lucid," "sincere," and "sweet" strike the modern ear as suggestive but insufficiently technical, while more troublingly, they imply the substitution of biographical content for the detailed analysis of form. For example, in his 1885 essay "Style in Literature," John Dennis praises Henry Fielding's style as "natural, vigorous, idiomatic,"[1] which might describe an affinity for plainspoken, unornamented speech. But rather than root his judgments in the observable features of a novel, Dennis continually explicates them through reference to Fielding's actual personality. Arguing from the premise that the "style proclaims the man" (74), Dennis notes that Fielding's "manliness is to be seen in his biography, and so also is the taint of vulgarity and coarseness" (74). His style, consequently, is "devoid of weakness and affectation" and yet "more homely than refined" – a literal embodiment of "its master" (75).

The biographical reductionism of Victorian stylistic criticism (along with much literary criticism before it) has helped give it a reputation for formal obtuseness, evidence of an aesthetically naïve "impressionism" that ought to be repudiated.[2] As John Guillory writes, stylistics remains "merely impressionistic" – that is, unsubstantiated and imprecise – when it attempts "to characterize style by means of figurative language, for example, by words such as 'curt'"[3] or, in this case, "natural" and "manly." However, the characterological terms of Victorian stylistic criticism often did double duty as descriptors with more precise, formalistic meanings – a mode of signification that has long been acknowledged in less obviously representational fields such as music.[4] For example, in a review of Thackeray's *Henry Esmond* (1852), George Brimley celebrates the style as "manly, clear, terse, and vigorous," not because the author was homely or truthful but because he "knows what he means to say, and does not give the public thoughts half-worked-out, or thoughts on matters where clear thinking is impossible."[5] In contrast to Dennis, Brimley draws on the non-biographical meaning of "manly" as it appears in classical and eighteenth-century rhetorical manuals, where it describes the strength of style that results from forthright and deliberate argument. As Hugh Blair writes of Jonathan Swift in his *Lectures on Rhetoric and Belles Lettres* (1783), "His style is of the plain and simple kind; free of all affectation and all superfluity; perspicuous, manly, and pure."[6] To be sure, the word "manly" could be equally used to denote the gentlemanly status of an author or the representation of masculinity within a work. But Brimley and Blair's use of the word is more technical than literal, referring to a style of presentation that exists apart from the personal history of an author or the subject matter he represents.[7]

For another example of this terminological double valence, consider the word "chaste" as it was used in the controversy over Algernon Charles Swinburne's "fleshly" poetry. In his scathing review of *Poems and Ballads* (1866), John Morley attacked Swinburne for possessing a genius turned "exclusively in the direction of libidinous song."[8] Whereas, Morley writes, "the Greek poets in their most impetuous moods never allowed themselves to be carried on by the swing of words" (146), Swinburne provides passion without sobriety, engendering poems of "hot lustfulness . . . aflame with the feverish carnality of the schoolboy" (145). For his part, Swinburne defends his style by animating the alternative meanings within Morley's own condemnatory lexicon. "Treated in the grave and chaste manner as a serious 'thing of beauty,'" he writes of the statue in "Hermaphroditus," "it can give no offence but to the purblind and the prurient."[9] Here, Swinburne uses the word "chaste" not in its moral sense of celibate or sexually pure, but as Quintilian does in the eighth book of the *Institutio Oratoria*, as *sanctus*,[10] to indicate a style of ornamentation that is "natural and unaffected" rather than "artificial" (8.Pr.19). Swinburne concludes by averring that "adult art" is neither "puerile nor feminine, but virile," being "noble and chaste in the wider masculine sense" (23), once again echoing Quintilian's injunction that "healthy" ornament be "manly, strong, and chaste" to achieve "health and vigour" (8.3.6–7). Through this strategic use of the classical stylistic lexicon, Swinburne was able to rebut accusations of formal (and not just personal) degeneracy.[11]

Clearly, two conceptions of style were circulating during the Victorian period: a referential or reductionist one, which envisions style as the embodiment of some predetermining material, and a more impersonal or autonomous one that ascribes to style an independent aesthetic character.[12]

Contents

Illustrations

Why, then, if virtue terms are so liable to lead to confusion between these two different conceptions of style, did they supply the interpretive vocabulary for both? The answer to this question lies at the heart of what "style" and "virtue" meant to a nineteenth-century audience and which it is the purpose of this book to recover. In literary contexts, we often think of style and virtue as opposed: style deals with the formal qualities of language and deportment, virtue with the moral qualities of characters or authors; style can be examined in relative isolation from a text's propositional content, virtue can only be considered with reference to a context for action. Consequently, approaches that yoke style and virtue together tend to be reductionist or moralistic in character, whether by delineating how stylistic choices reflect the overall "worldview" of a text or by revealing how different styles shape the moral imaginations of readers. These are compelling ways of thinking about style, which I shall consider in greater detail below, but they are not the focus of this book. Rather, I aim to show how style may be considered apart from the non-stylistic "content" of a text and yet still possess "virtues," understood, following Aristotle, as qualities that render it an excellent specimen of its kind. This generic conception of virtue can help us to see how style has uniquely aesthetic dimensions that are no less "ethical" for being so.

Though scarcely remembered today, stylistic virtues are, in fact, among our oldest rhetorical concepts. First defined by Aristotle, they refer to verbal properties, located in small-scale units such as the phrase or sentence, that constitute a distinguishing feature of a text. Because classical rhetoric presumes a speaker behind any communicative act, stylistic virtues have often been regarded as indices to the ethos, or character, of an author, conflating style as a literary form and style as an expression of the self (the referential conception). But stylistic virtues also encode a way of thinking about style that endows it with autonomous qualities that either do not express the self (whether that self is literal or "implied"), or else that express the self *exclusively* in relation to the production of aesthetic effects. An awareness of stylistic virtue in this second, autonomous sense helps substantiate aesthetic "impressions" that do not necessarily align with that which is delivered by other components of a text such as plot development, subject matter, character interaction, or thematic ideation – those larger-scale units of meaning that have long dominated criticism of the novel. Instead, they ask us to register the interpretive significance of a text's most ostentatiously non-mimetic features, in this way providing the foundations for more formalist approaches to fiction that are typically regarded as products of the twentieth century.[13]

At the same time, stylistic virtue remains an ethical category insofar as, within the framework of virtue theory, the aesthetic realization of character constitutes a substantive moral good. This idea, drawn from Aristotle and carried through the rhetorical tradition he initiated, widely influenced Victorian literature and culture and ultimately shifted the location of virtue from the production of style as the expression of individual genius to the appreciation of style as a meritorious act. If, as many writers argued, differences in character are inevitable and agreeable, and style is expressive of character, then the contemplation of style becomes a normative good linked to a range of values that have less to do with the expression of any *particular* stylistic character than with the fact that styles are expressive of character *per se*. In contrast to the philosophical tradition that sees aesthetic experience as either beyond ethics ("disinterested") or servile to it ("instrumental"), the union of "style" and "virtue" provides a new way of conceptualizing the ethical value of formalism, rooted not in the separation of art from life but rather in their unembarrassed contiguity.[14]

In its analysis of Victorian style, this book remains largely agnostic as to the actual effects of individual texts upon the virtues of writers or readers, nor does it attempt to argue what virtues (stylistic or otherwise) a text ought to contain or express. Rather, I use the concept of stylistic virtue to show how the verbal properties it traditionally addresses make an important but overlooked contribution to the ethos of prose fiction in ways that are best understood as formal or aesthetic, and (as a secondary claim) that they have ethical value for precisely this reason. To make this argument, which requires considerable historical excavation, the book is split into two halves. In the first part, I provide an intellectual history of stylistic virtue to clarify the major terms of the study (such as style, virtue, aesthetic, ethos, and character) and show how their formalist conjunction shaped an array of practices across rhetoric, criticism, and philosophy. While stylistic virtues may prove useful to further inquiries into poetry, my focus here is on their foundational but neglected role in constructing a "prosaics." In the second part, I use the recovery of what Caroline Levine calls an "historical heuristic"[15] – a portable way of reading rooted in the interpretive methods of the past – to provide revisionary readings of style in three major Victorian novelists. Although the writers I consider often draw on a well-established repertoire of stylistic virtues, my goal is not to revive an outdated vocabulary for its own sake. Rather, I use Victorian virtue terms as a way of understanding stylistic ethos more generally, elaborating a new and (I hope) workable methodology for conducting stylistic analysis and interpreting the meaning of style within a work.

Stylistic Virtue: A History

Today, the word "virtue" is typically associated with a pious moral culture and its rigid, theologically grounded codes of conduct – with the four cardinal virtues of temperance, prudence, courage, and justice, or the Mudie-esque imperative to inculcate virtuous habits in morally impressionable readers. But the word has a deeper history that underwrites this narrow usage, rooted in the Greek word *arete*, of which the Latin *virtus*, or "virtue," is a translation.[16] According to Aristotle, *arete* – also translated as "excellence," "strength," or "merit" – describes the quality of something that makes it good at what it is supposed to do.[17] For example, rods and cones are virtues of an eye because they allow it to discern color and light, while vision itself is a kind of virtue because "it is by the excellence of the eye that we see well" (*Ethics*, 1106a). Sometimes called the "function argument,"[18] this generic notion of virtue judges a property as "excellent" if it helps realize the inherent purpose, or *telos*, of the substance to which it belongs, whether it be a body part, a machine, a human being, or a literary text.

Aristotle first joins the words "style" and "virtue" in his *Art of Rhetoric*, where he uses the conjunction to describe verbal properties that are "excellent" because they contribute positively to the *telos* of a speech. As Aristotle puts it, "the first virtue of style is to be clear (since speech is a kind of indication; if it does not indicate clearly it will not be performing its function)" (1404b). Clarity is a virtue – a verbal property that is excellent and effective – because it makes a speech perspicuous to its audience, which helps it to achieve its desired effect. Subsequent rhetoricians followed Aristotle in locating style (*lexis*) at the level of the word or sentence, larger systems of organization being treated under other headings. As such, he laid the foundation for the central classical virtues of "propriety" (the style must match the subject matter), "purity" (sentences must be idiomatic and correct), and "beauty" or "ornateness" (the verbal qualities of a discourse must interest and please its hearers), along with several others.[19]

Present-day scholars are more likely to have encountered the term "virtue" through Aristotle's *Nicomachean Ethics*, where he uses the word *arete* to refer to the morally valuable traits of character that constitute a person's *eudaimonia*, or flourishing. *Eudaimonia* is the *telos* for human life, a condition that Thomas Hurka describes as occurring when the "properties that constitute [our] nature are developed to a high degree."[20] A person is said to flourish when his moral virtues (*ethikos*) and intellectual virtues (*dianoetikos*) become a habit (*ethos*), or settled disposition. As W.D. Ross notes in his translation of the *Ethics*, the word "morality" is an appropriate translation of *ethikos* insofar as it is "used not in the narrow sense of 'right versus wrong' but in the archaic sense of 'pertaining to character or *mores*'"[21] – similar to the modern use of the word "ethos" to refer to a characteristic way of seeing or being. Hence, from the start, a parallel was established between the "virtues" of a person and the "virtues" of a text: just as judgments about moral virtue evaluate a character trait for its contribution to flourishing – to what makes a human being an excellent or fully-functional example of itself – so do judgments about stylistic virtue celebrate verbal or linguistic traits that help to realize the "nature" or "character" of a discourse.

The parallel between moral and stylistic virtue has long shaped the rhetorical tradition. On the one hand, a close alignment between style and character undergirds the referential conception of style that interprets the former in terms of the latter – the conception that reads style as reinforcing the impression (*poios*) that a speech projects as furnished by its speaker, subject matter, or "thought" (*logos*) (*Rhetoric*, 1403b). For example, the virtue of propriety, which requires that the style "be neither mean nor above the prestige of its subject matter" (1404b), asserts the classical pre-eminence of matter over manner. Similarly, throughout the *Rhetoric*, Aristotle uses the word *ethos* in a moralistic way to describe one of three modes of proof (the others being *pathos* and *logos*) that appeal to the "character" of the speaker, presenting him as virtuous and therefore "worthy of credence" (1356a).[22] Although Aristotle views style as an essentially artificial construction – a shaping design to be imposed upon *logos* or used to bring *ethos* into being – later rhetoricians assumed a more organic unity of expression and underlying character. Quintilian, for example, argues that excellence in speech is only possible if the orator is a *vir bonus*, or "good man,"[23] while Seneca the Younger, when asked why "certain periods [have] seen the appearance of a corrupt style of speech," responds simply, "As are men's lives, so is their speech."[24]

However, the rise of stylistic organicism has sometimes eclipsed the extent to which Aristotle invests style with a considerable degree of autonomy, suggesting that it possesses an ethos independent of the speaker's virtue. For example, "frigidity" is both a stylistic vice (its antonym is clarity) and an aesthetic type, occurring whenever a discourse draws undue attention to itself through the use of poetical devices such as compound names, exotic words, and inappropriate metaphors. If "by speaking poetically men produce an absurd and ridiculous effect through the inappropriateness" (1406a-b), then frigidity refers neither to the cold-heartedness of the speaker, nor to the banality of an argument, but to the intrinsic properties of the stylistic devices, which signify poeticism and artifice whenever they occur in a prosaic context. The "frigid" style may be vicious because it lacks congruity with other parts of a speech, but that very incongruity reveals its capacity to generate a tonality independent of the speaker's established character, making "character" less a property of persons or ideas than a predominantly linguistic quality.

In the *Rhetoric*, Aristotle notes it was poets who "first began to develop the study of style and delivery" (1403b), and that "this sort of enquiry has just as much to do with rhetoric as to do with poetics" (1403b). But the treatment of style in the *Poetics* is relatively scanty, which means that the rhetorical account of style as "ethical" – that is, as linked to the expression of ethos or character – became the dominant paradigm for stylistic criticism well into the twentieth century.[25] Because the line between moral and formal character was never sharply drawn, ancient rhetoricians advance various admixtures of the two. For example, the Greek rhetorician Demetrius identified four "types" (*charakteres*) of style (the elevated, the elegant, the plain, and the forcible), each with a corresponding anti-type (the frigid, the affected, the arid, and the graceless).[26] Each type is defined by its unique constellation of "thought," "diction," and "appropriate composition" (89), combining thematic considerations with formal abstractions such as the rounding of periods (93) or the use of expletive particles (97). Later, Cicero and Quintilian would describe how the grand, middle, and plain styles – designations based on propriety – achieve a kind of independent embodiment in the "characters" of Atticism and Asianism.[27] Such conceptual hybridity reached its apex in Hermogenes of Tarsus, whose *On Types of Style* was one of the most influential texts of the Renaissance. Hermogenes begins by arguing that the style of a text must flow from its semantic content, asserting the primacy of content over form ("first of all, and the most important, is the thought").[28] But he also claims that style itself conveys a kind of content, classifiable within seven virtues (clarity, grandeur, beauty, rapidity, character, sincerity, force) that he elevates into full-fledged "types" (*ideai*). As Annabel Patterson notes, "Hermogenes uses the term 'idea' to mean both 'characteristic style' and 'essential nature,'"[29] suggesting that there are certain formal protocols that reliably indicate a stylistic character even when detached from a specific person or argument. "Character," for example, which Hermogenes identifies as a "type," refers simultaneously to the ability of a style to evoke the *ethos* of a speaker and to four stylistic sub-types (simplicity, sweetness, subtlety, and modesty) that possess an "essential nature"[30] or character of their own.

The stylistic history most directly relevant for this book begins in the eighteenth century, when the distance between matter and manner dramatically narrowed. Although the neoclassical period is often remembered as a time when style and content were separate – "Language is the dress of thought," as Samuel Johnson says[31] – as early as 1675, the French philosopher Bernard Lamy describes how "[t]he Idea's present to our Mind . . . are the Soul of our Words," with "the Sounds form'd by the Organs of our Voice" being their "material part" or "Body."[32] According to Archibald Alison, "matter is not beautiful in itself, but derives its beauty from the expression of mind,"[33] which resembles Adam Smith's claim that "the stile of an author is generally of the same stamp as their character."[34] Here, we see the vehicular or "mechanical" role of style that had been privileged in classical rhetoric give way to the more "organic" unification between style and subjectivity that became central to romantic and post-romantic aesthetics. On this view, language is no longer the dress of thoughts but, as Thomas Carlyle puts it, its "flesh-garment" or "body,"[35] an idea perhaps best encapsulated in de Buffon's famous pronouncement of 1754 that "the style is the man himself."[36]

Buffon's dictum became an apothegm of the Victorian age, but it is not as simple as it is often made to appear. In his "Discourse on Style," Buffon first defines style as "simply the order and movement one gives to one's thoughts," implying that whatever virtues the style possesses reflect the author's underlying mental processes or habits of thought: "If [the thoughts] are connected closely, and rigorously compressed, the style will be firm, nervous, and concise. If they are allowed to follow one another loosely and merely at the lead of the diction, however choice this be, the style will be diffuse, nerveless, and languid" (171). However, Buffon also argues that while the "knowledge" conveyed in arguments is essentially fungible, capable of being delivered in a variety of ways, style somehow remains constant: it "can be neither detached, nor transferred, nor altered by time: if it is elevated, noble, sublime, the author will be equally admired in all ages" (178). According to W.C. Brownell, Buffon's claim here is less that "the writer's personal temperament leaves a deep impression on his style" than that his style is "within his personal control in a sense in which data and discoveries are not."[37] That is to say, style is less an expression of personal mannerism than a particular *manner* of expression, consisting of semi-autonomous "types" that are impersonal (though linked to an author) and trans-historical (though deployed at a particular point in time).

We would be right to call Buffon's discourse "belletristic" insofar as the character-based words he uses to describe style – words such as "firm," "nervous," "elevated," and "languid" – were massively popularized by the rhetorical criticism of the eighteenth century known as belletrism.[38] Further evidence of the psychologization of rhetoric, belletrism paid careful attention to the way in which the external features of an author's writing correlate with the internal features of his character or disposition. As Blair explained it, "words being the copies of our ideas, there must always be a very intimate connection between the manner in which every writer employs words, and his manner of thinking; and that, from the peculiarity of thought and expression which belongs to him, there is a certain character imprinted on his Style, which may be denominated his manner" (I:368). This notion of style recalls Dennis's statement (itself modeled after Buffon's) that the "style proclaims the man" and anticipates Matthew Arnold's assertion that styles have a "physiognomy, which are an essential part of their author, which stamp an indelible impression of him on the reader's mind."[39]

However, the influence of belletristic rhetoric was paradoxical, for in reviving the technical study of style, which had for some time been considered inferior to the more "rational" parts of rhetoric such as logic and argument, it also elevated style as an object of independent aesthetic attention.[40] For example, Blair begins his lectures by identifying how sentence-level properties, such as precision, unity, and harmony, relate to the way an author discovers and arranges his ideas (I:183–271). Yet he then examines how different mixtures of these properties combine to create an impression of "general characters of style" (I:368) that apply less to a single individual than to a larger formal class. To distinguish between styles that are diffuse and concise, styles that are feeble, nervous, dry, and plain, and styles that are simple, affected, vehement, and neat, Blair considers whether they are rapid in pace, glowing in tone, or gaudy in texture, features that reveal less about an author's mental organization than whether the discursive presentation interests the imagination or pleases the ear. As Blair confesses, "these distinctions carry, in general, some reference to an author's manner of thinking, but refer chiefly to his mode of expression" (I:368). Styles, in other words, may go some way toward revealing the man "in his own natural character" (I:390), but they also convey a distinctive *aesthetic* character defined by verbal relations internal to a community of texts.

Influenced by Aristotelian theory as well as eighteenth-century rhetoric, the virtue terms of Victorian criticism reflect this rhetorical paradox. On the surface, words like naturalness, delicacy, sincerity, sweetness, and grace seem to suggest an impoverishment of formal analysis, relying upon general "impressions" of the underlying ethos that style is construed as representing. And, to be sure, nineteenth-century readers were fascinated by the idea that verbal forms could serve as a window to some underlying spirit or idea, whether it be the biographical personality of an author, the historical conditions of an epoch, or the *Weltanschauung* of a nation or culture.[41] When we say that Iago's style is obfuscating and therefore pernicious or that Trollope's style is transparent and therefore sincere, we produce moralizing stylistic analysis in this vein. But virtue terms were also employed by belletristic rhetoric for more formalist descriptions of prose, enabling critics to evince their sensitivity to how a style's literary or aesthetic character could be virtuous in intrinsic and non-referential ways. The dis-imbrication of form and content may be an ontological impossibility and yet their conceptual distinctiveness remains an analytical necessity; as Tzvetan Todorov has observed, "the fact that we find them together does not prevent us from distinguishing them."[42] Hence, it becomes necessary when discussing the Victorian criticism of literature to speak of two kinds of character – personal or moral or thematic character on the one hand, and aesthetic or technical or expressive character on the other – as well as to clarify the complex relations between them.

In its attempt to characterize aesthetic procedures in "ethical" or characterological terms, William Archer's essay of 1885, "Robert Louis Stevenson: His Style and His Thought," offers a typically Victorian illustration of how this might be done.[43] Archer begins his essay by noting the increasing prominence enjoyed by style, which he defines in an Aristotelian fashion: "We hear much in these days of an occult literary virtue yclept style: which term, by a figurative process whose name I forget, has come to include within its content the idea of excellence."[44] Neither simple grammatical competence nor expository prowess, style involves "an added grace, a supererogatory strength" that "is the result of the writer's individual sense of beauty and power in the collocation of words" (581). However, "so far, but so far only, was Buffon right in saying, 'Le style est l'homme même,'" for aside from the author's capacity to transform ordinary writing into something "literary," his real-life personality may have little bearing on the content of his art (582). Archer specifies: "The style need not truly proclaim the man, but it infallibly announces the artist, or in other words, one side, and often a subsidiary and incongruous side, of the character as a whole" (582).

Because style necessarily reflects the man-as-artist, and only incidentally reflects the man-as-person, there may be a difference between a person's manifest personality and her aesthetic sensibility. Moreover, style has a unique capacity to convey this potentially "incongruous" subset of character because its method of signification is not based on the expected variety of cognitive or referential content. As Archer explains, "Mr. Stevenson is not only philosophically content, but deliberately resolved, that his readers shall look first to his manner, and only in the second place to his matter" (583), suggesting, theoretically, that these two kinds of meaning may diverge. Reversing the usual equation, Archer implies that *res*, or content, is really just a vehicle for style, which may transmute this material into matter of its own: "He professes himself an artist in words, and thinks only those thoughts, tells none but those tales, paints those pictures alone, which adapt themselves to his peculiar manner. An impressionist on occasion, he is always an expressionist" (583). In Archer's view, the chief stylistic "virtue" that Stevenson expresses and models is "lightness of touch," a general term under which he organizes an array of more specific techniques: "a buoyant, staccato, touch-and-go elasticity" whereby the author "jots effects rather than composes pictures" (583); unexpectedly vivid words and expressions that "quicken the imagination, and pass into the reader's store of remembered experiences" (584); impressionistic scene-painting, characterized by "a few crisp, clean strokes and a wash of transparent colour" (584); and a "direct, rapid, [and] objective" mode of unadulterated "story-telling" that "plunges into the midst of things" rather than slowing the pace with intellectual analysis (585).

Like many Victorian critics, Archer supports his judgments with long textual excerpts, including the following description of Noyon Cathedral from Stevenson's 1878 travelogue *An Inland Voyage*:

> I have seldom looked on the east end of a church with more complete sympathy. As it flanges out in three wide terraces, and settles down broadly on the earth, it looks like the poop of some great old battle-ship. Hollow-backed buttresses carry vases which figure for the stern lanterns. There is a roll in the ground, and the towers just appear above the pitch of the roof, as though the good ship were bowing lazily over an *Atlantic* swell. At any moment it might be a hundred feet away from you, climbing the next billow. At any moment, a window might open, and some old admiral thrust forth a cocked hat and proceed to take an observation. (583)

Although Archer lacks specificity in the way he relates his stylistic impressions to details in the text, the passage is clearly intended to exemplify the virtues he describes. The verb "flanges," which initiates the metaphorical transposition of the passage, is "full of descriptive force" (584), transforming a noun that denotes a supportive or metallic disc into a lively feat of nautical animation. Stevenson similarly enlivens the flying buttresses by re-imagining the inert "vases" they carry as the suspended "lanterns" of the stern, flickering in and out of view with the rise and fall of the waves. As Archer argues, "bowing lazily" seems the "right" (583) figurative expression for describing the ship's movement, perhaps because it combines the mindless lumbering of a large vessel ("lazily") with a carefully concealed pun (the "bow" is the front of a ship). A series of unobtrusive assonances and pararhymes further support the dense yet deft evocations of the passage: in addition to "stern" and "lantern," the succession of "hollow," "roll," "bowing," "swell," and "billow," with their rounded vowels and liquid phonemes, evoke the sway of a foaming sea. The final two sentences, casually introduced with a repeated adverbial clause in the subjunctive mood ("at any moment"), create an illusion of spontaneity that is anything but: on the one hand, the ship might seem "a hundred feet away," yet in the next instant we might be close enough to witness the tiny mind that controls it from within. The imaginative and physical distance traveled in this relatively short passage is remarkable: the cathedral has become a ship, and the outside observer reappears as its pilot from within.

Readers of this passage may note stylistic characteristics that Archer does not, emphasizing (as I have) the figurative wit that transforms travel writing into an adventurous *jeu d'esprit*; and one may question whether "lightness of touch" is the right phrase to summarize its range of effects. But Archer embraces the virtue term because it captures how the aesthetic aspects of a text are characterological insofar as they represent a sensibility and structure of values uniquely communicable through artistic verbal forms. In the second part of the essay, Archer seeks to measure the effect of Stevenson's lightness on his actual performance of life; he argues, in fact, that Stevenson "is an artist in life as he is in words . . . carrying his life in accordance with that ideal" (588). Given the aestheticist injunction to treat life in the spirit of art, Archer's reflections are not surprising, and helpfully explain certain facts about Stevenson's opinions and themes (his "denunciation of the commercial spirit," for example, or his "apologies for idlers," (588)). But the term "lightness" is useful here not because it collapses formal and moral values but because it *compares* them, each embodying an ethos that resembles, but is not identical with, other kinds of characterological content.

Reading Victorian Virtue

The centrality of both "virtue" and "character" to Victorian studies is hardly new, and we are used to thinking of the Victorians as inhabiting a thoroughly moralized culture. Stefan Collini describes how, during the nineteenth century, "constant invocations of the virtues of character in fact presupposed an agreed moral code"[45] with an array of influences ranging from evangelical Christianity to romantic individualism. This preoccupation with moral rectitude naturally extended to fiction, with many of the most notable writers, such as Thackeray, Dickens, and Eliot, adopting some version of the sugared-pill theory of the novel, seeing the author as a secular parson responsible for cultivating the reader's moral education. Moreover, the conditions of Victorian publishing required that a best-selling novel contain no content that could not be admitted into the sanctity of the family circle, fostering a reviewing culture sensitive to moral appraisal.[46] The simplicity of this picture has been complicated in recent years by scholars such as Rohan Maitzen, Jesse Rosenthal, and Sarah Allison, who discern a much more complex relationship between the goals of practical ethics and the procedures of literary form.[47] Yet the aesthetic movement remains commonly understood as a reaction against morally reductive approaches that dominated the first part of the century, which treated works of art as socially didactic rather than as autonomous aesthetic events. We think, for example, of Pater's reminder in the Conclusion to the *Renaissance* (1873) that the wisdom of a "quickened, multiplied consciousness" comes most from "the poetic passion, the desire of beauty, the love of art for its own sake,"[48] or of Oscar Wilde's dictum in the Preface to *The Picture of Dorian Gray* (1891) that "no artist has ethical sympathies."[49]

The puzzle, however, is why critics who were motivated to emphasize art's autonomy would continue to use the moralized vocabulary of virtue and vice that they could otherwise repudiate. This, after all, is what happens in the twentieth century, when a more neutral vocabulary supplanted the personalistic metaphors of impressionism. But late Victorian formalists reveal their continued attachment to this language. The formal analyses in Pater's *Renaissance* are full of virtue terms – sweetness, lightness, grace, and finish – and his essay on "Style" proclaims that "the style, the manner, would be the man, not in his unreasoned and really uncharacteristic caprices, involuntary or affected, but in absolutely sincere apprehension of what is most real to him."[50] Similarly, in "The Critic as Artist," Oscar Wilde cites approvingly a mid-century authority on stylistic reductionism: "Forms are the food of faith, cried Newman in one of those great moments of sincerity that made us admire and know the man . . . It is not merely in art that the body is the soul."[51]

The early chapters of this book offer several reasons for why this vocabulary persists. For one, belletristic rhetoric was widely disseminated in the nineteenth century and channeled that aspect of the rhetorical tradition most concerned with the use of language as an independent *techne* or art. For authors and critics in this tradition, the deployment of virtue terms from belletrism indicates an intensification of stylistic formalism rather than its neglect, locating aesthetic character in the verbal properties traditionally attended by *elocutio*. In addition, virtue terms appealed to late-century formalists because these thinkers remained just as preoccupied as their predecessors with ideas of ethos and excellence in character. As Pater admits, his interest in the Renaissance is not merely for "its concrete works of art" but also "for its general spirit and character, for the ethical qualities of which it is a consummate type" (xxxii). By tracking the progress of stylistic virtue over the nineteenth century, I observe a process of "ethico-aesthetic drift" whereby the ethical character that most literally refers to the morality of persons gets gradually understood as an analogous yet substantively different kind of aesthetic phenomenon realized through stylistic form. Given the classical origins of stylistic virtue, it is not surprising that an Aristotelian conception of character flourished in the writings of many Victorian philosophers who resisted the dissociation of ethics from aesthetics by conceiving character as an aesthetic realization of the self. In contrast to the usual emphasis on Kant or Plato in understanding the moral background of Victorian aesthetics (and aestheticism in particular), I show how Aristotelian virtue theory provided an ethical justification for the character-based formalism that became so widespread in nineteenth-century Britain, along with the idea of aesthetic autonomy that it entrained.[52]

The word "virtue" has, in fact, enjoyed a revival in recent years among ethical critics influenced by Aristotle. In *Love's Knowledge*, Martha Nussbaum describes how novels model moral virtue and educate readers in ways that make them capable of virtuous action.[53] Similarly, Joshua Landy shows how fictions play a "formative" role in inculcating "virtue of character"[54] by training the mental capacities of readers. Andrew Miller alludes to virtue ethics when describing how literary texts solicit a "responsiveness to exemplary figures"[55] that has the potential to develop the self in morally improving ways, while Wayne Booth, in *The Company We Keep*, uses "virtue" in its broadest classical sense to refer to "the whole range of human 'powers,' 'strengths,' 'capacities,' or 'habits of behavior'" that are in some way excellent or admirable.[56] These works helpfully distinguish between a "narrowly moral" perspective on fiction, which focuses on doctrinaire questions of right and wrong, and the "broadly ethical" view that emphasizes the components of a life well-lived,[57] making them tributaries to the larger "eudaimonic turn" that has been observed across the arts and social sciences.[58] But their accounts of style tend to be reductive in character and focus on style's ethical consequences over and above its ontological singularity as a mode of signification. For example, while Booth argues that style can model "intellectual virtues" (his closest approximation of the virtues that I call "autonomous"), he valorizes them for the experience of "friendship" they provide – an experience that is tightly bound up with their providing a motive for "emulation" – rather than as examples of characterological excellence that secure a different sort of contemplation and pleasure.[59]

Several critics have also recognized the importance of "character" as a complex cultural category with particular salience in nineteenth-century Britain. Drawing on Lorraine Daston and Peter Galison's notion of an "epistemic virtue," or moralized trait, Amanda Anderson describes how an "ideal of critical distance" shaped the "cultivation" of Victorian "character" across a wide range of domains and practices.[60] Similarly, Matthew Bevis explores disinterestedness as "a method – a *form* of enquiry, rather than a repository for a settled political *content*,"[61] shifting attention away from concrete goods and outcomes to the characterological dispositions and attitudes that condition their expression. In this context, Elaine Hadley rightly uses the word "formalism" to describe the "strikingly formalized mental attitudes" (such as "disinterestedness," "sincerity," or "impersonality") that Victorians adopted as stances rather than "contents,"[62] a contrast familiar in moral philosophy, where, for example, Christine Korsgaard distinguishes between "a formal conception of morality" that "identifies it with a method of reasoning about practical issues" and "a substantive conception of morality" that "identifies morality in terms of its content."[63] The difference is relevant here because many Victorian formalists approached style as a containing concept rather than as a content, and, by treating the appreciation of style *qua* style as a virtuous activity, reshaped the object of criticism and elevated the ethical significance of both. For example, in the mid-Victorian period, the virtue of sincerity often referred to an earnest wholesomeness in realism, a good that is recognizably substantive. But sincerity, for Oscar Wilde, describes a dispositional commitment to the expression of transient states and moods and a corresponding receptivity in readers. The fact that Wilde professed indifference to the actual content of those expressions does not make these latter forms of sincerity any less "ethical" than the more substantive variety: their value derives not from the specific goods they identify but rather from the form of their expression (in an artwork) and the manner of their perception (by a reader).

An attention to the "formalist" dimensions of moral or political character has naturally prompted an attention to analogous verbal forms. As David Russell observes, scholars of Victorian liberalism have examined how "a style of reflexive reasoned deliberation" relates to "the shape of the life that would practice it," and he defines "tact" as a "stylistic approach to the incorporation of difference in social interaction."[64] Most strikingly, Jonathan Farina describes how "the style of a text could bear the weight of its moral, aesthetic, scientific, and political character, independently of the character of its author or content,"[65] suggesting the possibility of "autonomous" stylistic character that is a major subject of this book. However, insofar as these critics analyze style, it is usually as an index to something *other* than style, whether that be liberal agency (Hadley), or "nonprescriptive inclusiveness"[66] (Russell), or different ways of knowing (Farina). My use of a characterological vocabulary thus differs from these writers in ways that have important consequences for the study of style. First, in identifying a subset of virtues that I call "stylistic," I draw attention to the ways in which the sentence-level properties of texts reveal attitudes about style as a function of those sentences. I approach style as an historically constructed category that interacts with, but can be examined independently from, whatever else contributes to a text's unique way of being and seeing and whatever other contributions a text may make to the outside world. Second, I use the term "ethical" to refer to a specific hermeneutic practice within Victorian rhetoric and culture rather than to the much broader normative field associated with the "ethical turn" of the 1980s and 90s. One problem with ethical criticism is that its use of the word "ethical" to describe many of the things that texts "do" is so capacious as to become conceptually inert. In contrast, I use the word, first, as an adjectival form of the word "ethos," making it nearly synonymous with "characterological"; and second, as a way of describing how Victorian figures imagined style as possessing normative value not because it reconfigures the behavior of readers or serves some other moral or political end (though these remain real possibilities) but rather because it allows for a particular kind of aesthetic expression and appreciation that are also part of "the good life" for human beings.[67]

Reading Victorian Style

In a well-known essay called "Style and Personality in the Literary Work" (1985), Jenefer Robinson defends the common assumption that "style is essentially an expression of qualities of mind, attitudes, interests and personality traits which appear to be the author's own."[68] On this view, "a writer has a literary style in virtue of the fact that her style of performing a wide variety of artistic acts expresses the same qualities of (her) mind and temperament," understood as the projection of an implied (rather than actual) author.[69] Robinson's theory reinforces the referential conception of style in its most intuitive and formalistic formulation, buttressed by its surety in the organic unity of the underlying "author": "the many disparate elements of verbal style fit together," she claims, "only because they are being used to express the 'same' personality . . . which 'makes sense' out of (unifies) this multitude of artistic acts."[70] However, as we have seen, this argument is vulnerable to the objection raised by Archer that the verbal elements of an artwork have the capacity to express traits of character that may not, and need not, be commensurate. As Nick Riggle puts it, "artists are like persons with style" in that "they develop and present ideals in their work – but the ideals they present are *artistic* ideals, or ideals they have for their art."[71] There are, in other words, multiple levels of personality expressed in a literary work, including the form of personality that orients itself solely toward style as an autonomous rather than a referential concept.

Stylistic referentialism has long dominated the analysis of prose, and not without reason. In *Anatomy of Criticism*, Northrop Frye argues that all "literary structures" are endowed with "the quality of a verbal personality or a speaking voice," which he calls "style."[72] But, he claims, we are more likely to discern style in "thematic" or "non-literary prose" because the stylistic quality there, more than in drama or lyric poetry, "is felt to be the voice of the author himself."[73] Frye adds that style "had its great period in late Victorian times, when the primary connection between writing and personality was a fundamental principle of criticism,"[74] and it is notable that the two major collections of essays dedicated to the criticism of nineteenth-century prose style – George Levine and William Madden's *The Art of Victorian Prose* (1968) and Michael D. Hurley and Marcus Waithe's *Thinking through Style* (2018) – confine themselves to nonfictional sources.[75] While these collections are replete with close readings that affirm the "literary" or aesthetic value of essayistic writing, they perpetuate the axiom that style is the expressive dimension of an argument, idea, moral personality, or *logos* (Hurley and Waithe call it a "mode of thinking *through*"[76]) rather than a self-referring artefact.

In *Anatomy of Criticism*, Frye further distinguishes two forces within language, a centrifugal one directing the reader outward toward actual or symbolic content, and a centripetal one directing the reader inward toward the verbal pattern itself as the source of beauty, meaning, and interest.[77] The novel, which developed out of expository prose styles such as the sermon and the letter, is the most centrifugal among the literary arts, hence early criticism of the novel revolved around its verisimilitude, or truth-telling abilities. But one can see how the centrifugal qualities of the novel also work to reinforce a "thematic" conception of fictionality that ultimately privileges "the primary connection between writing and personality"[78] that Frye associates with rhetoric and nonfiction, with the author's "personality" or "voice" being located both within the text as its driving subjectivity and also outside the text as its object of representation. Hence, when the Russian formalists wished to free "literariness" from what Frye calls the "representational fallacy,"[79] they did so specifically by identifying it with deviations from a prose-based norm. In "Art as Technique" (1917), Viktor Shklovsky contrasts "poetic" speech, which is "strange and wonderful," with the language of prose, which is "ordinary" and "direct."[80] Similarly, in "Criticism, Inc.," one of the founding documents of New Criticism, John Crowe Ransom contrasts the "prose core to which [the critic] can violently reduce the total object" with "the differentia, residue, or tissue, which keeps the object poetical or entire."[81]

Structuralist narratology did much to correct the shortfalls of formalist methods in undertaking a "poetics" of fiction, but style, as an aesthetic concept, was subordinated to larger-scale forms of organization such as genre, story, and narrative point of view.[82] The rise of the "new stylistics" in the 1960s seemed more promising, dedicated as it was to the substantiation of critical "impressions" through a scrupulous attention to language.[83] But stylistics and mainstream literary criticism have not always functioned symbiotically. Their productive confluence was particularly hindered by a series of forceful essays launched by Stanley Fish in the 1970s that cast doubt on what he perceived to be stylistics' uncompromising scientism. According to Fish, stylisticians failed to recognize that the "formal patterns" they identified were "always the product of a prior interpretive act,"[84] thereby contaminating their methods with traces of the subjectivism they sought to remedy. Others, such as David Lodge, had already "abstained as far as possible from using the term 'style'"[85] due to similar considerations. Stylistics subsequently migrated to the margins of literary studies – though, as Michael Burke points out, it has built a reputable "house" of its own[86] – where its methodological specializations sometimes seem at odds with the traditional goals of literary criticism.[87] While literary critics certainly draw on corpus stylistics, cognitive poetics, and the varieties of "distant reading" popularized by Franco Moretti (to name just a few of the more contemporary methodologies), an approach to style that adequately balances the empirical rigor of "literary linguistics" with the range of purposes encompassed by "criticism and interpretation" has yet to be fully theorized.[88]

Stylistic virtue, then, is a useful concept because it points a way out of these divisions. According to Aristotle, the interpretation of stylistic virtue (like the interpretation of moral virtue) must always be evaluated relative to both a presentational context and a mean between deficiency and excess. For example, whether or not an epithet conveys "grandeur" depends not only upon the subject matter of a text (is the subject elevated or demotic?) but also upon frequency of mention (too many epithets can evoke frigidity while too few can lead to plainness). Such judgments depend upon further beliefs about a text's larger identity or *telos*, whether locally (what is this sentence meant to achieve?) or at a higher level (what kind of text is this?). Even further, judgments about *telos* are themselves subjective: whether (to take another example) one regards Dickens's language as excessive, superfluous, exaggerated, or anarchic depends in part upon which verbal features critics select for inspection (which are often similar or identical) and in part upon beliefs about the "function" of Dickens's work (which often differ radically).[89] Some might worry about an excess of subjectivity or bias in arriving at such beliefs, but I argue that variability among teleological judgments is inevitable and desirable. Like moral claims, judgments about style do not appeal exclusively to natural facts but rather to a combination of linguistic evidence and intersubjective, culturally mediated opinions, explaining how legitimate interpretive controversies can arise over the same "objective" properties. Disagreements about which sentence-level properties are salient in a text, or whether they count as excellences, are not a failure of stylistic criticism but rather a sign that stylistic interpretation is proceeding appropriately.

Because stylistic virtues require us to sharpen our knowledge of the *kind* of virtue (both descriptive and evaluative) under consideration, they allow for greater precision in analyzing aesthetic effects. This book is hardly the first to recover the interpretive value of Victorian critical concepts. In *The Physiology of the Novel*, Nicholas Dames discovers "a largely vanished way of theorizing the novel"[90] rooted in the physiological sciences. One could mention further studies by Benjamin Morgan and Daniel Wright, whose readings of novels are sensitively informed by their knowledge of materialist aesthetics and philosophical logic respectively.[91] Taken together, there can no longer be any doubt that the Victorian novel is, *pace* Henry James, "*discutable*" or supported by a rich background of nineteenth-century criticism and theory. However, this study differs from its predecessors in locating the "lens" or "framework" for interpretation not in some body of knowledge contemporaneous to the fiction of the Victorian period but rather in the longer history of rhetorical criticism and change that stands behind it. In this way, it makes formalism both the subject and object of its historicism and approaches style as the product of an internal history. This perspective adds a necessary diachronic or genealogical dimension to our understanding of style and its interpretation;[92] it also reveals how styles participate in feedback loops that deepen as well as limit their interpretive variability. For example, one might be tempted to debate whether epithets are "intrinsically" poetic – that is, whether they will signify "artifice" no matter what the content or context – but the question is irrelevant to the purposes of authors for whom epithets have been made synonymous with poetic grandeur through millennia of inherited practice and rhetorical instruction. Through their usage over time, stylistic "characters" accrue associations with authors, topics, and cultural conditions that influence their later use, helping to account for some of the particular meanings that they generate without entirely foreclosing their possibilities for change. Trollope, for example, praised Thackeray for the "ease" and "lucidity" of his writing, allying him with an Attic tradition that emphasized the delivery of "truth"; but Thackeray's own models were satirists who accessed the "truth" through distortion rather than transparency. Interpretive mistakes occur when critics take a one-style-fits-all approach that assumes a straightforward match between "content" and stylistic ethos when styles are also independent, bringing with them a characteristic atmosphere or tone or history, even as they are continually shaped by the surrounding textual environment and varying hermeneutic assumptions.

To be sure, the rise of realism in the nineteenth century encouraged many writers to commit to a general stylistic ideal of clarity, naturalness, and conversational ease, emphasizing mimetic transparency over stylistic self-regard. But the bias *within* the Victorian period toward speech-based idioms and written dialects – the two linguistic features of the period most prominently featured in histories of prose in English – does not warrant the assumption that Victorian language is, as James Sutherland once wrote, "on the whole universally intelligible"[93] and therefore in little need of special explanation or theory. It is a strange fact that historians of prose have paid more attention to the "emergence" of prose than to what happens after it arrives, even though a nineteenth-century critic would have found an idea as monolithic or transparent as "Victorian style" to be patently absurd. As in the twentieth century, Victorian readers were eager to establish the set of qualities and attitudes that distinguished one author's work from another, with essays and reviews comparing the tone, atmosphere, and characteristic feel of contemporaries (the "Bell" sisters), rivals (Dickens vs. Thackeray), schools ("sensation" novelists), and outliers (e.g. Edward Bulwer-Lytton or George Meredith). As Louis T. Milic notes, for much of its history the word "style" referred not to idiosyncratic expression but to impersonal verbal classes, with a "good" or "competent" style being one that conformed to models previously established for emulation.[94] Stylistic virtues reflect these ostensibly competing notions: by choosing to write in a particular style or to embrace certain virtues over others, writers could situate themselves within a broader stylistic tradition without denying the uniqueness of their work. The antiquated language of stylistic virtue reflects the influence of the classical, conscious-choice approach even as the more romantic notion of spontaneous stylistic individualism was becoming the norm.

In this light, stylistic virtues remain useful because, through their appeal to historicism, they refine the *kind* of form that "formalism" should address. Like style, the words "form" and "formalism" have long been problematic for criticism, though their casual ubiquity makes it impossible to imagine criticism without them. In her recent book *Forms*, Caroline Levine notes that "form has never belonged only to the discourse of aesthetics," but nonetheless finds a "common definition" across its uses: "'form' always indicates *an arrangement of elements – an ordering, patterning, or shaping.*"[95] Levine embraces the wideness of this definition because she seeks to reveal how concepts of form that seem distinctly literary are in play whenever "power" has a role in "governing social life"; this serves her moral goal of putting literary criticism at the service of more "just" arrangements in the world outside the text.[96] I share Levine's interest in the contours of literary form, but my methodology, both critical and philosophical, is rather different. Instead of examining how ideas about literary style are portable to other domains (such as styles of life or styles of politics), I seek to pinpoint the ways in which stylistic virtue functions as a specialized literary term that reinforces the distinctiveness of style as an object for aesthetic criticism. This program is not, as some might argue, inherently reactionary,[97] but instead serves three important functions. First, by retaining style's traditional focus on language rather than the content of representation or larger structures within or outside the text, it seeks to defend literary experience on distinctly aesthetic grounds, thereby resisting negative forms of politicization that degrade aesthetic values demonstrably worth preserving. Second, by identifying what renders a text artistically distinguished, the evaluative dimension of stylistic virtue does not commit the critic to making parochial judgments about the moral value of texts but rather shows how criticism can itself be "moralized" in ways that respect rather than violate the autonomy of art. Third, and most importantly, such an approach leads to new insights about the style in which a text is written, stabilizing that concept in the craft of organizing words and sentences. It restores the idea that style is a kind of quality or "beauty" (to use the *démodé* yet more unembarrassedly evaluative term) at once technical, conventionalized, and expressive, a quality that remains integral to literary experience, whatever one ultimately makes of it.

Overview and Author Chapters

The major arguments of this book unfold as follows. Chapter 1 claims that stylistic virtue is an important feature in the history of British rhetoric that had significant effects on the development of modern aesthetics, especially the disciplinary protocols of formalism. It provides an overlooked genealogy for the development of modern "English" and the importance of style within it. Chapter 2 argues that stylistic virtues remained popular because the virtue-theoretic paradigm was especially appealing to those who sought to place formalist methods on an ethically defensible ground. It tracks this progress primarily through the ethico-aesthetic ideas of the major critics educated at Oxford (Ruskin, Arnold, Pater, and Wilde), where Aristotle pervaded the curriculum. Chapter 3 examines virtue theory against the broader background of Victorian moral philosophy, where it helped establish the realization of character as an end in itself. In the process, virtue ethics became associated with "aesthetic" modes of reasoning that, for better or for worse, facilitated the separation of ethics from art in a way that has obscured the virtue-theoretic foundations that unite them. In the second half of the book, I turn to the novels of Thackeray, Trollope, and Meredith to demonstrate how stylistic virtues offer an historically embedded formalist hermeneutic that prompts new interpretations of literary style by highlighting the difference between stylistic meaning and other forms of content, re-contextualizing verbal features, and drawing out unnoticed properties. Taken together, these six chapters, along with the Afterword, which follows the fate of stylistic virtue in the post-Victorian period, provide a full account of what I call a "virtue-theoretic" approach to style and the arguments that may be used to defend it.

A word needs to be said about the selection principles guiding the individual case studies that comprise the second half of this book. As a generic category, stylistic virtues could be identified in any text simply by combining the description of salient stylistic patterns with their positive valorization. All texts have virtues, even if their authors are ignorant of them. But part of the purpose of this project is to reveal how an awareness of stylistic virtue circulated throughout Victorian culture, sometimes shaping an author's own attitude toward his or her work and sometimes instilling biases in the reception of that work that cast a shadow over subsequent interpretations. Consequently, I have chosen three authors who in one way or another have left an explicit record of their opinion toward style or whose style attracted contemporaneous attention in a way that sheds light on their formal method. One may not agree with an author's stylistic choices or views of them held by the author or others, but they provide essential pieces of archival data for the task of stylistic criticism.

Moreover, the three authors chosen – Thackeray, Trollope, and Meredith – are exemplary because they offer three representative and contrasting pathways within the landscape of nineteenth-century prose. While working, generally speaking, as realists of the middle-class and gentry, they offer a spectrum of possibilities concerning the relation of style to content and to the genealogy of stylistic choice. I begin with Thackeray because he was considered by many to be the period's most capable stylist, with *Henry Esmond* being his finest work, even though few readers today can make sense of this assessment. The fault lies in part with the traditions of Thackerayan criticism. Obsessed with the quality of his narrative voice, many have focused on Thackeray's unity (or disunity) of tone, leading to dubious interpretations of key early works. By re-thinking these interpretations, which stem from thematically oriented criticism, Chapter 4 shows that there is a difference between Thackeray's satirical personality and the protean adaptability of his stylistic guises. The consequence for Thackeray's reader is a hyper-awareness of "grace," a form of stylistic versatility and detachment that exists in productive tension with the author's more earnest (if also captious) ethical attitudes.

Of all Victorian authors, Trollope comes closest to aspiring to the "degree zero" style that has played such an important role in modern theorizations of prose. Committed to an ideal of stylistic transparency, Trollope sought the unmediated transmission of authorial thought-content, borrowing from the more psychological strains of belletrism. However, Chapter 5 challenges the moralization of Trollope's "disappearing" style as honest, objective, and forthright by cataloguing the acts of formal deception necessary to render such effects. Moreover, Trollope's own writings on style reveal an abiding interest in non-mimetic features of prose such as "harmony" and "rhythm," contrasting markedly with the utilitarian and subordinate function he putatively assigns to the virtues of "ease" and "lucidity" in his autobiography. Trollope's blend of Attic simplicity with Ciceronian schemes proves his style to be one of the most artfully mannered in Victorian English, conveying an impression of aesthetic virtuosity where many critics have seen only bourgeois pedestrianism.

The style of George Meredith represents an opposite extreme: dense with epigram and ornament, it is frequently denigrated as extravagant and obscure, violating the realist conventions that Trollope worked hard to establish. However, Meredith drew on the orthogonal virtues of Asiatic and baroque styles to create a new form of psychological realism characterized by what he called "fervidness," the intensity that arises when contradictory intellectual and imaginative principles are held in tension. On the one hand, Meredith gravitated to short forms like epithet and epigram, distilling complex thoughts into memorably philosophical phrases; on the other, he delighted in the flights of fancy permitted by prosaic expansiveness. Through a consideration of major and minor work, I show how fervidness is embodied structurally as a drama between conditions of freedom and constraint that impinge upon the development of central characters. While I stress the gap between moral and stylistic virtues in Thackeray and Trollope, Meredith's "fervidness" formally replicates a dynamic that plays out at other levels of the text, making his style much more referential in terms of its relation to content than that of either Thackeray or Trollope before him.

Besides offering three different attitudes toward style and examples of its handling, the authorial case studies demonstrate three different ways of making a stylistic argument. It is not simply that each author has a different stylistic genealogy, with Thackeray deriving his pastiche style from eighteenth-century novelists, Trollope inventing his disappearing style through the imitation of classical and Augustan authors, and Meredith drawing his difficult style from romantic and orientalist aesthetics. These chapters also show that analyzing the genealogical development *within* an author's career can prove analytically fruitful. The chapter on Thackeray, for example, examines his early work because there we clearly see the stylistic idiosyncrasies that he worked to contain in his most famous novel, *Vanity Fair.* It is partly because that novel is the only one narrated *in propria persona* that it moderates the stylistic flamboyance of the early work without actually repudiating its governing logic. In contrast, the chapter on Trollope focuses on a single novel from the middle of his career because unlike Thackeray, Trollope perfected a "classic" style that he repeated again and again; whether in a tragic text like *He Knew He Was Right* or an acrid satire like *The Way We Live Now*, Trollope's amoral harmonies and rhythms remain constant. Finally, the Meredith chapter covers the range of his career, from early to late, in order to demonstrate how he remained single-mindedly committed to the "fervid" ideal. While seemingly eccentric, Meredith's organicism provides a principle of unity within the author's work that also connects it to broader prosaic traditions.

All this being said, stylistic virtues represent only one way of looking at style, and even then only one aspect of that particular dimension. Grace is not the only virtue of Thackeray, nor is Meredith entirely defined by fervidness; and the double valence of stylistic virtue allows for the dual recognition of referentialism and autonomy. As with human character itself, stylistic virtue presumes an inherent multi-sidedness to literary works in which different virtues are activated according to different contexts and schemes of value. These chapters thus represent the beginning rather than the end point of their study.

CHAPTER I

Stylistic Virtue and the Rise of Literary Formalism

In *Studies in Early Victorian Literature* (1895), Frederic Harrison, the Oxford-educated positivist, praises Thackeray for his "almost perfect prose style – a style as nervous as that of Swift, as easy as that of Goldsmith, as graceful as that of Addison, as rich as that of Gibbon and Burke."[1] The conjunction of each adjective with its exemplar is meant to conjure truths already known, but what was once known may also be forgotten. Do words such as "nervous" and "graceful" refer to diction, syntax, or other linguistic properties of the sentence? To images, attitudes, or shades of authorial tone? To the general impression or character that the style conveys? Whatever the case, we can no longer be sure, as Harrison was, that Thackeray's "mastery over style – a style at once simple, pure, nervous, flexible, pathetic, and graceful – places Thackeray amongst the very greatest masters of English prose" (108), not because we doubt Thackeray's excellence or Harrison's acuity, but because we no longer understand the terms of art that he uses to make his judgment.

Harrison's virtue-based vocabulary was typical of his period, but it was not new. In this chapter, I discuss its dissemination through eighteenth-century Scottish rhetoric and belles lettres, which profoundly influenced nineteenth-century rhetoric and criticism. As Douglas Patey notes, the phrase "'literary criticism' itself is to be found scarcely anywhere in the eighteenth century,"[2] with "criticism" previously referring to a wide range of inquiries involving human experience and judgment, including discussion of the arts. According to Hayden White, "criticism" emerges in the nineteenth century as a specialized hermeneutic activity directed toward literary texts only through the "suppression" of the rhetorical tradition that preceded it and that persists in diminished form.[3] But the belief that eighteenth-century "rhetoric" and nineteenth-century "criticism" address themselves to different objects, or employ different methods for treating the objects that they share in common, is an anachronism that obscures the intimate connection between these fields during a formative period when their actual relationship was far more dialectical. Here, I argue that style became central to Victorian criticism because eighteenth-century rhetoric had already identified it as the defining feature of "literary" or "imaginative" texts, even if the ultimate migration of *elucutio* from rhetoric to criticism permanently attenuated relations between two fields that evolved in tandem.

In the introduction to this book, I described how classical rhetoric had always been tugged in two directions, between the referential conception of style that treats verbal features as the embodiment of underlying content and an autonomous one that sees style as conveying a characterological content of its own. In the eighteenth century, that division both intensified and blurred, as a mentalist approach to style emerged that, somewhat paradoxically, fostered a new appreciation for style's independent signification. This development begins in earnest with Adam Smith, who reads style as an index to character, and continues in the work of Hugh Blair, whose lectures on style emphasize its aesthetic qualities while popularizing the use of a virtue-based vocabulary to analyze them. More psychologically oriented rhetoricians such as George Campbell and Richard Whately, though influential in setting up an ever-hardening boundary between "rhetorical" and "literary" texts, also contributed to an idea of literature as a form of interpersonal communication, further ensconcing the centrality of style-as-character within it.

The theoretical questions that govern the Victorian criticism of style – whether style is subjective or objective, personal or impersonal, unconsciously determined or a matter of careful craft – reflect this imbrication of forces. Critics as diverse as De Quincey, Newman, Spencer, and Raleigh each draw on discourses about style to argue for the aesthetic specificity of literary material without detaching it from an ethics of character, establishing the tenets of a formalist methodology that remains with us today. An understanding of this method explains apparent contradictions within Victorian formalism concerning the nature of stylistic value, as when, in "The Principles of Criticism," John Addington Symonds argues, "It will not, therefore, do in the long run for the critic of art to apply the same rules as the moralist" while also claiming that "in man's soul – his intellectual and moral nature – must be sought those abiding relations which constitute great art, and are the test of right aesthetic judgment."[4] For Symonds, as for many of his contemporaries, the ability to appreciate a wide range of stylistic virtues reflects not only a specialized aesthetic sensibility – though that remains of the utmost importance – but also a commitment to an ethical humanism that begins with the spirit of the Renaissance (109).

A proper explanation of this unusual imperative will require this and the next two chapters to unfold.

The Belletristic Background

There are many reasons why rhetoric came to flourish in eighteenth-century Scotland. Culturally, the study of rhetoric allowed the Scottish middle class to emulate the educational formation of the English gentleman, serving as a vehicle for social acceptance and advancement.[5] Intellectually, rhetoric and related fields, such as moral philosophy and politics, provided an historically fruitful mode for studying the principles of human nature, which, in the British tradition, increasingly centered upon the faculty of "taste" as the seat of moral and aesthetic judgment.[6] Until this period, however, rhetoric was understood primarily as the analysis of argument, to be taught as a branch of philosophical logic or ethics.[7] Insofar as it existed, the formal study of "belles lettres" – a term, loosely meaning "fine letters" or "polite literature," that encompassed a wide swathe of humanistic writing, including imaginative literature[8] – was a minor rhetorical appendage, useful for illustrating principles of style and elaborating the general taxonomy of verbal genres.[9]

Out of this context, Adam Smith played a seminal role in reviving rhetoric as a method for studying the arts.[10] From 1748 to 1750, Smith delivered a series of public lectures at the University of Edinburgh dedicated solely to "rhetoric and belles lettres," and students would have been sensitive to the emancipation of these subjects from their customary philosophical setting.[11] In contrast to the courses of his predecessor, John Stevenson, Smith paid relatively little attention to the dominant rhetorical topics of invention and arrangement, choosing instead to focus the majority of his lectures on style, ranging from the structure of sentences, to techniques of description and ornament, to the characteristic features of authors and genres. Smith's own account of the rhetorical tradition is highly revisionary, underscoring his shift in emphasis:

> The Expression and Stile is what requires most skill and is alone capable of any particular directions. We see accordingly that Cicero, Quinctilian and all the best authors who treat of Rhetoricall composition, treat of the Invention of arguments, or Topicks, and the composition or arrangement of them, as very slight matter and of no great difficulty, and never see[e]m to be in ernest unless when they give us directions concerning the ornaments of Language and Expression. (139)

According to Vincent Bevilacqua, this statement offers "not a traditional theory of rhetoric . . . but a stylistic-belletristic one,"[12] as *lexis* triumphs over *logos* as the *telos* of rhetorical power and craft. It is also belletristic in its scope of application, for Smith considers the nature of style not just in pulpit or political oratory (the most instrumental components of rhetoric for a British audience) but in a wide range of historical, narrative, and other written (as opposed to spoken) texts.

Smith's character-based conception of style also became a fixture of belletrism. On the one hand, his view that "the stile of an author is generally of the same stamp as their character" (35) reflects an eighteenth-century fascination with language as a psychological medium. For example, Smith claims that "perfection of stile consists in Express<ing> in the most concise, proper and precise manner the thought of the author, and that in the manner which best conveys the sentiment, passion or affection with which it affects or he pretends it does affect him and which he designs to communicate to his reader" (55). Insofar as the author's thoughts and sentiments vary, so will the style, which then serves as an accurate index to everything that preceded it. (By allowing that an author might "affect" or "pretend" his feelings, Smith does not yet make a virtue of "sincerity," as many Victorian writers do, though he does affirm the "easy and natural" style as an enduringly popular ideal.) However, verbal styles vary even "when all other circumstances are alike" – that is, when two authors share identical thoughts, feelings, and communicative intentions – because "the character of the author must make the stile different" (40). For example, a "plain man . . . gives his opinion bluntly and affirms without condescending to give any reason for his doing so," whereas "the Simple man . . . is not over ready to give his opinion and when he does it 'tis with that unaffected modesty which displays itself in all his behavior" (36–37). Style thus provides a window onto character on two levels: first, in how an author generates and arranges his text for a particular end; and second, in the underlying temperament or tone that organizes that surface material.

Smith uses the connection between style and character as a way of legitimating its interest and beauty. Speaking of human diversity, Smith writes that "There are variety of characters which we may equally admire, as equally go<o>d and amiable, and yet these may be very different" (34). For example, because no one individual can encompass every appealing trait, we do not discredit the attractions of the simple man just because he lacks the virtues of the plain one. Instead, "the consideration of this variety of characters affords us often no small entertainment, it forms one of the chief pleasures of a sociall life" (34). If differences in character are inevitable and agreeable, and style is an extension of character, then the contemplation of different styles is also intrinsically pleasurable, with each offering a different specimen of its kind: "In the same manner the various stiles in stead of being condemned for the want of beauties perhaps incompatible with those they possess may be considered as good in their kind and suited to the circumstance of the author" (34). Of course, not all styles are equally pleasing. Sometimes an author affects a style that does not suit his "genius and temper" (56), resulting in defects or vices, and individual stylistic preferences will vary, just as social preferences do. There are also other sources of stylistic beauty, such as figurative devices and "smoothness of cadence" (37), that seem less intimately tethered to a characterological norm. But, on the whole, Smith establishes character as a primary determinant of stylistic quality and variety while explaining, for this reason, why readers should take pleasure in that diversity.

Smith's lectures were not published during his lifetime, but their influence was substantial, especially upon the writings of Hugh Blair, the first Regius Professor of Rhetoric and Belles Lettres at the University of Edinburgh and an intellectual associate of Smith.[13] In his *Lectures on Rhetoric and Belles Lettres*, published in 1783 but based on courses given in the preceding decades, Blair reaffirms the centrality of style within rhetoric, defining style similarly to Smith, as "the peculiar manner in which a man expresses his conceptions, by means of Language" (I:183). Also like Smith, Blair focuses upon written rather than spoken texts, interchangeably using the words "speech" and "writing," "eloquence" and "communication." Having begun with a brief overview of the aesthetic topics then in vogue – taste, sublimity, and the history and structure of language – Blair moves swiftly to providing a detailed overview of stylistic virtues and vices that relies heavily upon Cicero and Quintilian. "All the qualities of a good Style," he declares, "may be ranged under two heads, Perspicuity and Ornament" (I:184). Perspicuity, which privileges clearness in communication, incorporates purity (idiomatic diction), propriety (appropriateness in expression), and precision (the language expresses exactly what the author intends, and nothing more), both in diction and the structure of the sentence. Good sentence structure also depends upon unity (related members must be placed near each other), strength or "liveliness of impression," and harmony, which concerns "agreeableness to the ear" (I:247). Ornament, responsible for effects of "grace and beauty" (I:204), arises "from a graceful, strong, or melodious construction of words" (I:272), as well as from metaphor and other figures of speech.

From these constituent virtues, Blair next considers the "general characters of style" that "arise from the whole tenour of [an author's] language; and comprehend the effect produced by all those parts of Style which we have already considered" (I:368).

At their simplest, the "general characters" function like a signature through which "the best and most original writers are known and distinguished" (I:370). They are naturally connected to an author's "manner of thinking," as when the "diffuse writer unfolds his thought fully," or the concise writer "lops off, as redundant, every expression which does not add something material to the sense" (I:371). But they also reflect a more general attitude toward style itself as a component of verbal expression that has little to do with an author's "ideas" as they were commonly understood, reflecting what Archer would later call the "man-as-artist." For example, the concise writer does not "reject" ornament in principle, "but his ornament is intended for the sake of force, rather than grace" (I:371), reducing the impression of beauty. Similarly, the "nervous" writer produces prose characterized by a high degree of strength, but may, through a disregard for stylistic variety, fall into monotonous "harshness" (I:377). In contrast to Smith, Blair does not explain the general characters as concomitants of an author's physical body, environment, or behavior (what Smith calls "the circumstance of the author"), as when Smith claims that "Swifts naturall moroseness joined to the constant dissapointments and crosses he met with in life would make contempt naturall to his character" (48), fomenting a predilection for ridicule and satire. Instead, Blair interprets Swift's "genius" as that of an aesthetic sensibility, saying that "we must not look for much ornament and grace in his Language" because his "haughty and morose genius, made him despise any embellishment of this kind" (I:381). Blair's difference from Smith thus resides in his careful contrivance of the distance between what Wayne Booth calls the "real" and "implied" author – that is, between the actual living person and the persona established by the text. Blair describes Lord Bolingbroke, for example, as having "the Style *of one* who speaks, or rather who harangues. Indeed, all his Political Writings . . . carry much more *the appearance of one* declaiming with warmth in a great Assembly, than *of one* writing in a closet, in order to be read by others" (II:238, my emphasis). There is an obvious distance here between the real Lord Bolingbroke and the character who appears through his writings, just as Swift's "manner of writing carries in it the character of one who rests altogether on his sense" (I:476). It may be that Swift did possess such a character in real life, but that fact remains extrinsic to the character norm that is conjured by the text.

The evolution of the stylistic virtue of nervousness is telling, not least because its Victorian meaning shares little in common with either its earliest eighteenth-century incarnations or its current psychologizations. According to George Rousseau, the word has roots in the Latin translation of the Greek word for "sinew" or "tendon,"[14] which eighteenth-century physiologists thought were marked by sexual difference: masculine nerves were muscular and vigorous, while feminine nerves were languid and diffuse.[15] Rhetoricians subsequently began using the word "nervous" as "an ellision for all things masculine in language, tough, strong, assertive, taut, concise,"[16] updating an ancient stylistic type in accordance with modern physiological science. However, in part due to Blair's example, the word gradually shed its gendered character: for example, in 1895 Harrison contrasts the "chastened literary art" of novelists and historians, invoking a sexually diverse group that spans Thackeray (male), George Eliot (female), and Symonds (homosexual), with "the flat, ungainly, nerveless style of mere scientific research," all of whose exemplars are male (19). Harrison's use of the term suggests that "nervousness," like "manliness," eventually became a property of language and genre rather than gender, its significance shifting from the referential to the autonomous sphere.

Blair begins the second volume of his *Lectures* by declaring every other rhetorical topic – including eloquence (i.e. public speaking), delivery, and genres of historical, philosophical, poetical, and dramatic writing – as "the subjects upon which Style is employed" (II:1), implying the supremacy of style as an interpretive skeleton key.[17] But the *Lectures* were most innovative for containing, as the conclusion of the first volume, a hundred-page "Critical Examination of the Style of Mr. Addison, in No. 411 of the Spectator," in which Blair painstakingly analyzes the essay sentence by sentence, and sometimes word by word, to determine whether the expression is pleasing or disagreeable, clear or elegant, florid or plain, perspicuous or obscure. Blair's emphasis is not on the rectitude of Addison's argument, or even on the "manner of thinking" that gives rise to such thoughts and sentiments, but rather on the role played by style in shaping the conveyance of content, culminating in judgments of taste. This fine-grained application of stylistic theory to what later became known as "practical criticism"[18] was, in 1783, unprecedented in the history of nonbiblical hermeneutics, and helped make "belletrism" synonymous with the appreciation of style both as an expression of general character and as an autonomous – that is to say, intrinsically pleasurable – aesthetic experience. As Blair says of Bolingbroke's writings, "it is to be regretted . . . that the matter contained in them, should have been so trivial or so false; for, from the manner and style, considerable advantage might be reaped" (II:239). Hence, we find in Blair the foundations not only for a conception of autonomous style, but also for what David Wellbery calls the "theory of autonomous art," the view that "art is necessarily independent of external purposes" and "serves no other purposes than its own self-presentation"[19] – complicating Wellbery's claim that aesthetic autonomy was fundamentally incompatible with rhetoric.[20]

Blair's influence in the nineteenth century was enormous: running through at least 130 editions in Britain and America between 1783 and 1911,[21] the *Lectures* formed the backbone of the Victorian pupil's literary education, used as a textbook for study at home or in colleges and universities or pillaged for source material in a range of derivative works.[22] But his significance must be juxtaposed with another form of "new rhetoric" that was also circulating during this period. Like Blair, the Scottish law lord Henry Home Kames was present during Smith's lectures and a member of the Select Society of Edinburgh; his *Elements of Criticism*, published in 1762, offers a similarly capacious treatment of *elocutio* across a range of texts, focusing on literature, or "belles lettres." There is, however, a notable difference: unlike Blair, Kames delays the treatment of style to the second volume, using the first to provide an overarching theory of aesthetic response in line with the rising science of "aesthetics."[23] In this way, Kames subordinates the treatment of style to his study of emotions and reason, as he explains in the middle of the first volume: "having discoursed in general of emotions and passions, I proceed to a more narrow inspection of such of them as serve to unfold the principles of the fine arts . . . I carry my view no farther than to the elements of criticism, in order to show, that the fine arts are a subject of reasoning as well as of taste."[24] Though imaginative texts play a major role in his text, Kames uses the arts to provide insight into the nature of perception and judgment rather than the other way around. His emphasis is, to borrow terms first provided by Douglas Ehninger, more "psychological-epistemological" than "belletristic," focusing on the transmission of information and affect rather than on their manner of artistry.[25]

Kames's *Elements* was never as popular as Blair's *Lectures*, but he laid the groundwork for George Campbell's *Philosophy of Rhetoric*, first published in 1776 and, after Blair's *Lectures*, the second most-reproduced rhetoric of the nineteenth century.[26] Campbell, who spent his teaching life in Aberdeen, was influenced by the philosophical currents of the Scottish Enlightenment, and approached rhetoric as a branch of the human sciences; in the introduction, he declares that "no art whatever that has so close a connexion with all the faculties and powers of the mind as eloquence, of the art of speaking, in the extensive sense in which I employ the term."[27] Rhetoric is, undoubtedly, a fine art, using the imagination to please and persuade; but its study is primarily useful because it "not only traces the operations of the intellect and imagination, but discloses the lurking springs of action in the heart" (6). For Campbell, style plays a diminished role in rhetoric, valuable only insofar as it "must be applied for the conviction and persuasion of others" (5); on this view, the aesthetic dimension of style "is the pleasure which the artist or the critic enjoys, who can coolly and deliberately survey the whole" (125), rather than the less disinterested experience of the passionate listener whom a discourse has the capacity to move. For this reason, Campbell criticizes Kames for widening the scope of rhetoric beyond its instrumental uses, arguing that "the subject of the learned and ingenious author of that work is rather too multifarious to admit so narrow a scrutiny as would be necessary for a perfect knowledge of the several parts" (8). To wit:

> Everything that is an object of taste, *sculpture, painting, music, architecture*, and *gardening*, as well as *poetry* and eloquence, come within his plan . . . All those particular arts are examined only on that side, wherein there is found a pretty considerable coincidence with one another; namely, as objects of taste, which by exciting sentiments of grandeur, beauty, novelty, and the like, are calculated to delight the imagination. In this view, eloquence comes no farther under consideration, than as a fine art . . . But to treat it also as an useful art, and closely connected with the understanding and the will, would have led to a discussion foreign to his purpose. (8)

Given this position, it is hardly surprising that Campbell, while promising to discuss five qualities of style – perspicuity, vivacity, elegance, animation, and music – scarcely reaches farther than the second term. His discussion focuses on purity, clarity, and the avoidance of solecism and enervation, all fundamental to discursive transmission in a way that the "unessential" (6) stylistic beauties are not. For example, Campbell considers poetry to be a "particular mode or form of certain branches of oratory," and hence dismisses aspects of its literary specificity, such as versification, as "the more mechanical part of the poet's work, being at most but a sort of garnishing" (6).

Campbell's instrumentalization of rhetoric and demotion of literary style finds its chief legacy in Richard Whately's *Elements of Rhetoric*, which was also widely reproduced as a Victorian textbook.[28] Having taken holy orders in 1814 and then published a study of logic, Whately, of St. Alban's College, Oxford, was drawn to rhetoric as a tool of ecclesiastical oratory. If Campbell provides the theory, then Whately supplies the practice, bridging the gap between the philosophy of rhetoric and its practical applications in composition and sermonizing. Given Blair's own emphasis on providing models of stylistic analysis, it may seem surprising that Whately calls Campbell's work "incomparably superior" to Blair's *Lectures* in consideration of their "practical utility to the student."[29] But such a view becomes comprehensible when we contrast Whately's conception of rhetoric as an aid to the production of discourse with Blair's emphasis on the criticism of written texts. Of style – which comes at the end of Whately's treatise rather than, as in Blair's, at the beginning – Whately says that it encompasses "much that by no means *peculiarly* belongs to our present inquiry" (234), which he claims has "an especial reference to argumentative and persuasive works" (234). This qualification recalls Aristotle's own distinction between rhetoric and poetry and establishes a categorical difference between prose designed to establish a conviction in its reader (i.e. expository prose) and prose whose primary purpose is otherwise (i.e. literary or imaginative). Indeed, Whately registers the distance between the purposes of rhetoric and literary criticism when he states, at the start of his treatise, that "much of what we now call literature, or 'Belles Lettres,' was *formerly* included in what the ancients called rhetorical studies" (23, my emphasis). Against Blair's effort to widen the purview of rhetoric by elevating the study of style, Whately proposed its functionalistic re-narrowing, returning the academic study of rhetoric to the traditional ends of argumentative logic, persuasion, and composition (18–19).

From Rhetoric to Criticism

According to I.A. Richards, the study of rhetoric begins with Aristotle and "may perhaps be said to end with Archbishop Whately,"[30] whose account of style he finds particularly lacking: "Instead of a philosophic inquiry into how words work in discourse, we get the usual postcard's-worth of crude common sense: – be clear, yet don't be dry; be vivacious, use metaphors when they will be understood not otherwise; respect usage,"[31] and so on. Richards's summary dismissal of Victorian rhetoric is justified in the sense that no Victorian author produced an original rhetoric that could rival its classical or eighteenth-century predecessors in either authority or influence. As a result, it became commonplace throughout the twentieth century to assume that Victorian rhetoric lacked either intrinsic interest or special relevance to literary studies. In the *Encyclopedia of Rhetoric and Composition: Communication from Ancient Times to the Information Age* – a massive tome published by Routledge in 1996 – William M. Purcell notes that "nineteenth-century rhetorical studies have been dismissed by twentieth-century scholars"[32] while Linda Ferreira-Buckley describes how historians have "found little 'rhetoric' in the nineteenth century worth studying."[33] The polymath Alexander Bain attempted the period's most ambitious rhetoric in 1866, and even then he acknowledged that "the fulfilment of this design has ended in a work more closely allied to Campbell's Philosophy of Rhetoric, Blair's Lectures, and Whately's Rhetoric, than to the majority of recent works on English Composition."[34]

Bain's remark is revealing, however, for the way he casually elides the differences among forbears that clearly possess "classic" status. For, if there is anything original about Victorian rhetoric, it emanates from the unexpected ways in which the bellestristic and psychological-epistemological currents of the eighteenth century, which led to such different endpoints in the conceptualization of rhetoric itself, were recombined within the purview of Victorian literary criticism, where the "philosophic inquiry" into *elocutio* ultimately came to rest. Numerous scholars have already discussed the shaping impact of Scottish new rhetoric, and belletrism in particular, on the "institutionalization"[35] of "college English"[36] as a modern university discipline, which not only helped establish a canon of English literary works, but also allowed them to be seen as having more than merely "rhetorical or didactic" value[37] – that is, to be seen as "autonomous creations"[38] worthy of specialized disciplinary interest in a way that escaped Richards's notice. However, less has been observed about how style *in particular* became the privileged object for literary critics precisely because it was the area most closely identified with the practice of belletrism as an extension of classical *elocutio*, and thus most closely linked to the criticism of literary texts. While the treatment of style within manuals on "English composition" became increasingly mechanical and rote – the very situation that Richards lamented – it nonetheless flourished in the growing literary-critical establishment, which seamlessly co-opted the formalistic features of the rhetorical apparatus it presumed to supersede.

The first indications of this shift may be observed in two sets of essays published by Thomas De Quincey, one on "Rhetoric," occasioned as a review of Whately's *Elements* in 1828, and another on "Style," published in three parts in 1840–41.[39] In the essay on rhetoric, De Quincey adheres to the Whatelyan conception of rhetoric as an art of persuasion in which style plays a "ministerial" (147) or supporting role: in describing Donne as a "rhetorical" poet, De Quincey affirms that "we revert to the original use of the word *Rhetoric*, as laying the principal stress upon the management of the thoughts, and only a secondary one upon the ornaments of style" (147). On this view, style is most useful when it enhances the "perfect interpretation of the thoughts" or "conciliate[s] regard to the speaker" (147), in keeping with the classical hierarchy of *logos* over *lexis* and *ethos* as the appeal to character. However, in the multi-part essay on style, De Quincey expresses dissatisfaction with the limitations of rhetoric as the exclusive context for understanding style as an art of expression. De Quincey offers two reasons for its inadequacy. First, although Britain has an impressive history of "popular eloquence" (7) through which engaged citizens are exposed to stylistic excellence, "many a man is fascinated by the artifices of composition who fancies that it is the subject which has operated so potently" (7). A lack of theoretical sophistication, in other words, causes listeners to mistake the manner for the matter, a problem seemingly unremediated by the usual rhetorical training. Second, De Quincey argues that "*the modes of style appropriate to popular eloquence being essentially different from those of written composition*, any possible experience on the hustings, or in the senate, would *pro tanto* tend rather to disqualify the mind for appreciating the more chaste and more elaborate qualities of style fitted for books; and thus a real advantage of the English in one direction has been neutralized by two causes in another" (9). Here, de Quincey follows the examples of eighteenth-century rhetoricians in observing the stylistic differentiation of written (and, we may infer, non-expository) texts, but suggests that the emerging conception of rhetoric is ultimately too narrow to accommodate it.

That being said, De Quincey's approach to style, however emancipated from the confines of persuasive rhetoric, remains deeply shaped by the rhetorical tradition, in particular through his elaboration of an organic conception of style that is frequently associated with romanticism.[40] In the first part of "Style," De Quincey distinguishes between "the science of style as an organ of thought, of style in relation to the ideas and feelings," and "the science of style considered as a machine, in which words act upon words, and through a particular grammar" (37). These two sciences of style represent not two kinds of qualities found in a literary text but rather two ways of analyzing them: they correspond roughly to the difference between matter and manner, allowing that the "mode of expression" (to borrow a term from Blair) must suit the "thought" that precedes it. In the fourth part of the essay, however, De Quincey seems to conflate these two approaches when he distinguishes between "objective" and "subjective" texts. Objective compositions are those in which the matter is "generally equal to its own enunciation" and "tells without any manner" (226); there is no room for style in an objective text because the words serve an exclusively informational purpose. However, in a subjective text, such as "meditative poetry," which involves the projection of an "inner mind," "the manner of treating it not only transcends the matter, but very often, and in very great proportion, *is* the matter" (115); put differently, "the two elements are not united as a body with a separable dress, but as a mysterious incarnation" such that "the style becomes confluent with the matter" (119). The idealization of this imaginative unity is sometimes thought to be a German idea, disseminated in Britain by Hazlitt and Coleridge; but, as Douglas Patey explains, virtually "*all* eighteenth-century writers liken successful literary works to living creatures," according to which "higher levels are the formal cause of lower ones," as with "the relation of soul to body."[41] Indeed, Patey argues that the neoclassical virtue of propriety reflects an organic conception of style insofar as it demands that "all relations among levels – all relations of form to meaning – must be adequate relations of *expression* . . . and for expression to occur, for the reader to be able to move from form to intended meaning at any level in the work, formal choices must be *appropriate* and *natural*."[42] What De Quincey calls stylistic "confluence" recalls Blair's own belief that "the Style and thoughts of a writer are so intimately connected, that . . . it is frequently hard to distinguish them" (I:402), offering a restatement rather than a revolution of a basic rhetorical premise.

In the essay on "Style," De Quincey claims that the literary value of style is proportionate to textual subjectivity: the more the "content" of a work consists in thoughts or feelings as filtered through the "prism" (115) of the writer's mind, "precisely in that degree, and the more subtly, does the style or the embodying of the thoughts cease to be a mere separable ornament" (118–19). This idea became commonplace in Victorian criticism, further extirpating style away from functionalist expository texts and closer to imaginative art as the expression of an author's particular "genius."[43] When, therefore, in a later essay on "Language" (1858), De Quincey speculates that style may also have "an *absolute value*, like the product of any other exquisite art, quite distinct from the value of the subject about which it is employed, and irrelatively to the subject" (212), it remains ambiguous whether the second "subject" refers to the rhetorical *logos* as separable from style or rather to the neoclassical conflation of "subject" with the "subjectivity" of the author. Either way, De Quincey makes a strong case for autonomous stylistic value even as he intensifies its connection to authorial character.

This apparent paradox recurs in John Henry Newman's section on "Literature" in *The Idea of a University* (1852), which recapitulates many of De Quincey's ideas. Contrasting the subjectivism of literature, which represents "the personal use or exercise of language," with the universality of science, which "has to do with things,"[44] Newman defines style as a "thinking out into language" (276) according to which an author "uses language in its full compass" (275) to provide "not only the image of his subject, but of his mind" (280). Newman supplements this organic view of style with a celebration of the virtue of propriety: "the mere dealer in words cares little or nothing for the subject which he is embellishing, but can paint and gild anything whatever to order; whereas the artist, whom I am acknowledging, has his great or rich visions before him, and his only aim is to bring out what he thinks or what he feels in a way adequate to the thing spoke of, and appropriate to the speaker" (285). For Newman, the "artist" is equal parts genius and craftsman, a worthy individual whose capacity to master the art of expression makes possible his imaginative self-embodiment through form. Like others in this period, Newman cites Shakespeare as the greatest example of this sort of artist, describing him as "the master of the two-fold Logos, the thought and the word, distinct, but inseparable from each other" (291).

Newman's belief that style is fundamentally "personal," as unique as a person's own "shadow" (276), was hardly new; the line from Smith and De Quincey is not difficult to draw. But his collecting of these rhetorical principles under the heading of "Literature," within the context of the liberal university, reflects the drift of style toward a new disciplinary context. The evolution of the Regius Chair at the University of Edinburgh provides further evidence of this movement. When the Chair was first founded in 1762 to be occupied by Blair, it was called the Regius Chair of Rhetoric and Belles Lettres, which was doubly innovative: it marked the first time that belles lettres was formally recognized as a subject for university instruction and the first time that rhetoric had been officially released from the grip of philosophical logic. However, when David Masson assumed the post in 1865, its name was changed to the Regius Chair of Rhetoric and English Literature, the latter term having begun to appear in place of "belles lettres" toward the middle of the nineteenth century. This was no mere substitution of an English word for an outmoded French synonym; rather, it reflected how the rise of literary criticism depended, if not on the absolute "suppression"[45] of rhetoric, then on the selective assimilation of its methods and subject matter. For example, in his inaugural lecture, Masson promises to offer a synthesis of eighteenth-century rhetorical approaches: distinguishing between didactic, expository, oratorical, and imaginative writing, he seeks to combine "a theory of style, or of that art of expression in language which writers and speakers of all the 4 kinds have alike to practise" with a "science of the principles . . . whereby, according to the constitution of the human mind, this or that mental effect may be produced."[46] However, in practice, Masson revealed his greater debt to belletrism by dedicating over half of his lectures to the "History of English Literature," with a heavy focus on "Poesy," or the "imaginative" variety (243).[47] As he says in the first lecture, the tradition of English literature "finds its great beginner in Chaucer" (243) and then continues through Spenser, Bacon, Shakespeare, Milton, Scott, and Wordsworth; further inspection of the lectures reveals a canon including Defoe, Richardson, Austen, Dickens, Thackeray, and Emily Brontë.[48] This list is notable for two reasons. First, it resembles the one Masson proposed six years earlier in *British Novelists and Their Styles* (1859), which was the first full-length monograph on British fiction and thus a seminal piece of criticism. As Jack Downs observes, the earlier text was deeply shaped by "belles lettres-inflicted critical concepts"[49] such as stylistic comparison, propriety, and individual "genius" or character that subsequently get repeated in the lectures. Second, Masson gives equal (if not greater) representation to writers of prose as compared to poetry, a hangover from rhetoric's long-standing association with sentences rather than verse, best exemplified through Blair's analysis of Addison. The drift of belleletristic criticism toward style in the novel, and away from nonfictional prose where it was customarily dominant, owes something to this rhetorical convention.

Downs claims that Masson's "vast influence – as an editor, essayist, and academic – certainly helped sustain the belles lettres-inspired critical tradition throughout the latter half of the nineteenth century,"[50] citing, as just one example, *Episodes of Fiction* (1870), whose extracts, the anonymous editor describes, were "selected with the view of illustrating the general character of their style, and presenting the reader with an opportunity of comparing the present school of fiction with the past."[51] Blair's influence also infected the study of rhetoric proper, where the psychological-epistemological approach otherwise came to prominence. For example, one might expect Alexander Bain, one of the period's most eminent psychologists, to adopt a strictly Campbellian framework, noting, as he does in the overture to his *English Composition and Rhetoric*, that the three ends of speaking or writing – "to inform, to persuade, [and] to please – correspond to three departments of the human mind, the Understanding, the Will, and the Feelings" (19). However, Bain begins his text with an overview of "Style generally" because style pertains "to all modes of address" (19). Moreover, by describing styles in terms of their "qualities" (78) rather than their characters, Bain expands the possibility for autonomous stylistic signification to an even greater extent than Blair: "A composition abounding in any one of the figures would be described by an epithet from the name of that figure; as, Metaphorical, Antithetical, Epigrammatic, Hyperbolical, Ironical, Sarcastic, Elliptical. A profusion of figurative language generally would receive the designations – Figurative, Flowery, Ornate, Imaginative, Illustrative; to which are opposed the Plain, Dry, Bald" (78). Bain's sensitivity to the distinctiveness of stylistic artistry is further evident in the third part of his treatise, where he counts "aesthetic emotions" among the feelings that "oratory" (by which he means any persuasive discourse) seeks to move: "The preacher, for example, who has to draw out and strengthen the religious and moral sentiments, must proceed by appropriate descriptions, combinations, and narrations, in the manner of an artist" (255). Poetry itself generates its own characteristic emotion, namely the "pleasure" that is an end in itself (253).

It may seem ironic that the psychological-epistemological trend within rhetoric has played a greater role in shaping twenty-first-century approaches to Victorian style than belletrism. For example, Nicholas Dames finds an implicit "literary theory" buried in Bain's *Emotions and the Will* – a text that, as Dames admits, makes no reference to "literary language"[52] – rather than in the explicitly rhetorical account of style found in *English Composition and Rhetoric*. However, critics could be forgiven for gravitating to scientific contexts in seeking to explain Victorian formalism. Herbert Spencer's early essay "Philosophy of Style" (1852) is saturated in scientific protocols, seeking, as one Victorian editor described it, to "unroll the secrets of the human mind" by generating a single "law from which naturally flow the rules of rhetoric and good composition."[53] According to Spencer, that law is cognitive economy: "other things equal, the force of all verbal forms and arrangements is great, in proportion as the time and mental effort they demand from the recipient is small" (33). Such a view, which applies as much to syllables and diction as it does to metaphors and symbols, takes Campbellian mentalism to its logical extreme, and made Spencer a target for early formalists who felt he expressed a typically Victorian insensitivity to the particularities of literary form. For example, in "Art as Technique," Viktor Shklovsky counters Spencer's "economy of mental effort"[54] with the principle of defamiliarization, which aims to slow down perception rather than speed it up.[55] He argues that Spencer's application of a single principle to all uses of language – expository or imaginative, poetic or prosaic – demonstrates how he "failed utterly"[56] to distinguish between rhetorical and literary uses of language, as if the two must inevitably be opposed.

However, a closer reading of Spencer's essay reveals a firm commitment to the kind of belletristic literariness of which even Shklovsky might approve. In the much less-quoted second part and appendix of the essay, he reiterates many of the most influential points found in Blair. For example, just as Blair writes that "different countries have been noted for peculiarities of Style, suited to their different temper and genius" (I:184), Spencer reads "peculiarities" of style as "the hieroglyphics" in which temporal, national, or individual "characters are inscribed" (55). He recommends the "natural style – the style in which a writer speaks as he thinks and feels, and which depends on his temperament and nature of his subject" – as the best course for any "literary aspirant" (51). And, in an uncanny anticipation of Shklovsky's own remarks against him, he revels, like Smith and Newman before him, in stylistic diversity, claiming that a uniform or unchanging style reflects the ossification of an author's emotions and intellect: "Why is Johnson pompous, Goldsmith simple? Why is one author abrupt, another rhythmical, another concise? Evidently in each case the habitual mode of utterance must depend upon the habitual balance of the nature" (47). According to Spencer, the "perfectly-endowed" writer would "unconsciously write in all styles ... His mode of expression naturally responding to his state of feeling, there will flow from his pen a composition changing to the same degree that the aspects of his subject change" (48). This point of view echoes Blair's conception of the "general characters" of style as impersonal aesthetic norms to be studied and internalized, such that it becomes difficult to determine whether the matter drives the style or vice versa. As Spencer says, "fixity of style will disappear" once the "powers of speech" are "fully developed": then, he claims, "the perfect writer will express himself as Junius, when in the Junius frame of mind; when he feels as Lamb felt, will use a like familiar speech; and will fall into the ruggedness of Carlyle when in a Carlylean mood" (48).

An efflorescence of writings about style accompanied the consolidation of a culture of literary criticism in the last third of the nineteenth century.[57] In general, these reflect a typically Victorian effort to reconcile the ethical account of style with a more sophisticated appreciation of literature's aesthetic specificity.[58] For example, in an essay on "Style" published in 1877, T.H. Wright wonders "how is it that language, which is but the vehicle of thought, comes to have a force which is not the mere weight of that which it carries," where "the matter and the form seem to have independent claims upon the attention."[59] Wright's answer to this question is complicated. Like his belletristic predecessors, he views style as the "expression in language" of "countless little traits of character" that amount to "unconscious revelations of the hidden self" (83). There can therefore be no difference "between the speech and the mind that conceived it" (80). But, at the same time, style only exists because of the "imperfection" of language as a "vehicle of thought" (83). If language were able to express all that we think, there would be no need for style because every written expression would be "objective" in De Quincey's sense: declarative and self-disclosing. But "the countless devices of language, the gestures and tones of discourse, the thousand rhetorical figures of written composition, are really one and all simple propositions not capable of exact expression in the body of the narrative" (83). These distinctly literary qualities actually serve two purposes: they are, on the one hand, attempts to get closer to capturing a particular thought in words, but they are also, in themselves, "simple propositions . . . which are to tickle the imagination of the reader with suggested beauties" (83). These propositions are thus aesthetic in character, and "it is exactly in these refinements of expression that the deepest meaning of any author . . . his *self* resides" (83). Wright therefore disagrees with Spencer's evocation of an "ideal style" that would emanate from "an ideal being who is to be without personality" (84). Stylistic distinctiveness *is* the personality that defines the work of art as such.

In an essay called "Le Style C'est L'Homme" (1892), W.H. Mallock argues from different premises but arrives at much the same conclusion. According to Mallock, style is the "means by which one personality impresses itself on others" and thus functions as a "vehicle of character."[60] But rather than view style as a matter of conscious aesthetic effort, Mallock believes it to be psychologically determined: "the foundation of style, its essence, its colouring principle, is not the writer's skills as a writer, but his character as a man" (443). As a result, Mallock warns against the admiration of "mere technical skill" (443) in writing, signalling a general trend, even among artists, to decry the self-conscious appearance of effort, which was redolent of rhetorical artificiality.[61] Still, Mallock notes that "though the writing of the ordinary man not only can, but inevitably will, reveal his character up to a certain point, and will so far possess a distinctive style, it will do this and possess this up to a certain point only, and to rise beyond that point exceptional skill is needed" (448). Mallock pauses to address the apparent contradiction: "I urged that the colouring principle of style was not skill but character – was a human quality, not a literary accomplishment . . . But I did all this with the limited intention only of showing that style and skill were distinct things in essence, not of showing that the first had no need of the second" (448). As the subjectivity of the writer becomes richer and more complex, "the more does his style need skill to show itself, to embody itself, one may almost say to exist" (448). There is thus a proportional relationship between characterological and stylistic subjectivism, with the most "ethically" rich and distinctive style also being the most artistically accomplished.

In the 1890s, Walter Raleigh became the first Professor of Modern Literature at University College, Liverpool, and his essay on "Style" (1897) reveals just how thoroughly a belletristic approach to style had, by the end of the nineteenth century, migrated into the literary-critical domain. Describing style as the "body" that expresses "the informing soul," Raleigh claims that while mind and manner cannot be distinguished, as a matter of aesthetic judgment, they must be. "All style is gesture, the gesture of the mind and of the soul . . . But who shall impose laws upon the soul? It is thus of common note that one may dislike or even hate a particular style while admiring its facility, its strength, its skilful adaptation to the matter set forth."[62] Once again, the virtue of propriety constitutes an aesthetic merit that can be isolated from the referential properties that style conveys, suggesting, as in Bain, that style may be understood as a formal "quality" as well as a "general character." Consequently, in *The English Novel* (1894), a formative textbook published three years earlier, Raleigh re-imagines the history of fiction as a history of stylistic virtue, providing a literary-critical parallel to the more rhetorical-philological survey offered by John Earle in his massive *English Prose: Its Elements, History, and Usage* (1890).[63] On the second page, Raleigh laments how "there is no English version of any of the Charlemagne legends that reproduces the grave and unadorned simplicity of the French *chansons de geste* of the eleventh century."[64] English literature subsequently begins with Chaucer, whose poetry "was putting to shame, by its high artistic finish, the ambling monotony of the chanted recitations concerning Sir Eglamour, Sir Perceval, and Sir Isembras" (4). Here, the manner of presentation outweighs the matter, just as the stylistic characteristics of

John Lyly's *Euphues*, involving antithesis, alliteration, prolixity, epigram, allusion, digression, and simile, "set the first fashion in novel-writing" and yet were "vastly more important than the story" (33). Best described as a history of fictional prose styles rather than a history of the novel *per se*, *The English Novel* laid the foundation for twentieth-century surveys by George Williamson, Ian Gordon, and F.W. Bateson, placing stylistic formalism at the heart of literary study.

Conclusion

In his 1888 essay on Guy de Maupassant, Henry James repeats one of his favorite theories about "the whole question of the different classes of fiction."[65] There are, James writes, "simply as many different kinds as there are persons for practising the art, for if a picture, a tale, or a novel be a direct impression of life (and that surely constitutes its interest and value) the impression will vary according to the plate that takes it, the peculiar structure and mixture of the recipient" (523). Without alluding to the specifics of style (James briefly discusses Maupassant's "masculine firmness," 534), we can see how James's entire understanding of imaginative construction is nonetheless informed by it. Like Maupassant, he believes that "the first duty of the artist, and the thing that makes him most useful to his fellow-men, is to master his instrument, whatever it may happen to be" (525). But James also believes that it remains an open question whether the music of that instrument, however perfectly formed, be worth listening to. Judgments about art therefore involve both aesthetic and ethical dimensions, separate but inextricable.

As Debora Shuger argues with respect to seventeenth-century stylistic categories, their "significance . . . does not lie in their descriptive precision" but rather for the way "theorists use these terms to relate the formal characteristics of discourse to larger cultural issues."[66] For Victorian theorists of style, one of those issues is the nature of art itself, considered as both a morally valuable expression of the self and an aesthetically valuable formal practice. For all their differences, the recurring keynote of Victorian stylistic criticism is the way in which these two conceptions refuse to be clearly separated: as Robert Louis Stevenson argues, "the best that can be offered by the best writer of prose is to show us how the development of the idea and the stylistic pattern proceed hand in hand."[67] The precise meaning of "masculine" or "nervous" – the specific words or sentences to which they refer, or their utility as larger descriptive categories – is in many ways less important than the role that they played in drawing, from rhetoric, a conception of the literary rooted in stylistic character. This emphasis on character not only furthered the romantic celebration of stylistic individuality and genius – "it is when a man, as far as he can, expresses *himself*, that his communication is most worth having," says Wright[68] – but also helped readers appreciate that literary "communication" is admirable not only for the self that gets expressed but for the "technical elements" that make such expression possible.

CHAPTER 2

Stylistic Virtue between Moralism and Aestheticism

In *English Prose*, John Earle summarizes a common Victorian view: "The expression of Style is so various and differs by traits so delicate, that it naturally suggests a comparison with human sensibility, and the expression of emotion by the human face. By threads like these the mind is drawn to associate Style with moral character, and it is interesting to observe how frequently this idea has suggested itself" (353). In keeping with Victorian norms, Earle uses the phrase "moral character" here to refer less to the specific doctrines espoused by a text than to an author's disposition, character traits, and general habits of mind, reading style as a kind of physiognomy. But it remains ambiguous whether such character is fully a property of the artist, or in some degree the property of the text – and whether, if character is indeed a textual property, its content is distinctive enough to be governed by separate standards.

As we have seen, Victorian critics of style were increasingly likely to entertain some notion of difference between authorial *ethos*, representational content, and the ethos of style or form. This awareness stemmed from long-standing efforts to root a style's "general character" in the operations of words and sentences, which could be governed by their own internal logic. Hence, for some late nineteenth-century critics, the phrase "art for art's sake" was associated not just with aesthetic autonomy, understood as the indifference of works of art to questions of practical utility or commercial gain, but also with the stylistic autonomy that inheres in the meaning-making potential of distinctly aesthetic properties. In the Preface to *The Picture of Dorian Gray*, for example, Wilde asserts that "vice and virtue are to the artist materials for an art" (4) rather than its standard of meaning, and argues that books are neither moral or immoral, but only well or badly written. In the same vein, Robert Louis Stevenson, who regarded style as the "foundation of all literature," defines it not as personality but as "pattern": that is, as an artistic contrivance whose value exists apart from "the interest of the fact or fable" and that must be measured accordingly ("On Style," 551).

In the last chapter, I argued that virtue terms persist in nineteenth-century stylistic criticism because they were co-opted from rhetoric, which, by establishing style as the quintessential literary property, bequeathed a series of ready-made methods for analyzing it. Given the close connection between the style and the man promoted by nearly all rhetorical theory in this period, it is unsurprising that Victorian critics would embrace a set of terms that could be used to describe both. However, if the words used to describe general stylistic character lend themselves so easily to confusion between (conventionally) moral and aesthetic appraisal, one might expect aesthetically minded writers such as Wilde or Stevenson to disavow them in favor of a more neutral, less ethically inflected vocabulary. That the opposite occurs offers an intriguing puzzle in the history of criticism. In this chapter, I argue that the very doubleness of stylistic terms – the moral and aesthetic doubleness incipient in the mentalism of belletristic rhetoric and connoted by the idea of "general character" – made them appealing to those who sought to enhance the distinctiveness of aesthetic appreciation without depriving it of ethical force. On this view, stylistic formalism rises to prominence toward the end of the nineteenth century not as a reaction against mid-century moralism but rather as its logical extension.

This paradoxical extension is most visible in the writings of the four Victorian critics most influenced by Aristotle: Ruskin, Arnold, Pater, and Wilde, each of whom was educated at Oxford. According to some accounts of the period, Ruskin and Arnold were moralizing critics, reducing the value of stylistic features to the expression of spiritual or moral content, while Pater and Wilde, as exponents of "art for art's sake," held exactly the reverse position. But why, if Ruskin subordinated formal to moral values, is he considered the grandfather of aestheticism? And why, if Pater was dedicated to form "for its own sake," is his writing replete with claims about ethos and virtue? In answer, I argue that each of these thinkers draws on an Aristotelian conceptual framework that interprets style as the realization of character, whether ethos is understood in narrowly referential terms or broadly aesthetic ones. Following the romantic elevation of a "confluent" stylistic ideal, most critics in this tradition resist an absolute separation between aesthetics and ethics, style and content: Pater, for example, insists that no work of art addresses itself exclusively to "pure sense" or "pure intellect" but rather to a synthetic faculty that he calls (using a phrase from Arnold) "'imaginative reason,' through the senses" (*Renaissance*, 83). Hence, the ideal work of art is that in which "we are least able to detach the matter from the form, without a deduction of something from that matter itself" (87). Even so, the conceptual difference between content and form remains intellectually significant and helps foster a new sense of "matter" as being formally constituted – as having, so to speak, an aesthetic ethos that is integral to the "perfection" of its character. As literary criticism came to be seen as a creative act on a par with the production of art, it too became a morally valuable act, incorporated within a vision of "the good life" based upon the expression and appreciation of character in its richest and most diversified forms.

A Century of Aristotle

If eighteenth-century Britain was the "Augustan Age," when cultural figures patterned themselves after Roman models such as Virgil, Horace, and Cicero, the nineteenth century was marked by a turn toward Hellenism.[1] Politically, Victorians favored the civic virtues of Athenian democracy over the aristocratic privileges of the Roman imperium.[2] Theologically, Greek philosophy "provided both a surrogate for Christianity and a foil against Victorian utilitarianism and scientific naturalism."[3] Most obviously, the "spirit of Hellenism" manifested itself in new attitudes toward culture and the arts, which Angel Clare, in Hardy's *Tess of the D'Urbervilles*, describes as "the aesthetic, sensuous, pagan pleasure in natural life."[4] Because familiarity with classical culture remained the calling card of a small but influential social elite well into the nineteenth century,[5] the British educational system remained the most important conduit of its dissemination, with knowledge of Ancient Greek and Latin long being required for admission to Oxford and Cambridge. In 1800, Oxford formalized its commitment to keeping classics at the center of the curriculum through the launch of *Literae Humaniores*, otherwise known as "Greats," as a new requirement for the Bachelor of Arts.[6] While the required texts varied, the works of Aristotle were always dominant: according to Turner, its enduring place in "Greats" made the *Nicomachean Ethics* "the single most translated Greek philosophical text of the entire century,"[7] rivalled only by the interest in Plato's works in the 1850s and 60s that was stimulated by Aristotle's pre-eminence.[8] According to the classicist Jonathan Barnes (writing as "M.R. Stopper"), "Aristotle was never eclipsed. Oxford undergraduates, throughout the nineteenth century, spent more time on Aristotle than any other author, Plato included."[9]

Turner, among others, emphasizes Aristotle's compatibility with both liberal and conservative strains of Christianity in accounting for the uptake of the *Ethics* in a culture of religious seriousness. In a period when secularism posed a threat to evangelicalism, liberal theologians cited the *Ethics* as disclosing through natural reason what Christianity delivered through divine revelation. "The ethical writings of Aristotle," writes R.D. Hampden, one of the Oxford Noetics, "composed amidst the darkness of heathen superstition, abound with pure and just sentiments. Instead of depressing man to the standard of the existing depraved opinions and manners, they tend to elevate him to the perfection of his nature."[10] At the same time, the Tractarians drew on Aristotle's doctrine of the mean as supporting a view of the Church as offering a "Via Media" between evangelicalism and Catholicism, seeing an echo of their own confidence in "man's Moral nature as capable of advancing indefinitely towards its perfection."[11] The reverberation of the words "virtue," "character," and "perfection" in non-religious writings reveals Aristotle's general popularity as a moral signpost, best exemplified in the opening sentences of Samuel Smiles's *Character* (1871): "Character is one of the greatest motive powers in the world. In its noblest embodiments, it exemplifies human nature in its highest forms, for it exhibits man at his best."[12] This statement, with its emphasis on exemplary character as the ultimate *telos* of human perfection, reflects how thoroughly Aristotle's *Ethics* provided the template for the ethological, or character-based, approach to ethics that permeated Victorian culture and which I discuss more extensively in the next chapter. There can be little doubt that John Henry Newman articulated a general (if mostly forgotten) truth when he declared, in *The Idea of a University*, that "in many subject-matters, to think correctly, is to think like Aristotle, and we are his disciples whether we will or no, though we may not know it" (119).

The fact that less has been said about the influence of Aristotle's *Rhetoric* is ironic given that educated Victorian readers would have seen the *Ethics* and the *Rhetoric* as inextricably connected. Carol Poster notes that the requirement that students be examined on the *Rhetoric* in "Greats" in conjunction with the *Ethics* led to the "dramatic increase in publication of translations and editions of and student aids to the work from the 1820s through the 1850s at Oxford,"[13] to be followed by a second "flurry" of publications when the *Rhetoric* was added to the Cambridge Tripos in 1874.[14] This connection has an ancient history. The appeal to *ethos*, or to the character of a speaker, is central to the *Rhetoric*, where Aristotle argues that representing oneself as virtuous is essential for communicative success. Roman rhetoricians such as Cicero and Quintilian similarly defined rhetoric as the speech of a virtuous man, approaching rhetoric as a "profoundly ethical business" that both expresses and develops character.[15] Victorian readers would have felt the influence of the *Rhetoric* first through the classical rhetorical tradition extended by Cicero and Quintilian, then revived by Campbell and Blair, and second through its study as an "ethical"[16] text with insights into Greek and contemporary culture. For example, in his introduction to a new translation of the *Rhetoric*, published in 1867, Edward Meredith Cope distinguishes Aristotle's work from that of his predecessors by noting its "special characteristic," namely the "analysis" it provides of "human character, motives, and feelings."[17] Hence "it becomes closely connected with the study of Politics (including Ethics), which treats of moral and social phenomena, of man as an individual and as a member of society" (9).

It is surely not coincidental that the two men whom Poster credits with Aristotle's "nineteenth-century rehabilitation"[18] were Scottish academics associated with the rhetorical revival: James Moor, a professor of Greek at Glasgow University, colleague of Adam Smith, and former student of Francis Hutcheson, who did much to popularize the integrated study of moral philosophy and rhetoric;[19] and John Gillies, Moor's student and an historian of Ancient Greece, whose 1823 translation of the *Rhetoric* sought a unified approach to rhetoric, moral philosophy, and belles lettres. The interaction between communicative mentalism and belletristic aestheticism that conditions eighteenth-century rhetoric appears equally in Gillies's introduction to his text. First, Gillies writes that the study of rhetoric "comprises, within a narrow compass, the absolute and unalterable principles of good taste, the foundations of all correct moral reasoning, and, humanly speaking, the maxims of all sound practical wisdom,"[20] a thoroughly "ethical" characterization that reflects a Kamesian approach to criticism as a branch of humanist science. Yet Gillies also regards the *Rhetoric* as a hermeneutic document, seeking "to explain, on correct philosophical principles, the merits and demerits of literary composition; to investigate the rules of taste, and establish the canons of criticism" (6). In this context, it is worth noting that the *Rhetoric*, rather than the *Poetics*, served as the main point of access for understanding Aristotle's aesthetic views well into the nineteenth century, reinforcing a mutual relationship between ethics and aesthetics that cast a long shadow over Victorian criticism of the arts.[21] Only in Wilde's "The Critic as Artist" does the *Poetics* finally receive praise for treating the arts "not from the moral, but from the purely aesthetic point of view" (*Intentions*, 115),[22] but even this statement is misleading, for it was only by ethicizing the aesthetic that

Victorian critics in the Aristotelian tradition were able to isolate its characteristic meaning and value.

Ruskin and Ethico-Aesthetic Drift

During the period bracketed by De Quincey's essays on "Style" and "Language," Ruskin published the first four volumes of *Modern Painters*, *The Seven Lamps of Architecture*, and the first volume of *The Stones of Venice*. In them we can find the period's most explicit example of referential criticism insofar as Ruskin self-consciously reads formal features as an index to the spiritual condition, moral values, and mental characteristics of their producers. As he says in his Slade lecture on "The Relation of Art to Morals" (1870), the major topic of his criticism is to be "the relation of expression to character" and, at least in these lectures, how the "manual arts are as accurate exponents of ethical state."[23] The "other modes" Ruskin refers to here are linguistic, and one of his innovations as a critic was to extend the referential conception of style to works of art that lack representational or propositional content. Still, Ruskin insists that "you must have the right moral state first, or you cannot have the art" (80), a view that has caused some critics to worry that he subordinates formal considerations to judgments of moral or spiritual goodness. George P. Landow, for example, argues that Ruskin's theory of beauty as "theophany," or a symbol of the divine presence in earthly things, means that "contemplating beauty, like contemplating the Bible, God's other revelation, is a moral and religious act."[24] For Harold Bloom, Pater's "great achievement" was "to empty Ruskin's aestheticism of its moral bias," which he calls "irrelevant" and "ferocious."[25] While the high value Ruskin placed on aesthetic experience is not in dispute, his appeal to spiritually derived moral standards to ground and legitimize various kinds of aesthetic pleasure has long served to differentiate him from late Victorian aesthetes.

However, as David Craig has demonstrated, Ruskin's conception of morality was not delimited by the divinely inspired precepts of Christianity, nor confined to a set of permissions and prohibitions drawn from conventional morality. On the contrary, Ruskin belongs to the perfectionist tradition oriented toward "characters, virtues, and goods"[26] in which the central "moral task" is "to form one's character, to train one's desires, so as to be able to seek out the proper ends of a good and full life."[27] Craig notes how Ruskin consequently employs a "character-based critical approach"[28] to art that focuses on the possession and exercise of "virtues" across every aspect of aesthetic experience, from art-making to perception to qualities embodied by the work itself. When Ruskin uses the words "ethical" and "moral" interchangeably, as he does throughout the 1870 lecture, he should not be understood as invoking the parochial or pietistic morality sometimes attributed to him by detractors but as engaging the eudaimonistic tradition laid out in Aristotle's *Ethics*.[29]

Critics interested in Aristotle's influence on Ruskin usually focus their attention on the second volume of *Modern Painters* (1846), where Ruskin openly acknowledges his debt to the philosopher. Ruskin there confesses that what he calls the "theoretic faculty," which "is concerned with the moral perception and appreciation of ideas of beauty,"[30] comes from Aristotle's account of "*theoria*" (7), which exalts the contemplative life as the ultimate fulfillment of man's ethical good. As Katherine Gilbert explains, "Ruskin's use of the term Θεωρία [*theoria*] was in part polemical. He needed a word that should do two things: bind the enjoyment of art to the perception of external objects, and also fix the plane of that enjoyment on the highest level of human experience."[31] Because the theoretic faculty, as a "moral" faculty, contrasts with the "aesthetic" faculty, which involves the "mere operation of sense,"[32] Ruskin can use it to justify one's engagement with art as an enjoyment of "higher pleasures"[33] that is also a kind of virtuous exercise. Ruskin's accounts of typical and vital beauty are also distinctly Aristotelian. Typical Beauty refers to external features that convey an idea of divine attributes while Vital Beauty constitutes the expression of natural or human ones. Whether the "stamp" is divine or sublunary, all things that exist in or aspire to a state of "perfection" (which Ruskin defines, in Aristotelian fashion, as the fulfillment of a natural end or *telos*) will possess sensuous traces that are "illustrative or expressive" (87) of their source.

The theoretical framework of *Modern Painters* makes all criticism of art a criticism of virtue insofar as it attends, explicitly or implicitly, to the connection between underlying "moral dispositions or principles" (147) and the physical properties that express them. In practical terms, Ruskin begins with the observation of an object's attractive powers, enumerates its visible features, and then reasons backward toward an explanatory principle. For example, in the final section on "Typical Beauty," Ruskin observes that an object's "chasteness" (135), which he defines as freedom from violence or extravagance, is aesthetically pleasing because it conveys in material form the immaterial benevolence of a creator who willingly restricts his omnipotent power. Similarly, the aesthetic quality of "finish" (136) in the workmanship reflects the "care" (138) with which the deity tends to his creation. In this way, artistic style resembles action in

Aristotelian ethics, being the mode through which underlying moral dispositions and principles are given tangible external form; chasteness, as a stylistic virtue, is essentially reducible to "moderation" (138) as a moral one. Ruskin follows a similar procedure in *The Stones of Venice* (1851–53). The famous chapter on the Gothic argues that the external forms of Gothic architecture – its savageness, changefulness, naturalism, and so on – physically embody the moral sensibility of the Gothic worker, with his rudeness, love of change, and love of nature. Ruskin insists upon the union in great art of "mental expression" and "material form,"[34] and the highly moralized nature of his vocabulary – he considers the relation of "haughty" architecture to "humility" (II:207), for example, and distinguishes between styles of ornament that are "servile," "constitutional," and "revolutionary" (II:158) – indicates the extent to which for him, moral and stylistic virtues are fundamentally one.[35]

However, rather than dismiss Ruskin as an exponent of anti-aesthetic stylistic reductionism, we must keep in mind that for Ruskin, morality involves the entire set of qualities and characteristics, virtues and goods, that constitute an ideal vision of human flourishing. This framework possesses the theoretical potential to endow *aesthesis* with independent value, as exhibited by Ruskin's attachment to binary pairs that emphasize the technical separation between moral virtues and their stylistic exemplars. "Internal elements" and "external forms," "Mental Power" and "Material Form" (II:153), "principle" and "index" (II:158), feeling and "evidence of the feeling" (II:367): each duo insists upon a difference between idea and expression even as they are intimately connected, suggesting how far coldness, frivolity, seriousness, and the like might be regarded as autonomous rather than referential qualities. Ruskin himself gestures at this possibility when, in the third volume of *The Stones of Venice*, he worries about the false or empty formalisms that occur when similar surfaces differ in underlying motive. He contrasts the "true grotesque" of the Gothic, for example, with the "false grotesque" of the Renaissance, the former expressing the "*repose* or play of a *serious* mind" and the latter the "*full exertion* of a *frivolous* one" (III:143, original emphasis). As material forms the true and false grotesque emanate from dramatically different moral cultures, but their superficial similarities may betray a common aesthetic logic that leads to erroneous judgments of taste. Similarly, Ruskin notes how an underlying motive may be present even before it can be inferred from material forms, "the tendency to the adoption of Gothic types being always first shown by greater irregularity, and richer variation in the forms of architecture it is about to supersede, long before the appearance of the pointed arch or any other recognizable outward sign of the Gothic mind" (III:176). If the motive can be present in the absence of an obvious visual analogue, then the reverse situation may also obtain.[36]

As a second example of this possibility, consider Ruskin's discussion of skill in his lecture on "The Relation of Art to Use." At the beginning of the lecture, Ruskin takes pains to argue that although skill and beauty are necessary for great art, they are insufficient without truth or use. But the criteria of truth and use, being limited to mimetic fidelity and wholesome design, seem inadequate to the pleasure that skill and beauty inevitably afford. If, as Ruskin argues in *Modern Painters*, pleasure and admiration are overlapping experiences, then how does it become possible to divorce pleasure from goodness in judging the quality of art? The gap between beauty and utility suggests that skill may constitute a stylistic virtue with autonomous aesthetic value, even though Ruskin himself would declare that morally vicious styles cannot be aesthetically beautiful. Put another way, stylistic elements (such as irregularity and variation, or the beauty of craft), though imagined as embodying specific and predetermining moral qualities rooted in particular social conditions (such as late feudal individualism or functional design), may become detached from the concrete sources of these qualities without being deprived of their ethical significance. We might say, then, that just as Swinburne describes his poetry as figuratively (as opposed to literally) "chaste," Ruskin inspires a kind of semantic drift whereby virtues of style maintain a sense of ethical vitality even when they no longer refer to a particular person or culture.

Ruskin has always been a paradoxical figure for aestheticism because, as Kenneth Daley points out, he unites a "consistent and enthusiastic adulation of beauty" with a "direct opposition to any tendency toward aesthetic autonomy."[37] Daley describes how *Modern Painters* firmly establishes the idea that the contemplation of beauty is "disinterested" such that "the sense of beauty has nothing to do with private interest or desire for personal possession."[38] However, Daley suggests that around the time of the Slade lectures in 1870, Ruskin reacted to the excesses of the aesthetic movement partly by elevating utility in relation to beauty, emphasizing the necessary connection between art and practical use. As Ruskin says in the final lecture, "however pleasant, wonderful or impressive [art] may be in itself . . . it must never exist alone – never for itself" (116). But this shift in Ruskin's applied moral preferences, from theoretic contemplation to practical utility,[39] should not be seen as undermining his contribution to the aesthetic movement or, indeed, the emergent idea of stylistic autonomy. By insisting upon the ethical content of art, Ruskin sought an alliance between "disinterested" criticism and moralism, bridging a gap that remains pertinent today.[40] Yet the very success of this effort enhanced the prestige of *aesthesis* and demonstrated how well the self-contained work of art could provide a formalist origin point for the ethos and value it expresses.

Style and Criticism in Arnold

The influence of Aristotle on Matthew Arnold's thinking and criticism is so pervasive as to have, paradoxically, escaped detailed critical comment. Like other undergraduates at Oxford, Arnold was shaped by an educational program that relied heavily on Aristotle's texts. When Arnold enrolled in *Literae Humaniores* in 1841, Aristotle's "*Nicomachean Ethics* and *Rhetoric* were regarded as essential,"[41] and Arnold later reported that "we at Oxford used to read our Aristotle or our Butler with the same absolute faith in the classicality of their matter as in the classicality of Homer's form."[42] Yet as scholars have paid increasing attention to the Christian influences on Arnold's thought, the philosophical significance of his Hellenic formation has gone underappreciated. For example, Arnold refers extensively throughout his criticism to the *Imitation of Christ* by Thomas à Kempis as Christianity's most "exquisite" spiritual production,[43] but Arnold admired the Imitation in part because the Christian tradition of *imitatio Christi* paralleled Aristotle's own method of modeling one's virtue after the example of great men.[44] Indeed, when Arnold adopts this methodology in the middle chapters of *Culture and Anarchy* (1869), the credit goes to Aristotle rather than to Thomas. "Having been brought up at Oxford in the bad old times, when we were stuffed with Greek and Aristotle," he writes, "my head is still full of a lumber of phrases we learnt at Oxford from Aristotle, about virtue being in a mean, and about excess and defect, and so on" (64). Arnold then proceeds to analyze the virtues and vices of the major social classes in exactly these Aristotelian terms.

Referring to one of the lectures that became *Culture and Anarchy*, the philosopher Henry Sidgwick scoffed that "the root of culture, when examined ethically, is found to be a refined eudaemonism."[45] Just as Sidgwick would attack Aristotle's *eudaimonia* in *The Methods of Ethics* (1874) for lacking a clear conception of the good or rules for achieving it,[46] he criticizes Arnold for vagueness, for treating "the most profound and difficult problems of individual and social life with an airy dogmatism that ignores their depth and difficulty" ("Prophet," 158). Arnold's intention in *Culture and Anarchy* was to write a piece of social and cultural criticism rather than a moral treatise, but Sidgwick correctly recognizes the ways in which Arnold employs a eudaimonistic vocabulary to define and defend humanity's ultimate good. To begin, Arnold makes "culture" an ethical program when he defines it holistically as the "pursuit of our total perfection" (*Culture*, 5), and he equates perfection with virtue when he describes it as the "harmonious expansion of *all* the powers which make the beauty and worth of human nature" (36, original emphasis).[47] Arnold invokes the Aristotelian idea of the mean in stressing that perfection "is not consistent with the over-development of any one power at the expense of the rest" (36), and he directly contrasts perfection with Benthamism and egoism in specifying that it is an "inward condition of the mind and spirit" (37) and a "*general* expansion of the human family" (37, original emphasis). Arnold also follows Aristotle in understanding perfection as a condition of not only moral but also aesthetic excellence, in the sense that it constitutes what is "beautiful, graceful, and becoming" (38) in human beings: individual self-fashioning requires modeling oneself after an ideal standard rather than by some universal rule (38). Arnold continues the parallel between moral and aesthetic excellence when he writes that culture is akin to poetry and that "greatness," broadly conceived, commands "our love, interest, and admiration" (38), much like a work of art.

Like Ruskin's, Arnold's virtue-theoretic approach means he conceives of culture as ethos, or the expression of "spirits" and "tendencies" that conduce to or are constitutive of "excellence." Instead of the value-laden binary distinction between Gothic and Renaissance, he advocates a more synthetic relationship between Hellenism and Hebraism where the sweetness and light of the one work to enhance and counter-balance the fire and strength of the other.[48] "Sweetness and light" is itself but a more general term for a specific set of virtues – namely flexibility, disinterestedness, and the free play of the mind – which, Arnold argues, have been neglected in favor of the Hebraic virtues of obedience and action. Once again, Arnold follows Ruskin by inferring the presence (or absence) of virtuous motives beneath surface properties or sentiments, while at the same time extending Ruskin's mode of criticism to forms of cultural expression beyond the manual arts. Arnold argues, for example, that the qualities of the "Barbarians" – individualism, chivalry, love of sports, and care for personal appearance – reflect, on the one hand, virtues of courage and high spirits, but, on the other, an "insufficiency of light," or of self-reflective intelligence (76–77).

One of the more confusing features of Arnold's writing is that the Hellenic virtues described in *Culture and Anarchy* are precisely those attributed to criticism in "The Function of Criticism at the Present Time" (1864). In that earlier essay, Arnold describes criticism as aiming to perform exactly the same kind of work as the Hellenic spirit, namely "to keep man from a self-satisfaction which is retarding and vulgarizing, to lead him towards perfection, by making his mind dwell upon what is excellent in itself, and the absolute beauty and fitness of things."[49] The critical faculty is thus both analytic, in that it strives to "see the object as in itself it really is" (258), but also ethical, in that it constitutes an "attitude" to be adopted "towards things in general," a "right tone and temper of mind" (282) that should be applied not just to art objects but also to people and cultures. According to Timothy Peltason, Arnold thereby belongs to "a long tradition of moralized epistemology – especially rich in the British nineteenth century – according to which we must lose ourselves to find the object, an analog or version in small of the spiritual narrative of Christian rebirth."[50] Though this account minimizes the Hellenic influences on Arnold's thought, the phrase "moralized epistemology" accurately captures how ways of knowing, even those that stress objectivity and neutrality, are actually virtues within a broader framework of what is good for human beings to think and do.[51] Arnold's criticism thus performs a function analogous to, but much broader than, Ruskin's theoretic faculty by treating the apprehension and evaluation of aesthetic excellence as expressing an ethical norm.

We see the consequences of Arnold's virtue-based orientation for the analysis of style in the evolution of his literary criticism. In the 1853 Preface to *Poems*, Aristotle's influence on Arnold is largely limited to the *Poetics*. Because Arnold agrees with Aristotle that poetry is the representation of action, he writes that no poet "can make an intrinsically inferior action equally delightful with a more excellent one by his treatment of it,"[52] suggesting an approach to reading poetry that is predominantly thematic. He argues for the superiority of Greek poetry because "their expression," or style, "is so admirably kept in its right degree of prominence; because it is so simple and so well subordinated; because it draws its force directly from the pregnancy of the matter which it conveys" (5). Modern poetry, in contrast, values expression over action, such that "we have critics who seem to direct their attention merely to detached expressions, to the language about the action, not to the action itself" (7). Arnold most deprecates poets who choose as their action the state of their own minds, asserting that no felicity in expression could ever elevate the poverty of the subject matter.

Shakespeare, for example, was a great stylist because he knew how to conceive of an excellent action, but the poet fails when his "fondness for curiosity of expression" makes it "impossible for him to say a thing plainly, even when the press of the action demands the very directest language" (11).

In the 1853 Preface, then, Arnold identifies two targets: a literary criticism that privileges expression over action and a romantic-expressive theory of poetry in which the author, rather than an action, is taken as subject. However, in "The Study of Poetry" (1880), Arnold affirms a very different point of view, influenced, I believe, by his gradual acceptance of a virtue-based aesthetics (the word "virtue" appears fifteen times in the essay). Now calling poetry a "criticism of life" (163), Arnold approaches it not only *with* the critical spirit but as an example *of* spirit, as something colored by the "character" of the author in terms of both substance and style: "The characters of a high quality of poetry are what is expressed *there* . . . Both of these, the substance and matter on the one hand, the style and manner on the other, have a mark, an accent, of high beauty, worth, and power" (170–71, original emphasis). While Arnold continues to insist that in poetry "the idea is everything" (161), the word "idea" now encompasses more than a mimetically represented action. "Truth and seriousness," like sweetness and light, involve both action and expression, in an equal rather than a hierarchical relationship: "The superior character of truth and seriousness, in the matter and substance of the best poetry, is inseparable from the superiority of diction and movement marking its style and manner . . . So far as high poetic truth and seriousness are wanting to a poet's matter and substance, so far also, we may be sure, will a high poetic stamp of diction and movement be wanting to his style and manner" (171). We can see how Arnold, like Ruskin, uses different words to describe stylistic virtues and the "substance" to which they correspond despite the assertion of referential monism. Chaucer's "divine liquidness of diction" and "divine fluidity of movement" (174), for example, are formal manifestations of a sensibility that is "large, free, simple, clear yet kindly" (174).

In "Arnold and Pater" (1930), T.S. Eliot expresses confusion over whether Arnold ought to be understood as a moralist or an aesthete: "Art for art's sake," Eliot writes, "is the offspring of Arnold's culture: and we can hardly venture to say that it is even a perversion of Arnold's doctrine, considering how very vague and ambiguous that doctrine is."[53] However, Arnold's doctrine is not so ambiguous if one considers the eudaimonistic tradition from which it emanates. To "see the object as in itself it really is" is an ethical imperative guided by the critical spirit, whose work consists in "going back upon the actual instincts and forces which rule our life, seeing them as they really are, connecting them with other instincts and forces, and enlarging our whole view and rule of life" (*Culture*, 106). Arnold's recognition that style as much as substance can be a vehicle for virtue is part of this framework, for style is itself a kind of object: though Chaucer may lack high seriousness, Arnold nonetheless appreciates his "exquisite virtue of style and manner," indicating the potential for style's "detached expression" to contribute to the total value of a work and evincing the greater catholicity of taste required by the critical spirit. Indeed, for Arnold, criticism is virtuous not only because it stimulates "the best which has been thought and said" but because it expands our capacity to appreciate these creations, enlarging our imaginations and, in this way, advancing our "perfect" self-development. The practice of "criticism" thus provides, in more secularized terms than Ruskin, a moral ground for the appreciation of style as constitutive of "poetic truth."

The Form of Virtue and the Virtue of Form in Pater

Although Pater is often remembered as the prophet of aestheticism, identified with a doctrine of autonomy that "does not move beyond the work of art to its wider or deeper human relevance,"[54] references to ethical value permeate his work. In the Preface to *The Renaissance* (1873), for example, Pater writes that fifteenth-century Italy draws his interest "not merely for its positive results in the things of the intellect and the imagination, its concrete works of art, its special and prominent personalities, with their profound aesthetic charm, but for its general spirit and character, for the ethical qualities of which it is a consummate type" (xxxii). Like Ruskin and Arnold, Pater treats examples of "culture" broadly conceived – works of art, nation-states, even individual personalities – as expressing an underlying "spirit" whose "ethical qualities" warrant attention and, potentially, admiration (xxxii). Hence Pater explains his attraction to a "spirit of general elevation and enlightenment" that "gives unity to all the various products of the Renaissance," a spirit that, following the Arnoldian precedent, manifests an "intimate alliance with mind, this participation in the best thoughts which that age produced" (xxxiii).

Pater's identification of style with ethos is nowhere more evident than in his essay on "Style" (1888), which recapitulates the major themes of Victorian stylistic criticism from De Quincey to Arnold.[55] He begins by distinguishing imaginative writing from "unimaginative" writing (7): in unimaginative literature the writer merely transcribes external facts, while in imaginative or literary writing he transcribes his "sense of fact," "the representation of such fact as connected with soul, of a specific personality, in its preferences, its volition and power" (10). Like Buffon before him, Pater believes that the "style is the man" (35), and he consequently defines the finest writing as that which is "really characteristic or expressive" (36) of its author and in which "it is impossible to distinguish the form from the substance or matter, the subject from the expression" (37). Style, in other words, should be understood as "the finer accommodation of speech to that vision within" (10), a vision composed of both neoclassical "mind" (which selects the design or form) and romantic "soul" (which less consciously determines the atmosphere and color). Pater's extended analysis of Gustave Flaubert toward the end of the essay serves not to celebrate the author as a detached stylist, pursuing the beauty of words and images for their own sake, but rather to confirm the definition of literary "beauty" as "truth" to "some personal sense of fact" in which there is "that absolute accordance of expression to idea" (34). Flaubert's supremacy therefore consists in moralized stylistic virtues, such as the perseverance with which he searches for *le mot juste* – Pater plays on the double meaning of *juste* to underscore the "justice" (30) of Flaubert's quest for the perfect word – and the "tact" (31) with which he bends his language "to the inherent perplexities and recusancy of a certain difficult thought" (32).[56]

If Pater's essay on style is notable not for how it departs from predecessors but for the familiarity of its central tenets, then we should not be surprised that much of Pater's criticism continues the mid-Victorian effort to delineate the relationship between a work's moral and aesthetic character. His "Sir Thomas Browne" is redolent of Hugh Blair, marveling at how "we have the manner of Sir Thomas Browne, in exact expression of his mind! – minute and curious in its thinking, but with an effect, on the sudden, of a real sublimity in depth" (*Appreciations*, 126). Similarly, Pater admires Wordsworth for "that perfect fidelity to one's own inward presentations, to the precise features of the picture within, without which any profound poetry is impossible" (51). In the Postscript to *Appreciations*, Pater argues that "if 'the style is the man' it is also the age" (261), which may be taken as the guiding motive for the artist-specific essays of his earlier book on *The Renaissance*. In the essay on Luca della Robbia, Pater defines expression as "the seal on a man's work of what is most inward and peculiar in his moods, and manner of apprehension," something possessed by "artists of the fifteenth century . . . in an unmistakable way" (46). The classical and belletristic language that Pater uses to identify the qualities of Renaissance artists – "sweetness" and "strength" in Michelangelo (47), "finish" or "*finesse*" in Leonardo (70–71), "grace" (104) in Joachim du

Bellay – underscores the fusion between form and idea (i.e. "truth"), with elements of style deriving their "beauty" and "power" from the "ethical qualities" that originate them. Hegel's influence on Pater here only serves to reinforce the familiar Victorian idea that a generative *ethos* may be embodied in concrete sensuous form.[57]

The Preface to *The Renaissance* defines the aesthetic manifestation of ethical qualities specifically as "virtues," underscoring the ethico-aesthetic overlap implied by the word. But, as in the later criticism of Arnold, Pater empties "virtue" of its narrowly moral connotations by describing it more abstractly (though in keeping with one of its proper senses) as a "power" or "force" capable of producing "pleasurable sensations," an "active principle" of a "more or less peculiar or unique kind" that conveys a work's special quality (xxix–xxxi). In these terms, it is not the literal content of the virtue, the view of life that it expresses, that counts, but rather its authenticity and uniqueness, the fact that it expresses a view. This more abstract conception of virtue, which became consequential for Oscar Wilde, Pater repeatedly describes as a function of sincerity. In "Style," for example, Pater writes, "the style, the manner, would be the man, not in his unreasoned and really uncharacteristic caprices, involuntary or affected, but in absolutely sincere apprehension of what is most real to him" (36). Sincerity thus depends upon the author conveying what he has distinctly thought or felt, but it differs from "mere" subjectivity or mannerism because the "intensity of a veritable apprehension" renders style "in a real sense 'impersonal'" (37), objectifying a subjective impression into a universal aesthetic norm.[58]

As we have seen, the principle of sincerity was not original to Pater. In *The Principles of Success in Literature*, first published in *The Fortnightly Review* in 1865, G.H. Lewes devotes an entire chapter to it, arguing that "the principle is universal, stretching from the highest purposes of Literature down to its smallest details."[59] Although Lewes was shaped more by Campbell and Coleridge than by Hellenism, his language closely parallels Pater's: "In all sincere speech there is power," he writes, "not necessarily great power, but as much as the speaker is capable of" (91); moreover, "the art of writing is not, as many seem to imagine, the art of bringing fine phrases into rhythmical order, but the art of placing before the reader intelligible symbols of the thoughts and feelings in the writer's mind" (101); and finally, "whatever is sincerely felt or believed, whatever forms part of the imaginative experience, and is not simply imitation or hearsay, may fitly be given to the world, and will always maintain an infinite superiority over imitative splendour" (102). Like Pater, Lewes was concerned with the dishonesty of verbal artifice and tricks, as well as with the insincere espousal of doctrines to which an author does not genuinely subscribe; but his comments also validate a broader ethical principle of dispositional authenticity – a condition of right feeling and attitude – that guarantees the legitimacy of expression. Lewes reveals the virtue-theoretic background of this position when he adds that "the principle of sincerity comprises all those qualities of courage, patience, honesty, and simplicity which give momentum to talent, and determine successful Literature" (89–90). Superiority of style reflects ethical and not just aesthetic excellence, following the belletristic precedent that regards them as inextricable.

Given Pater's highly ethicized and monistic conception of style, how is it that he remains among the least likely of Victorian critics to whom we would attribute a practice of moralistic reductionism? Pater's exhortation to "treat life in the spirit of art" (*Appreciations*, 62) provides one clue to this puzzle. Unlike Arnold, who sought to treat art as a criticism of life, Pater elevates art over life and, in the process, assimilates the ethical realm to the private world of sensory experience, thereby subjecting it to a new set of hedonistic and anti-utilitarian laws. For example, in the most doctrinal chapter of *Marius the Epicurean* (1885), Pater describes how the claims of Marius's "'aesthetic' philosophy" may go "against those of the received morality," perhaps even "breaking beyond" its limits.[60] A similar inference may be made with respect to Pater's Conclusion to *The Renaissance*: "Of such wisdom, the poetic passion, the desire of beauty, the love of art for its own sake, has most. For art comes to you proposing frankly to give nothing but the highest quality to your moments as they pass, and simply for those moments' sake" (153). This statement, when not taken as a straightforward endorsement of amoral hedonism, has been submitted as evidence for a view of life that places a premium on disinterested aesthetic experience – that is, on emotion and sensation valued "for their own sake" and not requiring any further justification, moral or otherwise.

However, an awareness of the virtue-theoretic tradition reveals just how moralized Pater's notion of aesthetic autonomy really is. For example, Pater's conception of moral perfection in the "New Cyrenaicism" chapter of *Marius the Epicurean* presents Aristotle as mediated by Ruskin and Arnold and with his own emphasis on powers and capacities. Pater begins by defining culture as "a wide, a complete, education . . . directed especially to the expansion and refinement of the power of reception" (117); adds that the "products of the imagination" must be central to such an education because they present "spirit and matter alike under their purest and most perfect conditions" (118); and concludes that in making artworks the object of "impassioned contemplation," we realize "culture," or "the vision of perfect men and things" (118). Taken together, this vision or "Θεωρία" (118) – transliterated as "*theôria*" in the first two editions and untranslated from Ancient Greek in the third – is a sort of aesthetic religion that, in the Christian context of the novel, retains much of the divine scaffolding attributed to it by Ruskin. As a second example, consider the statement to "treat life in the spirit of art," which appears in Pater's essay on Wordsworth at the very moment when Pater admits ironically that "lessons" may be drawn from the poet even though the poet's task is not to moralize (*Appreciations*, 59).[61] According to Pater, the lesson that Wordsworth "conveys more clearly than all" is "the supreme importance of contemplation in the conduct of life" (59), by which Pater means two things: first, the self-conscious endorsement of ethical intentions over ends, so that the actions one takes are the product of right reasons regardless of the fruit they bear ("whatever may become of the fruit, make sure of the flowers and the leaves," 61–62); and second, the cultivation of a "certain disposition of the mind" (62) that takes a withdrawn or "disinterested" attitude toward the "spectacle" of life and witnesses it with "appropriate emotions" (63). These two conditions for contemplation or "theoria," drawn directly from the virtue tradition, are overlapping and complementary: both are fundamentally dispositional, requiring that the perceiver "contemplate" life by treating means as ends and valuing individual moments more than outcomes. As Marius confesses, "he would at all events be sure that the means, to use the well-worn terminology, should have something of finality or perfection about them, and themselves partake, in a measure, of the more excellent nature of ends" (117). The aesthetic imperative to "treat life in the spirit of art" is simply to privilege ways of thinking and feeling, which are reflective and volitional, over outcomes and results, which are incidental and subject to chance.

Pater's statement in *Appreciations* that "the end of life is not action but contemplation – *being* as distinct from *doing*" (62), echoes Marius's insistence that it is "not what I do, but what I am" that pleases the gods (121). Both remarks follow not only Arnold's division (following Heine) between Hellenism and Hebraism but also Aristotle's famous distinction between "activities" and "products": "Every art and every inquiry, and similarly every action and pursuit, is thought to aim at some good . . . But a certain difference is found among ends; some are activities, others are products apart from the activities" (*Ethics*, 1).[62] Aristotle adds that "where there are ends apart from the actions, it is the nature of the products to be better than the activities," but Pater, more than Arnold, treats "culture" as an activity above all and contemplation as a "disposition of the mind." In this way, Pater transforms the *form* of moral life – the conditions that make moral behavior possible, and the spirit with which it is willed – into its manifest *content*. This is what Marius means when he says that "the means should justify the end" (117) and why Pater's ethical instructions in the Conclusion to *The Renaissance* focus solely on attitudes and activities: "The service of philosophy, of speculative culture, is to rouse, to startle it to a life of constant and eager observation . . . What we have to do is to be for ever curiously testing new opinions and courting new impressions . . . Only be sure it is passion – that it does yield you this fruit of a quickened, multiplied consciousness" (152–53). The "fruit" is the experience of consciousness itself – not the object as Arnold sees it, but our own impressions being realized distinctly and intentionally.

Once we recognize the formal character of Pater's ethics, we can understand the privileged place it accords to art as both a model of virtue (because means and ends are identical within it) and a stimulant to virtue (because we must mirror the spirit of art in order to understand and appreciate it). The central importance of style also becomes clearer. If the purpose of life is to harmonize means and ends so that "one's existence, from day to day, came to be like a well-executed piece of music" (*Marius*, 118), then one must first "know one's own impression as it really is, to discriminate it, to realize it distinctly" (*Renaissance*, xxix). However, because the perceptual experience of every individual is different, segregated as one is behind "the walls of the closely shut cell of one's own personality" (*Marius*, 117), what matters is not the content of one's impressions but whether one realizes them sincerely and integrally. Hence Marius concludes that "a true understanding of one's self [is] ever the first condition of genuine style," according to which "words should indeed be things . . . in exact proportion to the transparency with which [they] conveyed to others the apprehension, the emotion, the mood, so vividly real within himself" (122). Style embodies not the man in his eccentricities and mannerisms but man as exercising the dispositional virtues of sincerity, openness, and strength, exhibiting that diversity of human personality that Adam Smith found inevitable and agreeable. All varieties of style, from the musical to the meditative to the mundane, if sincerely intended and tactfully conveyed, will communicate some element of these perfectionist, "contemplative" preconditions.

In "Arnold and Pater," T.S. Eliot criticizes Arnold for getting "all the emotional kick out of Christianity one can, without the bother of believing it:"[63] if forms are all we have to go by, whither ethics? However, an awareness of the virtue-theoretic tradition that shapes Pater's statements about the relationship between ethics and art mitigates the danger implied by this objection. Virtues of style are genuine virtues, not because they are reducible to mental states or social conditions, not because they merely index underlying values, but because they constitute examples *in themselves* of human excellence in aesthetic form. To embrace Christianity, Marius does not need a conceptual understanding of its doctrines; he needs only the intuitive recognition that its stylistic forms, "the ritual system of the church ... ranks as one of the great, conjoint, and (so to term them) *necessary,* products of the human mind" (243). In Kierkegaardian fashion, Marius is impressed by the "wonderful spectacle ... of those who believe" (246) not because of what they believe in, but for the act of belief itself. If the triumph of Christianity at the end of *Marius the Epicurean* was unconvincing to Eliot, it was for Pater the necessary consequence of a formalist ethics that takes an agnostic position with respect to cognitive beliefs and puts greater store in the conditions for virtuous worship – an ethics that makes morals a function of manners (*Appreciations*, 61). As Lucian says in "A Conversation Not Imaginary," "All alike are in search of Happiness – what kind of thing it is. One says one thing, one another ... And Happiness may indeed be one of those things. But it is possible also that it may be still something else, different and distinct from them all" (*Marius*, 266). Faced with this kind of metaphysical "vacuity" (245), form replaces content as the ultimate end, and virtues of style become valuable "for their own sake" (*Renaissance*, xxxiii), each encapsulating a worldview, a mode of being, a way of life that is, in Pater's terminology, deeply subjective and yet ultimately "impersonal" (*Appreciations*, 37).[64]

Wilde and Stylistic Multiplicity

Perhaps no Victorian figure is more closely associated with the doctrine of aesthetic autonomy than Oscar Wilde, in part due to the attacks on moralism contained in his most elaborate theoretical statement, "The Critic as Artist," published in 1891. According to Gilbert, who serves as a mouthpiece for the author, "the first condition of criticism is that the critic should be able to recognise that the sphere of Art and the sphere of Ethics are absolutely distinct and separate ... Art is out of the reach of morals, for her eyes are fixed upon things beautiful and immortal and ever-changing" (*Intentions*, 188–89). These statements suggest not only that art and ethics take different objects, but, potentially, that art itself cannot be an object of ethics – an erroneous interpretation stemming from the ambiguity of these terms. For, as Julia Prewitt Brown has shown, Wilde uses the words "ethics" and "morality" to refer to "the puritan and philistine moralities of the period"[65] – particularly, we might add, those that treat works of art as vehicles for narrowly moral content or "views" – rather than to the Aristotelian eudaimonism that formed the backbone of Wilde's Oxford education and in which aesthetics play a major role.[66] Indeed, Wilde (through Gilbert) claims that "aesthetics are higher than ethics" (210) not because aesthetic judgments exclude normative claims about thought or behavior but because the thoughts and behaviors it concerns "belong to a more spiritual sphere" (210). The nature of aesthetic experience thus becomes a central topic of the essay, with Gilbert providing the period's most elaborate explanation of why formalism is ethically valuable.

Wilde graduated from "Greats" with a double first in 1878, and "The Critic as Artist" reflects the beliefs of his predecessors. Wilde's aesthetic theory combines an Arnoldian celebration of the "critical spirit" with a Ruskinian commitment of the contemplative life (*theoria*) to recommend a Paterian catholicity of taste as integral to human perfection.[67] The essay seems to begin in desultory fashion, with Wilde exalting "egotism" over the philistine values of self-effacement and conformity with others. "In literature mere egotism is delightful," Wilde claims, because it acquaints the reader with different personalities and their corresponding "mode[s] of thought" (96). As in belletristic rhetoric, Wilde celebrates style as the expression of character, saying "there is no art where there is no style, and no style where there is no unity, and unity is of the individual" (122). However, in keeping with the title of the essay, he gives this formulation an Arnoldian flourish: just as the work of art represents the distinctive personality, so too does the critical impression represent "the record of one's own soul" (138), thus becoming, "as the Greeks would put it, in itself, and to itself, an end" (137). Wilde's teleological language here recalls Aristotle as mediated by Pater in *Appreciations*; like his Oxford tutor, Wilde emphasizes the form of impression-making – its inherent subjectivism and dispositional sincerity – over the particulars of its content. "Who cares whether Mr. Ruskin's views on Turner are sound or not? What does it matter? That mighty and majestic prose of his, so fervid and so fiery-coloured in its noble eloquence ... is at least as great a work of art as any of those wonderful sunsets ... greater indeed, one is apt to think at times ... on account of the fuller variety of its appeal, soul speaking to soul in those long-cadenced lines" (139–40).

Throughout the essay, Wilde insists that "emotion for the sake of emotion is the aim of art" (166), which means that all art consists in the expression of a particular "mood." The word functions analogously to "personality" or "character" in earlier stylistic criticism but refers to something more mutable and transient: "Beauty has as many meanings as man has moods" and "when one has found expression for a mood, one has done with it" (143). The substitution of "mood" for "character" is one moment in which Wilde deliberately eschews the vocabulary of his predecessors to distinguish his own conception of ethos from a narrowly moral one. Referring to the *Poetics*, for example, he writes that "the ethical effect of art, its importance to culture, and its place in the formation of character, had been done once for all by Plato; but here we have art treated, not from the moral, but from the purely aesthetic point of view" (115). Nonetheless, the artistic expression of mood parallels the process through which, according to Pater, a subjective "inward sense" can be transformed into an impersonal aesthetic form, leading to one of the essay's most striking (yet now familiar) paradoxes: "I would say that the more objective a creation appears to be, the more subjective it really is. Shakespeare might have met Rosencrantz and Guildenstern in the white streets of London ... but Hamlet came out of his soul, and Romeo out of his passion. They were elements of his nature to which he gave visible form ... not on the lower plane of actual life, where they would have been trammelled and constrained and so made imperfect, but on that imaginative plane of art" (181). The relationship that obtains between subjective and objective forms is, as the language suggests, somewhat mystical, but it highlights an important difference between the artist's and the critic's work. The goal of the artist is to purify one subjective mood to make it available for appreciation, something that art alone can accomplish; the goal of the critic, in contrast, is to cultivate "a temperament exquisitely susceptible to beauty" (190) so that we can "multiply our personalities" (188) by assimilating the moods of others. "The true critic," Wilde writes, "will seek for beauty in every age and in each school, and will never suffer himself to be limited to any settled custom of thought or stereotyped mode of looking at things. He will realise himself in many forms, and by a thousand different ways, and will ever be curious of new sensations and fresh points of view" (187–88).

"Creation limits, while contemplation widens, the vision" (202): the phrase "art for art's sake" is surely inadequate to capture the ethical complexity of this position, which identifies the "critical faculty" with the expansion of personality and "contemplation" with the appreciation of beautiful moods. On the one hand, it harkens back to Adam Smith's belief that an appreciation of style is akin to an appreciation for human variety writ large, an intrinsic pleasure that arises from our delight in the *natura naturans* of the human *telos*. In this way, the openness and catholicity of the critic resemble the activity of literature itself, which, Wilde argues, is "the perfect expression of life" because it "most fully mirrors man in his infinite variety" (112). If Aristotle is right to argue that moral perfection consists in the realization of total human potential, and "the aesthetic critic alone can appreciate all forms and modes" (202), then Wilde logically concludes that "it is through Art, and through Art only, that we can realise our perfection" (165). However, this "perfection" involves more than enjoyment or pleasure, which Wilde makes clear toward the end of the essay when he offers two interconnected defenses for its ethical necessity as a *summum bonum*. First, contemplation is valuable because "art does not hurt us" (165). Recalling Aristotle's definition of *catharsis* as the purgation of pity and fear, Wilde writes that "the tears that we shed at a play are a type of the exquisite sterile emotions that it is the function of Art to awaken" (165). In other words, art manages to put us in touch with our essential humanity without corrupting that experience through potentially harmful interactions with others; in emphasizing the experience of emotion over its direction toward an object, Wilde follows Pater in defining "the way to live" as "not DOING but BEING, and" – in recognition of his emphasis on the ever-restless and fluctuating nature of emotions and moods – "not BEING merely, but BECOMING" (173). Second, Wilde argues that criticism "makes us cosmopolitan" (207). Because "there must be no mood with which [the critic] cannot sympathise" (170), the contemplation of art emancipates the critic from the confines of his own subjectivity and puts him into contact with (quoting Arnold) "the best that is known and thought in the world" (173). Wilde deliberately contrasts this form of cosmopolitan critical sympathy with the "emotional sympathy" that "limits knowledge" (175) by attaching itself to a narrow set of prejudicial objects: "It is too variable, and too closely connected with the passions; and a board of arbitrators who, for the general welfare of the race, are to be deprived of the power of putting their decisions into execution, will not be of much avail" (208). In contrast, Wilde claims that "it is only by the cultivation of the habit of intellectual criticism that we shall be able to rise superior to race-prejudices" (208) because the catholicity of the critical spirit celebrates human excellence in all its available forms. "If we are tempted to make war upon another nation," Wilde writes in a passage whose moral stakes could hardly be clearer, "we are seeking to destroy an element of our own culture" (209).[68]

In "The Art of Fiction," Henry James argues that "if we pretend to respect the artist at all, we must allow him his freedom of choice."[69] For

Wilde, that freedom is most perfectly realized not by the artist, but by the "criticism that, recognising no position as final, and refusing to bind itself by the shallow shibboleths of any sect or school, creates that serene philosophic temper which loves truth for its own sake, and loves it not the less because it knows it to be unattainable" (209). While such a position may appear relativistic, it is based on a standard of excellence that inheres not in the content of an author's views (what James calls his "donnée"), but in the quality of its aesthetic expression (James's "execution"), a standard that might seem arbitrary if it were not for its freedom from harm and cosmopolitan respect for "the unity of the human mind in the variety of all its forms" (209). In *De Profundis*, Wilde makes his highest spiritual claim for aesthetic experience when he argues that there is an "intimate and immediate connexion between the true life of Christ and the true life of the artist"[70]: endowed with "an intense and flamelike imagination," Christ "realized in the entire sphere of human relations that imaginative sympathy which in the sphere of Art is the sole secret of creation" (165), thereby providing a synthesis between two realms supposedly opposed. But Christ is ultimately less comprehensible as a figure for the artist than as a figure for the critic insofar as he possesses "the unerring instinct that reveals to one all things under their conditions of beauty" (*Intentions*, 168), seeing "no difference at all between the lives of others and one's own life" (*De Profundis*, 170). By universalizing our subjective experiences, Christ "gave to man an extended, a Titan personality" (170), providing a spiritual basis for the critical appreciation of style as an ethical norm.

Conclusion

In overlapping ways, Ruskin, Arnold, Pater, and Wilde all use the language of excellence, perfection, virtue, and contemplation to account for the ways that aesthetic experience, and particularly the critical spirit with which we must approach it, fits within a normative conception of "the good life." This remarkably unified critical tradition can only have occurred by adopting a concept of virtue elastic enough to reach from the moralistic reductionism of Ruskin to the ethical autonomy of Wilde, who exalts the critical spirit precisely because it is "never trammelled by any shackles of verisimilitude," never hindered by "reference to any standard external to itself" (*Intentions*, 137–38). Thus we see that the idea of style as an end in itself assumes a central importance in nineteenth-century criticism not because it offered an alternative to ethics, but because it offered an alternative ethics to narrower forms of morality that either excluded aesthetic perception from their ideal of human perfection or reduced the aesthetic value of style to some ulterior end. Whereas Pater stresses the monumental "impersonality" of a perfectly expressed temperament, and Wilde argues that man finds "unity" in the "constant change" of momentary moods, all critics in this tradition recognize the presence of ethical virtues in stylistic form because they express, model, and invite us to exercise an aesthetically inflected conception of *theoria*, or the contemplative life, that is superior to, and ennobling of, ordinary experience. By making a "virtue" of style itself, these critics invest "the aesthetic" with a new kind of ethical value, a key innovation of Victorian criticism that was deeply supported, as the next chapter argues, by the philosophical development of virtue theory.

CHAPTER 3

Virtue Theory and the Nature of the Aesthetic

In the last chapter, I argued that Hellenic thought offered Victorian critics a conceptual framework for understanding the relationship between moral and formal value. The ethos-based formalism so characteristic of Victorian criticism, which reads style as the expression of character, has roots in an Aristotelian analogy between persons and texts, which shaped the contours of a critical tradition that sought to invest aesthetic appreciation with ethical significance. Here, I further situate this tradition within the contexts of nineteenth-century British philosophy, whose contribution to aesthetic theory is not always appreciated. Despite recent challenges to the Kantian model, which has long dominated aesthetics, Aristotelian virtue theory remains a missing piece in our understanding of Victorian intellectual and artistic thought and its contemporary relevance.[1]

In a seminal essay of 1958, Elizabeth Anscombe claims that nineteenth-century British philosophy was dominated by two systems of moral reasoning: consequentialism, associated with Bentham and Mill, which asserts that the rightness of an act depends on the nature of its consequences, and deontology, identified with Kant, which judges the rightness of an act according to its conformity with a moral norm or rule.[2] During the period, these systems were more commonly known as "utilitarianism" and "duty ethics," and Anscombe argues that their inadequacies indicate the exigency of reviving the "aretaic" (from *arete*) or virtue ethics of Aristotle. However, as this chapter demonstrates, virtue-based thinking had long provided both moral systems with a point of departure as well as a substantive alternative. More to our purposes, it contributed directly to the formation of a distinctly British notion of "the aesthetic" that centered upon the connection between artistic appreciation and the realization of characterological excellence, imagining aesthetic "autonomy" as an ethical value linked to the *telos* for human beings.

To make this argument, I begin by focusing on a crucial event in the history of British philosophy: the publication in 1874 of Henry Sidgwick's

The Methods of Ethics, which, in order to establish the supremacy of rule-based utilitarianism, strictly opposed it to the "aesthetic intuitionism" of perfectionist approaches associated with Aristotle. In one light, Sidgwick's rational codification of utilitarian principles represents the culmination of a mode of moral reasoning that was deemed inhospitable to art. From Dickens to Eliot, Ruskin to Wilde, major figures in the Victorian art-world regarded utilitarianism – especially the quantitative hedonism so rigorously delineated by *The Methods* – as anathema to aesthetic values. But Sidgwick's most unsympathetic features shed light upon a rival tradition that has long identified moral virtue with art and an aesthetic disposition. This tradition begins with Plato and Aristotle, for whom *kalon* signifies the beauty of the good, and it continues through the British sentimentalists who argue that moral and aesthetic judgments are fundamentally similar, rooted in common sensations of liking and aversion (which Sidgwick calls "sentiments of admiration"). In the Victorian period, this way of thinking comes to fruition in the work of four philosophers not typically seen in tandem – J.S. Mill, John Grote, T.H. Green, and Bernard Bosanquet[3] – all of whom regard the realization of excellence as fundamental to our attainment of the good. In place of twentieth-century ideas of formalist autonomism, which rigorously police the boundary between ethics and art, these thinkers elaborate a more appealing virtue-theoretic approach that sees them as analogous and often united, with the "aesthetic" mode of reasoning derided by Sidgwick providing an ironic justification for the ethical value of style in both its referential and autonomous modes.

Utilitarianism, Aesthetic Intuitionism, and Excellence

The importance of *The Methods of Ethics* to the history of philosophy can hardly be underestimated. In 1930, the Cambridge philosopher C.D. Broad called *The Methods* "the best treatise on moral theory that has ever been written."[4] Fifty years later, John Rawls described it as "the first truly academic work in moral philosophy which undertakes to provide a systematic comparative study of moral conceptions" and praised it for offering "the clearest and most accessible formulation of what we may call 'the classical utilitarian doctrine.'"[5] In *A Short History of Ethics*, Alasdair MacIntyre finds that even Sidgwick's limitations constitute a source of interest: although his "defects are the defects of his age," MacIntyre writes, "no philosopher expressed the moral situation of nineteenth-century England – and to some extent we are still in the nineteenth century – better than Henry Sidgwick."[6] These statements bear out Roger Crisp's more recent claim that *The Methods of Ethics* is a "philosophical goldmine, and we are only at the beginning of uncovering its treasures."[7]

The situation that the young Sidgwick faced included the rise of religious skepticism, which questioned the foundations of inherited moral beliefs, and the authority of intuitionism as espoused by William Whewell, whose *Elements of Morality* (1845) was required reading for undergraduates at Trinity College, Cambridge. In a set of manuscript notes appended to the sixth edition of *The Methods of Ethics*, Sidgwick describes his dissatisfaction with "Intuitional moralists," whom he found "hopelessly loose (as compared to mathematicians) in their definitions and axioms."[8] In contrast, Sidgwick was drawn to J.S. Mill's account of utilitarianism because it offered a simple and apparently inarguable conception of the good in the principle of human happiness (xvii). Moreover, it provided a clear decision principle for choosing among alternative actions by instructing agents to act so as to maximize the greatest happiness for the greatest number (the principle of utilitarianism).

Even so, Sidgwick remained troubled by Mill's failure to provide a convincing justification for why one should sacrifice one's own good for the sake of others – a tension between egoistic and universalistic hedonism, or self-interest and benevolence, that *The Methods of Ethics* never fully resolves. However, as the book's title suggests, Sidgwick was more interested in the *methods* of practical reasoning than in the specific goods that ethics strives to attain.[9] Indeed, in Sidgwick's view, the common-sense rules that arise in every period and culture testify to the natural inclination among human beings toward virtue and moral standards. The difficulties occur when they must decide among conflicting maxims or defend their reasons for action in ways that are clear and can be accepted by everyone.[10] Hence, in the third part of the *Methods*, Sidgwick develops a formal test to verify whether a stated reason can be accepted as such: it must be clear, self-evident, and worthy of universal assent.[11]

Though its significance may be difficult to appreciate today, Sidgwick saw this test as revolutionary because it brought a new level of scientific validity to the study of moral reasoning. As he claims in his proof of Utilitarianism, his aim was "to shew a natural transition from the Morality of Common Sense to Utilitarianism, somewhat like the transition in special branches of practice from trained instinct and empirical rules to the technical method that embodies and applies the conclusions of science: so that Utilitarianism may appear only as the scientifically complete and systematically reflective form of that regulation of conduct, which through the whole course of human history has always tended substantially in the same direction" (395–96). Sidgwick found his results worthy of these aspirations: after conducting an inductive survey of the moral beliefs of his era, he concludes that only utilitarianism can explain the bulk of the accepted rules while also satisfying his formal standard of validity. The proof is the empirical fact that most moral rules aim at the promotion of happiness; that arguments for or against different rules tend to appeal to the principle of utility; and that, whereas all other intuitions are ultimately subjective or controvertible, only the utilitarian intuition is "clear and certain" (274) enough to count as a fundamental axiom to which anyone can appeal in cases of moral disagreement.

Integral to Sidgwick's establishment of a new method for ethics was his rejection of a set of opposing methods that he characterized as "aesthetic." The OED indicates that the first use of "aesthetic" in English was relatively recent, in a 1764 translation of Baumgarten, for whom the word signified the sensory as opposed to the rational or noumenal branch of knowledge;[12] but, in part owing to its uptake by moral philosophers, the meaning of "aesthetic" changed over the nineteenth century, so it is important to clarify the precise meaning that Sidgwick assigns to it.[13] First, he uses the word to argue against an analogy between debates about rightness in conduct in the moral sphere and the recognition of beauty in art. Whereas, Sidgwick says, "we can describe the beautiful products when they are produced, and to some extent classify their beauties, giving names to each," we cannot, as we must in ethics, "prescribe any certain method for producing each kind of beauty." This is because, in Sidgwick's view, "the highest excellence [in the fine arts] is always due to an instinct or tact that cannot be reduced to definite formulae" (198). In other words, there is a gap between the principles of aesthetic excellence and the rules for its production, it being impossible to specify a straightforward rule or maxim to guarantee success across multiple instances. While a scientific approach to ethics requires precise definitions and laws, beauty is too complex, specific, and context-dependent to be encoded by a set of common instructions.

In the second, related definition, Sidgwick takes issue with the aesthetic as one of the possible "points of view" from which morality "may be contemplated" (442). Whereas the rational or "jural" perspective focuses on what is right, obligatory, or required, the aesthetic point of view emphasizes what is good, praiseworthy, or excellent. This difference may seem trivial, but in Sidgwick's view, the latter expressivist perspective leads to ethical systems poisoned by subjective and cultural bias, best exemplified by the virtue ethics of Aristotle. We may, for example, be taught to admire the moral virtue of courage by inspecting the objective features of a situation (such as battle) and the subjective qualities of an agent (say, a volition to serve his country in the face of danger). But because there is no irreducible account of "courage" that transcends situation or subject – because its status as a virtue depends wholly upon the contexts for agency – it is impossible to specify a determinate rule for its exercise:

> And hence the attempt to state an explicit maxim, by applying which we may be sure of producing virtuous acts of any kind, must fail; we can only give a general account of the virtue – a description, not a definition – and leave it to trained insight to find in any particular circumstances the act that will best realize it. (198)

Sidgwick does not wish to claim that the virtues are irrelevant to human morality – his own interest in recuperating common-sense morality indicates the opposite – but rather that the form of virtue ethics does not present their "truth" in a way that provides a reliable guide to conduct. Virtues are, as he says, descriptive rather than definitive, character traits that are admirable but not obtainable by self-evident prescription, and thus susceptible to non-moral bias.[14]

Sidgwick calls virtue ethics a form of "aesthetic intuitionism" (198) because, as a practical doctrine, it is characterized by the "fluctuations and discrepancies of opinion, in which we acquiesce in aesthetic discussions, but which tend to endanger seriously the authority of ethical beliefs."[15] In a later chapter, Sidgwick further elaborates this point, showing how Aristotle's doctrine of the mean – the closest that his philosophy gets to formulating a general rule for conduct – is incapable of meeting his idea of a rational standard: "For example, Common Sense may seem to regard Liberality, Frugality, Courage, Placability, as intrinsically desirable: but when we consider their relation respectively to Profusion, Meanness, Foolhardiness, Weakness, we find that Common Sense draws the line in each case not by immediate intuition, but by reference either to some definite maxim of duty, or to the general notion of 'Good' or Wellbeing: and similarly when we seek at what point Candour, Generosity, Humility cease to be virtues by becoming 'excessive'" (2nd ed., 364).[16] As Sidgwick admits, virtues and vices can be perceived through the combination of native sense and special training, but this perception, as in the Humean account of taste that it resembles, involves aesthetic rather than ethical judgment, relying as it does upon the thick description of qualities and values in their context-dependent particularity rather than action-guiding principles derived from immediate intuitions of the good.

Sidgwick's distinction between rational and aesthetic intuitionism, a first in the history of ethics, helped cement a landscape in which aretaic approaches were increasingly opposed to utilitarianism. Against the rule-based reasoning of hedonistic consequentialism, Sidgwick sets the context-dependent description of culturally mediated values intended to serve some ultimate good of excellence or perfection. Because Sidgwick regarded this confusion of aesthetics and ethics to be one of the central problems of modern moral philosophy, he was particularly vigilant in spotting this flaw in others. For example, in his review of *Culture and Anarchy*, he denounced Arnold's Aristotelian conception of cultural perfection as "ambitious, vague, and perverse";[17] he criticized T.H. Green for introducing art as a moral virtue in his assessment of Greek ethics (*Lectures*, 89–90); and he worried that James Martineau expanded the scope of ethics beyond the right conduct of willing persons to treat excessively abstract notions such as goodness and badness broadly conceived (*Lectures*, 330). Interestingly, however, Sidgwick omits from *The Methods* any mention of the aesthetic aspects of the philosophical writings of his predecessor, J.S. Mill, perhaps because he was unable to conceive how the great popularizer of Utilitarianism could have admitted doctrines so antithetical to Sidgwick's own anti-intuitive methods.

In its essential points, Sidgwick's text may certainly be regarded as a rigorous defense of the main assumptions of classical utilitarian doctrine as espoused in *Utilitarianism*, which Mill published in 1871. Like Sidgwick, Mill seeks to reduce the complexity of moral rules to fundamental principles, criticizing intuitionists for failing to "make out a list of the *a priori* principles which are to serve as the premises of the [moral] science."[18] Like Sidgwick, Mill accepts the principle of utility – that the good for human beings is happiness, and that human beings ought to pursue their good – as the only one that is intuitively defensible (157, 189). And like Sidgwick, Mill believes that the rightness of an act must always be evaluated with respect to the consequences it produces (178). He also believes, not surprisingly, that utility is the only principle that may be "invoked to decide between [secondary principles] when their demands are incompatible" (185) and that virtue is valuable only insofar as it conduces to states of happiness but not as something to be pursued for itself (201).

However, while *Utilitarianism* is a key text for Sidgwick's ethical theory, Sidgwick leaves out of *The Methods* any sustained discussion of one of Mill's other preoccupations in *Utilitarianism*, namely the distinction between higher and lower pleasures. Mill introduces this distinction to defend utilitarianism from the popular perception, dramatized in

Dickens's 1854 novel *Hard Times*, that it reduced human happiness to swine-like philistinism. By distinguishing between bodily pleasures and those associated with the exercise of "higher faculties" (163) – "the pleasures of the intellect, of the feelings and imagination, and of the moral sentiments" (162) – he appeals to a (supposedly) intuitive sense that "some *kinds* of pleasure are more desirable and more valuable than others" (162). Yet by arguing that it is better to be Socrates dissatisfied than a pig satisfied, Mill also implies that the higher pleasures as such are *intrinsically* valuable, worth having less because they produce pleasure than because they contribute to a "sense of dignity, which all human beings possess in one form or other" (164). In this way, Mill introduces a perfectionist or idealist element into utilitarianism that Sidgwick, with his commitment to a strict quantification of empirical pleasures, could not accept.[19]

In *Utilitarianism*, Mill seeks to show how the principle of utility can act as an "umpire" between spurious moral systems that perilously "afford a free scope for the actions of personal desires and partialities" (185). However, in the earlier *On Liberty*, published in 1859, the free scope of subjective character is precisely what Mill seeks to protect and enhance. The second chapter develops at greater length the perfectionist elements that return in Mill's later work, arguing that cultivation of individual character is vital to happiness because it exercises those higher faculties that are innately constitutive of humanity:

> The human faculties of perception, judgement, discriminative feeling, mental activity, and even moral preference, are exercised only in making a choice . . . He who lets the world, or his own portion of it, choose his plan of life for him, has no need of any other faculty than the ape-like one of imitation. He who chooses his plan for himself, employs all his faculties.[20]

What is at stake here is not simply the idea of moral autonomy but a broader imperative that the individual follow his "desires and impulses" (76) in order to develop the "varieties of character" (72) that are latent in human diversity and which distinguish us as a higher species. Against the abnegation of individuality asserted by Calvinism, Mill offers "a different type of human excellence" drawn from "a Greek idea of self-development" that transforms the generic human being into an individualized and *sui generis* ideal (80).

Mill argues that the development of individual character is consistent with utilitarianism insofar as it promotes happiness, but this conception of happiness differs sharply from that which depends upon the pleasurable mental states described by Bentham. As his language and references indicate, Mill's idea of "excellence" has more in common with Aristotle's understanding of eudemonia as the ethically admirable condition of a life well lived (*êthikai aretai*). Just as Aristotle describes how happiness consists in the cultivation of virtue, so does Mill ascribe a similar value to the exercise of the higher capacities: "it is not by wearing down into universality all that is individual in themselves, but by cultivating it and calling it forth ... that human beings become a noble and beautiful object of contemplation" (80). Few statements better capture what Sidgwick meant to deride with the phrase "aesthetic intuitionism." But Mill differs from Aristotle in a way that underlines even further how much his perfectionist conception of character is a nineteenth-century product. Unlike Aristotle, who felt that virtue was best cultivated by following culturally accepted models, Mill argues on post-romantic lines that true uniqueness of character can only be developed in relative independence from custom, tradition, and example. In an age when the public is "more disposed than at most former periods to prescribe general rules of conduct" (89), Mill encourages individuals to challenge the "despotism of custom" (91) and take responsibility for their own potentially eccentric self-development.

The perfectionism of Mill's approach is further illuminated by the analogy he draws from religion. If there were a Supreme Being, Mill suggests, we should take it on faith that "he gave all human faculties that they might be cultivated and unfolded, not rooted out and consumed, and that he takes delight in every nearer approach made by his creatures to the ideal conception embodied in them" (80). The ideal realization of the higher faculties is difficult to square with the kind of hedonism indicated by certain aspects of *Utilitarianism*, but it is entirely consistent with that mode of ethical reasoning that Sidgwick calls "aesthetic." Excellence of character is a descriptive rather than a rational goal, something too vague and variable in definition to meet Sidgwick's standard of self-evidence or universality; moreover, it depends for its attainment not on prescriptive rules but on the absence of such prescriptions. "It really is of importance," Mill says, "not only what men do, but also what manner of men they are that do it" (76), it being up to the individual "to find out what part of recorded experience is properly applicable to his own circumstances and character" (74). The creation of an ethical self is thus context-dependent and rule-independent, recalling a passage from George Eliot's *Mill on the Floss*, published the following year, in which she calls for a similar type of practical virtue involving the use of higher faculties: "All people of broad, strong sense have an instinctive repugnance to the men of maxims; because such people early discern that the very mysterious complexity of our life is not to be embraced by maxims . . . And that the man of maxims is the popular representative of the minds that are guided in their moral judgment solely by general rules . . . without the trouble of exerting patience, discrimination, impartiality."[21]

While Mill's utilitarianism thus possesses elements of what Sidgwick calls aesthetic intuitionism, it is also aesthetic in a second sense, imagining self-development as a quasi-artistic act. "Among the works of man, which human life is rightly employed in perfecting and beautifying," Mill writes, "the first in importance surely is man himself" (*On Liberty*, 76). In his view, a unique and cultivated character elicits a sort of admiration and pleasure analogous to that produced by the well-executed work of art, with the free exercise of human faculties mirroring the free play of imagination described by Arnold and later Bosanquet. The disinterested contemplation of beauty is usually opposed to utilitarian egoism, but here it is adduced as one of its principal outcomes, just as it is for critics such as Spencer and Wilde. This strange fact highlights how virtue ethics could be understood as an aesthetic mode of judgment for which the realization of character through the exercise of one's higher faculties constitutes an intrinsic good.

Moral Taste and the Relation between Ethics and Aesthetics

In *The Ideology of the Aesthetic*, Terry Eagleton writes that "the ruling ideology of Victorian England is a virulently anti-aesthetic Utilitarianism, the belated offspring of Enlightenment rationalism. Self-interest wins out over moral sense, as custom, tradition and sensibility are subjected of the cold light of rational critique."[22] This view may be based more on a caricature of Bentham or Sidgwick than of Mill, but it captures how the philosophical opponents of utilitarianism worried that its narrowly hedonistic doctrine evacuated ethics of beauty, sentiment, and other values that did not directly bear upon the consequentialist calculation of right or wrong. This fear spurred an intense reaction in which moral philosophers looked to different philosophical traditions in order to recuperate the values that utilitarianism seemed to exclude – traditions, emanating from Aristotle, in which moral philosophy does not oppose the aesthetic but helps to define and constitute it.

The most charitable of the philosophical critics of utilitarianism may be John Grote. In the posthumously published *An Examination of the Utilitarian Philosophy* (1870), Grote stressed that his "disagreement with utilitarianism has mainly reference to its claim to supersede all other philosophy, and to occupy the whole ground of morals to itself."[23] Grote did not "deny the importance, in regard of actions, of their conduciveness to happiness" but rather objected to "the philosophy which would assert that there is no other original and primary reason which can make us take interest in actions, and consider them good or valuable, except this" (119). Like other followers of Whewell, Grote wished to expand moral philosophy to include non-hedonic sources of value. Mill had argued that one can evaluate virtue from two different perspectives – an objective one, insofar as it contributes to utility, and a subjective one, insofar as it expresses something admirable about the intentions of the moral agent – but Grote believed that this artificially separated the right from the good (126). Grote consequently calls for an ethics that can "solve the difficulty of the relation between right actions and good feeling or character" (130) by returning to the true subject of moral philosophy, which is "the 'ars artium,' the great art of living" (348), as found in Aristotle.

In *A Treatise on the Moral Ideals* (1876), Grote begins by distinguishing between two "sciences" within the single subject of ethics: eudaimonics, which treats happiness as a function of man's pleasures and pains in his existence as a sentient being, and aretaics, which examines virtue as man's activity with respect to a uniquely human ideal.[24] In this view, aretaics corresponds to the Aristotelian notion of "eupraxia," or living well (*Examination*, 347), in a moral landscape shaped by words such as virtue, duty, ought, and should (*Treatise*, 15). Grote notes that the science of duty, or deontology, can be analyzed separately from aretaics, although, in emphasizing that which should be done rather than the ideal itself, they amount to the same thing (*Treatise*, 102). Most of the *Treatise* consists in determining what a man's duties are, but in the final section he treats "ethics" in light of its original meaning in Aristotle as the science of human character, which joins aretaics to complete the study of moral philosophy (433–34).[25]

Following a method derived from what he calls Aristotle's "moral biology" (*Examination*, xxiv), Grote describes how a distinct character emerges as a result of natural feelings, dispositions, and temperaments being shaped by culture and experience and hardening into more permanent customs and habits. Scientifically speaking, character "should be described as a matter of fact, without praise or blame" (*Treatise*, 445). But Grote notes that "our perception of the actual facts of character is greatly hindered by our universal tendency of immediate criticism of them" (445). Indeed, such criticism is the essence of moral philosophy: an adequate science of action (aretaics) can only be developed in light of the character, or ethics, that animates it (446). This, Grote believes, is where Aristotle fails. "The science of character is, as I have said, the true and original *Ethics*, as in Aristotle" (448), but Aristotle's ethics is arbitrary because he does not tell us, for example, "upon what principle we are to ascertain what amount of [some virtue] is desirable. His reference is only to feeling and character and the general estimation shown in actual language" (449). As Sidgwick observes, Aristotle may confuse admiration with moral reasoning, but Grote seeks to recuperate Aristotle through a different understanding of the aesthetic:

> Surely, if it is worth while having principles upon which to make our judgments in nature and art, it is equally so as to human character. There is an evident analogy, as we have seen already in speaking of the face and form: we talk of features of character, painting character, etc.: and so, in regard to the description of character as in regard to art, there are two kinds of correctness, accuracy as to the facts, rightness as to the ideal or standard of judgment. (447)

The challenge is not to describe different types of character accurately but to determine an appropriate standard by which to judge them, which involves the science of aretaics (virtue and duty) in relation to ethics (character). Judgments about character, therefore, involve the exercise of "moral taste" (447), beginning with superficial descriptions on the basis of positive or negative feeling and ending, after they are shaped by experience and education, as refined evaluations with respect to an imaginative and action-guiding ideal. Rather than distinguish between character, virtue, and duty, Grote tries to align them, resulting in a synthesis involving common imaginative ideals, feelings, and judgments.

Grote's theory of "moral taste" has roots in eighteenth-century sentimentalism, which was inclined to regard morality and beauty as ideas derived from parallel, sometimes overlapping, senses. In a revealing coincidence of phrasing, Reginald Rogers uses the term "aesthetic intuitionism" to describe the moral sense theories of Shaftesbury and Hutcheson;[26] the phrase is anachronistic, for the word "aesthetic" did not emerge until the end of the eighteenth century, but it highlights just how much these philosophers found inquiries into morality and beauty to be mutually illuminating.[27] Shaftesbury, for example, posits the existence of a special faculty that is capable of being affected by the moral qualities of actions in the same way we have a faculty capable of being affected by the beautiful qualities of objects. The discernment of beauty, like the discernment of goodness, is as necessary and unmediated as our responses to other external sensations such that "to deny the common natural Sense of a SUBLIME and BEAUTIFUL in Things, will appear an Affectation merely, to any-one who considers duly of this Affair."[28] Moreover, the moral and aesthetic senses are broadly interconnected. As Michael B. Gill explains, "[Shaftesbury] suggested that the positive reaction we have when observing a moral action or character is the same as (or one example of) the positive reaction we have when observing the beauty of nature or works of art, and that the motive to act virtuously is the same as (or one example of) an artist's motive to create beauty. Shaftesbury also said that the virtuous person is one who attempts to make her life a thing of moral beauty in the same way that an artist tries to make beautiful works of art."[29] In Rogers's simpler formulation, for Shaftesbury "moral goodness is beauty in the sphere of the affections."[30]

As a philosopher of aesthetics, Hume is remembered mostly for his essay on taste, but he shared Shaftesbury's, and also Hutcheson's, view that ideas of beauty and morality are fundamentally similar, motivated by common feelings of approbation and displeasure.[31] In his effort to assert the primacy of sentiment as a motive for action in *An Enquiry Concerning the Principles of Morals* (1751), Hume naturally draws analogies between moral and aesthetic feelings. Both aesthetic and moral judgments arise from basic feelings of desire or aversion, but these feelings need to be trained or cultivated to ensure that they conform to a reasonable standard. Hume even uses the phrase "moral beauty" to emphasize the similar way in which "much reasoning" must be employed "in order to feel the proper sentiment"[32] with respect to both kinds of value. Hume also stresses the dual role played by sympathy in moral and aesthetic reasoning. Morally speaking, sympathy is the principle that makes possible and animates the social feelings that give rise to utilitarianism; by the same logic, it allows art to engage the emotions since "no passion, when well represented, can be entirely indifferent to us" (45). Sympathy even has physiological manifestations, such as the displeasure one feels upon hearing "jarring sounds" because they suggest that someone "suffers from the pronunciation" of the words (46).

Most significantly, Hume proffers a version of the doctrine of "moral taste" that reappears in Grote. In his appendix on the nature of moral sentiment, Hume describes how the knowledge of moral relations, like the knowledge of relations in a matter of external beauty, is not enough to stimulate a moral or aesthetic response. Moral or physical beauty "is only the effect, which that figure produces upon the mind, whose peculiar fabric or structure renders it susceptible of such sentiments" (86). In other words, following Shaftesbury and Hutcheson, the ideas of morality and beauty inhere in mental states of liking or aversion that depend on the unique effects of external sensation acting upon internal structure, resulting in feelings of pleasure or pain. In this light, Hume concludes that we make judgments of both beauty and morality through the faculty of taste rather than reason:

> Thus the distinct boundaries and offices of *reason* and of *taste* are easily ascertained. The former conveys the knowledge of truth and falsehood: The latter gives the sentiment of beauty and deformity, vice and virtue. The one discovers objects, as they really stand in nature without addition or diminution: The other has a productive faculty, and gilding and staining all natural objects with the colours, borrowed from internal sentiment, raises, in a manner, a new creation. (88)

By uniting the internal senses of morality and beauty within the single faculty of "taste," Hume argues that moral and aesthetic sentiments are essentially the same. They each supply the motivational underpinnings for the judgments of liking or aversion to which category words such as "beauty" and "vice" reduce. Neither, moreover, is entirely disinterested with respect to persons or objects: "taste, as it gives pleasure or pain, and thereby constitutes happiness or misery, becomes a motive to action, and is the first spring or impulse to desire and volition" (88). Taste therefore matters not only as an expression of a personal feeling but also as a normative judgment that has action-guiding force, a claim that differs sharply from Kant's belief that judgments of the beautiful, being "merely contemplative," do not elicit desires that lead to action.

In histories of English, Kant is often credited with giving rise to the notion that works of art are "autonomous," that is to say, non-instrumental and auto-telic.[33] For example, Harold Schweizer claims that "the notion of literary autonomy – popularized through the 'art for art's sake' movement in the nineteenth century – is the result of what one might call productive misappropriations of Immanuel Kant's (1724–1804) immensely influential aesthetic theory in his Critique of Judgment (1790)."[34] However, the sentimentalist tradition in Britain contains much of what became operative in a Victorian notion of the "aesthetic" more or less independently of the continental tradition that developed alongside it. For example, Trevor Ross locates the roots of the valorization of aesthetic autonomy in Blair's belletrism, which "popularized the notion of an autonomous aesthetic experience" by treating literary works as having "an authority that preceded the reader's."[35] For Blair, the literary text did not have "designs" on readers in the usual "rhetorical" sense of persuading her to adopt a belief or execute an action but rather existed as objects to satisfy the intrinsic goodness of human contemplation and "taste."[36] Since the exercise of taste was good in itself, akin to a moral capacity, then rhetoric could, as David Wellbery argues, be "naturalized and psychologized"[37] in a way parallel to the *Critique of Judgment*, though not directly conversant with it. Similarly, the concept of "disinterestedness" gets its start with Shaftesbury, who describes a situation in which "contemplative delight ... relates not in the least to any private interest of the creature, nor has for its object any self-good or advantage of the private system," but "turns wholly upon what is exterior and foreign to ourselves," including "the love of truth, proportion, order and symmetry" (202–03).[38] This position – which David Fenner believes leads directly to formalism[39] – predates the continental sources now most associated with it.

While the British and German traditions have important points of interaction, the relative unimportance of Germanic aesthetics is ironically implied by Rosemary Ashton's *The German Idea*, which shows how German philosophy had a significant impact upon only a small set of writers who were capable of reading it in the original language.[40] In the early nineteenth century, Coleridge read Kant and Schiller's essay on aesthetics and propagated their ideas in his writings, generating further interest among Carlyle, De Quincey, and Lewes. But their understanding of Kant's doctrines was partial at best, leading Carlyle to complain in 1827 that German writers were generally "not understood"[41] in England. German philosophical ideas continued to circulate in the Lewes circle – Eliot's translations of Strauss and Feuerbach offer further examples – but, as Stephen Prickett notes, the philosophy of Kant, Hegel, and others "remained largely untranslated until mid-century, and much of the writings of the German Romantics, including Novalis, the Schlegels and Schleiermacher, remained so until the twentieth century."[42] Jonah Siegel concedes that "a powerful native tradition of aesthetic thought, including authors such as Shaftesbury, Addison, Smith, and Burke, which itself contributed to German idealist formulations, was bound to be a direct and indirect influence on British thinkers."[43] Indeed, J.S. Mill exemplified what Carlyle decried in the British public's lack of receptivity to German ideas, the prominent philosopher's hostility ensuring that "English interest in German Idealism in general, and in Hegel in particular, remained marginal"[44] until at least the 1860s.

The 1860s, however, do mark the point at which German idealism came to assume a more prominent position in academic circles. In 1862, F.D.

Maurice completed the second volume of his *Moral and Metaphysical Philosophy*, which began as a three-part series for the vast *Encyclopedia Metropolitana*, whose goal was to realize, "on a methodical plan projected by Samuel Taylor Coleridge," a "system of universal knowledge" that encompassed the history of Western philosophy.[45] Maurice's volume includes a large section devoted to Kant and ends with a survey of German philosophy from Fichte to David Strauss. In 1865, J.H. Stirling further popularized the work of Hegel through *The Secret of Hegel*, which was, according to William Sweet, "epoch-making" for "younger scholars"[46] such as Benjamin Jowett, then Master of Balliol College, Oxford, and his pupil T.H. Green. It was likely through Jowett's lectures on Hegel that F.H. Bradley and Bernard Bosanquet (who first translated Hegel's *Introductory Lectures on Aesthetics* into English), both of whom matriculated in Oxford in the mid-1860s, were first exposed to German ideas. However, as Frank M. Turner has shown, the first of Hegel's texts to assume any traction among British readers was the *Philosophy of History*, whose conception of historical development primarily served to reinvigorate interest in the Greeks.[47] It was, in fact, Alexander Grant, one of the century's most prominent Aristotelians, who argued as early as 1858 that "modern German thought, whatever may have been its extravagances, has, to say the least, this advantage, that it puts those who have the slightest degree caught its influence on a better level for understanding Parmenides and Heraclitus, Plato and Aristotle."[48]

That the influence of German thought should reinforce a Hellenic revival already heavily underway in Britain is not especially surprising. The central concept of Hegelian metaphysics – that history represents the unfolding of the Idea in sensuous form – is essentially Platonic in nature, and it is no coincidence that Jowett and Pater, who both took up Hegel readily, were also most closely associated with Neoplatonism. In terms of British antecedents, Hegelian ideas find their most striking anticipations in the work of Thomas Reid, whom J.B. Schneewind claims dominated British moral philosophy until at least the 1830s.[49] Reid is a significant figure for nineteenth-century virtue aesthetics because he provides an indigenous bridge from Hume's conception of moral taste to the perfectionist tendencies of Mill and later Green, consolidating the ethico-aesthetic synthesis that would also be developed by Alison. In *Essays on the Intellectual Power of Man* (1785), Reid begins with the classical presumption that "there is no real excellence which has not its beauty to a discerning eye, when placed in a proper point of view," using excellence broadly to refer to moral and natural beauty, intellectual beauty, and beauty in works of man as well as God.[50] Reid is more careful than his predecessors to distinguish between the internal and external aspects of beauty; for him, the assertoric nature of aesthetic statements (e.g. "*The Georgics* is beautiful") suggests that beauty is a property of the objects it describes, but at the same time, judgments of beauty depend upon the working of an internal sense with what seem to be cognitive components. Reid's attention to the language of aesthetic judgment is an interesting application of Hume's method, but his true innovation consists in demonstrating the extent to which aesthetic qualities "derive" from the moral qualities that occasion similar feelings.

Reid's basic theory is that aesthetic qualities, insofar as they reside in the properties of objects, are admirable when they disclose the existence of excellent qualities in the mind that produced them. "It is in the oral and intellectual perfections of mind, and in its active powers, that beauty originally dwells; and that from this as the fountain, of all beauty which we perceive in the visible world is derived" (750). In other words, the "beauties of mind" – such as the higher faculties described by Mill – may be invisible in themselves, but they become sensible in objects that indirectly express them. In the case of *The Iliad*, for example, "its sublimity was really in the mind of HOMER. He conceived great characters, great actions, and great events, in a manner suitable to their nature, and with those emotions which they are naturally fitted to produce . . . The grandeur of his thoughts is reflected to our eye by his work, and therefore it is justly called a grand work" (732). Roger Gallie explains Reid's position as claiming that art imitates the human expression of emotion without actually imitating an emotion;[51] put differently, one could argue that art, in the qualities that merit approbation, expresses something deeper than the concrete external forms in which those qualities are objectively manifested. While the perception of sublimity (or "grandeur") depends on the scale of admiration that the percipient feels toward an object, Reid elaborates that beauty inheres in the perception of qualities that merit love or esteem (445). The list of such qualities is long, including amiable moral virtues (such as innocence or public spirit), amiable intellectual talents (such as knowledge and cheerfulness or even excellence in the fine arts) and perfections that indicate the fitness of the mind and body (such as health and agility). Reid argues that there is "a real intrinsic excellence" (729) in these qualities of mind, rendering beautiful any person or thing that expresses them, but this expression is oblique at best. In music, for example, the word "harmony" describes relations between simultaneously sounded notes, but it takes a secondary judgment to determine what quality this property reflects, such as amity and friendship in the "relations of minds and affections" (753). The fact of concord, therefore, has two meanings, one aesthetic (describing the relation between a first and a fifth) and one ethical (signifying a virtue). The first results from a surface judgment with primarily affective components (i.e. pleasure); the second adds a cognitive judgment that explains where that pleasure comes from. The roots of Ruskin's aesthetic theophany, along with ethico-aesthetic drift, have been laid.

In his *Essays on the Nature and Principles of Taste* (1790), Archibald Alison acknowledges a debt to Reid and agrees with the doctrine that "matter is not beautiful in itself, but derives its beauty from the expression of mind."[52] Whereas Reid could be vague in establishing how aesthetic and moral qualities were connected, Alison offers derivations that are explicitly associationist, treating aesthetic qualities as signs, indices, or metonyms of underlying mental excellences. After establishing that "it is only ... through the medium of matter that, in the present condition of our being, the qualities of mind are known to us" (444), he suggests that matter may express mind in two ways: through direct signs of the mind's powers or emotions (as in a design that exhibits complexity or a melody that evokes joy), or as indirect associations that are "less universal and less permanent" (445): for example, a luxury product may seem beautiful because it testifies to the wealth of the owner, a color may be particularly suggestive of an emotion, or we may have contingent associations with certain objects because of their use in fashions, rituals, or "our own private affections or remembrances" (446). Alison's examples may seem unconvincing given our greater appreciation for cultural variability in the experience of art, but his significance lies in showing how, along with Reid, an expressivist aesthetics could evolve out of eighteenth-century moral philosophy without necessarily being assimilated to that philosophy.[53] For Alison argues that the "emotions of taste" prompted by beauty and sublimity need not be identical to the emotions that influence moral judgment, as they seem to be in Hume. Aesthetic judgment is ethical not because aesthetic judgments should be reduced to moral claims or moral feelings, but because their distinctive affect can only be explained with reference to the underlying qualities of mind that provide a foundation for both types of judgment.[54] Dabney Townsend goes so far as to say that "Alison frees aesthetics from its moral connections to virtue – ironically, given his own moral purposes," and argues that elements of his theory influence British aesthetics "through Ruskin and the pre-Raphaelites and into the particularly British versions of post-Kantian idealism."[55] However, the importance of virtue in nineteenth-century philosophy ensures that the link between aesthetics and the ethical broadly conceived – virtue, character, and admirable "qualities of mind" – is never fully severed.

Green's "Self-Realisation" and Bosanquet's "Aesthetic"

According to Sidgwick's *Outlines of the History of Ethics* (1886), the distinctive form of idealism to which Townsend refers finds its "most elaborate and important expression in Green's *Prolegomena to Ethics,*"[56] published posthumously in 1883. This work, along with F.H. Bradley's *Ethical Studies* of 1876, marks the advent toward the end of the nineteenth century of a non-hedonic alternative to utilitarianism that took "self-realization" to be the ultimate good and self-satisfaction as its corresponding happiness. British idealists were strongly influenced by Kant and Hegel, but the Aristotelian character of their work is often overlooked, despite the fact that one of Sidgwick's major criticisms of Green concerned his use of Greek ethics.

T.H. Irwin, in "Eminent Victorians and Greek Ethics," reviews some of these differences, beginning with the fundamental discrepancy in attitude between Sidgwick and Green with respect to Aristotle's ethics. While Sidgwick uses Greek ethics "primarily for a negative, even cautionary, purpose,"[57] Green "thinks Greek moral philosophy embodies, in undeveloped form, the outlook that Green himself takes to be correct."[58] While Sidgwick criticizes virtue ethics as a form of "aesthetic intuitionism" in which admiration for the virtues substitutes for rational analysis, Green sees Aristotle's account of the virtues as actualizing, in undeveloped form, a true conception of the good.[59] While Sidgwick thinks Aristotle's conception of moral excellence is too vague and historically conditioned to be useful, Green regards it as consistent with the idea that self-satisfaction consists in the full realization of the rational agent's capacities, including an obligation to the common good.[60] Sidgwick, in short, sees utilitarianism as delivering a fundamental break from aesthetic intuitionism while Green sees idealism as integrating virtue ethics with Kantian notions of freedom and a categorical conception of moral law. For this reason, D.G. Ritchie aptly describes Green as having "corrected Kant by Aristotle and Aristotle by Kant."[61]

At the center of this chiasmus is Green's ideal of self-realization. On the Kantian side, Green believes that "reason is the self-objectifying consciousness" and "constitutes . . . the capability in man of seeking an absolute good and of conceiving this good as common to others with himself: and it is this capability which alone renders him a possible author and a self-submitting subject of law."[62] Green, in other words, sees man as a noumenon, free to act in accordance with norms that reflect his autonomy. But, in a more Aristotelian mode, Green argues that rational self-legislation consists in "a progress *of* personal character and *to* personal character – a progress of which feeling, thinking, and willing subjects are the agents and sustainers, and of which each step is a fuller realisation of the capacities of such subjects" (212). Freedom, in this view, consists in the exercise of capacities that realize "the will to be perfect" (467), the "fuller realisation of the capacities of the human soul" (457) with an eye to the "perfection of the human spirit" (470). This theory, as David Brink observes, "makes the content of the good consist in the exercise of the very same capacities that make one a rational agent, subject to reasons for action, in the first place,"[63] thereby enabling Green to offer a perfectionist alternative to utilitarianism that blends Kantian deontology with the virtue ethics found implicitly in Mill and explicitly, as aretaic ethics, in Grote.

The Aristotelian influence is arguably stronger than the Kantian, particularly as Green equates his theory with "the theory of virtue as an end in itself" (470). In the chapter comparing "Greek and Modern Conceptions of Virtue," Green underlines the centrality of Aristotle for his system, arguing that "for the present our concern is rather to point out the greatness – in a certain sense the completeness and finality – of the advance in spiritual development which the Greek philosophers represent" (300). Green offers four reasons why virtue is at the center of this approach. First, he explains that "the real value of the virtue rises with the more full and clear conception of the end to which it is directed, as a character not a good fortune, as a fulfillment of human capabilities from within not an accession of good things from without" (291). The question, Green says, is not "what ought to be done" but "what should I be? – a question of motives and character" (374). Second, Green specifies that "the highest possible realisation of [man's] faculties is the common ground of every form of true virtue" (298), thereby defining virtue as the exercise of his capacities: virtue is the mechanism by which man attempts to realize or express the perfection of soul that is his ultimate good. Third, Green argues that the virtues are actuated by a will "directed not to anything external, or anything in respect of which it is passive, but to its own perfection, to the attainment of what is noblest in human character and action" (330). This ideal, which he calls a "disinterested interest in the good," explains why virtue is to be pursued for its own sake and not for some consequential reward like pleasure or fortune: it too is intrinsically good, expressing the intrinsic good of the ideal it realizes.[64] Fourth, Green argues that the realization of a good will involves different modes of virtuous action, interpreted broadly to mean not only the deliberative capacities, as Brink suggests,[65] but "other faculties indeed than those which are directly exhibited in the specifically moral virtues – faculties which find their expression not in his dealings with other men, but in the arts and sciences" (456).

Following the last point, Green massively expands the range of things that can be interpreted as expressing the will to perfection, spanning from judgments, aspirations, and institutions (206), to "various forms of recognised duty and beneficent work" (207), to other "modes of life" and "forms of the imagination" (382).[66] As a fellow of Balliol College in 1862, Green wrote a prize-winning essay called *An Estimate of the Value and Influence of Works of Fiction in Modern Times*, which has prompted Leigh Dale to call him "one of several British idealists who saw in poets and poetry a parallel enterprise to that of idealist philosophy."[67] Although he devotes little attention to the traditional subject of beauty in the *Prolegomena*, Green's multiple references to art as an expression of the good reveal how, in his philosophy, aesthetic products can be understood as actualizing the intrinsic goodness of the virtues that motivate them, similar to the schemes of Reid and Alison. Moreover, as Green indicates, the goodness expressed may be "other" than that which is "specifically moral" (456). The broad conception of excellence that characterizes Aristotelian ethics means that there are non-moral sources of value, realized through the exercise of capacities and sometimes expressed through works of art, that are "disinterested" or worth pursuing for their own sake because they contribute, in part, to the "full realisation of human capabilities" (457).

In this light, it is not difficult to see how the aesthetic "character" of a literary work can emerge out of the perfectionist account of character that receives its fullest treatment in Green. In a double meaning the word refers to both ethical and aesthetic excellence, the latter being valued disinterestedly, or for its own sake, because it has already been established as virtuously expressive of the ultimate good. Such an understanding of "art for art's sake" is rather different from that usually assumed within literary studies, in which aesthetic autonomy (or "non-instrumentality") suggests the indifference of art or of the aesthetic disposition to moral or political ends. Exponents of this view tend to argue that mid-nineteenth-century writers such as Flaubert and Mallarmé liberated "style" from its service to subject matter in order to establish the independence of the aesthetic sphere;[68] yet, as we have seen, an aretaic or virtue-based conception of art identifies style with the "aesthetic" not to isolate it but to explain its peculiar moral status. For Victorian theorists of art, virtues of style allude at once to the moral character of a speaker's ethos and to distinctly aesthetic values that are counted good for the capacities they express or the faculties they engage when abstracted away from an individual source. Critics of literature who recognize the role played by virtue in the novel often attend to the first category without recognizing the existence of the second.

Green's philosophy provides the period's fullest statement of how aesthetic value could be ethically relevant within a non-utilitarian paradigm. His work was continued by his student, Bernard Bosanquet, an historian and philosopher whose work in aesthetics combines Aristotelian ethics with German idealism in a uniquely British synthesis. In 1889, Bosanquet published an article called "The Part Played by Aesthetic in the Development of Modern Philosophy" in which he lamented the relative vacuity of formal aesthetic philosophy in Britain. Unlike Germany, which had Kant and Fichte, Winklemann and Schiller and Goethe, in Britain there is a "different atmosphere" where "the history of philosophy, of religion, of fine art, of civilization, is conspicuous by its absence."[69] In 1886, Bosanquet had begun to remedy this defect by translating into English *The Introduction to Hegel's Philosophy of Fine Art*, and his 1889 article bears distinctive traces of Hegel's influence. Bosanquet argues that the problem of modern philosophy, first established by Kant, is the reconciliation of the sensuous world of nature with the suprasensuous world of freedom, or the reality of sense with the ideal realm of thought (369). There is, in other words, a gap between the ideals of spirit or the universal mind and the sensuous world we inhabit. Bosanquet interprets Kant's aesthetics as attempting to overcome this gap, an effort continued by Winkelmann and especially Schiller, who first "impressed upon the age ... the idea that in beauty, and in the mind which is perceptive of beauty, there is an actual and existing reconciliation of such opposites as sense and thought, natural necessity and moral freedom, matter and form" (376). This is the conception of beauty von Hartmann calls "concrete idealism" and that Hegel, in Boanquet's paraphrase, defines as "the Idea as it shows itself to sense."[70]

In 1892, Bosanquet published *A History of Aesthetic*, the first English work on the subject and an important defense of "aesthetic" as a distinct branch of philosophical inquiry. Bosanquet begins by noting that although the word "aesthetic" did not emerge until the second half of the eighteenth century, the "thing existed before the name" (1), his purpose being to untangle genuine "aesthetic interest" from approaches governed by extrinsic values such as moral goodness, utility, or sensual gratification. According to Bosanquet, "aesthetic interest" should be understood as a posture of disinterestedness with respect to art, with the pleasure that attends beauty being independent from "all satisfaction attaching to practical relations with reality, whether moral, non-moral, or immoral" (62). It exists in Plato "only in so far as he recognizes a peculiar satisfaction attending the very abstract manifestations of purely formal beauty" (53), such as in non-imitative colors, shapes, and tones (32), and in Aristotle to the extent that he appreciates an "ideal unity of structure such as to display the events of life in their essential connection" (75). But the ancients were limited by their mimetic theory of art, which degraded it to a mere copy of reality, as well as by their identification of virtue with beauty. For this reason, Bosanquet criticizes Shaftesbury, an early champion of disinterestedness, whose "extension of the terms 'beauty' and 'sense' to the goodness of morality and the faculty by which we judge of it, is fatal of course to a distinct demarcation of the aesthetic region" (177).

Bosanquet's *History* offers the nineteenth century's most comprehensive defense of disinterestedness as the attitude appropriate to the "aesthetic consciousness," but, as John Dewey observed, its author struggles to reconcile the ancients' appreciation for abstract formal qualities with the modern notion that aesthetic reflection is "characteristic" or expressive of "life in its entire range."[71] On the one hand, there is a difficulty in determining what exactly Bosanquet's aesthetic "Idea" consists of;[72] on the other, one wonders how a person's attitude toward such a broad-ranging spiritual ideal could be entirely disinterested. The paradox, however, is not so puzzling when one recalls two concepts from Bosanquet's mentor Green: first, that morality be defined as a "disinterested interest in the good," and second, that virtuous action consist in the agent's "full realisation" of his capacities (*Prolegomena*, 300). Within this framework, it becomes possible to establish a mutually reinforcing connection between ethics and art: in the realm of morality, a love of virtue provides the motive to realize the good for its own sake, while in the realm of aesthetics, a love of beauty provides the motive to appreciate, with a "peculiar satisfaction," the idea in sensuous form. Bosanquet's understanding of disinterestedness, therefore, is not an example of the doctrine of art for art's sake that divorces art from the ethical realm but rather a defense of the idea that aesthetic interest, like the practice of virtue, is intrinsically valuable as an expression of the ultimate good.

In an essay called "On the Nature of Aesthetic Emotion," Bosanquet focuses on the artist as the origin of aesthetic interest, defining art as feeling that is "only articulate through that of which it is the feeling, viz. a presentation more or less individual" (*"Science and Philosophy,"* 397). A presentation that articulates a feeling will evolve a new "correlative emotion (pure feeling as qualified by the presentation itself)" and this emotion is distinctly aesthetic:

> If this is so, it would seem that every emotion exists only as correlative to its expression; or that strictly speaking we do not first have an emotion and then proceed to express it; but that an emotion assumes its character, or becomes what it is, through the mode and degree of its expression; and therefore that aesthetic emotion first arises in and is essentially constituted by, expression for expression's sake, or in other words, when its discharge takes the form of a positive production or action which has no purpose beyond that of uttering the content of our feeling. (397–98)

Because of passages like the above, Bosanquet's theory has been called "expressivist," though it remains ambiguous whether the emotion is aesthetic because it results in an aesthetic emotion, is motivated by an aesthetic interest, or is recognized as aesthetic by the right kind of person. As his career progressed, Bosanquet's interest shifted to explanations of the latter variety. In his chapter on the Middle Ages in *A History of Aesthetic*, he clarifies his position with respect to the aestheticist creed by implying that disinterestedness is less a virtue of artistic creation than the requirement for its adequate appreciation: "So far from its being true that there is no genuine art-consciousness where there is no intentional aim at beauty for beauty's sake, it is probable that such intentional aim is at least a grave danger to art, if not a sure symptom of decadence" (*History*, 167). Similarly, in *Three Lectures on Aesthetic* (1915), he argues that the aesthetic attitude is "the attitude of a mind which freely tracks and pursues the details of experience for the sake of a particular kind of satisfaction,"[73] such that the feeling of pleasure derived from the object is attributed to it as one of its properties (25). As in Wilde, "form is the beginning of things" because aesthetic expression makes ethical character intelligible and admirable. But it is through aesthetic appreciation and criticism that we best express those qualities which bring us closer to the ideal, and which are in actuality a precondition for form:

> The imagination is precisely the mind at work, pursuing and exploring the possibilities suggested by the connections of its experience. It may operate, of course, in the service of logical enquiry and of exact science itself . . . The only difference is that when the imagination is free, when the mind is operating, for instance, not in the service of theoretical truth, but in that of aesthetic feeling, then it altogether ceases to be bound by agreement with what we call reality as a whole. It cannot help starting from what we call experience . . . but its guiding purpose is the satisfaction of feeling. (27)

This portrait of the creative imagination, however Kantian in its outlines, is infused by Green's notion that "satisfaction" depends upon the exercise of overtly ethical capacities, as long as we remain disinterested in the appropriate way (that is, for the sake of the ideal itself). Thus, we can see how the country's leading exponent of aesthetic autonomy provided a thoroughly ethical justification for the creation and criticism of art.

Conclusion

Bosanquet lamented the absence of aesthetic theory in British philosophy but noted that there are "great writers" who have "occupied a sort of prophetic position" at least as influential as the logicians, psychologists, and moral philosophers ("*Science and Philosophy*," 387). These writers include Wordsworth, Carlyle, Ruskin, Morris, and Pater, as well as (we may add to Bosanquet's list) Arnold and Wilde. With moral philosophy dominated by the rise of, and opposition to, the relatively arid prescriptions of empirical utilitarianism, non-philosophical writers naturally conducted a different kind of aesthetic business. But in doing so they drew on the various forms of perfectionism and idealism, most thoroughly articulated by moral philosophers, that sought to regain a space for virtue within the broader ethical landscape.

We now have a synoptic view of the literary-critical and philosophical history and theory of stylistic virtue. We have seen how style began as a rhetorical category referring to the qualities of a text's words or sentences; how these sentences combine to convey an impression of general stylistic character; and how stylistic character played a central role in driving the formalist methods used to describe it. We have come to appreciate the difference between a referential conception of style, which interprets it as the embodiment of an underlying *ethos* or personality, and an autonomous one that interprets ethos in the light of aesthetic values such as beauty, craft, and "impersonal" stylistic norms. And we now understand why style, as the essence of the aesthetic, emerged as the major discourse in which a virtue-theoretic approach to art was manifested, not in spite of the aesthetic independence attributed to style but because of it. In the next three chapters, which examine stylistic virtues in Thackeray, Trollope, and Meredith, I shall be less interested in *why* some thinkers came to value style for its realization of aesthetic character than in *how* it actually does so. The usefulness of stylistic virtue as an interpretive tool can only be measured by the results of its literary-critical application.

CHAPTER 4

Thackeray's Grace

Upon the publication of Thackeray's last novel, *The Adventures of Philip* (1861), critics noted the familiarity and predictability of Thackeray's manner, warmly citing "the old humour, the old irony, the old extensive knowledge of men and things, the old ease of writing, and the old excellence of telling a story."[1] But Thackeray's early writings, published anonymously or under pseudonyms, were most distinctive for their versatility, exhibiting a stylistic restlessness that effectively masked the author's real identity until the publication of *Vanity Fair* (1848). In the first part of this chapter, I suggest that the variousness of Thackeray's early work, combined with the conditions of early Victorian publishing, spurred a long-standing effort to define Thackeray's "personality" and ethos – that is, to stabilize the attitudes, character, and values of the author "implied" by his works. But I shall go on to argue that there are important differences between Thackeray's authorial personality as conveyed by the "certain characteristic way" in which he "delineated"[2] human life and the aesthetic character embodied by his stylistic virtues, which diverge from, and sometimes contradict, the impression of formal consistency.

Wayne Booth argues that the ethos of a "fiction" or "work of art" is synonymous with that of the implied author,[3] which disposes the reader to look for unity of thought and tone, much as we would with a real person. However, in the middle sections of this chapter, I examine several instances where the presumption of stylistic referentialism has prejudiced interpretations of Thackeray's early works in problematic ways. First, I argue against the common belief that "Crinoline," in *Novels by Eminent Hands*, is a "self-parody," showing instead how Thackeray uses style to avoid establishing a personal signature; second, I claim that *Catherine*, Thackeray's early novella, is not a manifesto for moral realism but a stylistic account of its limitations; and third, I explain why *The Luck of Barry Lyndon*, Thackeray's first major novel, should not be judged according to the standard set by its putative prototype, Fielding's *Jonathan Wild*, arguing, rather, that it belongs to the tradition of fictional memoir established by Defoe. I focus on the early works because they contain, in exaggerated form, the stylistic virtues of grace and ease that characterize Thackeray's later novels, even as I seek to detach these qualities from the realistic description, satirical distortion, and ironic authorial tone that have traditionally been regarded as hallmarks of the "Thackerayan."[4]

In 1935, Lord David Cecil described Thackeray's style as "flexible enough to cover without awkwardness all the vast variety of mood and incident which Thackeray's subject matter entails," such that it can "soar and drop and brood and perorate and weep and laugh with equal ease."[5] Even among his earliest critics, this kind of style prompted accusations of "pococurantism" or gentlemanly privilege that still require some measure of special pleading.[6] For example, Amanpal Garcha sees Thackeray's style (which he regards as regular rather than changeable) as offering an oasis of "consistency and stasis" amidst the turmoil of the modern marketplace, enacting a "fantasy of living timelessly, outside the contingency and overwhelming humbug responsible for the subject's decentered existence."[7] I take a different view, claiming that Thackeray, despite his merciless attacks on all kinds of pretension, sham, and affectation in his representations of social life, paradoxically accepted that stylistic grace – its protean ease and dextrous versatility – necessarily involves a kind of tolerable hypocrisy or "humbug." In fact, the malleability of Thackeray's style, with its unembarrassed embrace of parody, burlesque, and *bricolage*, is an aesthetic achievement more postmodern in character than conservatively oriented toward the past, despite the author's preoccupation with eighteenth-century models. In the chapters on Trollope and Meredith, I focus more on the mechanics of style than on the authors' attitudes toward style as a concept, but I hope to show here how productively we can understand one through the other.

One Thackeray or Many?

In January 1846, a year before the serialization of *Vanity Fair*, *Fraser's Magazine* published a review of *Notes of a Journey from Cornhill to Grand Cairo*, a travelogue that Thackeray authored under his most popular pseudonym, Michael Angelo Titmarsh. Before analyzing the work itself, the reviewer asks a question that his audience shared: "But who is TITMARSH? Such is the ejaculatory formula in which public curiosity gives vent to its ignorant impatience of pseudonymous renown. Who *is* MICHAEL ANGELO TITMARSH? Such is the note of interrogation which has been heard at intervals these several seasons back."[8] The question is only partly tongue-in-cheek: in 1846, only a handful of readers knew that Titmarsh was Thackeray (who was not yet a public figure) and few, if any, were familiar with the full range of his authorial personae. The reviewer continues by describing Titmarsh as a literary chameleon of astounding versatility, producing works under the guise of the Anglo-Indian colonial, Major Goliath Gahagan; the adventurer Augustus Fitz-Boodle (himself presumed to be a disguised Barry Lyndon, whose memoirs he purports to "edit"); James Yellowplush, the footman, and James de la Pluche, Esq., that footman as an upper-class snob; and *Punch*'s "Fat Contributor." "Here," the reviewer continues, "a feeling of incredulity will naturally come upon the reader. Must he admit all this multiformity in single-handed authorship, and do not so many irreconcilable phases stagger belief in one persisting individuality?" (88).

Upon the threshold of publishing *Vanity Fair*, Thackeray was primarily known for lacking a determinate personality, or for possessing so many distinctive personalities that they merited comparison to the "various incarnations of Visnou, in imitation of whom this wayward genius may be supposed to incorporate himself in a variety of manifestations" (88).[9] Hence, as the first work that Thackeray published under his own name, *Vanity Fair* has played a central, if misleading, role in stimulating critics to identify what exactly is "Thackerayan" about it. In a review for the *Spectator*, Robert Stephen Rintoul wrote that "the novel is distinguished by the more remarkable qualities which have created the reputation of the author, – his keen perception of the weaknesses, vanities, and humbug of society, the felicitous point with which he displays or the pungent though goodnatured satire with which he exposes them."[10] At the same time, the novel added something new, "a depth and at times a pathos which we do not remember to have met with in Mr. Thackeray's previous writings."[11] In a more sweeping gesture, Abraham Hayward treated *Vanity Fair* as a point of origin rather than a culmination, dismissing the rest of the author's work as mere juvenilia: "in forming our general estimate of this writer, we wish to be understood as referring principally, if not exclusively, to *Vanity Fair* (a novel in monthly parts), though still unfinished; so immeasurably superior, in our opinion, is this to every other known production of his pen."[12] Hayward believed that *Vanity Fair*, unlike the "multiformity" of the journalistic writings, with their diverse personae and styles, revealed the author speaking in his own voice, with "much that is most characteristic in his style of expression and mode of looking at things and people" now being traceable to facts that could be known about his actual biography (49–50).

In his two-part biography of Thackeray (1955–58), Gordon Ray enshrined the tendency to divide Thackeray's career into pre- and post-*Vanity Fair*, beginning with the "Uses of Adversity," in which Thackeray rises to prominence, and concluding with the "Age of Wisdom," in which he bears the fruits of his success.[13] For partisans of the later period, this dichotomy provides a useful framework in which to trace the evolution of Thackeray's themes and techniques from crudeness to maturity, buttressed by the pre-eminence, at least until recently, of the novel over more ephemeral forms such as the essay, short story, or review.[14] However, an equally strong tradition of criticism holds that *Vanity Fair* had negative consequences for Thackeray's life and art, adducing the major novels that followed – *Pendennis*, *Henry Esmond*, *The Newcomes*, *The Virginians*, and *Philip* – as evidence that Thackeray eschewed the caustic satire of the early works in a bid to satisfy the more genial tastes of a bourgeois reading public.[15] In either case, Thackeray's critics elide the "multiformity" that once defined Thackeray's achievement around the pivot of *Vanity Fair*, which, as M.G. Sundell puts it, has meant "'Thackeray' for years"[16] in both the literal and literary senses.

Critics have sought to stabilize Thackeray's personality in part because early Victorian reviewers, insofar as they emphasized life-like mimesis and authorial truth-telling, placed a premium on "sincerity" or earnest communication. Such attitudes contributed to Victorian complaints of Thackeray failing to take either reality, or his artistic representations of it, seriously.[17] They also provoked interest in Thackeray's narrators, beginning with Brownell's defense of Thackeray's intrusions on the grounds that "the evil is lessened in proportion to the interest of the personality so obtruded."[18] However, with several exceptions, few commentators adequately distinguish between the narrator of *Vanity Fair*, presumed to be closest to Thackeray himself, and the homodiegetic character-authors, from Fitz-Boodle to Pendennis, whom he uses to narrate the fictions.[19] In fact, the conviction that Thackeray's larger *oeuvre* is pervaded by the "fine display of the personal ego"[20] accounts for a third group of critics who seek to transcend unsettling divisions by insisting that Thackeray must, as George Saintsbury first argued, be read "all of a piece."[21] For example, in *Thackeray the Novelist*, Geoffrey Tillotson seeks "to define the Thackerayan oneness" by uniting Thackeray's "constant" style with the "I" whose "presence is felt everywhere";[22] James Wheatley argues that "parody is both conceptually and biographically fundamental to Thackeray's career";[23] while Judith Law Fisher describes how Thackeray's ironies reveal "a rhetorical intent that ties narrative technique and story together as mirror images of each other."[24] While increasingly sensitive to style and language, these studies nonetheless minimize the diversity of Thackeray's output in pursuit of some underlying notion of authorial intention that can unify its enormous variety.

This diversity has posed a problem to those seeking to stabilize the list of periodical and occasional writings that may be attributed to Thackeray, a notoriously difficult task owing to his frequency of anonymous publication.[25] It is particularly telling that Gary Simons, who once referred hopefully to "'smoking gun' expressions or language" or a localized "Thackeray 'fingerprint,'"[26] finds that what makes Thackeray "Thackerayan" is less a function of linguistic regularity than of subject matter and authorial tone: "a mixture of sense and sentiment, the recognition of the ludicrous in human nature and human activity, an attack on pomposity and pretense, the deft handling of a witty subversive phrase or an insightful contrast, and the underlying affection for honesty and the search for truth that later became Thackeray's hallmark as a novelist."[27] While there is nothing objectionable about this list, it excludes the possibility that Thackeray's protean style may signify something apart from those characteristics that critics have so consistently sought to localize in the coherence of an underlying ego, which has long dictated a referentialist approach to the style presumed to express it.

The sentence that G.H. Lewes selects as "very characteristic of the author"[28] in his 1848 review of *Vanity Fair* is particularly revealing in this context. Lewes quotes from the narrator's comments on the character of Old Miss Crawley: "Picture to yourself, oh fair young reader, a worldly, selfish, graceless, thankless, religionless old woman, writhing in pain and fear, and *without her wig!* Picture her to yourself, and ere you be old learn to love and pray!" (797). As an isolated sample, the sentence is recognizably Thackerayan in its arch address to the reader, the mock-horror and bathos implied by "without her wig," and the larger *topos* of *vanitas vanitatum* – all features of subject matter and tone. But stylistically, the excerpt is both "characteristic" of Thackeray and empty of individual character. The address to the reader parodies the kind of decorous apostrophe that typified silver-fork fiction and that Thackeray lampoons elsewhere; the run of adjectives defining the woman recalls Swift in its diction and manner; the italicized phrase is deliberately double-voiced, impersonating the worldly shock of the vain woman at her own state of dishabille; while the final exhortation offers a parody of Biblical sermonizing that, given the declared triviality of the subject matter, is questionably serious. The passage, to use Trollope's phrase, "has a strong flavour of Thackeray,"[29] but for all that it is difficult to say whether any of these elements is distinctly "Thackerayan." The novelist's mind stands behind the style in its constant attack on social pretension and worldly values, but the style itself is more of a shell than a body, encompassing different sociolects, allusions, conventions, and rhetorical techniques.[30] If the Thackerayan "touch" only shows its marks when these elements are brought together for a thematic or tonal purpose, then perhaps there is another form of the "Thackerayan" that we have not yet learned to feel.

The Evasion of "Personality" in *Novels by Eminent Hands*

The treatment given to Thackeray's "self-parody" in *Novels by Eminent Hands* (1847)[31] offers a signal example of how style gets simplified when it is "explained" as an index to the "mind" of an implied author rather than as the embodiment of an attitude toward art. As is well known, Thackeray produced this series for *Punch* in order to mock the styles and attitudes of the voices then dominant in contemporary fiction. "George de Barnwell" parodies the grandiloquent diction and dubious philosophizing of Bulwer's *Eugene Aram*. "Codlingsby," in which every person of note turns out to be Jewish, is a rather direct burlesque of Disraeli's *Coningsby*. In "Phil Fogarty," Thackeray exaggerates Charles Lever's swaggering military manner, while in "Barbazure" he imitates the romantic archaism of G.P.R. James. "Lords and Liveries," perhaps the most successful parody, skewers the Frenchified pretensions of Catherine Gore's "silver-fork" fiction, and "The Stars and Stripes" makes sport of James Fenimore Cooper. The last remaining story, "Crinoline," is usually treated as a "self-parody" to maintain consistency with the group. Juliet McMaster, the most careful student of the series, writes that "'Crinoline' is Thackeray's take-off of himself. He writes in his old familiar *Punch* guise, as the ill-spelling footman, Jeames; and his protagonist is another incarnation of himself, this time as a Frenchman, Jools de Chacabac."[32] McMaster's analysis may be influenced by the fact that Thackeray did later use one narrative alter ego to narrate the adventures of another with Arthur Pendennis and Philip Firmin in *Philip* – perhaps the closest that Victorian fiction comes to the mirror-games of Philip Roth. But she overlooks the peculiar status of an author's "self-parody" when the style parodied is not the author's "own" but that of a fabricated character who employs language that is already highly stylized.

Charles Yellowplush, Thackeray's fictional footman, first makes his appearance as the author of a literary review that draws attention to his stylistic peculiarities. In "Fashnable Fax and Polite Annygoats," published in *Fraser's* in 1837, Thackeray used the persona to pen a devastatingly satirical analysis of John Henry Skelton's *My Book; or, the Anatomy of Conduct*, a manual for correct behavior in what Yellowplush calls "gen'-l'manly society."[33] The editor defends Yellowplush's credentials to review the book, in spite of his "orthographical irregularities," because "he who stands behind a fashionable table knows more of society than the guests who sit at the board" (128). But those very "irregularities" in spelling and grammar construct the satirical contrast between Skelton's rarefied manner and Yellowplush's more naturally expressed, salt-of-the-earth opinions. Yellowplush quotes a particularly offending passage from Skelton in which the author laments certain topics that had to be considered: "I would that with propriety much might be expunged, but that I felt it is all required from the nature of the work" (120). In response, Yellowplush comments: "Miss Simkins, my lady's *feel de chamber*, says it's complete ungrammatticle, as so it is. 'I would that,' etc., 'but that,' and so forth: what can be the earthly meaning of it?" (120). The reader laughs here not at Yellowplush's own solecisms and faulty French, but at the way his unaffected language and sentiments undermine the pretentiousness of Skelton's self-consciously literary prose. Yellowplush continues with a distortion of Skelton's name that highlights his style's relative aridity: "'Graceful manners,' says Skeliton, 'is not intuitive,' Nor more an't grammar" (120).[34]

In subsequent papers, Yellowplush consciously, though modestly, sets himself up as an arbiter of linguistic taste. In a review of a play by Lytton Bulwer, he explains that "I (being remarkabble for my style of riting) should cretasize the languidge" (141), which he does harshly: "Away with this canting about great motifs! Let us not be too prowd, my dear Barnet" (146). Thackeray often ridiculed Bulwer for his high-flown style and airs, which are here deflated by Yellowplush's artlessness. In another number, after being complimented by literary men for his work in *Fraser's*, Yellowplush even acknowledges tentative efforts to write his own "novvle" (118), which, given the popularity of his papers in *Punch*, does not seem an ill-conceived idea.

After an interval of several years, Thackeray revived the footman not as the author of satire but as its object. In "A Lucky Speculator,"

Fraser's reports that the one-time manservant has had a sudden reversal of fortune after speculating on railroads and is now a wealthy gentleman of the City. Rechristening himself as "C. Jeames de la Pluche, Esq." (in deference to a supposed ancestor who "came over with the Conqueror," 161), and later as "Fitz-James de la Pluche," Yellowplush adopts the same manners of speech and behavior he had earlier criticized in Skelton and Bulwer. Accused of jilting his fiancée, Fitz-James defends himself ignominiously: "Has for marridge. Haltered suckmstancies rendered it himpossable. I was gone into a new spear of life – mingling with my native aristoxy. I breathe no sallible of blame aginst Miss H. but his a hilliterit cookmaid fit to set at a fashnable table?" (166). Now on the other side of the "table" first mentioned in "Fashionable Fax," Yellowplush's language is no longer endearingly artless. Instead, his newly acquired class-based idioms ("altered circumstances," "native aristocracy"), still mangled by more conscientiously executed pronunciation and spelling (including the hyper-correcting h-insertions in front of "impossible" and "illiterate"), convey his snobbish betrayal of an earlier way of life. Whereas in "Fashionable Fax," Yellowplush's working-class style successfully undermines Skelton's elegant affectations, throughout *Jeames's Diary* its traces perform the opposite function of self-satirizing burlesque.

Considered in this light, "Crinoline" is not a self-parody in the sense that Thackeray foregrounds the quintessential elements of his verbal signature. Nor is it, like the others, a parody that uses an artificial author-persona to exaggerate the style and mannerisms of another author, living or fictional. Instead, "Crinoline" offers a novella written in ostensible earnest by "Je-mes Pl-sh, Esq.," the "second" Yellowplush who aspires to wealth, position, and literary notoriety. The style and manner are characteristic of Yellowplush, not distorted but simply applied to a new context. "I'm not at libbaty to divulj the reel names of the 2 Eroes of the igstrawny Tail which I am abowt to relait to those unlightnd paytrons of letarature and true connyshures of merrit," he begins, "But I pledj my varacity that this singular story of rewmantic love, absobbing pashn, and likewise of GENTEEL LIFE, is, in the main fax, TREW."[35] Each element of this sentence – polite circumlocutions ("libbaty to divulj"), conventionalized emotions and expressions ("abobbing pashn"), and fawning epithets ("unlightnd paytrons of letarature") – is consistent with Fitz-James's earlier writings, but here they are re-purposed for an affectedly upper-class authorial performance, even if his phonetic spelling and colloquialisms (the second paragraph begins, "Welthen") continue to undermine his pretensions. "Crinoline" is thus less a parody of Thackeray's writings than a satire on authorship itself: by telling the story "straight," Plush reveals a lack of awareness that his desire to write a "novvle," like his desire to become a gentleman, constitutes a parodic distortion of an earlier self.

In this way, the reader of "Crinoline" is doubly distanced: the text is an unwitting parody of professional authorship written by a pretender who fails to distinguish himself fully from an earlier incarnation that is itself a fictional creation. In this hall of mirrors, the actual Thackeray is nearly lost; and indeed, the version of the author that the story provides – the Anglophobic journalist Jools de Chacabac, whose visage resembles Thackeray's (see fig. 4.1) – is yet another decoy, resembling the author in an earlier form (when Thackeray too was a penny-a-liner in Paris) but

Fig. 4.1 Thackeray's self-portrait (with glasses) as the French journalist Jools de Chacabac, in *Punch, or the London Charivari* 13 (28 Aug. 1847), 73.

being something other than his external projection. Unlike the knowing moralist of *Vanity Fair*, the early numbers of which were also then appearing in *Punch*, Jools is a naïve tourist whose commentary combines hypocritical enjoyment with unabashed prejudice. "I will go see with my own I's," Plush quotes him as saying, "that infimus hiland of which the innabitants are shopkeepers, gorged with roast beef and treason" (63–64). It is nigh impossible to determine whether Jools's xenophobia is an hilarious exaggeration of Thackeray's own supposed cynicism or a depiction of a French stereotype that existed ready-made in the mind of Thackeray's readers, a stock literary character who is no more Thackeray than Thackeray is Jeames.

"Crinoline" is inconsistent with the other parodies in *Novels by Eminent Hands*, then, not only because the author "parodied" is a fictional persona but because its mode of mockery is not straightforward parody, in which the resemblances between texts are satirically proportional, but rather complex irony, in which the relations between authors, characters, and pseudonyms are refractory and evasive. As if to emphasize this difference, at the moment within "Crinoline" when Thackeray promises to give us the "Thackerayan" – the appearance of the Frenchified magazine-writer – he offers yet another parody through the uncanny author-surrogate of Jools. As James Wheatley summarizes Thackeray's technique in *Vanity Fair*, "the argument of style, the point it makes, is that there is no escape from roles. Just as there is no single language that by itself can indicate the narrator's true role, there is no role that is somehow not a role."[36] However, "Crinoline" extends the possibility that the author's desire may be to play every possible role while also disclosing his fantasy of ultimately being role-less. Trollope, as we shall see, pursues this fantasy by developing a prose style that strives after total invisibility, receding behind the objects of representation. Thackeray's strategy is different. By foregrounding the extent to which all literary language is conventional and marked, he eliminates the "self" from "self-parody."

Stylistic Multiformity in *Catherine*

Critics have long recognized the significance of *Catherine* (1840) to Thackeray's literary practice, particularly to the development of his realism. In an influential essay, Robert A. Colby argued that Thackeray's first full-length work serves as a kind of "credo" for the themes and techniques of his longer fiction. Exposing criminality in all its repellent baseness, *Catherine* attacked the tendency of Newgate novels to romanticize their subject matter; stylistically, it is a "novel-on-novels where the idiocies of popular romance are whipped like the wretched Count Galgenstein."[37] Thackeray's parodic targets resemble those in *Novels by Eminent Hands*: hyper-inflated passages of scenic description (as found in Ainsworth), intellectual pedantry and classical allusion (as in Bulwer), affected speech and the over-use of unintentionally imperfect French (as in silver-fork fiction), and the ostentatious inclusion of actual historical figures to give the work the flavor of authenticity (as in Bulwer's *Eugene Aram*).[38] In Colby's view, Thackeray uses the distortions of parody to advance his evolving conception of morally didactic realism, using literary satire to undermine "romanticism and sentimentality in any guise."[39] If readers were confused by "sudden and perverse shifts of mood and tone," or put off by "the chameleon-like narrator who is successively jester, lay prophet, chronicler, and theatre manager," this was because Thackeray had not yet learned to make "order" out of youthful "jumble," as he would in more mature works.[40]

Following Colby, style in *Catherine* has been primarily regarded as an instance of literary apprenticeship or realistic argumentation, and despite the common classification of the work as a "parody," most critics interpret it as an essay in truth. Hence Frederick Cabot identifies a tension not between style and subject but between moralism and realism: Thackeray employs parody to ensure our disgust with the fashionable presentation of vice, but his mimetic powers compel him to create in Catherine a character of such "psychological complexity"[41] that she engages the reader's interest and sympathy in spite of Thackeray's desire that we should loathe her. Thackeray himself argued that the work was a "mistake all through" because "it was not made disgusting enough,"[42] but this does not mean, as A. Savkar Altinel argues, that the work is more valuable as realistic social critique rather than as parody.[43] Even Jack P. Rawlins, who takes parody seriously as fundamental to Thackeray's *oeuvre*, regards Catherine as a failed experiment in moral realism, hinging his analysis on Thackeray's interpolation of actual journalistic prose at the novel's end – an argument worth examining in more detail precisely for the way it assumes that parody serves realism but not that realism might itself be a kind of parody.

Already highly metafictional, *Catherine* transitions into pure pastiche in its final two chapters, originally published as a single instalment in February 1840. By setting Catherine's murder of her husband entirely off-stage, Thackeray deflects attention away from the moment of action and onto the manner of telling. In the penultimate chapter, called "Chapter the Last," the single sentence that alludes to the murder – "Some scuffling and

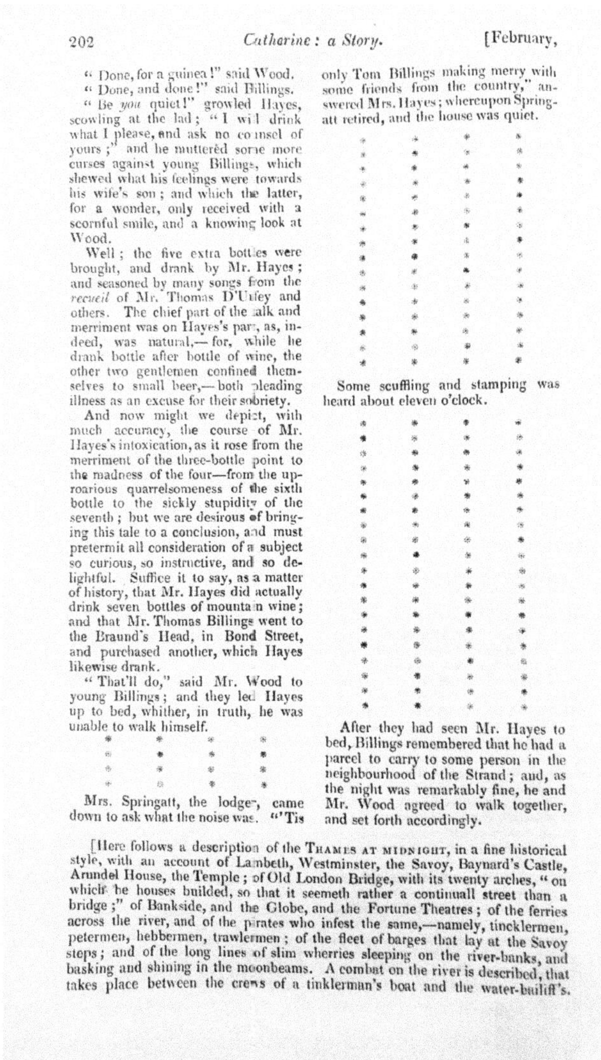

202 *Catherine: a Story.* [February,

"Done, for a guinea!" said Wood.

"Done, and done!" said Billings.

"Be *you* quiet!" growled Hayes, scowling at the lad; "I will drink what I please, and ask no counsel of yours;" and he muttered some more curses against young Billings, which shewed what his feelings were towards his wife's son; and which the latter, for a wonder, only received with a scornful smile, and a knowing look at Wood.

Well; the five extra bottles were brought, and drank by Mr. Hayes; and seasoned by many songs from the *recueil* of Mr. Thomas D'Urfey and others. The chief part of the talk and merriment was on Hayes's part, as, indeed, was natural,—for, while he drank bottle after bottle of wine, the other two gentlemen confined themselves to small beer,—both pleading illness as an excuse for their sobriety.

And now might we depict, with much accuracy, the course of Mr. Hayes's intoxication, as it rose from the merriment of the three-bottle point to the madness of the four—from the uproarious quarrelsomeness of the sixth bottle to the sickly stupidity of the seventh; but we are desirous of bringing this tale to a conclusion, and must pretermit all consideration of a subject so curious, so instructive, and so delightful. Suffice it to say, as a matter of history, that Mr. Hayes did actually drink seven bottles of mountain wine; and that Mr. Thomas Billings went to the Braund's Head, in Bond Street, and purchased another, which Hayes likewise drank.

"That'll do," said Mr. Wood to young Billings; and they led Hayes up to bed, whither, in truth, he was unable to walk himself.

* * * *
* * * *
* * * *
* * * *

Mrs. Springatt, the lodger, came down to ask what the noise was. "'Tis only Tom Billings making merry with some friends from the country," answered Mrs. Hayes; whereupon Springatt retired, and the house was quiet.

* * * *
* * * *
* * * *
* * * *
* * * *
* * * *
* * * *
* * * *
* * * *
* * * *
* * * *
* * * *
* * * *
* * * *
* * * *
* * * *

Some scuffling and stamping was heard about eleven o'clock.

* * * *
* * * *
* * * *
* * * *
* * * *
* * * *
* * * *
* * * *
* * * *
* * * *
* * * *
* * * *
* * * *
* * * *
* * * *
* * * *
* * * *
* * * *
* * * *
* * * *
* * * *

After they had seen Mr. Hayes to bed, Billings remembered that he had a parcel to carry to some person in the neighbourhood of the Strand; and, as the night was remarkably fine, he and Mr. Wood agreed to walk together, and set forth accordingly.

[Here follows a description of the THAMES AT MIDNIGHT, in a fine historical style, with an account of Lambeth, Westminster, the Savoy, Baynard's Castle, Arundel House, the Temple; of Old London Bridge, with its twenty arches, "on which the houses builded, so that it seemeth rather a continuall street than a bridge;" of Bankside, and the Globe, and the Fortune Theatres; of the ferries across the river, and of the pirates who infest the same,—namely, tincklermen, petermen, hebbermen, trawlermen; of the fleet of barges that lay at the Savoy steps; and of the long lines of slim wherries sleeping on the river-banks, and basking and shining in the moonbeams. A combat on the river is described, that takes place between the crews of a tinklerman's boat and the water-bailiff's.

Fig. 4.2 The murder of Hayes, in *Fraser's Magazine* 21.122 (Feb. 1840), 202.

stamping was heard about eleven o'clock" – is surrounded on both sides by an extensive cluster of asterisks[44] (see fig. 4.2). Then follows not the expected *dénouement* but a digression in square brackets in which the narrator, posing as a journal editor, provides a condensed account of "fine writing" that appears extraneous to the central story: "Here follows a description of the Thames at Midnight, in a fine historical style; with an account of Lambeth, Westminster, the Savoy, Baynard's Castle, Arundel House, the Temple" (120). The narrator continues this diversion, transforming the novel's climactic moment into an attack on historical gimmickry: "A combat on the river is described," followed by yet "another episode" in which "two masked ladies quarrel at the door of a tavern overlooking the Thames" (121). These ladies "turn out to be Stella and Vanessa," who, having "followed Swift thither," find him "in the act of reading *Gulliver's Travels* to Gay, Arbuthnot, Bolingbroke, and Pope" (121). This putative last chapter, in which fashionable writing substitutes for the grisly murder, is followed by "Another Last Chapter," which promises closure by proceeding with the expected *dénouement*. Having murdered her husband, Catherine seeks a reunion with the Count, but the narrative is exaggeratedly sentimental, characterized by the stock elements of melodrama. There are climactic revelations ("Max," she said, "*I am free*!"), emotional repetitions ("No, no, not dead"), dramatic exclamations ("but, oh Heaven! I deserved this ... It is too much – too much, oh Heaven!"), and visually striking, if comically implausible, tableaux ("And the wretched woman fell back almost fainting"). The scene ends with the apparition of Hayes's head ("and on the summit, strangely distinct, and smiling ghastly, was a livid human head") and the Count's subsequent committal to an antiquated mental asylum where he moans and howls under chain and lash (121–24).

In Rawlins's view, Thackeray's use of parody in *Catherine* highlights how artificial or excessively "literary" discourses provide an unreliable guide to moral truth. He argues that Thackeray's decision to include, after the fine writing and melodramatic set piece, a factual account of Catherine's murder, trial, and execution – based on the ordinary of Newgate's account, which Thackeray condenses and summarizes, intermixed with direct quotations from the *Daily Journal* of 1726 – constitutes a deliberate critique of the preceding parodies. "After hundreds of pages of stifling tedium," Rawlins explains, "Thackeray offers us two 'artful' perspectives on the deed of murder, and then faces us with the truth of the murder in its naked newspaper form, with no 'art,' in the sense of cunning distortion."[45] However, Rawlins does not believe that this generic contrast is successful. *Catherine* is a "failure ... to write precisely the literal truth of life" because Thackeray's "views on style are based on a realistic aesthetic that is simply untenable – that there is an 'honest' style, a style without style, where words stand for things and things are demonstrably real."[46]

Rawlins needles Thackeray for holding fast to the possibility of a "styleless style,"[47] but his argument misreads Thackeray's parodic technique within the novel, assuming, like Colby, that because the work is early it must be imperfectly conceived. This error may be conditioned in part by *Catherine*'s textual history. The final two chapters, as they appeared in *Fraser's*, are rarely reprinted unexpurgated. In the 1869 edition of Thackeray's works, issued by Smith, Elder and Company six years after the author's death, and then reproduced in the 1911 centenary edition, both the ordinary's summary and the newspaper description, along with some surrounding material, were excised with the following explanation:

> The description of the murder and the execution of the culprits, which here follows in the original, was taken from the newspapers of the day. Coming from such a source they have, as may be imagined, no literary merit. The details of the crime are simply horrible, without one touch of even that sort of romance which sometimes gives a little dignity to murder. As such they precisely suited Mr. Thackeray's purpose at the time – which was to show the real manners and customs of the Sheppards and Turpins who were then the popular heroes of fiction.[48]

The note is a remarkable mélange of contradictory appeals. The editor assumes that newspaper reports have no literary merit because they lack "that sort of romance" that is in fact the object of *Catherine*'s satire. While the editor acknowledges that such unvarnished reporting "precisely suited Mr. Thackeray's purpose at the time," he does not believe, as Rawlins does, that the newspaper report offers an alternative to the hackneyed styles parodied in the penultimate chapter. Rawlins's analysis thus serves to correct this error by defending Thackeray's inclusion of the un-romantic prose on moralistic grounds, with newspaper writing representing the epitome of "honest" or "styleless" prose.

Yet Rawlins leaves out important details concerning the expurgated material that suggest that the newspaper quotation is a continuation of pastiche rather than its salutary alternative. As originally published, the inflated description of Catherine's reunion with the Count is followed immediately not by the ordinary's narrative but by metafictional commentary on the author's success in getting readers to "weep and whimper" over "a poor, illiterate country wench, who has come from cutting her husband's throat" (124). To effect this immoral pathos, the narrator facetiously argues, is "the proper end of fiction, and one of the greatest triumphs a novelist can achieve" (124). But *Catherine*'s stylistic commentary is not confined to one genre. If the novel is the best vehicle for treating character and sympathy, the theater is a better fit for the Gothic visual effects suggested by the apparition of Hayes's head. In majuscule typeset that resembles program notes or a script, Thackeray offers "the following scene ... as affording a pretty thrill of horror" (124): "WESTMINSTER AT MIDNIGHT. (*Organs heard in Westminster Abbey.*) THE MEETING AMONG THE TOMBS. THE RISING OF THE STORM! THE SETTING OF DITTO!! THE RISING OF THE MOON!!! **The Head! The Head!**" (125). Thackeray then quotes from the *Daily Post* of March 3, 1726 to prove, ironically, that such a spectacle "is strictly historical," and finally introduces the ordinary's report by explaining that it adds even more incidents "which will make the fortune of any theatrical piece, especially if set off with a little broad comedy, and some good songs and jokes" (125). The ordinary's report does not, therefore, offer an alternative to literary artificiality or a corrective to Thackeray's pastiche. Instead, it supplies the raw materials for its most elaborately theatrical continuation.[49]

After Thackeray signals the end of the ordinary's report with a series of asterisks, he provides yet another theatrical frame by presenting "a series of delightful subjects for the artist and the theatre" in the form of scenic descriptions (some "might go nicely into one plate"), including Hayes dancing (with a comic song), Hayes in Bed, and a drinking chorus; a "grand tableau" with Mrs. Catherine cutting off her husband's head; different scenes involving the murder and its aftermath, with gratuitously gothic details (e.g. "Catherine kissing her Husband's Head!"), followed by her burning at the stake (130; see fig. 4.3). As in *Vanity Fair*, the curtain then falls, disposing of the "dramatis personae" (131) like so many puppets. As the putative editor's comments make clear, the ordinary's narrative is fully integrated into the narrator's theatrical conception: for those who wonder why Solomons expatiates on the early part of Catherine's story but not the climax and catastrophe, the "'ordinary' narrative as above condensed by him, is far more emphatic than any composition of his own could be" (131). In other words, each literary form that Solomons employs – from the historical style, to fine writing, to gothic melodrama, to newspaper reporting, to engraved scene – coalesces to produce the same pseudoclassical objective, namely the "*Catherine* cathartic" which induces a "wholesome nausea" at the glorification of vice (132). The scare quotes around "ordinary" indicate the editor's insight into Solomons's technique: the ordinary's narrative is only superficially "ordinary," for its contents are just as spectacular and grotesque (actually more so) than any other genre he could have turned to the same rhetorical purpose. The conclusion of

1840.] *Catherine: a Story.* 209

[All this presents a series of delightful subjects for the artist and the theatre:—

These four might go nicely into one plate.
1. Hayes dancing.
(*Comic Song. Wood, Billings, and Mrs. Cat, in chorus.*
2. Hayes in Bed. "Now's the Time!"
3. The first Stroke with the Axe!!
4. The Finisher. (*Drinking Chorus*).

A Grand Tableau.

MRS. CATHERINE CUTTING OFF HER HUSBAND'S HEAD.

---

1. The Carrying of the Pail.
2. The Thames at Midnight. The Emptying of the Pail.
3. The Thames at Low-water. Discovery of the Head.
4. St. Margaret's by Moonlight. The Head on the Pole!

Grand Tableau.

THE MANIAC AMBASSADOR.

---

1. Old Marybone Fields—evening.
2. The Carrying of the Legs!
3. The Bearers of the Trunk!
4. The Discovery at the Pond!

Grand Tableau.

THE SEIZURE, AND THE APPEARANCE BEFORE THE MAGISTRATES.

---

1. The Death of Wood in Prison.
2. Catherine kissing her Husband's Head!
3. The Way to the Scaffold!
4. The Gallows and the Stake!

Grand Tableau. Finale. Blue Lights. Green Lights. The whole strength of the Band.

CATHERINE BURNING AT THE STAKE! BILLINGS HANGED IN THE BACKGROUND!! THE THREE SCREAMS OF THE VICTIM!!!

The Executioner dashes her brains out with a billet.

The Curtain falls to slow Music.

God save the Queen! No money returned.

Children in arms encouraged, rather than otherwise.]

Fig. 4.3 Plans for a theatrical representation of the story's climax and conclusion, in *Fraser's Magazine* 22.122 (Feb. 1840), 209.

Catherine is thus not an appeal to realism but an acknowledgement of realism's ultimate conventionality. Sandwiched between melodramatic program notes and Hogarthian stage directions, the "realistic" quotation draws attention to the way in which all representations are intrinsically stylized.

Critics are no doubt right to notice some divisions between Thackeray's aims and accomplishments in *Catherine*. The author correctly observed that he failed to make his protagonist adequately repulsive, not only because he entertained a "sneaking kindness" for her that elicits the reader's sympathy but also because stylistic self-consciousness does not always produce the proper effect. Instead of being disgusted by the narrative's conclusion, the reader is likely to be impressed by the concatenation of stylistic discourses, each offering its own account of the same grisly act. The result is to be distanced from the acts themselves, which appear intensely artificial at both the melodramatic and factual extremes. But knowledge of the impossibility of a neutral or honest style is not simply incidental to *Catherine*'s satire; it is an integral part of its narrative texture, with metafictional moments literally bracketing the text. In the first chapter, Solomons apologizes to the reader for "introducing them to characters that are so utterly worthless . . . In this we have consulted nature and history, rather than the prevailing taste and the general manner of authors" (19). At the end of the last chapter, the putative editor assures the reader that Solomons feels "the greatest disgust for the characters he describes" and hopes "to cause the public also to hate them" (133). While these moments appeal to documentary-style realism, they also foreground it as a literary construction, recalling the pivotal recognition scene between Catherine and the Count: "Now I know what I could have done," the narrator speculates, "I can turn out a quotation from Sophocles (by looking to the index) as well as another: I can throw off a bit of fine writing too" (96). After experimenting with several styles, he concludes: "instead, however, of all this rant and nonsense, how much finer is the speech that the Count really did make? 'It is a very fine evening, – egad it is!' The 'egad' did the whole business" (97).

The "egad" does the business not just for Thackeray but for those of his critics who treat this passage as indicative of his moral and aesthetic purpose, that ordinary and colloquial speech is both more accurate and more appropriate for the realistic representation of life. But the narrative concentration on "egad" is ironic given that, as a hackneyed deformation of the sixteenth-century expression "A God!", the word is as arbitrarily conventional of the "ordinary" as a correspondingly "fine" expression is of the sublime. The quotation marks that defamiliarize "egad" as an index of the quotidian could surround virtually any phrase in Thackeray's text, some elevated, some bathetic, none stylistically neutral or naturally dominant. The real irony of *Catherine* is thus not its failure to accomplish its moral objective but the amoral outcome of its stylistic pastiche: by drawing attention away from the message and onto the medium itself, the novel makes style in all its powerful conventionality, rather than vice in its repellent ugliness or character in its meretricious attractions, its central theme.

Style and Irony in *Barry Lyndon* and *Jonathan Wild*

It has long been asserted that Thackeray's role model was Henry Fielding, and no text has been perceived as more exemplary of his discipleship than *The Luck of Barry Lyndon* (1844). In his biography, Ray writes that in his conception of *Barry Lyndon* Thackeray "found the example of *Jonathan Wild* invaluable,"[50] and Loofbourow goes so far as to call Thackeray's novel a direct "imitation"[51] of Fielding's satirical portrait. But Thackeray's debt to Fielding is also interpreted as deficient. In the same way that critics condemn *Catherine*'s stylistic pastiche as a digression from the author's apparent attachment to moral realism, they have also criticized *Barry Lyndon* for failing to live up to the ethico-aesthetic ideal supposedly provided by Fielding.

The origin of this invidious comparison may be traced to George Saintsbury's 1908 introduction to *Barry Lyndon*. Saintsbury openly declared that he liked *Barry Lyndon* least of Thackeray's works,[52] in part because of the way it deviated from Fielding's model. What Saintsbury admires in *Jonathan Wild* (1743) is the consistent clarity with which the narrator maintains an ironic distance from his characters: "He never confuses himself with them: and you never confuse them with him."[53] Thackeray's error was in allowing Barry to tell his story in the first person, obscuring the author's "attitude toward the story": "Thackeray's sermons never bore me when they are his, or Mr. Pendennis's, or those of anybody *congruous*. But that Barry should preach me I own surprises me."[54] Saintsbury thus identifies a contrast between the obvious gap between author and narrator in *Jonathan Wild* with the moral ambiguities that characterize Thackeray's relationship to his protagonist. In Fielding, there is never any doubt that the epithet "great" as applied to the hero means anything other than "villainous" in the reader's parlance, but Barry's sympathetic views about pacifism or honesty chime less easily with his otherwise criminal character.

It is surprising that Saintsbury paid so much attention to affinities between *Barry Lyndon* and *Jonathan Wild* when there is no direct evidence of their connection. Of course, Thackeray greatly admired Fielding and admitted, in retrospect, that he had unconsciously taken him as a general model.[55] Both authors began their careers as parodists and both novels have been understood as rogue narratives or burlesques of criminal biographies. But until the *Lectures on the English Humorists*, in 1851, there are only two notable references to *Jonathan Wild* in Thackeray's letters or works: an article in the *Westminster Review* in 1839, in which he admires Fielding's "great comic epic" for providing "a more curious picture of the manners of those times than any recognized history of them";[56] and in the conclusion to *Catherine*, where he writes approvingly that "in the dreadful satire of *Jonathan Wild*, no reader is so dull as to make the mistake of admiring, and can overlook the grand and hearty contempt of the author for the character he has described" (133). Saintsbury's views have influenced many of *Lyndon*'s twentieth-century critics on the strength of the latter assertion, though there are dangers when theories from one text are applied to another.

In an influential article, Eva Beach Touster argues that among Thackeray's works *Barry Lyndon* was most indebted to Fielding's example, to wit: *Lyndon* is an effort "to correct the faults of *Catherine* and to write a novel which would satirize simultaneously the rogue in all his rascality and the popular criminal biography which presented the rogue in altogether too attractive colors ... as Fielding had done in *Jonathan Wild*."[57] Like Saintsbury, Touster regards the work as a failure because Thackeray's "Victorian sensibilities"[58] compelled him to make Barry excessively sympathetic, such that "irony disappears altogether and is replaced by almost sentimental restraint."[59] In a similar argument, David Parker writes that "Barry is not allowed uninterruptedly to function as a vehicle for satire"[60] and hence "readers are not constantly astonished and delighted by the effortless grace with which ironies are brought forth, as we are when we read its prototype, *Jonathan Wild the Great*."[61] When Lyndon expresses sentiments that feel more uprightly Victorian than scurrilously eighteenth-century, "the artifice of rogue literature is broken" and "Thackeray the moralist stands openly before us."[62] Lidmila Pantůčková agrees that Thackeray attempted but failed to "do the same thing as Fielding had done in his *Jonathan Wild*" by satirizing rogues and rogue literature in *Barry Lyndon*, but attributes Thackeray's failure of nerve to the author's gradual rejection of Fielding's satirical lash for the more genial conception of kind and loving "humor" as elaborated in the *Lectures on English Humorists*.[63] *Barry Lyndon* is thus an early symptom of "just how far his identification with the hypocritical Victorian bourgeois society"[64] would go.

The assumption that Fielding was Thackeray's model has not worked to Thackeray's advantage. In each case, critics attribute stylistic differences between *Lyndon* and *Wild* to Thackeray's Victorian "betrayal" of eighteenth-century values, with humor replacing satire, moralism supplanting irony, and bourgeois realism overtaking the authenticity of "coarse truth."[65] Perhaps because he was a contemporary, Trollope's view diverges diametrically from those of Thackeray's more recent critics.[66] Instead of treating *Lyndon* as a moral (and therefore aesthetic) failure, he sees it as a stylistic success in which the reader's moral sentiments are just one sort of material available for aesthetic manipulation. "In imagination, language, construction, and general literary capacity, Thackeray never did anything more remarkable than *Barry Lyndon*,"[67] Trollope claims, admiring above all Thackeray's creation of an objectively nefarious narrator for whom "it is almost impossible not to entertain something of a friendly feeling" (71). Like Blake with Milton's Satan, Trollope finds Barry so charismatic and ingratiating a *raconteur* that he rejoices in his successes and grieves with his losses even as he remains conscious that Barry is "a man possessed by all meannesses except cowardice" (71). This sympathy occurs not in spite of the first-person narration but because of it. By speaking directly to readers with a voice that is "never unnatural, astounding us rather by its naturalness" (75), Barry draws the reader into his confidence. For Trollope, to see things from Barry's point of view is to be seduced by the "frankness and energy" (71), the "gusto" and the "liveliness" (75), of his prose.

In *The Rhetoric of Fiction*, Wayne Booth claims that "some narrators, like Barry Lyndon, are placed as far 'away' from their author and reader as possible, in respect to every virtue except a kind of interesting vitality."[68] But this remark errs not only by overlooking how critics have emphasized the protagonist's discomfiting proximity to the implied author and his norms, but also, more importantly, because it neglects how such proximity derives from stylistic virtues such as "vitality" and its cognates. Consider, for example, the treatment of irony in *Jonathan Wild* as compared to *Barry Lyndon*. In Fielding's text, the narrator is so determined to ensure that his ironies remain explicit that he continually explicates his verbal strategy. In the first chapter, Fielding uses perfectly balanced parallel clauses and antitheses to establish a relationship between the good and bad qualities of mixed characters: "Since we shall often find such a Mixture of Good and Evil in the same Character, that it may require a very accurate Judgment and elaborate Inquiry to determine which Side the Ballance turns . . . yet far the greater Number are of the mixt Kind; neither totally good nor bad; their greatest Virtues being obscured and allayed by their Vices, and those again softened and coloured over by their Virtues."[69] The quality of the prose – at once analytic and aphoristic – sets the pattern for every subsequent appraisal of Wild's "virtue," which is defined by the semantic inversion of good for bad: Fireblood is known "to be an accomplished Rascal, as the Vulgar term it, a complete Great Man in our language" (119); or "The Justice having thus luckily and timely discovered this Scene of Villany, *alias* Greatness, lost not a Moment" (141); or "while a great Man and a Great Rogue are synonymous Terms, so long shall *Wild* stand unrivalled on the Pinnacle of Greatness" (180). An explanatory impulse governs the rhetoric of these examples, in which the reader is not left to infer the meaning of "greatness" on the basis of Wild's conduct or the author's tone but stands directly informed of the precise ways in which the narrator's perverse ideal deforms the reader's common-sense understandings.

Barry Lyndon adopts the opposite strategy, neither offering an explanatory gloss on the narrator's use of language nor preventing Barry from articulating thoughts that the reader might share in varying degrees.[70] In some cases, the ironic gap between the norms of narrator and reader is obvious, as when Barry speaks admiringly of his son's tantrums, cursing, and "precocious" drinking of champagne.[71] In other cases, the gap hardly exists at all, as when Barry eschews the "passionate style" of writing in favor of artless honesty to describe Lady Lyndon's charms ("truth compels me to say, that there was nothing divine about her at all. She was very well, but no more," 188). The majority of cases, however, involve an odd combination of moral and aesthetic ambiguity, in which the reader may be repelled by the content but attracted by the form. Consider, for example, Barry's reflections on his management of his wife's estate:

> Her death would have been no comfort to me, as I leave any person of common prudence to imagine; for that scoundrel of a young Bullingdon . . . would have inherited every penny of the property, and I should have been left considerably poorer even than when I married the widow; for I spent my personal fortune as well as the lady's income in the keeping up of our rank, and was always too much a man of honour and spirit to save a penny of Lady Lyndon's income. Let this be flung in the teeth of my detractors, who say I never could have so injured the Lyndon property had I not been making a private purse for myself. (256)

The ironies that recall *Jonathan Wild* come from the passage's numerous perverse surprises: the death of Barry's wife would be no "comfort" because it would deprive him of income; Barry congratulates himself on squandering her fortune; Barry thinks his degrading treatment of her constitutes a defense in the face of "detractors." But however much the reader may stand in moral condemnation, there is a bizarre consistency to Barry's prudential logic and his final conclusion is a legitimate deduction that does exonerate Barry from a crime (i.e. deserting a sinking ship) he rightly regards as vicious. In the same way, when Barry praises himself for being "always too much a man of honour and spirit to save a penny of Lady Lyndon's income," the reader understands "honour" and "spirit" to indicate self-serving vanity and feckless enthusiasm. But the words have a less impeaching connotation, too, in the sense that Barry neither presents himself in a cunning light nor strains himself to defend any aspect of his reprehensible conduct. "Few men are so honest as I am," Barry continues, "for few will own to their real motives, and I don't care a button about confessing mine" (188). Although we may abjure his motives, we recognize, and even admire, the "honesty" with which Barry fully embraces the confessional mode, replacing Fielding's carefully poised rhetoric with unabashed conversational candor.

If the main flaw in *Catherine* was Thackeray's inability to make his heroine sufficiently repulsive, then it seems unlikely that several years later he would seek to "correct" this error by giving readers unmediated access to his next protagonist's inner thoughts and reflections. The shift from the third to the first person (despite numerous similarities in setting and subject) indicates that *Lyndon* is a different sort of book from *Catherine* and different, too, in the nature of its ironies. As Trollope suggested, it is directly the result of Barry's lack of self-conscious moral awareness – his insensibility to his own venality and vice – that the reader comes to enjoy his unabashed brazenness, unconstrained by the dour effects of self-laceration or doubt. "Irony" arises not from the clash between the reader's moral sensibility and the narrator's, but from the thoroughness with which the narrator wins the reader's sympathy in spite of this clash, as well as from the narrator's ostensible naïveté with respect to both. Barry is, in his own words, "all frankness and aboveboard" (256), and his moral triumph, in this sense, is a stylistic one.

Unlike *Jonathan Wild*, then, *Barry Lyndon* captures the reader's interest by its speaking voice – a voice as "distinctive" as the one that David Kurnick observes throughout Thackeray's narratives but possessing little of its "melancholy" or "disenchantment."[72] In this first-person narration, frankness of tone, transparency of reasoning, a distinctive personality, and characteristic modes of thought and expression matter more than plot, symbolic action, or satiric structure. Not Fielding but Defoe – an author who, as Wayne Booth observes, excels in "dramatic, realistic impersonation,"[73] and who, like Thackeray, created multiple personae under a variety of pseudonyms – presides over *Barry Lyndon.* In his combination of reckless logorrhea and carefully constructed confession, egoistic self-congratulation and earnest self-castigation, Lyndon bears a far greater resemblance to Moll Flanders and Roxana than to the un-self-conscious and essentially voiceless protagonist of Fielding's text. Thackeray's sentence structure also resembles Defoe's, with its accumulation of explanatory, often self-exculpating clauses, intermingled with third-person imperatives, and strung together with commas and semi-colons, as may be observed in Roxana's description of her behavior toward the Quaker woman:

> Let no reader wonder at my extraordinary concern for this poor woman, or at my giving my bounty to her a place in this account. It is not, I assure you to make a pageantry of my charity, or to value myself upon the greatness of my soul, that should give in so profuse a manner as this, which was above my figure, if my wealth had been twice as much as it was; but there was another spring from whence all flowed, and 'tis on that account I speak of it.[74]

To appreciate the difference between Defoe and Fielding is thus to become sensitive to the difference between stylistic and non-stylistic ethos as governing principles of Thackeray's work. The razor-sharp ironies of *Jonathan Wild* exist because they enact the work's satiric intent, while the moral ambiguities of a work like *Roxana* result from an author's fundamental interest in unmediated character-based ventriloquism.

Defoe wrote in an environment when people were more susceptible to representational *trompe l'oeil.* For Thackeray's readers, the obverse of *Barry Lyndon*'s verisimilitude was an enhanced awareness of the literary construction of fictiveness and a desire to clarify the relationship between the represented world and the author's intention. Concerned that *Lyndon*'s earliest audience would struggle to stabilize his shifting ironies, Thackeray felt compelled to add the explanatory footnotes that, in Fielding's jocular manner, clarify the gap between Barry's values and those of the "editor," G.S. Fitz-Boodle, reducing the "moral of the story" (278) to a series of ironic adages (e.g. "honesty is *not* the best policy," 310).[75] Yet, when the novel was published in a single volume in 1856, Thackeray eliminated the footnotes, suggesting that he wished to renew the interpretive ambiguities associated with the work. Distancing himself from the "moralizing" passages within the novel that have so confounded critics, Thackeray ultimately refused to moralize on his own thematic purpose. In this way he taught readers to appreciate the stylistic virtues of Barry's prose – its vitality, frankness, energy, and spirit – whether they deemed him a lovable rogue or a hateful knave.

Conclusion: Grace and the Beauty of Cliché

In 1929, Virginia Woolf confessed her puzzlement at the high value that many nineteenth-century critics attributed to Thackeray's third major novel, *The History of Henry Esmond* (1852): "The critics often say that *Esmond* is Thackeray's most perfect novel. But the affectation of the style, with its imitation of the eighteenth century, hampers one, so far as I can remember; unless indeed the eighteenth-century style was natural to Thackeray."[76] Woolf had hoped that an inspection of the novel's manuscript would decide this question[77] – incidentally, her being prevented from doing so provides the origin story for *A Room of One's Own* – but the contrast between stylistic naturalness and affectation is for Thackeray a false dichotomy. Written entirely as a pastiche of eighteenth-century prose models, *Esmond* impressed critics as a technical accomplishment because they had become increasingly capable of appreciating stylistic virtues as an autonomous literary merit.[78] As Theodore Martin put it, "in point of style, [*Esmond*] is equal to anything in English literature; and it will be read for this quality when the interest of its story is disregarded."[79]

We have already seen how Thackeray uses parody in *Novels by Eminent Hands* to treat all styles as impersonal constructions; how he uses pastiche in *Catherine* to expose "realism" as just one sort of literary convention; and how he replaces didactic satire with the exuberance of naïve ventriloquism in *The Luck of Barry Lyndon*. Not ironically, the features that render *Esmond*'s pastiche style so "characteristic" of Thackeray – authorial personae (*Esmond* is a memoir edited by a fictional character), linguistic parody, burlesque, stylization, and double-voicing – are precisely those that account for the diversity of the early work.[80] These analyses confirm a point made long ago by John Loofbourow, that the "most important source of narrative content in Thackeray's prose is the satirical allusion to typical literary conventions," such that "very often, style is the story."[81] However, *pace* Loofbourow, who argues that Thackeray is the first Victorian to unify content and form in a way that anticipates the Modernist novel,[82] Thackeray held a more binary, eighteenth-century view: style for Thackeray, like clothes to the man, was something that could be actively deployed for different purposes and different pleasures, and though individuals vary in what lengths they can pull off one fashion or another, their garments are always, from some point of view, in quotation marks.

Thackeray makes this point most forcibly in an 1841 essay called "Men and Coats," in which he reverses the expected causal relationship between internal character and outward expression. Arguing that an author's style may be influenced by sartorial choices, Thackeray purports to write different parts of the essay while wearing different suits of clothes. "Now," he asks, "will the reader be able to perceive any difference in the style of writing of each chapter?"[83] An affirmative answer is only half-facetious, for Thackeray's approach to style shares more in common with the dualistic framework implied by Samuel Johnson's dictum that "language is the dress of thought"[84] than with the mystical monism asserted by Carlyle's revision, "Language is called the garment of thought: however, it should rather be, language is the flesh-garment, the body, of thought" (57).[85] According to Thackeray, a man no doubt enjoys a feeling of "exultation" when wearing a "new garment," but "a man does not have a new suit every day" (209): the subtle modulation of recyclable elements is just as important as the invention of original means.

Hence, we must not mistake the "high-bred ease" of Thackeray's style for an aristocratic sensibility that, in the view of George Saintsbury, had been essential for the development of style, nor must we mistake his "continual flexibility and grace, and adaptation to the matter in hand" for a nostalgic *sprezzatura*.[86] Grace, in particular, has less to do with the formal manners of an elevated class than with a more democratic spirit of adaptive metamorphosis – an effortless mobility that finds itself comfortable in every quarter. This meaning has deep roots. For Lord Kames, grace is "undoubtedly connected with motion; for when the most graceful person is at rest, neither moving nor speaking, we lose sight of that quality as much as of colour in the dark" (363). Hence, "grace" may refer to the agility of the body in dance (which Whately calls "airs and graces," 250) or else to the fluidity of Hogarth's "waving curve";[87] it may also be psychologized, as when the American philosopher Henry Noble Day observes grace in "the mind of the speaker . . . moving freely in its conceptions and its representations."[88] In a later text, Day goes so far as to identify "grace" with the "free activity of rational being,"[89] freedom being attached to the word's theological origins in the gift of salvation from an unpredictable but purposeful god. Thackeray's grace thus implies the effortless management of constant change, a versatility that is liberally virtuosic.[90]

In the preface to *Pendennis*, Thackeray avers that a writer is to be judged "by the tenor of his general bearing and conversation . . . Is he honest? Does he tell the truth in the main? Does he seem actuated by a desire to find out and speak it? Is he a quack, who shams sentiment, or mouths for effect? Does he seek popularity by claptraps or other arts?"[91] This statement encapsulates how Thackeray's skepticism of every sort of pretension in modern life – in dress, position, speech, and indeed style – became linked to realism and satire, which operate with and against the assumption of the "sincerity" of the author's attitudes. But the gracefulness of Thackeray's style, which knows no bounds in terms of the speech-patterns it represents, suggests that absolute sincerity is itself a hypocritical ideal. Because language is a shared commodity, every usage bears the trace of prior persons, characters, and contexts; because social life is inherently intertextual, the dream of an absolutely neutral or idiosyncratic style is the ultimate vanity.

In this light, it is significant that the character often taken to be Thackeray's alter ego, Arthur Pendennis, begins his literary career by writing a novel that is itself, to borrow Loofbourow's phrase, a tissue of "allusive conventions."[92] *Walter Lorraine* is a romance in the "fashionable style," and the single excerpt included in the text is a clumsy bricolage of archaic clichés: "'False as thou art beautiful! heartless as thou art fair! mockery of Passion!' Walter cried, addressing Leonora; 'what evil spirit hath sent thee to torture me so? O Leonora'" (519). Upon hearing this passage aloud, Pen commands Warrington to cut it out, confirming the reader's negative judgment of its merit. But he quickly reconsiders, "Well! don't read it out at any rate" (519). Warrington, himself the possessor of an important secret, baits his friend for "humbug," which he associates specifically with the literary profession. "All poets are humbugs, all literary men are humbugs; directly a man begins to sell his feelings for money he's a humbug. If a poet gets a pain in his side from too good a dinner, he bellows Ai Ai louder than Prometheus" (520). Pen objects to the statement, but, as before, acts the hypocrite: he throws *Walter Lorraine* onto the fire as a worthless piece of trash, first having ensured that the flames were too weak to consume it. The back-and-forth of Pen's actions mirrors the back-and-forth nature of his connection with Blanche Armory, the thinly disguised heroine of *Walter Lorraine* and herself the author of a derivative and sentimental collection of poems, *Mes Larmes*. It also reflects his indecision with respect to the value of his own prose. *Walter Lorraine* may be trash but it remains "as good as most books of the kind" (321), just as the crocodile tears of the author of *Mes Larmes* never cease to move him.

That Thackeray selects Pen to be the "author" of *The Newcomes* shows how thoroughly and unabashedly he committed himself to the inevitability of literary humbug. An infinitely adaptable journalist and social chameleon, Pen has mastered his culture's various sociolects and can use them to build a novel. The first chapter of *The Newcomes*, for example, begins with a beast fable, transitions to Carlylean jeremiad ("There was once a time when the sun used to shine brighter than it appears to do in this latter half of the nineteenth century") and ends with Dickensian animism ("that uplifted cane of the Colonel's had somehow fallen on the back of every man in the room").[93] Realism, as practiced by Pen, assumes a distinctly polyphonic texture in which every type of action has an associated literary convention: chivalric archaisms for courtship scenes, Bulwer-esque grandiloquence for regret and reflection, Swiftian catalogue for emotionally charged scene-painting, sentimental apostrophe for moments of familial tenderness or special portentousness. That is not to say that all of Pen's styles are derivative or parodic. He shares, for example, Thackeray's technique of inventing individualized but representative characters to indicate that a scene or a person is generic: "There was a time ... when to know Thompson, who had written a magazine-article, was an honour and a privilege; and to see Brown, the author of the last romance, in the flesh, and actually walking in the Park with his umbrella and Mrs. Brown, was an event remarkable" (*Newcomes*, 7). But a thorough immersion in Pen's world sensitizes one to the significance of cliché: no word, expression, or turn of phrase feels "original" or "authentic" because they are always derived from a broader linguistic web – just as the sight of Mrs. Brown is simultaneously an "event remarkable" and utterly banal.

Tonally, Thackeray does not satirize his cliché-loving narrator but conveys an admiration for the ease with which he masters different idioms and registers, not in order to "make them new" but to weave them into a socially determined tapestry whose pleasures are thoroughly stereotyped. "Ah! Yes: all stories are old" (278), Pen sighs, but with affection rather than resignation or contempt. "There was not one woman there who was not the heroine of some discreditable story . . . There they were, the Fauns and Satyrs: there they were, the merry Pagans: drinking and dancing, dicing and sporting . . . As those guileless virgins of romance and ballad, who walk smiling through dark forests charming off dragons and confronting lions, the young man as yet went through the world harmless; no giant waylaid him as yet" (272–73). If Pen readily acknowledges himself as world-weary, it is because his world is full of generic events, human types, and set pieces drawn from literature and life. He admires Clive not because he is a great artist but for the ease with which he can inhabit and move among different milieux, "as much at home in a fine drawing-room as in a public-house parlour," able to "talk as pleasantly to the polite mistress of the mansion as to the jolly landlady dispensing her drinks from the bar" (173).

In his obituary for Thackeray, Dickens admitted that he thought Thackeray "too much feigned a want of earnestness, and that he made a pretence of undervaluing his art, which was not good for the art that he held in trust."[94] But I believe this confuses Thackeray's attitudes toward the social significance of artists and art, which were thoroughly anti-romantic, with the aesthetic effects of his stylistic practice.[95] A preoccupation with Thackeray's moral views has eclipsed the way in which his use of style both enacts and undermines what in other lights might appear to be a relatively simplistic hostility to humbug in any form, calling to mind a literary comparison that is not often made. Like Flaubert, Thackeray was obsessed with style but refused to succumb to its romantic charms. Like Flaubert, he was capable of impersonating an enormous range of literary discourses in an effort to write authentically ordinary prose. And like Flaubert, his lasting achievement is not to denigrate style, nor to lament the necessity of cliché, but to instill in readers a heightened appreciation for the expressive potential of style *qua* style even in its susceptibility to corruption. In his book on Thackeray, Trollope describes how "as one reads, one sometimes is struck by a conviction that this or the other writer has thoroughly liked the work on which he is engaged" (75). The virtues of Thackeray's style – its ease, dexterity, versatility, and grace – communicate that kind of pleasure with, as Thackeray says of *Pendennis*, "a little more frankness than is customary" (lvii).

CHAPTER 5

Trollope's Ease and Lucidity

The virtue of transparency stands at the center of an evaluative controversy with respect to nineteenth-century realism. Transparency is both the primary condition of effective verisimilitude, something required if we are to be convinced that the created world of a text is natural and believable, but also the illusion through which the text naturalizes and makes believable facts and values that are not necessarily meritorious, obvious, or true. In *Critical Practice*, Catherine Belsey dismantles the myth of transparency that bedevils what she calls the "commonsense criticism" of classic realism. This practice of reading, she argues, assumes that literary texts "tell truths – about the period which produced them, about the world in general or about human nature – and that in doing so they express the particular perceptions, the individual insights, of their authors."[1] For Belsey, transparency is the fiction at the heart of fiction, an apparent clarity that pulls the wool over our eyes. The effect of transparency is to create the impression that we have unmediated access to an author's particular perception of total reality, manipulating us into taking for granted that which we have been arbitrarily given at either end.

If, in the twentieth century, transparency has been exposed as an art of deception, in the nineteenth century it was taken as a sign of an author's commitment to impartiality or objectivity in mimesis. In his critical writings, Trollope clearly subscribes to the latter view, quoting Nathaniel Hawthorne approvingly for having summarized the intended effect of his work. "Have you ever read the novels of Anthony Trollope?" Hawthorne asks.[2] They are "just as real as if some giant had hewn a great lump out of the earth and put it under a glass case, with all its inhabitants going about their daily business, and not suspecting they were being made a show of" (144). This assessment, which Trollope praises for capturing "with wonderful accuracy the purport that I have ever had in view in my writing" (145), draws attention to two aspects of realism that for Trollope are interrelated. First, the feeling of verisimilitude, or truth-to-life, depends upon the depiction of the ordinary activities of regular people; the subject matter is transparent in the sense that anyone can recognize and understand what the author represents. At the same time, realism requires a transparent style because it ensures that the author's meaning will be easily understood, preventing language from disrupting the illusion of verisimilitude or interposing itself like a screen between the perception of the work and its comprehension. "I hold that gentleman to be the best dressed whose dress no one observes," Trollope says, and "I am not sure but that the same may be said of an author's written language" (*Thackeray*, 200). For Trollope, effective realism involves looking through a glass not darkly, but clearly, which is only possible when the literary medium itself seems to disappear behind the imaginative reality it conveys.

It may be true that Henry James, in *Partial Portraits*, derided Trollope for being so transparent as to lack a distinctive point of view. "The striking thing," James writes, "was that his robust and patient mind had no particular bias, his imagination no light of its own."[3] But even though, James argues, Trollope saw things neither pictorially or grotesquely like Dickens, nor satirically like Thackeray, nor philosophically like Eliot, he adds in a backhanded way that there is something remarkably "*honnête*" – decent, decorous, and also honest – in the very banality of Trollope's style. "He thinks, he feels, he judges like a man, talking plainly and frankly about many things, and by no means destitute of a certain saving grace of coarseness" (528). In general, Trollope's twentieth-century critics have followed James in praising the author for his truth-telling plainness, with prose so carefully unpretentious that it "disappears" behind the world it represents. In *The Moral Trollope*, Ruth apRoberts celebrates Trollope because he "makes us forget the words while we apprehend effortlessly the most tenuous delicacies of nuance in psychology or social situations";[4] James Kincaid exalts the "plain, nondescript style" for "creating the illusion of a direct participation with reality";[5] and Walter Kendrick admires Trollope's style for "forcing writing to efface itself between the equal realities of the reader's real and the writer's represented world."[6] Kendrick goes on to argue that Trollope regards the novel as a rhetorical rather than a representational kind of art, even if he dedicates all his rhetoric to persuading the reader that the novel is representational rather than rhetorical. But the very plainness of the style serves as a kind of warning that "anyone who regards writing as more than an invisible vehicle will fail in the art of the realistic novel," making Trollope more "honest" about the norms of realism than his "artful or artificial" peers.[7]

The critical attachment to Trollope's "disappearing" style was justified insofar as Trollope was himself inclined to moralize transparency by associating it with representational honesty. In *An Autobiography*, he criticizes many of his contemporaries for impregnating their writing with the "flavour" of "mannerism" (259), arguing that the unmarked or nondescript style is truest to life because it least betrays the author's shaping presence. The books of Disraeli, for example, "smell of hair oil" (259) rather than reality, whereas a less mannered style offers positive proof that an author is committed to the impartial depiction of the outside world rather than the projection of his personality upon it. Even conceding that an author's conception of reality must, by necessity, emerge from his particular imaginative furniture, Trollope still insists that the transparent style is most likely to convey that content completely and accurately.[8] Echoing the basic tenets of neoclassical rhetoric, he explains that the language of fiction "should be so pellucid that the meaning should be rendered without an effort to the reader; – and not only some proportion of meaning, but the very sense, no more and no less, which the writer has intended to put into his words" (*Autobiography*, 234–35). However, in recent years critics have retreated from the post-Jamesian conception of Trollope as technically naïve in order to illustrate how his mastery of stylistic transparency produces sophisticated, often contradictory, effects. For example, Jonathan Farina (building upon seminal work by Hugh Sykes Davies) shows how Trollope's deployment of seemingly ordinary words and phrases (such as "but") animates an ethos of tactfulness undergirded by epistemological skepticism,[9] while Daniel Wright examines Trollope's use of tautology in order to demonstrate how this seeming "apotheosis of lucidity" contains the seeds of its own "critique."[10] Still, these and other examples of a formalist turn in Trollope studies continue to emphasize a mutually reinforcing relationship between the author's moral and stylistic virtues.[11]

In this chapter, I launch an even stronger critique of the usual view that Trollope's style offers, as he wished, an "honest" representation of authorial thought content, with the illusion of transparency serving the goals of traditional verisimilitude. Instead, I suggest that Trollope's struggle to achieve stylistic transparency depended upon his careful orchestration of two stylistic virtues, ease and lucidity, whose particular characters can be examined quite apart from the rubric of realism. By analyzing examples of these virtues in *Can You Forgive Her?*, an exemplary work from the middle of his career,[12] I show how Trollope's attempts to balance ease and lucidity in prose mark his style in predictable, often exaggeratedly mannered ways, calling into question the very possibility of the honesty and transparency with which he is so often associated, and helping to dismantle the myth of transparency that continues to shape criticism of his style. In the second half of the chapter, I parallel Anna Kornbluh's recent effort "to think realism aslant of reference"[13] and suggest that Trollope's interest in the ancient rhetorical virtues of harmony and rhythm further shapes his prose according to non-mimetic values. Because Trollope's style is often assumed to be nondescript, and because both he and his critics regard stylistic neutrality as integral to realist conventions, he offers an especially revealing case for the excavation of autonomous stylistic character – a character that Trollope, as a realist and a moralist, does his best to diminish and dismiss.

It Isn't Easy Being Easy

"I hate books I can't understand," says Bell Dale in *The Small House at Allington*, "I like a book to be clear as running water, so that the whole meaning may be seen at once."[14] Positive assessments of Trollope's perceived honesty often depend upon similar appeals to the author's stylistic clarity, which, by avoiding the rhetorical polarities of grandiloquence or burlesque, implies unmediated plainness and objectivity. Referring to the praise offered by Hawthorne, Trollope explains why the clarity of the glass case provides an apt metaphor for his transparency of manner and motive:

> I have always desired to "hew out some lump of the earth," so that my readers might recognize human beings like to themselves, and not feel themselves to be carried away among gods or demons. If I could do this, then I thought I might succeed in impregnating the mind of the novel-reader with a feeling that honesty is the best policy; that truth prevails while falsehood fails; that a girl will be loved as she is pure, and sweet, and unselfish; that a man will be honoured as he is true, and honest, and brave of heart. (*Autobiography*, 145)

Trollope here equates the accurate reproduction of nature with moral righteousness and personal virtue, suggesting that "honesty is the best policy" not only for readers and characters but also for the writers who teach and depict them.

Throughout his nonfiction, Trollope associates sincerity with accuracy and accuracy with realism, which ought to run a recognizable "middle course" between the depths of the ludicrous and the heights of the sublime (*Thackeray*, 187). Yet despite his emphasis on observation, memory, and the inculcation of "true honour, true love, true worship, and true humanity"

(*Autobiography*, 218), Trollope remains acutely aware that the success of realism depends upon complex acts of stylistic deception.[15] "Realism in style has not all the ease which seems to belong to it," he writes in *Thackeray*, shifting from a vocabulary of reproductive transparency to one of illusion and dissemblance. "In very truth the realistic must not be true, – but just so far removed from truth as to suit the erroneous idea of truth which the reader may be supposed to entertain" (184–85). This gap between the appearance of truth and truth itself influences not only the objects of novelistic presentation (such as story and character) but also the novelist's management of language, where, for example, dialogue must "steer between absolute accuracy of language" and "the slovenly inaccuracy of ordinary talkers" if it is to produce "a sense of reality" (*Autobiography*, 240). Purporting to be a straightforward account of Trollope's writing life, *An Autobiography* says little more about the verbal sleights of hand that realism requires. But in *Thackeray*, a work of extended literary criticism, Trollope provides much greater insight into the technical challenges of achieving a realist style.[16]

For Trollope, this challenge revolves around the contradictory demands imposed by the two chief "virtues" of style, ease and lucidity, that he argues are "very different" (196).[17] The easy style is that "by which the writer has succeeded in conveying to the reader that which the reader is intended to receive with the least possible amount of trouble to him." The lucid style "conveys to the reader most accurately all that the writer wishes to convey on any subject" (196). The difference between the two styles is thus one of transparency, exactitude, and comprehensiveness: the easy style is simple and straightforward, having an appearance of unlabored naturalness, whereas the lucid style is precise and complete but potentially overwrought. To illustrate the difference, Trollope describes an author who wishes to "give an idea that a certain flavour is bitter." If he communicates without trouble that the flavor is disagreeable only, then he has been easy, but he is only lucid if he also conveys the specific concept of bitterness (196).

The complexity of realistic fiction, Trollope adds, means that "the inexperienced writer is puzzled at every turn to express himself" (196), and hence Trollope defines literary production as an agonistic struggle for mastery between the author and his recalcitrant tongue. "Who among writers has not to acknowledge that he is often unable to tell all that he has to tell? Words refuse to do it for him. He struggles and stumbles and alters and adds, but finds at last that he has gone either too far or not quite far enough" (196–97). Although in *An Autobiography* Trollope seems confident in the power of language to provide an honest transcription of reality, in *Thackeray* he expresses an underlying anxiety about its inadequacies and limits. How is an author to "tell all that he has to tell" when he must constantly struggle between the competing demands of ease and lucidity, which Trollope describes as the "necessity of choosing between two evils"?

> He must either give up the fulness of his thought, and content himself with presenting some fragment of it in that lucid arrangement of words which he affects; or he must bring out his thought with ambages; he must mass his sentences inconsequentially; he must struggle up hill almost hopelessly with his phrases, – so that at the end the reader will have to labour as he himself has laboured, or else to leave behind much of the fruit which it has been intended that he should garner. (197)

It is telling how the style of Trollope's sentence mimics both the virtues and the vices he describes. The clause preceding the semicolon is relatively short, direct, and digestible, but the "fulness" of conceptual illustration gives way to abstract entities that the reader must imagine ("some fragment," "that lucid arrangement of words"). The second part of the sentence achieves greater precision through amplification, but the anaphora, archaic diction ("ambages"), weighty adverbs ("inconsequentially," "hopelessly"), and expanding metaphors ("struggle up hill," "leave behind much of the fruit . . . that he should garner") overload the sentence, evoking a feeling of exertion and upward strain. It is difficult to say whether this sentence is easy, or lucid, or both. The easy component lacks lucidity and the lucid component lacks ease, but taken together they ably imitate the concepts they seek to express.

The subtle manipulation of style to register substance represents a possible solution to the contest between ease and lucidity that Trollope thought was central to realistic writing, and that, once recognized, can be widely observed throughout his work. Published in 1864 at the height of his literary fame – and serving as a bridge between the Barchester and the Palliser series – *Can You Forgive Her?*, by its very title and subject matter (jilting), seems to foreground matters of morality and reference at the expense of surface or style:

> Whether or no, she, whom you are to forgive, if you can, did or did not belong to the Upper Ten Thousand of this our English world, I am not prepared to say with any strength of affirmation. By blood she was connected with big people, – distantly connected with some very big people indeed, people who belonged to the Upper Ten Hundred if there be any such division; but of these very big relations she had known and seen little, and they had cared as little for her.[18]

At first glance, this sentence seems to lack the ease that Trollope requires. The inverted opening has the effect of delaying the introduction of the main subject ("I"), creating an odd sensation of suspense for an opening salvo; the narrator's evasive rhetoric ("I am not prepared to say") fails to stabilize the series of brief, staccato units, with their back-and-forth motion ("whether or no," "to forgive, if you can," "did or did not"). The expectation that we forgive Alice is strangely qualified by the possibility that we might not be able to do so, and the longest portion of the second sentence exhaustively serves to define what we are told least relates to her. However, a second reading of the sentence conveys an opposite impression. The binary formulations in the sentence's first part evoke the novel's central topic – vacillation – while the narrator's lack of information foregrounds the problem of epistemological uncertainty (a point reinforced by the subjunctive and conjectural "if you can"). The abundance of adversatives and hesitations serves to confirm the notion that Trollope's is a "tactful" style – inquisitive, skeptical, and considerate – but the second sentence serves a comedic purpose in addition to its informational and ethical ones. In each successive clause, modifiers increase the distance between Alice and her relatives, creating a comical incongruity between the bigness of their size and the littleness of her association with them: "she was *connected* with *big* people, – distantly *connected* with some very *big people* indeed . . . but of these *very big* relations she had known and seen *little*, and they had cared as *little* for her" (my emphasis). The repeated words string the loosely connected units together, creating a crescendo that is undermined by the bathos of the final parallelism.

Trollope's predilection, particularly in his earlier novels, for mock-heroic style further justifies the apparent lack of ease. The hypotactic inversion of the opening evokes grandeur, ironically applied to the Upper Ten Thousand; naturally enough, then, as we turn from Alice's "very big relations" to her parochial and country-dwelling grandfather, Trollope shifts to a less artificial style that relies on coordination rather than subordination, replacing the jerky rhythms of the novel's first sentence with a propulsive forward movement that communicates, through the placement of accents on negatives and nasals ("never . . . no . . . any"), the obstinate and ornery character of her relative: "Her grandfather, Squire Vavasor of Vavasor Hall, in Westmoreland, was a country gentleman, possessing some thousand a year at the outside, and he therefore never came up to London, and had no ambition to have himself numbered as any one in any exclusive set" (39). Furthermore, the direct nature of the description of the Squire – "a hot-headed, ignorant, honest old gentleman" (39) – starkly contrasts with the subsequent depiction of Alice, in which an abundance of qualifying phrases suggests a struggle for precision: "It was not that her face was old, but that there was nothing that was girlish in her manners ... Her hair was brown, but very dark ... Her eyes, too, were dark, though they were not black, and her complexion, though not quite that of a brunette, was far away from being fair" (45). The writing here replicates Alice's tendency to define things provisionally and sharpen them through contrast, helping to establish this aspect of her character in the reader's mind while simultaneously foregrounding lucidity as a topic of thematic and representational concern.

An example like this prompts us to rethink our understanding of Trollope's honesty. On the one hand, his techniques of linguistic imitation – syntactical (coordination versus subordination), aural (rising and falling rhythms, strategic accents), conceptual (qualifiers, adversatives), typographical (capitalization) – satisfy the competing demands of ease and lucidity by combining conceptual depth with surface economy. Unlike the inartistic writer, who forfeits the complexity of his idea for ease of comprehension or else becomes fulsome or laborious in struggling to express its entirety, Trollope balances the two through a concentration of rhetorical techniques that simultaneously reinforce and undermine each other, creating the felicitous illusion of "natural" writing. On the other hand, Trollope's very success in realism depends upon his concealing the tension between exactitude and complexity that strikes to the heart of his prosaic practice. The author is frank ("*honnête*") about everything except this underlying problem that his style attempts to solve, which only sustained analysis can recover. Although one might contend that Trollope's honesty does not, for the sake of efficiency, go so far as to reveal the hidden mechanics behind his illusions, that view would be difficult to defend in light of his narrators' metafictional interventions throughout the novels and the revelations of rapid and regimented writing in *An Autobiography* that so injured his authorial reputation.[19] Transparency, it appears, was the one illusion that Trollope was especially motivated to preserve.

In *Thackeray*, Trollope sets the virtues of ease and lucidity against their opposites of obscurity and bombast, creating room for tension between transparency and complex thought. But because Trollope believed that the best style draws the least attention to itself, many of his characteristics as a writer – those eccentricities he was quick to denigrate in others as "mannerism" – serve to neutralize or mask the devices (typically *schemata verborum*, or "rhetorical schemes") that militate against it. In the following sentence from *Can You Forgive Her?*, Trollope combines anaphora (i.e. the repetition of the same word at the beginning of successive clauses) with anastrophe (i.e. the inversion of the usual order of words) to build toward a contrast that defies expectation: "With women he could be happy. With women he could really associate. A woman he could really love; – but I doubt whether for all that he could treat a woman well" (189). The surprise here occurs between the positive assertions of the first three phrases and the doubtful cast of the fourth, and the effect is heightened by the shift from the inverted phrases ("with women he could") to the narrator's final judgment ("he could treat a woman"). The very presence of inversion, however, is naturalized – made invisible – through George's swaggering, speech-based idiom, such that the return to the narrator does not restore order but moves from one colloquial discourse to another, concealing the verbal trick. In a similar example, Trollope buries a subtle conceptual modification in an idiom that strikes the reader as anything but refined:

> "Aunt Greenow always seems to me to be a very good sort of woman."
> "She may be a good woman, but I must say I think she's of a bad sort." (89)

The repetition of vague words such as "good" and "sort" gives this exchange the air of spontaneous and imprecise speech, but the antithesis is sharpened by the migration of "sort" to the end of the second sentence: its displacement allows the speaker to concede to Aunt Greenow some basic element of goodness, but not the kind that is the subject of their exchange.

These examples highlight how Trollope uses parallelism and antithesis in order to secure prosaic ease in ways that deter the reader from noticing their means of production, thereby creating the illusion of stylistic invisibility. But Trollope's extensive use of repetition in other contexts has not escaped attention. Critics have called Trollope's repetitive devices monotonous and superficial, attributing them to the slovenliness induced by rapid writing, and there may be some truth to these assertions.[20] But viewed within the context of the contest between ease and lucidity, Trollope's reliance on repetition becomes critically explicable.

Consider one instance where Trollope nominalizes one word so as not to supply another: "Two classes of people she had chosen to avoid, having been driven to such avoidings by her aunt's preferences" (44). Or a shift in tense that conveys a change in emotional tone while the substantive words remain constant: "But she had not been happy in accepting it. She was not happy now that she had accepted it" (379). Or the concentration of repetition used in the representation of individual consciousness, as when Alice, the heroine of *Can You Forgive Her?*, reflects upon her divided feelings toward her jilted lover:

> *She had* no *wish* to go back from her pledged word. She thought that *she had* no such *wish*. She *loved him* much, and admired him even more than *she loved him*. He was noble, generous, clever, *good*, – so *good* as to be almost *perfect*; nay, for aught *she knew* he was *perfect*. *Would that he had* some *faults*! *Would that he had! Would that he had! How could she*, full of *faults* as *she knew* herself to be, – *how could she* hope to make happy a man *perfect* as he was! (59–60, my emphasis)

This passage is striking for Trollope's effectiveness in rendering Alice's inner voice in a moment of feverish hopelessness: the simple and repetitive diction, creating the impression of continuous but circular thought; the recurring exclamation "Would that he had!", more hopelessly beseeching with every appearance; and the breathless use of dashes all convey a mind in agitated paralysis, veering and swooping over the same set of limited and intractable ideas. But this passage only exaggerates those techniques that are typical of Trollope at his least discursive moments. The repeated words and phrases in consecutive sentences, and the dashes and semicolons that introduce short clauses of supplementary information with repeated sentence openers, all evince Trollope's endemic reluctance to vary elements of diction or syntax in his style considered at large.

In such passages, Trollope's patterns of repetition push toward a sense of conceptual over-determination, as a single word is forced to bear the weight of multiple meanings and cumulative discriminations. This problem escalates in the case of abstract nouns, which are less characteristic of Trollope's diction. In *Can You Forgive Her?*, delicacy and its variants offer an example. Alice introduces it first, accusing George of lacking delicacy for flirting with her while she is engaged. His answer rejects the social pretense of the word, yearning for something more genuine: "Oh, indelicate! How I do hate that word. If any word in the language reminds me of a whited sepulchre it is that; – all clean and polished outside with filth and rottenness within. Are your thoughts delicate? that's the thing" (96). Shortly after, delicacy is used in a completely different sense to refer to both physical fragility and an appropriate femininity. In a jibe at Alice, Mr. Bott censures her for exposing Lady Glencora to the elements in the Priory ruins:

> "The frost was so uncommonly severe," said he, "that any delicate person like Lady Glencora must have suffered in remaining out so long."

> The insinuation that Alice was not a delicate person and that, as regarded her, the severity of the frost was of no moment, was very open, and was duly appreciated. (316)

The extent of Lady Glencora's delicacy thus becomes an important topic, but not only because Alice is presumed to have compromised her health; delicacy is also a euphemism for selfishness and puerility. In response to an accusation from Mrs. Marsham, Alice says of Glencora:

> "I believe she has very good health, which is the greatest blessing in the world. By delicate I suppose you mean weak and infirm."
>
> "Oh, dear, no, – not in the least, – not infirm certainly! I should be very sorry to be supposed to have said that Lady Glencora is infirm. What I mean is, not robust, Miss Vavasor. Her general organization, if you understand me, is exquisitely delicate. One can see that, I think, in every glance of her eye." (467)

Yet pages later, Trollope's narrator defends Lady Glencora's delicacy, by which he means neither physical weakness nor infantilism but a virtue closer to tactfulness and honor: "As to many matters her mind was wrong. In some things her taste was not delicate as should be that of a woman. But, as regarded her money, no woman could have behaved with greater reticence, or a purer delicacy" (470).

It is difficult to determine the precise ways in which Trollope's repetitive procedures contribute to any concept of formal or moral honesty. On the one hand, we may praise the author for circling around a single word as it accrues a range of possible interpretations, sensitizing the reader to the relativity of its meaning with respect to speaker and circumstance and to the provisional nature of any possible definition. In this view, stylistic self-restriction is a form of moral forthrightness, even if what is communicated is the impossibility of direct or reliable communication. On the other hand, Trollope's belabored repetitions may constitute the spectacular failure of a device that cannot efface the traces of its presence, turning rhetorical ease into prosaic error. Significantly, such a failure may indicate more than a lapse in realism because it points to a failure within language itself – a failure that exists "outside" of Trollope's realism and the morality he associates with it.

The Limits of Honesty

In her seminal study *The Moral Trollope*, apRoberts examines the relationship between Trollope and Cicero, the subject of a critical biography, *The*

Life of Cicero, that Trollope first published in 1876. According to apRoberts, both writers appreciate the "complexities of morals, and the necessity for relativism," with the "artistic correlative of this position [being] that complex of things we call *irony*."[21] Although apRoberts argues for congruence between Trollope and Cicero in terms of their moral and modal sensibilities, she denies that they are stylistically similar: "what is usually thought of as Ciceronian style is distinctly not Trollopian," she claims, seeing Trollope's style as an extension rather of Cicero's letters ("easy, intimate, witty") than his oratory.[22]

My analysis suggests that apRoberts misses the ways in which Trollope's style is highly influenced by Ciceronian oratory, notwithstanding the tonal differences between the oratory and the letters. For Trollope shared more with Cicero than a sensibility, even if, ironically, Cicero's style influences him more in sensibility than technique. Just as for Trollope the contest between ease and lucidity becomes a problem not only for the normative agenda of realism but also for language analyzed independently as a realm of form, so for him Cicero becomes an aesthetic, as opposed to broadly ethical, example. To examine Trollope's use of Cicero is thus to appreciate how much Trollope regards style as a domain of autonomous aesthetic literary experience, allowing us to re-conceptualize his "honesty" in uniquely formal terms.

In *The Life of Cicero*, Trollope praises *Orator* (which he describes as Cicero's fifth book on rhetoric, along with *De Oratore* and *Brutus*) as the Roman's most "finished" rhetorical treatise.[23] In *Orator*, Cicero famously mediates between Asiatic style (florid and ostentatious) and Attic style (plain and spare); "tempered" style keeps a "mean" between the two, allowing for simple ornaments of thought and diction but avoiding rhetorical extremes.[24] Cicero also provides his most comprehensive analysis of prose rhythm, which is judged by the ear rather than the intellect (475). As with the three manners of treatment (which Trollope translates as the "simple," "moderate," and "sublime" [*Life of Cicero*, 328]), Cicero advocates a middle course: prose "ought not to be rhythmical as a poem is, nor entirely without rhythm as is the speech of the vulgar – for one is too strict and confined, so that it seems artificial; the other is too loose, so that it seems rambling and vulgar" (*Orator*, 471). He confesses that his ear "rejoices in a full and rounded period" and both "feels a deficiency, and does not like an excess" (447). And truly rhythmical prose is that which "does not halt or waver, but advances steadily and uniformly" (473).

Although Trollope drew on *Orator* to establish the hierarchy of genres that appears in *Thackeray*, *The Life of Cicero* suggests that he most admires

Cicero for his "lightness of touch," an ability to "run hither and thither, while he always pleases us, whatever attitude he may assume, whatever he may say, and in whatever guise he may speak to us" (326–28). Morris Croll notes that nineteenth-century critics identified "Ciceronian" style with the periodic sentence that suspended its subject until its conclusion – one aspect of an elaborate, convoluted syntax that tends to foreground sound and schemes over simple and direct expression.[25] Trollope, in contrast, emphasizes Cicero's syntactical agility, conjuring the image of a nimble stylist who creates an illusion of lightness while achieving singularly persuasive feats. He quotes from *Orator* to prove that Cicero "knew how to use language as no one has done since":

> There is the opposing and the loosening. There is the avoiding, the holding back, the sudden exclamation, and the dropping of the voice. And the taking an argument from the case at large and bringing it to bear on a single point; and the proof and the propositions together. And then there is the leave given; – and then a doubting, and an expression of surprise. There is the counting up, the setting right; – the utter destruction, the continuation, the breaking off, the pretence, the answer made to oneself, the change of names, the disjoining and rejoining of things, – the relation, the retreat, and the curtailing. (319–20)

Ironically, this passage conveys much about Cicero's rhetorical style using syntax that, from the nineteenth-century point of view, is utterly un-Ciceronian. The paratactic structure creates an impression of informality and spontaneity (enhanced by the solecism of the third sentence) and the sequential accumulations feel unplanned. The only main verbs come from the "there is" expletives, and in the third sentence even this minimal element is dropped. Trollope's translation thus assumes the verbal form that is sometimes called a "loose" sentence,[26] with front-ended main clauses, coordinating conjunctions, and an unbounded structure that allows component parts to be freely added or removed.

Unlike some examples of the Ciceronian sentence in Latin, the interest of this passage lies not in its diction or grammar (which are quotidian and loose) but in its rolling, mimetic rhythms. It falls naturally into two parts: the first three sentences grow to include more and more beats, mimicking the climax of the orator coming to his point (with the alliteration of "proofs and propositions together" enhancing the feeling of fullness and fruition). The short fourth sentence then begins the process anew, expanding massively in the interjection (as the orator dazzles with his array of devices) before falling off with a rapid "curtailing" in the final member. Alliteration and echoes ("bring to bear," "disjoining and rejoining," "the relation, the retreat") achieve an impression of euphony, and the entire passage might be described as musical – not in the technical sense of having regularly timed beats but in its possession of a rhythmic flow that is ordered but not monotonous, expanding and contracting to embody the stream of thought.[27]

In *An Autobiography*, Trollope states that a novelist's language must be intelligible and harmonious, linking the fulsome melodiousness of the Ciceronian style with its presumed, "Attic" opposite. As Trollope remarks, a novel written in a "rough style" may be intelligible but fatiguing for readers, so harmony shares with "ease" a connotation of effortless and pleasant reading (236). Yet harmony is primarily aural (its antonyms include "rough" and "harsh"), and requires a blend of practice, instinct, and skill: "The harmony which is required must come from the practice of the ear. There are few ears naturally so dull that they cannot, if time be allowed to them, decide whether a sentence, when read, be or be not harmonious. And the sense of such harmony grows on the ear, when the intelligence has once informed itself as to what is, and what is not harmonious" (236). Notably, Trollope's comments on harmony do not encompass the sonic qualities of words; there is no mention of such figures of speech as alliteration, assonance, or onomatopoeia that might suggest a poet's attention to the phonetic texture.[28] For Trollope, harmony is mostly a matter of rhythm and pacing, influenced by his deep immersion in classical rhetoric rather than English poetry:

> [The writer] must so train his ear that he shall be able to weigh the rhythm of every word as it falls from his pen. This . . . will become so habitual to him that he will have appreciated the metrical duration of every syllable before it shall have dared to show itself upon paper. The art of the orator is the same. He knows beforehand how each sound which he is about to utter will affect the force of his climax. If a writer will do so he will charm his readers, though his readers will probably not know that they have been charmed. (236–37)

The above statement demonstrates the importance to Trollope of classical models of *elocutio*, persuasion, and metrics, pointing to the musical dimension of his Ciceronian affinity.

Stephanie Shirilan observes that "contemporary prose scholars seem particularly averse to the study of prose rhythm, even as they concede that this is the very feature that lends 'literary' prose its defining quality."[29] This lack of interest belies the importance that belletristic rhetoricians placed on musical properties such as harmony and rhythm, in keeping with the classical precedent. As Hugh Blair writes in his *Lectures on Rhetoric*, whenever ancient rhetoricians "treat of the Structure of Sentences, it is always the music of them that makes the principal object . . . The other qualities of Precision, Unity, and Strength, which we consider as of chief importance, they handle slightly" (I:318). According to Blair, then, "there are two things on which the music of a Sentence chiefly depends. These are, the proper distribution of the several members of it; and the close or cadence of the whole" (I:323); moreover, "in the harmonious structure and disposition of Periods, no writer whatever, antient or modern, equals Cicero" (I:316). In the Renaissance, it was commonplace to associate the musicality of prose with Cicero's distinctly oratorical style, which, as Croll argues, relies on schemes rather than tropes, these being "chiefly similarities or repetitions of sound used as purely sensuous devices to give pleasure or aid the attention."[30] However, following Blair, who praises Cicero's style for its "remarkable union . . . of harmony with ease" (I:323), Victorian writers allowed for a far greater consilience between aural and informational styles, helping to explain how a plain style might also be musical. For example, in an essay for *Fraser's* in 1857, William Forsyth describes how a lasting style will give utmost consideration to the "relation of sentences to each other. A rhythmical structure ought to exist, not only in the separate but in the collective periods; and the warp and woof of the entire texture should be so woven as to preserve a continuity of pattern, and produce the effect of an harmonious whole."[31] Yet the writer who best exemplifies the rhythmical "charm" of this "easy, natural, unaffected manner" is none other than the "historian," David Hume.[32]

We have already seen how Trollope creates antitheses that tend to mask their own sharpness, how he amplifies language through retrospective modification, and how he employs repetition to create an illusion of simplicity where there may be unsettling indeterminacy. Trollope also possesses a "characteristic cadence"[33] in the length and order of his clauses and, particularly in passages of free indirect thought, through the use of punctuation (such as dashes, semicolons, and question marks) to provide cohesion and manipulate intonation. Consider the reflections of Alice's grandfather in *Can You Forgive Her?*:

> His grandson George had offended him very deeply, – had offended him and never asked his pardon. He was determined that such pardon should never be given, unless it were asked for with almost bended knees; but, nevertheless, this grandson should be his heir. (337)

This passage, one of many possibilities across the corpus, reveals the extent to which Trollope thinks in Ciceronian periods rather than individual sentences.[34] The first clause feels unfinished because it has not one but two "feminine" end-words ("very" and "deeply"), creating an expectation for a stronger finish; the unit after the dash provides such an ending, by amplifying the preceding clause ("had offended him") and explicating the meaning of "very deeply" by a substitution that brings the sentence to a more determinate conclusion ("and never asked his pardon"). The second sentence looks backward once again, picking up the notions of "pardon" and "never," but unlike the first sentence it ends with a weak subjunctive clause that is defined by its lack of strong stresses. The weak word "almost" literally signifies diffidence and hesitation, artfully enhancing the effect. The final unit balances the weakness of the conditional with a positive declaration that packs as many strong stresses into seven syllables as the previous clause did into twelve, bringing to completion that expectation created at the start.

Nearly any paragraph by Trollope consists of similar internally connected units, aptly demonstrating his assimilation of Cicero's teachings. Within a sentence, dashes tend to introduce tightly coordinated members, particularly in the representation of conscious thought: "How might she best make herself useful, – useful in some sort that might gratify her ambition; – that was now the question which seemed to her to be of most importance" (342). The unfinished nature of the first unit, which is then amplified by the second and completed by the third, is a characteristic Trollopian rhythm. In some cases, strategies of verbal cohesion complement a character's effort to rationalize or order his or her experience, as when John Grey reviews his romantic feelings for Alice and discerns a satisfying pattern of continuously nested commitments: "From the day on which Alice had accepted his first offer, – nay, from an earlier day than that; from that day on which he had first resolved to make it, down to the present hour, he had never been stirred from his purpose" (777).

As one becomes attuned to the rhythms of Trollope's syntax, the preeminence of lucidity as a cognitive value recedes in favor of harmony and ease as virtues of form rather than content, but form considered in isolation from authorial *ethos*. That is to say, the criterion in relation to which honesty must be judged is no longer generic or ethical (Trollope is accurate or sincere), but aesthetic (Trollope is harmonious or musical), and if there is such a thing as an "ethics of form" it can only be considered "honest" in the sense that a musical phrase can be described as "pure" – possessing an aesthetic quality valorized by ethically inflected description, but in this case a description that does not subordinate the aesthetic to ethically determined ends. Trollope's honesty, from this perspective, derives from his fidelity to a set of stylistic ideals with a history and heritage independent of traditional realism, particularly as realism was moralized during the nineteenth century (and for which Cicero, whom even Trollope associated with rhetorical mercenariness, was distinctly unsuitable as patron). Truth in representation may come not only from the faithful reproduction of nature that is enhanced by stylistic invisibility, but also through the harmony and rhythm that create a different sort of pleasure and manifest specifically as stylistic effects.

As a final example of this point, consider the following passage of scenic description from *Can You Forgive Her?*, in which intelligibility is replaced by musical principles of repetition, expansion, and phonetic beauty:

> There is a special winter's light, which is very clear though devoid of all brilliancy, – through which every object strikes upon the eye with well-marked lines, and under which almost all forms of nature seem graceful to the sight if not actually beautiful. But there is a certain melancholy which ever accompanies it. It is the light of the afternoon, and gives token of the speedy coming of the early twilight. It tells of the shortness of the day, and contains even in its clearness a promise of the gloom of night. It is absolute light, but it seems to contain the darkness which is to follow it. (341)

There are several notable distinctions between this passage and those that surround it: the sentences are longer, the vocabulary is more varied, and the content expressed is of a more emotive and sensuous kind. Instead of syntactic compression, the mood is one of almost prolix dilation, with the central idea being subtly modeled and changed. The sheer length of the passage draws attention to the triteness of its main (nay, only) concept; but if one succumbs to the almost incantatory repetition of the same phonetic units ("it," "light," "twilight," "night," "contain"), the thought content recedes behind the surface effects. As the grammatical units shorten, the density of assonance increases, until every repeated sound occurs at least once in the final sentence. The impression conveyed is paradoxical: the syntax suggests a mind that is, as Davies says, in a "process of approximation and qualification,"[35] but this shifting momentum is ultimately subordinated to schemes that instill a feeling of predominantly aesthetic purpose. Such passages imply that every value at the level of form may not have a corresponding value within a broader social or moral category. There is little room for honesty where the very banality of content serves to enhance the autonomy of style – unless, from an aesthetic perspective, it be honest to concentrate intensively and exclusively on form.

Conclusion: Hiding in Plain Sight

In 1977, Roger Fowler coined the term "mind style" to describe texts of any kind that formally embody particular ways of seeing, thinking, and feeling. According to Fowler, mind style is a "distinctive linguistic representation of an individual mental self," involving not only "*what* is apprehended" but also "*how* that world is apprehended, or conceptualized" through noticeable verbal patterns.[36] What is Trollope's "mind style"? Ever since James argued that Trollope had no discernible mind (and therefore just as little style), critics have sought to restore integrity to his authorial imagination. They have pointed to his achievements in multiple plotting, complex characterization, and moral irony, and have praised the author for his delicacy, nuance, and social insight. Yet far too often the identification of mind with style has caused style to be read as an instantiation or reduction of mind; and the aesthetic dimension of certain problems of style – whether it be the contest between fullness of expression and intelligibility of meaning, or the persuasive "charm" that emanates from different rhythmic organizations – has tended to be eclipsed by thematic or tonal considerations that ignore the extent to which prosaic style has an artistry independent of, though intimately connected with, its deployment in a realistic novel.

A little-known experiment in Trollope's career sheds additional light on this matter. After having a major success with *Can You Forgive Her?* in the mid-1860s,[37] and at the height of his celebrity, Trollope published a series of novels anonymously to see whether he could "obtain a second identity" (*Autobiography*, 204) as a writer of fiction. Critics have offered a number of explanations for this foray into anonymous publication, ranging from a psychological determination to best himself,[38] to a desire to portray controversial subject matter behind the "smokescreen of unguessable identity,"[39] to a mischievous intent to upset the complacency of mid-Victorian critics[40] or to avoid over-saturating the market with his wares.[41] Whatever the case, Trollope seems to have been earnest in his belief that he could produce a successful novel in a style not recognizably his own, so it is all the more surprising that he was almost instantly identified as the author of the works. The first novel, *Nina Balatka*, may have departed from Trollope's usual subject matter by being set in continental Europe and treating the controversial topic of religious intermarriage in a sympathetic light; it also contained long passages of urban description and archaisized speech not found in his earlier novels. But, as at least one critic attested, what gave Trollope away were micro-stylistic elements that may have been beyond the realm of his conscious control. "No one who knows his style," wrote R.H. Hutton in *The Spectator*, "can read three pages of this tale without detecting him as plainly as if he were present in the flesh."[42]

Hutton's presumption can be verified in various ways. Louis Milic has shown that "style is most consistent at those levels where the unconscious is greatest,"[43] and *Nina Balatka* matches *Can You Forgive Her?* in its elemental features. Quantitative stylistics is helpful here. In a sample comprising the novels' first ten thousand words, a high proportion of sentences begin with "but" or "and" (13% in *Nina Balatka*, 11% in *Can You Forgive Her?*), with the word "but" appearing almost equally (99 and 95 times respectively); for comparison's sake, Dickens's novel *Our Mutual Friend*, published contemporaneously with *Can You Forgive Her?*, contains half as many sentences with such an opening. The excerpt from *Nina Balatka* also exhibits Trollope's expected lexical plainness, containing only 1639 distinct words, or 16% of the total number; the figure is similar for *Can You Forgive Her?* (18%), and considerably lower than that for Dickens (26%). But there are also, as Hutton suggested, more obvious traces of Trollope's presence.[44] The first page of *Nina* offers a striking example of witty repetition that elegantly demonstrates Trollope's finesse in balancing ease with lucidity by revising statements already made:

> Josef's wife, Nina's mother, had long been dead, having died – so said Sophie Zamenoy, her sister – of a broken heart; of a heart that had broken itself in grief, because her husband had joined his fortunes with those of a Jew. Whether the disgrace of the alliance or its disastrous result may have broken the lady's heart, or whether she may have died of a pleurisy, as the doctors said, we need not enquire here.[45]

The passage is familiar in the (apparently) effortless care with which the clichéd phrase is stated, analyzed, and undermined as it is repeated in each successive clause, from the adjectival "broken heart," to the reflexive verb phrase "heart that had broken itself," to the non-reflexive transitive construction "may have broken the lady's heart." The balanced and alliterative phrasing ("long been dead, having died," "joined his forces with those of a Jew," "whether the disgrace of the alliance or its disastrous result") conceals the sly transference of responsibility from impersonal fortune to uxoricidal recklessness. Given the euphuistic patterning, the medical term "pleurisy" – which contains the only bilabial stop (i.e. the letter "p") in the period – literally explodes as a bathetic punch-line, yet the passage ends, as did the overture to *Can You Forgive Her?*, with the ironic refusal to provide determinate information. The sardonic tone of the passage is recognizably Austenian; Trollope, after all, confesses in *An Autobiography* that he thought *Pride and Prejudice* "the best novel in the English language" until shifting that honor to *Henry Esmond* (41). But the handling, with its loosely assembled phraseology, subtly varied repetitions, indirect assertions, and tentative but devastating conclusions, is evidently Trollopian.

Trollope's desire, and failure, to mask his own style suggests two important conclusions. First, the very assumption of stylistic transparency that lies behind so much criticism of Trollope may be driven by thematic interests rather than accurate stylistic observations. As the experiment with anonymity shows, Trollope's style is anything but nondescript, but certain normative conceptions of his realism require that it be so. Second, the analysis of style may be poorly served by using virtue terms that overlap as signifiers of moral value. Because transparency is associated with honesty – "honest and transparent" is one of numerous ethico-aesthetic pairings in the language – it is difficult to determine whether one's appreciation of its manifestation in textual terms is driven by an aesthetic or morally reductionist interest. As with Thackeray, there are aspects of style that are not necessarily the man, or at least that reflect the man as a practical artist rather than as a moral ideal, pointing to the critical advantage of hewing closely to Trollope's own rhetorically conditioned vocabulary.

In probing how stylistic description may overlap with moral evaluation in the case of Trollopian "honesty," we initially found good reasons, encouraged by Trollope himself, for generating moral interpretations of form. Honesty and accuracy may rightly refer to the intentions of an author, the subject matter he represents, or his manner of representation. But when one sets aside the "middle course" of realism and the demands of morally didactic verisimilitude, we can see how Trollope's procedures in prose are governed by other preoccupations that are artistically independent. As the tradition of Trollopian criticism indicates, it is tempting to treat every structure valued at the level of form as an aspect of authorial ethos. But this strategy will only work when we learn to expand that ethos to include certain aspects of style that are qualities of language regardless of genre or intent.

CHAPTER 6

Meredith's Fervidness

The prose style of George Meredith is so eccentric as to have cost the author his once secure place within the first rank of Victorian authors.[1] In contrast to the graceful flexibility of Thackeray, and the ease and lucidity of Trollope, Meredith's style is typically described as difficult, unnatural, extravagant, artificial, and obscure, frustrating straightforward communication between author and reader. In an 1897 issue of the *Yellow Book*, John Robertson defined preciosity as "an assertion of individual or special personality as against the common usage of talk," and excoriated Meredith's style as "the most pronounced outbreak of preciosity in modern English literature."[2] Whereas Trollope strove to privilege the illusion of objective and unmediated content, Meredith's "egoism" and "tortuosity" scorn it at every turn, brazenly cultivating the mannerism to which Trollope so strenuously objected.

Yet when Meredith was asked to define his style for others, he claimed that he had none. "It must be rather your liking than discrimination which gives me a claim to this title [of stylist]," Meredith wrote in a letter to George Bainton. "I have no style, though I suppose my work is distinctive."[3] In making this statement, Meredith distanced himself from accusations of both egoism and artificiality, proclaiming his adherence to the Victorian principle of imaginative sincerity and not to the self-conscious cultivation of "style": "I have never written without having clear in vision the thing put to paper; and yet this has been the cause of roughness and uncommonness in the form of speech" (130). In another letter, Meredith confesses that "thought is tough, and dealing with thought produces toughness,"[4] the causal sequence suggesting that he regarded stylistic difficulty as the natural by-product of referential fidelity rather than as an end in itself.

Unlike Thackeray, whose detached conception of style encouraged him to draw from a vast array of expressive means, and Trollope, whose commitment to formal honesty compelled him to create a style whose objectivity and regularity was a hard-worked deception, Meredith saw style as more romantic and organic. The perceived "excrescence"[5] of the style thus indicates artistic failure at best and willful deformity at worst. However, in this chapter, I draw on Morris Croll's conception of "baroque" style to explain how the "difficulty" of Meredith's prose – often construed as pedantry or obscurity – actually provides the "natural" embodiment of a dialectical tension within Meredith's mind between two opposing impulses. The first, identified with metaphor and epigram, gravitates toward the philosophical intensity of poetic condensation, while the second, identified with plotting and syntax, seeks the imaginative freedom of discursive prose. Though it may seem exclusively a matter of artistic construction, this dialectic repeats itself thematically as a constant drama between conditions of constraint and freedom that impinge upon the development of central characters, many of whom (in the later novels) are women at odds with the paternalistic structures of bourgeois Victorian social life. The question to ask in dealing with Meredith is not "How can a poet and lover of nature who despised egoism write in a prose style that strikes many as both highly artificial and willfully egotistical?" but rather, "How does the appearance of Meredith's style provide an organic account of the ethical and aesthetic impulses that divided him?" As I shall show, for Meredith, both style and theme coalesce around the virtue of "fervidness," the sense of earnest energy or "boiling over" that results from the contest, and uneasy synthesis, between related but opposing forces.

Shagpat as Laboratory

As we have seen, reviewers praised the appearance in 1852 of Thackeray's *Henry Esmond* as an extraordinary feat of literary ventriloquism. John Foster, writing in the *Examiner*, expressed his "appreciation of the skill and taste with which *Esmond* is written . . . In his most habitual moods Mr Thackeray is a very easy, polished writer; he has lately been engaged in a close study of the authors upon whose style he founds his present manner; and the result displayed in the volumes before us is a novel of which the literary workmanship commands unstinted praise."[6] While reviewers generally treated *Vanity Fair* as satire, they regarded *Esmond* as an earnest homage to the age of Queen Anne and a manifesto for the persistence of its values. Some of the thematic and stylistic virtues that critics believed Thackeray shared with his eighteenth-century predecessors included clarity of thought, conversational directness, and an autumnal quality of self-reflection and Stoical detachment – elements of the Augustan prose style favored by Addison and Steele, who also appear as characters in Thackeray's novel.

In 1856, George Meredith delivered an equally convincing impersonation based upon a very different model. *The Shaving of Shagpat*, published by Chapman and Hall (who had brought out some of Thackeray's early works), carried the subtitle "An Arabian Entertainment," with a prefatory note explaining that "the only way to tell an Arabian Story was by imitating the style and manner of the Oriental Story-tellers."[7] Although such a work might "read like a translation," Meredith insisted that the novel was "in every respect an original Work" (vi). In her highly favorable review, George Eliot agreed. "Mr. Meredith has not simply imitated Arabian fictions," she wrote, "he has been inspired by them; he has used Oriental forms, but only as an Oriental genius would have used them who had been 'to the manner born.'" As specific points of excellence, she cited "exuberance of imagery," "picturesque wildness of incident," "significant humour," and "aphoristic wisdom."[8] In the 1890s, Edmund Gosse echoed this praise, writing that "the variety of scenes and images, the untiring evolution of plot, the kaleidoscopic shifting of harmonious colours, all these seem of the very essence of Arabia, and to coil directly from some bottle of a genie."[9]

Although no reviewer explicitly compared *Esmond* to *Shagpat* – the one a seasoned production by a literary celebrity, the other a first novel by a poet of limited renown – taken together these texts represent two possible directions within mid-century fiction. The stoic impersonality of *Esmond* paves the way for the "disappearing" style of Trollope, in which representational transparency stands for natural and high-bred ease, while the phantasmagorical exoticism of *Shagpat* signifies a movement away from realism and its stylistic conventions. Indeed, the story within *Shagpat* can be extremely difficult to trace, leading most reviewers – and contemporary readers – to comment exclusively on Meredith's use of sensuous imagery and ornament for their own sake, something they regret Meredith did not repudiate when he turned to mainstream realism, with its more legible characters, subject matters, and settings. However, to dismiss *Shagpat* as a freakish prodigy is to miss how it constitutes a laboratory for Meredith's later attempts to base his novels on stylistic principles that differ markedly from Thackeray's eighteenth-century assumptions. Under the cover of "Arabian" escapism, *Shagpat* foreshadows how Meredith would enlarge rather than undercut social and domestic realism by developing a theory of ornament that treats it as psychologically revelatory rather than merely decorative.

The Shaving of Shagpat recounts the efforts of its hero, Shibli, to surmount supernatural forces in order to deliver political justice to a city held in thrall to a terrible monster (the eponymous Shagpat). As every reviewer noticed, the text owes its feeling of verbal luxury to the rhetorical techniques associated with what Cicero called the "Asiatic" or magnificent mode of writing. Archaisms, neologisms, and poetical interpolations pervade the text, elevating and exoticizing the tone, while the use of sonic schemes such as alliteration and onomatopoeia creates an atmosphere of sensual richness. Above all, critics noted how Meredith lavished the text with similes and metaphors, often deploying multiple comparisons in tandem. Sometimes these comparisons simply repeat the sense of the original similitude, as when Baba Mustapha's arm was "hovering round Shagpat like a bird about the nest; and he was buzzing as a bee ere it entereth the flower, and quivered like a butterfly when 'tis fluttering over a blossom";[10] more often they enlarge and refine it, as in this description of the sorceress Goorelka's mouth: "On the couch lay one, a woman, pure in loveliness; the dark fringes of her closed lids like the living flashes of darkness, her mouth like an unstrung bow and as a double rosebud, even as two isles of coral between which in the clear transparent water beds the pearls shine freshly" (136).

Henry Able suggests that Meredith's closely grouped similes are influenced by Welsh Triads, a medieval form wherein three distinct objects share a common point of likeness.[11] Meredith's father-in-law, Thomas Love Peacock, with whom he was living at the time of composition, favored this form of wit, and Meredith's comparisons in *Shagpat* resemble Triads in their intellectual structure and folk-like content. But although they impersonate a wisdom form, Meredith's triads are mostly doggerel, meaning they are less interesting for what they communicate than for the unexpected directions they follow. For example, when Shibli refuses to heed Noorna's command to alight from the Horse Garraveen lest he be thrown over a cliff, she admonishes him:

> Lo, now, the greatness and the happiness thou art losing for this idle vanity is to be as a dunghill cock matched with an ostrich; and think not to escape the calamities thou bringest on thyself, for as is said,
>
> "No runner can outstrip his fate;"
>
> and it will overtake thee, though thou part like an arrow from the bow. (122–23)

Though the three comparisons are tightly bound in the same syntactic unit, they are neither parallel nor obviously coherent. Noorna compares

Shibli first to a "dunghill cock" whose proverbial boldness exceeds his actual strength, then to a "runner" who cannot evade the inevitability of his defeat, and finally to an "arrow" that races smoothly from the bow. The overall scheme of images is meant to chasten Shibli, but the aerial elegance of the arrow, which appears in a mitigating clause, is conceptually far from the earthbound degradations of the cock. In a similar example, the narrator introduces Noorna, disguised as a hag, as follows:

> Now, he was in the pits of despondency, even as one that yieldeth without further struggle to the waves of tempest at midnight, when he was ware of one standing over him, – a woman, old, wrinkled, a very crone, with but room for the drawing of a thread between her nose and her chin; she was, as is cited of them who betray the doings of Time,
>
> Wrinkled at the rind, and overripe at the core, and every part of her nodded and shook like a tree sapped by the waters, and her joints were sharp as the hind-legs of a grasshopper; she was indeed one close-wrecked upon the rocks of Time. (3)

The metaphorical density of this passage exceeds that of the previous examples. It begins with two hackneyed metaphors from spiritual allegory (the "pits of despondency" and "waves of tempest"), continues allusively (the "thread" recalls the spinning and cutting of the Greek Fates), pauses momentarily on an aphorism (the aged as overripe fruit), and nears completion with similes that elaborate the crone's appearance (like a withered tree or bony grasshopper). However, by the end of the passage, an unexpected transfer of spiritual import has occurred, because rather than Shibli being "close-wrecked upon the rocks," it is the crone. The energy contained in the earliest comparisons has been suspended throughout the passage, only to be released upon a different object.

Through his use of interconnected comparisons, Meredith reveals two inclinations: first, toward the intellectual pith of wisdom genres such as proverbs, which juxtapose statements in an elliptical or analogical relationship, requiring that the reader reflect upon them more carefully in order to apprehend their full import; and second, toward the imaginative freedom of continuous figuration, which flies away from compression in its rapid re-imagining of an image or concept. This double movement at the level of ornament replicates the same problem that Meredith would later theorize at the level of the sentence, namely how to find a mean between Attic concision on the one hand and Asiatic copiousness on the other.[12] The Bainton letter is filled with equivocations on this score (130–32). In favor of concision, Meredith claims that he thinks "it preferable, especially in these days of quantity, to be largely epigrammatic rather than exuberant in diction" and praises the "pellucid prose" of the French author La Bruyère; at the same time, he recommends "the wonderful sweep of a sentence by Gibbon" and warns against the "Addisonian style" that "can run only in the bounds of a brook." On the side of brevity, he tells writers to "be condensed, yet not obscure" and mocks Italian prose as "verbose, a coil of sounding phrases"; at the same time, he believes a writer can learn to "pour copiously, yet not overwhelm" and should not "too violently compress or restrain his nature" during youth. Ultimately, Meredith recommends a middle course between "the pregnant brevity which pricks imagination and the wide discursiveness which exhausts it," yet even this compromise is divided. The left half of the dichotomy partially enfolds the right, because curt passages open up to wider imaginative vistas than their brevity in space suggests; but the right half also gestures to the left, because "exhaust" can mean both "tire" and "expound."

Meredith's contemporary James Moffat strikes to the heart of this apparent contradiction when he observes that Meredith's best works "testify to the great 'note' of his mind, to the extraordinary *penetration* and *wide grasp* which inform the *luxuriant* fancy and *terse* energy of the style upon the higher levels of his prose or verse."[13] Notably, at the end of *Shagpat*, Meredith finds an objective correlative – the Sword of Aklis – for this synthesis of competing vectors. To seize the Sword, Shibli must first pass through the Cave of Chrysolites, which mystifies him with its confusing coruscations: "So they advanced beyond him, and lo! The Cave of Chrysolites, irradiate with beams, breaks of brilliance, confluences of lively hues, restless rays, meeting, vanishing, flooding splendours, now scattered in dazzling joints and spars, now uniting in momentary disks of radiance" (200–01). The sword itself is as bejeweled as the Cave in which it is found, yet its surface manages to "arrest" and concentrate the energies of its raw materials without any apparent loss of dynamism or vitality:

> Lo! The length of it was as the length of crimson across the sea when the sun is sideways on the wave, and it seemed full a mile long, the whole blade sheening like an arrested lightning from the end to the hilt; the hilt two large live serpents twined together, with eyes like somber jewels, and sparkling spotted skins, points of fire in their folds, and reflections of the emerald and topaz and ruby stones, studded in the blood-stained haft. (201)

Ornate but far from inert, the Sword is light to the touch and expands and contracts at will, and "its sharpness was such that nothing stood in its way, and it slipped through everything as we pass through water" (202) – even, as Shibli discovers, through inner thoughts. Although Meredith clearly seeks inspiration in what Lewes deprecatingly called "the luxuriant redundancy of Oriental expression,"[14] the ornamental Sword of Aklis suggests that sybaritic ornamentation can also be honed to sharpness.

With its stylized archaisms and fantastical digressions, *The Shaving of Shagpat* participates in a tradition of Orientalist narrative that seems to have little to do with our understanding of Meredith as a realist. ("We may think *Moby Dick* 'greater' than *The Egoist,*" writes Northrop Frye, "and yet feel that Meredith's book is closer to being a typical novel"[15]). But H.M. Cecil was right to claim that it contains much that became characteristic of Meredith's later work.[16] For Meredith, the choice between concision and copiousness was both a stylistic and a psychological problem: what linguistic forms and generic structures are adequate to a mind that seeks the intensity of condensation in short forms and the freedom of association in long ones? At this early point in his career, the richness of eastern romance offered a possible solution to this dilemma. But Meredith's commitment to the reality principle (perhaps anticipated in his selection of a lowly barber for hero) caused him to reject the Oriental setting and the rhetorical grandiloquence it entrained. Instead, he drew from *Shagpat* the idea of a bejeweled prose style in which "difficult" ornaments like simile and metaphor could play a double role, focusing the mind with analytic precision but pricking the imagination into further flights of fancy.

Meredith as Baroque: Between Curt and Loose Forms

"The problem of Meredith," wrote Arthur Symons in 1897, "is the problem of why a poet has spent most of his life in writing novels,"[17] a sentiment he was not alone in voicing. For Oscar Wilde, Meredith was a "prose Browning" (*Intentions*, 104) while Virginia Woolf called him a "poet-novelist" whose "mind was too self-conscious, and too sophisticated to remain lyrical for long" ("Novels," 232). The idea that Meredith was somehow hindered or trapped by his poetic sensibility recurs throughout the criticism. Henry James memorably wrote that Meredith hitched his lyrical gift "to the chariot of his prose – steeds who prance and dance and caracole, who strain the traces, attempt to quit the ground, and yearn for the upper air."[18] Similarly, Donald Fanger argues that Meredith "showed a lifelong hesitation over a full commitment to the prose form," but concludes that this led Meredith to strain "for a synthesis of the two – which at once limited the ensuing productions to only partial success."[19]

Meredith's attitudes toward prose were certainly influenced by poetic values. In the Bainton letter, for example, his conception of the sentence mirrors his conception of the line as governed by stress and meter: "Impress on your readers the power of the right use of emphasis, and of the music that there is in prose, and how to vary it" (130). Meredith also claims that "the best training in early life is verse. That serves for the management of our Saxon tongue; and may excuse the verse of Addison, in consideration of what he did" (130). More significantly, he once described his primary ideal in poetry as "concentration and suggestion,"[20] which parallels the idea of "pregnant brevity." Yet the implications of Meredith's poetic temperament can be overstated. "Writing prose, then, as if it were poetry," Symons says of Meredith, "with an endeavour to pack every phrase with imaginative meaning, every sentence, you realize, will be an epigram" (674). But few critics would refer to the epigrams of Oscar Wilde as especially poetic.

Given that Meredith dedicated most of his writing life to prose – prose that was regarded as some of the most notable, if also notorious, in the language – then the history of prose (including prose drama) offers a more productive starting point for understanding his novelistic style than the history of poetry.[21] As we have seen, Meredith was deliberate and self-conscious in the unusual way he launched himself into this tradition, beginning his novelistic career in a style orthogonal to prevailing norms. At the same time, his later works retained two key features of this early style, namely, condensing forms such as proverb and apothegm and amplifying forms such as imaginative comparison and description. While these two forms may seem opposed in strategy and technique, they represent – as Morris Croll once said of the Anti-Ciceronians – "two sides of the seventeenth-century mind: its sententiousness, its penetrating wit, its Stoic intensity, on the one hand, and its dislike of formalism, its roving and self-exploring curiosity, in brief, its skeptical tendency, on the other."[22] Indeed, Croll's work on "baroque" prose helps provide a stylistic genealogy for Meredith that avoids the usual pitfalls of regarding him as either a failed realist on the one hand or a failed poet on the other.

In his influential essay on "The Baroque Style in Prose," Croll identifies two seventeenth-century reactions to the rhetorical artfulness of Ciceronianism. The first, which he called "curt" or "serried" style, is defined by an aspiration toward brevity that is enhanced by a lack of syntactic connectives. Each member of a period "is as short as the most alert intelligence would have it" and is deployed "as a series of imaginative moments occurring in a logical pause or suspension."[23] Tending to "aphorism, or *pensée*, in its ideal form," curt sentences emerge like "flashes of a jewel or prism as it is turned about on its axis and takes the light in different ways."[24] In contrast, the "loose" style is defined by an abundance of syntactic ligatures, especially coordinating conjunctions and absolute constructions;[25] these allow a thought to be pursued in a flexible, even casual manner. Whereas in Ciceronian style each member of a period is essential to its logical development, loose periods include unexpected pauses, digressions, and other "natural" movements, accumulating an idea rather than succinctly expressing it. While the curt and loose styles seem obviously opposed, Croll argues that they both reflect the "baroque" fascination with states of motion rather than states of rest, especially with respect to psychology and intellectual life. For example, the loose style, in contrast to the formal eloquence it disdains, portrays "not a thought, but a mind thinking,"[26] spontaneously and through time, while the curt style, in its concentrated leaps, forces the mind to follow a "chain of 'points'" or "paradoxes" or "metaphors" that lead to a "more vivid imaginative realization."[27]

The conversational informality of Trollope's prose could not have existed without seventeenth-century innovations in syntactic looseness, though the placidity and poise of Trollope's style owes more to the spirit of Ciceronianism (and to the Attic spareness which Croll calls "Cartesianism") than to baroque forms, which in their irregularities (semantic contrast, staccato rhythm, rhetorical incongruity) foreground "the energy and labor of minds seeking the truth."[28] To be sure, the intellectual character of baroque styles makes them especially appealing to philosophers and essayists. But Croll's mentalist conception of baroque style also provides a starting point for understanding how stylistic difficulty can be compatible with a novelistic commitment to psychological realism. For example, in the first chapter of his first major novel, *The Ordeal of Richard Feverel* (1859), Meredith uses the narrative potential of loose forms to develop a theory of curt ones as it pertains to Sir Richard, the author of a book of maxims called *The Pilgrim's Scrip*:

> Modern Aphorists are accustomed to make their phrases a play of wit, flashing antithetical brilliancies, rather than condensing profound truths. This one, if he did not always say things new, evidently spoke from reflection, feeling, and experience: the Triad which gives a healthy utterance to Wisdom: and omitting one of which, or with the three not in proper equipoise and junction, admirable sentences may survive as curiosities, and aptly quoted may clinch a debate, but are as Dead Sea Apples to a thirsting mind, and to men at large incomprehensible juggleries usurping dominion of their understandings without seal of authority.[29]

As with the "two sides of the seventeenth-century mind," which "are generally not separated one from the other,"[30] here Meredith's synthesis of baroque forms is complete. Thematically, the sentence expounds a definition of aphorism as a "condensing form" leading to "profound truths" rather than a mere "play of wit," sneering at comparatively artificial styles in which syntactical involution can be mistaken for semantic insight. The overall structure of the second sentence is loose: the member that follows the first colon ("The Triad which gives a healthy utterance to Wisdom") is appositional to the preceding clause as well as the subject of the second; and this second clause, which is itself an absolute construction (and thus a hallmark of a loosely additive style), proceeds entirely by coordinating conjunctions. The members introduced by the colons do not re-state the thought but amplify it, establishing significance, stating conditions, and pointing out risks in a way that could hardly be predicted from the start.

At the same time, the sentence – like so many of Meredith's sentences – replicates the imaginative condensation it praises through its aphoristic use of figurative language. The simile "as Dead Sea Apples to a thirsting mind" enlarges the scope and pitch of the passage by invoking the fruit of Sodom that turns to dust and which Milton, in *Paradise Lost*, transfers to new ground in Hell;[31] while the subsequent metaphor – "incomprehensible juggleries usurping dominion of their understandings without seal of authority" – radicalizes this theme, turning Meredith's critique of modern wit into an epic warning against the seditiousness of partial truths. The style, which Meredith might describe as "largely allusive or guardedly imaginative" (qtd. in Bainton, 130), feels "intellectual" because the images ask the reader to analyze the central proposition in unexpected ways. As in proverbs, Meredith "impregnates" the "brevity," so to speak, with imaginative potential by making amplifying forms such as metaphor integral to his aphoristic constructions. Moreover, whereas Wilde's epigrams depend upon the rhetorical schemes that Meredith criticizes, such as chiasmus and antithesis, Meredith's own curt sentences rely considerably more on tropes. This is one reason why the view persists that his epigrams are more poetic than prosaic in character.[32]

Vanessa Ryan claims that Meredith's novels "dwell not on what is *in* the mind but rather on what the mind does,"[33] and though she makes no allusion to baroque styles her approach certainly suggests Meredith's affinity with them. But where Ryan argues that the "cognitive difficulty" of the style allegorizes the "opacity"[34] of the mind, with readers forced to engage in a mental effort that highlights the resistances of knowledge and truth, Meredith himself was likely to attribute *more* interpretive clarity to his elliptical formulations, not less. The Prelude to *The Egoist* (1879), for example, celebrates condensation as a literary principle precisely because it offers an antidote to the novelist's "constant tendency . . . to accumulate excess of substance," which, by "obscuring the glass it holds to mankind, renders us inexact in the recognition of our individual countenances."[35] According to Meredith, the world is constituted by the big "Book of Egoism" which can only be made legible through "a powerful compression" (35):

> [T]he realistic method of a conscientious transcription of all the visible, and a repetition of all the audible, is mainly accountable for our present branfulness, and that prolongation of the vasty and the noisy, out of which, as from an undrained fen, steams the malady of sameness, our modern malady . . . Shall we read [the book] by the watchmaker's eye in luminous rings eruptive of the infinitesimal, or pointed with examples and types under the broad Alpine survey of the spirit born of our united social intelligence, which is the Comic Spirit? Wise men say the latter. (34–35)

Here, Meredith credits an overweening realism with such an excess of transcription that it actually obscures the diversity of human character by blurring the distinctions among types. In contrast to externally oriented realism, which is "inexact" in its unmitigated detail, he calls for the use of an "inward mirror" (34) that will present human beings in their essential individuality. At the same time, the "condensing spirit" of Comedy must organize these unique character traits into recognizable groupings ("examples and types") to "give us those interminable milepost piles of matter (extending well-nigh to the very Pole) in essence, in chosen samples, digestibly" (34).

The criticism of Meredith's imagination as extravagantly overproductive can eclipse the extent to which his work is pervaded by aphoristic forms. In some cases, Meredith invents vehicles within the plot for the presentation of maxims, such as the apothegms of *Shagpat* or the aphorisms of *The Pilgrim's Scrip*. In other cases, a character's defining feature may be a gift for epigram or wit, as with Mrs. Mountstuart in *The Egoist* or Diana Warwick in *Diana of the Crossways* (1885). In still other cases, Meredith makes the relationship between brevity and discursiveness the subject of overtly metafictional remarks, such as when Carinthia, the child of nature in *The Amazing Marriage* (1895), criticizes the more urbane letter-writing style of her cousin Henrietta: "She was oppressed by wonder of the writer who could run like the rill of the mountains in written speech;

and her recollection of the contents perpetually hurried to the close, which was more in her way of writing, for there the brief sentences had a throb beneath them."[36] Finally, and perhaps most obviously, Meredith's narrators deploy pointed remarks and pithy observations to develop character, analyze motivation, and communicate universal truths, as when the narrator of *Diana* opines: "The state of aimlessness in hot perplexity demands a show of action."[37]

In an 1887 lecture, John Morley defines aphorism as "the compression of a mass of thought and observation into a single saying," putting into memorable form that which is called "the wisdom of life, or the wisdom of the world, or the wisdom of time and the ages."[38] Neither "flat," like a truism, nor "enigmatical," like a riddle, aphorism nonetheless draws on both to state the commonplace "in a form so fresh, pungent, and free from triviality, as to have all the force of new discovery" (7–8). In Morley's view, aphorism is not only compatible with realism but an aid to it, and "it is in the novel that, in this country, the faculty of observing social man and his peculiarities has found its most popular instrument" (22). However, Morley laments the fact that although British novelists concern themselves with articulating truths about human character, they rarely possess – as he says of Tacitus – "the art of condensing his thought and driving it home to the mind of the reader with a flash" (16). Lacking a counterpart to either a "maxim writer" like La Rochefoucauld or a "character writer" like La Bruyère, "our own generation in Great Britain has been singularly unfortunate in the literature of aphorism," although "one living writer of genius has given us a little sheaf of subtly-pointed maxims in the *Ordeal of Richard Feverel*" (19–20).

Morley's essay bears a striking resemblance to Meredith's "Preface" to *The Egoist*, which establishes an organic relationship between techniques of verbal compression and the dramatization of character as "types." In his earlier *Essay on Comedy*, Meredith discusses the application of character typology to realism, citing Menander and Molière as the finest comedic dramatists for their ability to find a mean between the realistic representation of actual character and the idealistic distillation of universal features: "Menander and Molière have given the principal types to Comedy hitherto . . . The reason is, that these two poets idealized upon life: the foundation of their types is real and in the quick, but they painted with spiritual strength, which is the solid in Art."[39] Now, however, Meredith goes further in arguing that just as a typological approach can condense "volumes in a character," so too can an aphoristic style "condense[] whole sections of the book [of wisdom] in a sentence" (*The Egoist*, 35). As with the two sides of baroque style, comedy is at once a "stillatory," slowing things down so that the author can "interrogate" the "throbs of your pulses," but also a quickener, providing a means of "reading swiftly and comprehensively" over the book of life (35–36).

The best example of Meredith's typological brevity occurs in the second chapter of *The Egoist*, where Mrs. Mountstuart, a devotee of Sir Willoughby's court, successfully distils the essence of his character into the single epithet: "*he has a leg*" (43, original emphasis). When first made, this utterance is praised for its curtness: "In seeming to say infinitely less than others, as Miss Isabel Patterne pointed out to Lady Busshe, Mrs. Mountstuart comprised all that the others had said, by showing the needlessness of allusions to the saliently evident" (43). Given that the reader knows little of Willoughby, an account of "the saliently evident" might seem to be in order; but Meredith argues that a suggestive metaphor is a superior stimulus to the imaginative apprehension of character than a factual description of personal traits. "A simple-seeming word of this import is the triumph of the spiritual," declares the narrator, "and where it passes for coin of value, the society has reached a high refinement: Arcadian by the aesthetic route" (43). What might seem "laboured or literary" (42), in other words, actually takes us closer to Nature, and thereby closer to Meredith's idealized realism – a point that Meredith himself makes in the form of an aphorism ("Arcadian by the aesthetic route").

However, in keeping with the "loose" aspect of Meredith's mind, the narrator immediately goes on to examine how the epithet might be "amplified," providing a veritable instruction manual for the aphorism's unpacking. "Dwell a short space on Mrs. Mountstuart's word," says the narrator, "and whither, into what fair region, and with how decorously voluptuous a sensation, do not we fly, who have, through mournful veneration of the Martyr Charles, a coy attachment of the Court of his Merrie Son, where the leg was ribboned with love-knots and reigned" (44). Beginning as a series of questions, this sentence answers itself by transporting the reader out of the immediate context and into Jacobean and then Restoration England; "yet have we dreamed of it," Meredith continues, "as the period when an English cavalier was grace incarnate; far from the boor now hustling us in another sphere" (44). The nostalgic evocation of seventeenth-century court culture is how Mrs. Mountstuart "touched a thrilling chord" (44). Having established that Willoughby's leg is that of the "born cavalier," Meredith continues to mine the sentence for meaning: "You *see* it; or, you see *he* has it. Miss Isabel and Miss Eleanor disputed the incidence of the emphasis" (44). Accentual analysis is one way of examining a phrase; elaborating it through modification, connotation, personification, and metaphorical expansion are others, each of which Meredith performs for the reader. "It was a burning leg . . . He has the leg of Rochester, Buckingham, Dorset, Suckling; the leg that smiles, that winks, is obsequious to you, yet perforce of beauty self-satisfied . . . It is a leg of ebb and flow and high-tide ripples" (44–45). And just as the reader thinks this flight of fancy may be winding down, Meredith begins anew, moralizing ("You see eminent in him what we would fain have brought about in a nation that has lost its leg in gaining a possibly cleaner morality"), comparing ("Well, footmen and courtiers and Scottish Highlanders, and the corps de ballet, draymen too, have legs"), decorating ("Our cavalier's is the poetic leg, a portent, a valiance . . . It is a lute to scatter songs to his mistress"), playing ("It is a peep, a part revelation, just sufferable, of the Olympian god") (46).

Anticipating the Prefaces of Henry James, Arthur Symons writes that Meredith "conceives his characters as pure intelligences," which means that "his novels are always in action. To him and his people . . . every conversation is a hurry of mental action: the impressiveness with which nothing happens, when nothing is happening, is itself a strain on the energy" (676). But while Symons sometimes found Meredith's style personally enervating, he also deemed it "alive in every fibre" (677). In my view, the unique vitality of Meredith's style evinces the dynamism and energy of baroque prose, which as Croll famously argues "is a progress of imaginative apprehension, a revolving and upward motion of the mind as it rises in energy, and views the same point from new levels."[40] However, Meredith sought to adapt this aesthetic sensibility to the circumstances of nineteenth-century fiction. On the one hand, he celebrated short forms by drawing on the conventions of New Comedy and neoclassical drama to develop a theory of brevity as the verisimilar condensation of character; at the same time, he used the narrator's role as commentator and the novel's expanded discursive field to track the imaginative unfurling of an idea over time. Despite some efforts to resuscitate Meredith by repudiating the presence of a "clear stylistic fingerprint"[41] or "idiosyncratic mannerisms that are everywhere present like a signature,"[42] his synthesis of curt and loose forms by way of unexpected metaphors is highly characteristic.

Catachresis and the Fascination of What's Difficult

For contemporary readers, Meredith may be most interesting for his socially progressive views about women. While not exactly a feminist,[43]

Meredith aspired toward more equal relations between the sexes, something he registers throughout his novels in both content and structure. *The Egoist*, for example, stages a marriage plot in reverse, beginning with Clara's engagement to the domineering Sir Willoughby but dedicating the bulk of its pages to the sympathetic narration of her attempts to break the connection. In *Diana of the Crossways*, he examines the effects of a tyrannous marriage on the spirit of an intelligent woman. Similarly, the "marriage" in Meredith's last novel is "amazing" not because it exemplifies the Victorian ideal of complementary companionship but because it is so implausible. When Fleetwood, a sophisticated man of culture, proposes impetuously to Carinthia, a mountain girl, she thoughtlessly accepts, only to spend the rest of the novel in a strenuous bid for her partner's recognition and fair treatment. While Meredith's novels do not entirely dismantle the marriage plot, they alter its elemental structure by focusing less on the search for an ideal partner than on the exigencies of adjusting to a real one.

The Amazing Marriage repeats these dissonances at the level of style by having the story be told by two distinct narrators: the effervescent "Dame Gossip," who believes in the inscrutability of character and the inherent interest of action, and the more measured male "Novelist," who prizes the intimacy of psychological analysis.[44] As with Carinthia and Fleetwood, the novel forces an accommodation between these two styles of narration that seem to have little in common, and the dueling narrators formally echo the dynamics of freedom and restraint that Meredith orchestrates in the plot. On the one hand, the normative male novelist struggles to contain the intrusions and eruptions that are constantly threatened by his irrepressible female counterpart, who stochastically interposes with her unaffected garrulity; but the story closes with Dame Gossip having the last word, and the novel, like the individuals it describes, ultimately abides the "clash of forces" (492) that clamor within it.

Some critics have adopted a dialogic approach to Meredith, noting that his texts abound in competing discourses, ideologies, and styles. For example, Jacob Korg describes *The Ordeal of Richard Feverel* as "essentially a debate of addled minds, like a Peacock novel, and the narrative style pretends to take part in this fools' symposium by fractioning the authorial voice heard in the conventional novel into a series of parodic styles embodying untenable attitudes."[45] Similarly, Neil Roberts argues that "where Meredith *is* self-conscious about style, and *does* show mastery, is not in imposing his own stylistic personality on the text but in registering and organizing what Bakhtin calls the 'language of heteroglossia.'"[46] However, both Korg and Roberts assume that for these discursive contests to work, Meredith needs to maintain an ironic distance from them, "pretend[ing] to take part"[47] through stylized impersonation or "registering and organizing"[48] the voices of others but not directly contributing. These recusals seek to rebut the accusation that Meredith is a "precious" or a "Decadent" writer, cultivating a style that is egoistic or "deliberately abnormal" (Symons, 677). But they neglect the ways in which Meredith embraces dissonance as both a formal and a thematic principle, being an author who delights, as baroque writers do, in "heavy masses and resistant materials."[49]

Indeed, Meredith's characters often evince an erotic fascination with what is difficult or paradoxical. In *Diana of the Crossways*, Percy Dacier is drawn to Diana because she violates his standard conception of femininity: "As to her sex, his active man's contempt of the petticoated secret attractive to boys and graylings, made him believe that in her he hunted the mind and the spirit: perchance a double mind, a twilighted spirit; but not a mere woman. She bore no resemblance to the bundle of women" (177). Later on Lady Esquart goads Percy's feelings for Diana by describing her as a "riddle to the world" (189). Similarly, in *The Amazing Marriage*, Fleetwood first falls in love with Carinthia after reading a description of her in Gower Woodseer's notebook as "*a beautiful Gorgon – a haggard Venus*" (78, original emphasis). The oxymoronic nature of the phrases exerts a catachrestic fascination on the traveler. "Who would imagine a comparison of a woman to a rock!" (79), he exclaims. And yet the linguistic novelty of the comparison ("You have done what I thought impossible – fused a woman's face and grand scenery, to make them inseparable") causes him to have greater confidence in the authenticity of its source, which he assumes must be similarly original: "You could not create an idea of a woman to move you like that . . . I want only to hear she lives, she is in the world" (79).

Catachresis, which derives from the Greek word for "misuse," most commonly refers to "words transferred from some other realm to name improperly what has no proper name,"[50] or "figurative substitutes for a literal term that does not exist."[51] Viewed negatively, catachresis is an "abuse" of language that renders it unintelligible and illogical, "a rhetorical term for the misapplication of a word or phrase with seeming disregard for its ordinary denotation or grammatical function, as in Milton's 'blind mouths.'"[52] But catachresis also allows speakers to defamiliarize what we already know through the non-intuitive use of language (e.g. Shakespeare's "I will speak daggers to him") or to generate new terms for previously unnamed ideas and sensations. In the *Institutio Oratoria*, Quintilian defends catachresis as a "necessary" trope because it fills the gap where "there was previously no word" (8.6.34). Similarly, George Steiner associates the challenges of catachresis with a certain kind of "tactical difficulty" in writing, where the poet aims "to charge with supreme intensity and genuineness of feeling a body of language, to 'make new' his text in the most durable sense of illuminative, penetrative insight."[53] Catachresis was an important term for deconstruction because, as Paul De Man argues, its "monstrous" transfers of meaning reveal the inherent power of language to "dismember the texture of reality and reassemble it in the most capricious of ways."[54]

In his discussion of *The Egoist* in *Ariadne's Thread*, J. Hillis Miller describes how catachresis is essential to Meredith's method of characterization as "only figurative, that is, improper language can name the movements of the soul . . . Its 'nature' is to have no nature, to be what it is not."[55] For Miller, then, *The Egoist* "entails a recognition that selfhood is projected by prosopopoetic catachresis,"[56] an argument I follow insofar as language, especially difficult or improbable language, becomes the primary medium in Meredith for revealing underlying acts of mind.[57] When characters are struck by new sensations or feelings, Meredith frequently dramatizes the process by which they grasp at figurative language in an attempt to embody those feelings in words. For example, when Percy meets Diana, "he could not think of her without shooting at nature, and nature's very sweetest and subtlest, for comparison" (177). More dramatically, Meredith provides one of his most notorious sets of similes when Gower Woodseer encounters a gambling table at a fashionable resort:

> Philosophy withdrew him from his temporary interest in the tricks of a circling white marble ball. The chuck-farthing of street urchins has quite as much dignity. He compared the creatures dabbling over the board to summer flies on butcher's meat, periodically scared by a cloth. More in the abstract, they were snatching at a snapdragon bowl. It struck him, that the gamblers had thronged on an invitation to drink the round of seed-time and harvest in a gulp. Again they were desperate gleaners, hopping, skipping, bleeding, amid a whizz of scythe-blades, for small wisps of booty. Nor was it long before the presidency of an ancient hoary Goat-Satan might be perceived, with skew-eyes and pucker-mouth, nursing a hoof on a knee. (97–98)

In his review of *The Amazing Marriage*, Edmund Gosse quotes this passage, complaining that "the Alexandrian extravagance of Mr. Meredith's style has now reached such a pitch that it is difficult to enjoy and sometimes impossible to understand what he writes."[58] Similarly, V.S. Pritchett criticizes the "four attempts to find a metaphor for gambling when one alone is required."[59] He continues: "Too many images brawl" which leads to "the final impression . . . of great messy orchestral clash, ending in anti-climax."[60]

Although Korg and Roberts claim that "orchestral clash" is indeed central to Meredith's method, the cited passage actually makes explicit a sequential logic that slows down the reading experience so that the process of thinking (as opposed to the thoughts themselves) can be minutely analyzed.[61] First, Woodseer compares the gamblers to "summer flies on butcher's meat, periodically scared by a cloth," an image that captures the lack of "dignity" of gamblers at play as well as the "cloth" of the roulette table. Then, he imagines them "snatching at a snapdragon bowl," which is "more in the abstract": on the one hand, the "snapdragon" plant is so called because its red flower is said to resemble a dragon's mouth that threatens to swallow up any insect that dares to draw its pollen, and in this way visually parallels the flies on the butcher's meat; at the same time, Woodseer's metonymic imagination recalls the parlor game of snapdragon, according to which players attempt to snatch raisins out of a bowl of burning brandy and then eat them alight. In an article for the *Tatler* (1709), the fictional Isaac Bickerstaff (Sir Richard Steele) describes snap-dragon as a menacing game in which "the wantonness of the thing was to see each other look like a demon, as we burnt ourselves, and snatch out the fruit,"[62] an effect enhanced by the dimming of lights during play; in Robert Chambers's *The Book of Days* (1864), this demonic aspect was amplified by a picture of a dragon attempting to "snatch" his "feast of plums" from a snapdragon bowl.[63] Woodseer's second comparison is "abstract," then, not because it fails to be lucid but because its lucidity depends upon the reader following this unique chain of verbal associations, resulting in an unexpected fusion of pastoral and demonic imagery that casts a satiric light on the entire scene.

In his more cursory analysis, Pritchett argues that the first two images of the passage "collide" unmusically with the third in which Woodseer pictures the gamblers as "gleaners," "thronged on an invitation to drink the round of seed-time and harvest in a gulp . . . hopping, skipping, bleeding, amid a whizz of scythe-blades, for small wisps of booty" – an "inapt" image "unless in the mind of a farmer."[64] But this image emerges directly from the dark pastoral of the first: no longer harmless scavengers, easily shooed by a cloth, the gamblers are now like the desperate folk of a Hardy novel, threatened by institutions that both co-opt and exploit them. (A progressive, Woodseer here makes an oblique comparison between the exploitation of the rural poor and of gambling addicts; the "whizz of scythe-blades" also resembles the turn of the roulette table.) Hence the inevitability of the final image ("nor was it long") of the "ancient hoary Goat-Satan" who presides over the scene, which strikes Pritchett as so gratuitous, but which actually unifies the seemingly disparate conceits of the passage. The demon of play, coolly surveying the darkly festive snap-dragon bowl, evokes both Pan and Mammon with their mad rural laborers and scavenging pests.

Whether or not catachresis is justified or "excrescent" is ultimately a matter of context and taste; even if one perceives the coherence of this apparently illogical paragraph, one might still object to it as the prodigal output of an "artist showman."[65] But Meredith is drawn to catachresis precisely because it captures, both thematically and formally, the vital energy that arises from the clash of differences. In *The Amazing Marriage*, the troubled protagonists and combative narrators suggest that sexual union is considerably more tempestuous than novelists make it seem, and that harmonious coupling is a literary ideal rooted in unrealistic social foundations. At the same time, verbal catachresis attunes readers to the linguistic dissonances that undergird the apparently seamless surface of psychological experience itself, interrupting it, as Dame Gossip does, in order to protest its narrative authority. One recalls Trollope's ambition, as stated in *An Autobiography*, to write in a style so transparent that "I might succeed in impregnating the mind of the novel-reader with a feeling that honesty is the best policy; that truth prevails while falsehood fails; that a girl will be loved as she is pure, and sweet, and unselfish; that a man will be honored as he is true, and honest, and brave of heart" (145) – a style, in other words, that guarantees the legitimacy of the sexual categories that the novel strives to enforce. In contrast, Meredith's self-conscious catachreses and verbal playfulness, his narrative disturbances and elliptical comparisons, directly challenge these literary and sexual complacencies.

Conclusion: The Meaning of Fervidness

In Meredith's final work, the unfinished novel *Celt and Saxon*, he once again gravitates to the uneasy accommodation of opposites as embodied by literary style. The journalist Rockney has lately been challenging the London establishment with an approach more Attic than Ciceronian:

> But after all, the main secret was his art of writing round English, instead of laborious Latinised periods: and the secret of the art was his meaning what

> he said. It was the personal throb. The fire of a mind was translucent in Press columns where our public had been accustomed to the rhetoric of primed scribes. He did away with the Biscay billow of the leading article – Bull's favourite prose – bardic construction of sentences that roll to the antithetical climax, whose foamy top is offered and gulped as equivalent to an idea . . . And he was not devoid of style. Fervidness is the core of style . . . An encounter between Swift and Johnson, were it imaginable, would present us probably the most prodigious Gigantomachy in literary polemics. It is not imaginable among comparative pygmies. But Rockney's combat with his fellow-politicians of the Press partook of the Swiftian against the Johnsonian in form. He was a steam ram that drove straight at the bulky broadside of the enemy.[66]

Here, we find recapitulated some of the most salient points in the evolution of nineteenth-century prose. Rockney boldly dismisses what he calls the "bulky broadside" of Johnsonian style: the formulaic structures, the rolling crescendo, the logical climax, the Latinate vocabulary. In contrast, he proposes a Swiftian riposte governed by simplicity, directness, and sincerity, its "style" guaranteed by the author's "meaning what he said." As Meredith writes a few paragraphs later, "had not Rockney been given to a high expression of opinion, plain in fervor, he would often have been exposed bare to hostile shafts" (208). But because he is "fervid" and sincere, "Style cast her aegis over him. He wore an armour in which he could walk, run and leap – a natural style" (208).

This passage helps explain what Meredith means when he says "I have no style," even though he is usually faulted for the opposite. In his haughtiness toward "style," Meredith rejects a kind of literary formation that *precedes* the thought it contains, and to that extent shapes it, a rhetorical framework that only presents itself *after* the labor of matching form and content has been achieved. In contrast, the "natural" style is one that follows the mind in the process of imaginative intellection: it may resemble an "armour," weighty and cumbersome rather than limpid and light, but in liberating the brain's contents it allows them to "walk, run, and leap" on the page. Meredith's style feels both intellectual and alive, not because it represses disruptive forces but because it acknowledges and frequently thematizes them, drawing attention to style – in a way that many Victorian readers would find both familiar and paradoxical – as the organic embodiment of dialectical forces that never fully resolve.[67]

Meredith has often puzzled critics because the content of his works seems so stereotypically Victorian while their style feels negligently out of time: as Oscar Wilde said, "a child of realism not on speaking terms with his father" (*Intentions*, 17). However, from the earliest stages of his career Meredith searched for an alternative set of formal means to embody what we might regard as standard objects of representation. Ironically, his poetic commitment to "concentration and suggestion," in which every line is tightly packed with allusive meaning, first encouraged him to turn to a seemingly opposite prosaic form, namely the copiousness of Asiatic romance. Such a form allowed for the conventional incorporation of the versified *sententiae* that would appear in Meredith's subsequent works as unrhymed aphorisms and epigrams; it also permitted Meredith to expand massively the quantity and scope of the figurative ornaments, such as simile and metaphor, that he privileges on a local scale. *The Ordeal of Richard Feverel* represents a turn away from florid conventions and to what critics have rightly called a more dialogic style. But rather than erase Meredith's stylistic imprint, *Feverel* shows the marks of the stylistic maturity associated with *The Egoist* in Meredith's unrelenting synthesis of curt and loose forms, which represent a baroque commitment to laying bare acts of imagination and thought that are complicated or difficult.

That Meredith found in this style a suitable vehicle for expressing conflict between the sexes, and in particular the plight of women, is one of the great achievements of late Victorian fiction. We see it not only in Diana Warwick's efforts to find a style that suits her own self-conception as an author, but also in Meredith's daring use of style to challenge what we might designate, recalling Wilde, a paternalistic view of realism. Although *The Amazing Marriage* mounts this challenge most explicitly, there is a moment in *The Egoist* that, characteristically of Meredith, does so more memorably because of its brevity. In the chapter called "The Wild Cherry-Tree," Clara first awakens to the magnitude of Willoughby's egoism. Clara at last "understood she was expected to worship him and uphold him for whatsoever he might be, without any estimation of qualities: as indeed love does, as young love does . . . That was before her 'little brain' had become active and had turned her senses to revolt" (149). Clara, in other words, loved Willoughby without question before she had a brain to think with, not because she was incapable of thought, but because, as Meredith writes, "a shadow of the male Egoist is in the chamber of [girls'] brains overawing them" (153). In such a condition, she could only think "in blanks" (153), and part of the point of the novel is to trace for the reader how Clara fills in those blanks both morally and textually.

The method turns out to be a strange one. While in search of another character, Clara finds him asleep with a book under a double-blossom wild cherry tree. At first her attention is drawn to his book, but she soon turns her face upward toward the blossoms, which Meredith describes with lyrical intensity. "From deep to deeper heavens of white," he writes, "her eyes perched and soared" (154) into realms of ever-increasing and paradoxical complexity:

> Wonder lived in her. Happiness in the beauty of the tree pressed to supplant it, and was more mortal and narrower. Reflection came, contracting her vision and weighing her to earth ... She would rather have clung to her first impression: wonder so divine, so unbounded, was like soaring into homes of angel-crowded space, sweeping through folded and on to folded white fountain-bow of wings, in innumerable columns; but the thought of it was no recovery of it; she might as well have striven to be a child. (155)

In this extraordinary description, Meredith provides a vision of imaginative freedom so unhinged that it skips the bounds of earth as well as of grammar, "sweeping through folded and on to folded white fountain-bow of wings," into a space as open as it is dense. What matters is less the content of Clara's image (though the imagery may be a sly reversal of Patmore's "The Angel of the House") but rather the way in which she imagines, loading symbol *and* digression with the full intensity of her fervid vision.

"Fervidness" may seem a vague criterion of style but it captures the odd way in which Meredith himself both assimilated and resisted various features of the realist landscape. On the one hand, it refers to the passion that comes from sincere belief; on the other, it alludes to energy, heat, and the possibility of over-boiling with excess enthusiasm. This is the criticism that has often been made against Meredith's style, but rather than regard it as a symptom of preciosity or decadence, we ought to see it, as Meredith did, as the natural expression of a peculiar sensibility. This is how Rosamund learns to appreciate the works of Carlyle at the beginning of *Beauchamp's Career*. "Why should he hug a book he owned he could not quite comprehend?"[68] she wonders of Nevil. But her description of the work contains the answer:

> His favourite author was one writing of Heroes, in (so she esteemed it) a style resembling either early architecture or utter dilapidation, so loose and rough it seemed ... sentences without commencements running to abrupt endings and smoke, like waves against a sea-wall, learned dictionary words

> giving a hand to street-slang, and accents falling on them haphazard, like slant rays from driving clouds; all the pages in a breeze, the whole book producing a kind of electrical agitation in the mind and the joints. (19)

Neglected as both a theorist and a practitioner of style, Meredith teaches us to appreciate the pleasure, and the predicament, of clashing forces in a period when fervidness was itself often clashing with a countervailing stylistic ideal.

AFTERWORD

Stylistic Virtue and Literary Value

In the first half of this book, I argued that the concept of style was integral to the emergence of the "literary" as a distinct area of value in the nineteenth century, but the nature of this value remains contentious and complex. For some ethical critics – the kind I have called reductionist – style is valuable because it reinforces or co-constitutes the "central values"[1] of the implied author. As we saw with respect to Thackeray's irony, Trollope's verisimilitude, or Meredith's psychology, there are many cases in which stylistic virtues are best understood referentially, and one can stage numerous arguments about why the verbal properties that allegorize underlying values are subsequently "good" to experience.[2] But, as I have also shown, the language of virtue persisted in part because it resists the centrifugal pressure on style to refer to something other than itself. Stylistic virtues resemble moral virtues in designating a characterological ideal, but, unlike moral virtues, that ideal may inhere in a realm of aesthetic accomplishment, such as a line of music or a stanzaic scheme, that cannot be easily translated into a cognitive proposition, behavioral norm, or action-guiding "pattern of desire."[3]

This book recasts the history of nineteenth-century aesthetic criticism as a series of interlocking efforts to account for the unique nature of this aesthetic value through the framework provided by virtue theory. Earlier critics such as Ruskin and Arnold began their careers committed to the pre-eminence of spiritual and social content over formal abstractions. But over time they gradually transferred the burden of ethical significance from outcomes to processes, which they conceived as virtuous ways of being, seeing, and thinking. Pater and Wilde completed this process of ethico-aesthetic drift by establishing criticism as an activity on par with the production of art, investing both performance and contemplation with normative value. In interpreting these figures, the phrase "art for art's sake" is best understood as "art for virtue's sake" because it designates aesthetic experiences of a certain kind to be worthy and valuable.

The ideas of this period are shot through with Aristotelian appeals to *eudaimonia*, or flourishing, a holistic view of "the good" that includes whatever helps realize excellence, or *arete* (i.e. strength, merits, powers, qualities) in human character. Rather than hew to the established lists of virtues and vices, thinkers in this tradition use a more generic concept of virtue to identify traits that are admirable *because* they may be characteristically developed. Throughout the eighteenth and nineteenth centuries, such Aristotelian ideas were already part of what Alan Donagan calls the "common morality," the "system of mores, actual and possible . . . by which everybody ought to live,"[4] but, in aesthetic contexts, they were more specifically disseminated through the prism of belletrism and an education that (for men of privilege, mainly) revolved around the classics. In more rarefied inquiries, academic philosophers further identified Aristotle with "aesthetic" modes of reasoning that base moral judgments on subjective feelings of liking or aversion rather than rationalist deductions of right and wrong. Moral perfectionists such as Mill, Green, and Bosanquet imagined the realization of human character as a virtuously aesthetic act, lending credence to the idea that the distinguishing feature of literary material – stylistic character itself – could also constitute a kind of excellence.

Various forces in the twentieth century caused this ethico-aesthetic synthesis to disintegrate, but its constituent assumptions were not so much annihilated as re-animated under other guises. Consider, for example, the role played by "personality" in two phases of T.S. Eliot's career. In "Tradition and the Individual Talent" (1919), Eliot rejects the "prejudice" that we "praise a poet, upon those aspects of his work in which he least resembles anyone else,"[5] seeming to prefer a classical approach to style over the romantic one. In claiming that "the most individual parts of [a poet's] work may be those in which the dead poets, his ancestors, assert their immortality most vigorously" (40), he echoes the Paterian paradox that the most perfect style is also the least personal. However, Eliot specifically indicates that "the poet has, not a 'personality' to express, but a particular medium, which is only a medium and not a personality" (42), revealing a strenuous effort to shed any remnants of stylistic reductionism. By defining poetry as "an escape from personality" rather than its ethical "expression" (43), Eliot seeks a more robustly autonomous formalism than his predecessors: the "mind of the poet" is no more than "a receptacle" (41), or "a shred of platinum" (41) for the catalysis of a "new art emotion" (43), which is entirely internal to the history of that form.

If the essay on tradition realizes one extreme of autonomous style – stating as a decisive point of difference what is really an evolutionary extension of the process of ethico-aesthetic drift initiated by Ruskin – "Religion and Literature," published in 1935, reveals what happens when moral evaluation returns to occupy a more central position in the function of criticism. Concerned by the "secularization"[6] of twentieth-century literature, Eliot counters that "the 'greatness' of literature cannot be determined solely by literary standards" (31) because "what we read does not concern merely something called our *literary taste*, but . . . the whole of what we are" (36). For the later Eliot, the "separation" between literary and moral judgment "is not, and never can be, complete" (35); "literary standards" may be necessary for determining what counts as "literature" (31), but they alone cannot tell us whether there is sufficient other value in the "world as seen by a particular mind" (38). When addressing the moral or spiritual influence of art, Eliot self-consciously (and, one might argue, regressively) returns to the vocabulary of personality and ethos, describing how great works embody the "views of life" of "divers [sic] and contradictory personalities" (39) that shape our sense of self. Through this appeal to "personality," Eliot seeks a sharper line between the happenstance of personal taste ("what we like") and the norm-setting work of ethico-evaluative standards ("what we *ought* to like," 40), opposing autonomous aesthetic value to the broader view of life that contains it.

Like the later Eliot, I.A. Richards regarded value judgments as central to the project of criticism, but he struck a more satisfactory balance between "aesthetics" and "morality." Indeed, according to Joseph North, I.A. Richards innovated a "new paradigm for literary criticism" that allowed "the connection between tastes and values to be taken up and insisted upon in a thoroughly new way,"[7] but the novelty presumed by this statement belies Richards's immense debt to the thought of his Victorian predecessors. For example, in *Principles of Literary Criticism* (1924), Richards rejects the tendentious moralizing that leads to literary censorship and cites an alternative tradition, beginning with Plato and Aristotle, that regards aesthetic activity as continuous with other "moral" goods;[8] they are, in fact, species of the same stripe, consisting equally in "the exercise of impulses and the satisfaction of their appetencies" (44). However, Richards is quick to distance himself from a simplistic notion of psychological hedonism of the kind associated with Utilitarianism. If "the full exercise of an activity is commonly its own 'satisfaction,'" then "what pleasure may accompany it is derivative and incidental" (39 n. 1); "happiness," on this view, consists in the "free and untrammeled activity" of a person's impulses (40–41), which individuals will "co-ordinate" (38) differently according to their nature and culture. The outlines of the Aristotelian perfectionist tradition are clearly discernible in this "psychological theory of value" (32). Like Arnold, Richards seeks a rich and harmonious integration of competing impulses rather than a single-minded scheme that demands too great a "sacrifice" (42) of other potential experiences; and like Pater, he ranks highest "the widest and most comprehensive co-ordination of activities" (45) because it encourages that "plasticity" (45) of character that keeps our lives "well-balanced" (40), "rich and full" (42).

The work of art has a special place in this scheme because it provides "the chief means" (43) by which individuals are exposed to, and influenced by, forms of "organization and systematization" (43) that are not their own. Works of art do not provide experiences that are discontinuous with ordinary life; rather, their experiences are "more highly and more delicately organized" (59), co-ordinating "a greater number of impulses" (85) with more harmony, and less interference from opposing impulses, than would otherwise be possible. By widening our range of superior experiences, great works expand our sense of human possibility and induce a momentary (and possibly permanent) restructuring of our mental organization (101–02). This conception of literary value, keenly shaped by virtue aesthetics, also grounds Richards's theory of the poem as a "pseudo-statement,"[9] or a complex of attitudes that is continuous with ordinary experience but simultaneously immune from the requirements of moral rectitude or scientific truth-telling. "The business of the poet," Richards tells us, "is to give order and coherence, and so freedom, to a body of experience" (*Science and Poetry*, 55), and the content of that experience "is justified entirely by its effect in releasing or organizing our impulses and attitudes" (59). The poem, in other words, is value-neutral with respect to the content of the impulses it represents but not with respect to their mode of organization, recalling the nineteenth-century idea that imaginative texts present a simulacrum of human character whose artistic value derives less from the "views" communicated than from the criteria (such as richness, harmony, complexity) that define their formal presentation.

That Richards wrote a *Philosophy of Rhetoric* is not surprising given his prior training as a psychologist and the weight of the rhetorical tradition. However, he regarded the "old rhetoric," from Aristotle to Whately (*Philosophy*, 5), as overly vague and often obtuse, and sought to re-describe "most of the more recondite virtues of prose style" (50) in terms of their linguistic functions (such as "feeling" or "tone") rather than as free-floating units of meaning. Later practitioners of the "new stylistics" would follow Richards in seeking to extirpate the belletristic vocabulary from the discourse of criticism – rejecting "many of the rather mysterious terms that are usually employed in discussing these matters, *harmony, rhythm, grace, texture, smoothness, suppleness, impressiveness*" (*Philosophy*, 50) – but it may be impossible to factor out what Richards called the "*critical* part" of a literary experience, which describes its "value," from the "*technical* part," which describes the properties of the aesthetic object (*Principles*, 15, original emphasis). As Frank Sibley argues, aesthetic criticism is inevitably populated by "descriptive-merit terms" that are neither purely descriptive (such as "red") nor purely evaluative (such as "excellent") but that fall somewhere between the two (such as "harmonious").[10] These terms, which "are generally held to name properties which constitute merits or defects vis-à-vis certain spheres of assessment,"[11] perform a function similar to virtue terms in ethics, leading the philosopher Daniel Statman to opine that "proponents of VE [virtue ethics] need to explain in what way ethical judgments are nevertheless different from aesthetic ones."[12]

There are essentially two planes upon which this difference may be investigated: according to the content of the judgments (i.e. the outcomes, goods, and values they identify) or according to their form (i.e. the meta-ethical and meta-aesthetical explanation we can give of the underlying assumptions that govern their determinations of value and that account for their common vocabulary and structure). In the last twenty years, aesthetic philosophers in the Anglo-American tradition have primarily pursued their analyses on the plane of content. A variety of positions – autonomism, moralism, contextualism, ethicism, and so on – have been postulated to clarify the relationship between the moral values of a work of art and its aesthetic quality or assessment.[13] To take just one example from the literature, a "moderate autonomist" would argue that a work of art may possess moral defects that never affect its aesthetic value; on this view, the offensiveness of a racist joke does nothing to compromise the aesthetic value of a well-made punch-line. In contrast, a "moderate moralist" would say that the immorality of the joke constitutes an aesthetic defect if it prevents the joke from being "taken up" by a morally sensitive audience or from satisfying the expectations of its genre (i.e. to make someone laugh). These are helpful, if over-simplified, clarifications, but the aspirational precision of analytic categories can fail to capture the complexity of literary and ethical experience as they vary across time, place, and audience. In the case of the racist joke, how can we determine what a "morally sensitive" audience would be? How can we verify if the joke were "taken up" by them? On what grounds could we decide whether the joke satisfies or subverts its genre, and whether it does so deliberately or by accident? These are basic literary questions that are notoriously difficult to settle and that advertise the need for caution whenever we seek to make definitive statements about the "morality" of a work, whether manifest or prescribed.

Following a series of recent essays by Peter Goldie, a smaller number of philosophers have turned to virtue theory as a way of explaining the ethical value of art, taking advantage of the more capacious definition of "ethics" implied by the idea of *eudaimonia*. In "Towards a Virtue Theory of Art" (2007), the first essay in this series, Goldie argues that "the connection between ethics and art is more than just analogy."[14] In Goldie's argument, "artistic activity, as an expression of the virtues of artmaking and art appreciation, will, along with ethical activity and what Aristotle called contemplative activity, be a constituent part of what goes to make up human well-being."[15] Here, Goldie describes aesthetic experience as just one of several components of "the good life," each of which is non-trivial: "art, like ethics, is not a luxury good: without art, as without ethics, one cannot do well."[16] There are, of course, important differences between ethical (i.e. traditionally moral) and aesthetic "virtues" in that "ethical virtues are motivationally *demanding* in ways that the artistic virtues are not."[17] That is to say, most of us would not fault someone for failing to exercise creative skill or good taste in the same way that we would fault someone for failing to behave honestly or respond to the suffering of others, suggesting, as Sidgwick believed, that moral reflection provides principles for action in ways that aesthetic modes of reasoning do not.[18] But differences aside, Goldie insists that "the virtues of art-making and art appreciation are, in important ways, intimately interwoven with the exercise of the more familiar ethical and intellectual virtues."[19] They are, as he states in a later essay, "an excellence" that is integral to "well-being" and thus "possessing these traits, or at least exercising them in the right way, is intrinsically or non-instrumentally valuable."[20]

Goldie is quick to couple the virtues of art-making with those of art appreciation, but, as Dominic Lopes argues, there is a difference between "beautiful states of affairs" and how we feel about them.[21] Indeed, as Oscar Wilde stressed so memorably, the skills, habits, and dispositions required for the creation of stylistic virtues are not commensurable with those required for their criticism and interpretation, so an "ethical" defense of appreciation must seek its own justification. For Lopes, appreciation is intrinsically good because it exhibits a "pro-attitude"[22] toward the intrinsic goodness of beauty. A virtuous critic does not merely admire the work of art but positively supports its existence (through such activities as admiring, contemplating, interpreting, sharing, and so on) as an instance of the beautiful. Such an approach is most useful if we think of the "beautiful" less as what is subjectively pleasing than as what we regard as aesthetically valuable, with "appreciation" being the activity that specializes in the recognition of aesthetic merit. At this point, the "formal" plane of virtue theory starts to assume its pre-eminence, as the ability to "appreciate" need not require one to like or enjoy any particular stylistic virtue but only to recognize the virtuousness of its existence as such.

For some scholars, the moral and political consequences of the virtues involved in aesthetic appreciation remain paramount. For example, the philosopher Alison Hills defends the familiar view that "art might be a good training ground for morality" because aesthetic virtues such as "discernment, sensitivity, strength of will, imaginatively exploring alternatives to the most obvious options, are plainly skills that play a role in moral virtue too."[23] For Elaine Hadley, virtues such as impersonality or disinterestedness are driven by a "political liberalism that posits liberal subjects living liberalized lives,"[24] a view that David Wayne Thomas associates with "liberal agency . . . as a form of life that engages meaningfully with the idea of plural forms of life."[25] As we have seen, virtue theory does not prescribe a constant set of stylistic values (such as "order" or "harmony") but rather establishes the procedures for debating stylistic merit, and there may be non-aesthetic advantages to participating in these debates. It is, for example, quite possible that the kind of virtue aesthetics I am advocating here, and which Wilde also advocated – an aesthetics of appreciation predicated on tolerance, understanding, and the commitment to pluralism known as "many-sidedness" – is fundamentally liberal in character, particularly when one attends to the emphasis on freedom found in so much of this critical heritage.[26] But whether the virtues exercised in acts of appreciation are good for social or political life is only contingently related to the question of whether they enhance our experience of art. From this point of view, the critical cosmopolitanism of someone like Wilde is salutary not because it supports or reflects an underlying political project but because it makes possible and enhances the range of aesthetic experiences to which it is sensitive. The moral and political dimensions of this commitment are not to be dismissed or underestimated, but neither do they underwrite its legitimacy as an interpretive practice.

If styles represent aesthetic ethos as character, and the contemplation of aesthetic character is an ethical good in the widest sense, then critical appreciation is a virtue when it expands the repertoire of styles that we can understand and enjoy. Yet it remains worth emphasizing how much the stylistic realization of character is marked by the ontological *difference* between works of art as pseudo-statements, whose impact upon actual states of affairs is indirect and diffuse, and the beliefs and propositions of ordinary morality, which, as Richards suggested, enjoy far fewer degrees of freedom than acts of literary imagination. A vicious moral character may have no redeeming virtues, but a thoroughly vicious style, as in parody or burlesque, may very well make a merit of its viciousness. Or, as de Quincey put it (on Aristotle's authority, no less), even murder may become admirable when considered as a fine art.[27] Hence, we do not judge Thackeray's grace, Trollope's ease and lucidity, and Meredith's fervidness as *beautiful* because they reflect the virtuous character of their authors or the righteousness of their subject matter or because they impel us to moral action. Rather, I argue that we should judge them as *virtuous* because they realize an aesthetic function that is "excellent" (i.e. worthy, pleasing, beautiful, characteristic, valuable, accomplished) in itself. Virtue theory warrants our attention today, then, not simply because it helps us understand the technical meanings that govern a critical lexicon dismissed by many as obsolete, but because it provides this meta-critical account of aesthetic experience, autonomy, and judgment, revealing how the history of style, as a formal value no less than a moral one, is also a history of ourselves.

Notes

Introduction: What Is Stylistic Virtue?

1. John Dennis, "Style in Literature," *Time* 13.7 (July 1885), 75.
2. "Stylistic impressionism" was a frequent target of the linguistically oriented prose criticism that rose to prominence in the 1950s and 60s. For example, Richard Ohmann sought to "save[] the study of style from having to rely *only* on those impressionistic, metaphorical judgments which have too often substituted for analysis: dignified, grand, plain, decorative, placid, exuberant, restrained, hard, and the whole tired assortment of epithets which name without explaining." Richard Ohmann, "Prolegomena to the Analysis of Prose Style," in *Style in Prose Fiction*, ed. Harold C. Martin (New York: Columbia University Press, 1958), 14. Ohmann and others acknowledged that stylistic "impressions" could be substantiated through verbal evidence, but worried that they encoded parochial non-literary judgments. See, for example, Louis T. Milic, "Stylistics," in *Encyclopedia of Rhetoric and Composition: Communication from Ancient Times to the Information Age*, ed. Theresa Enos (New York: Routledge, 1996), 703.
3. John Guillory, "Mercury's Words: The End of Rhetoric and the Beginning of Prose," *Representations* 138.1 (Spring 2017), 62.
4. For more on the poly-functionality of figurative language across a wide range of human purposes, see Raymond W. Gibbs, Jr., *The Poetics of Mind: Figurative Thought, Language, and Understanding* (Cambridge: Cambridge University Press, 1994). For accessible examinations of metaphor in relation to musical meaning, see Frank Sibley, "Making Music Our Own," in *The Interpretation of Music: Philosophical Essays*, ed. Michael Krausz (Oxford: Oxford University Press, 1993), 165–76; Stephen Davies, *Musical Meaning and Expression* (Ithaca: Cornell University Press, 1994), chap. 3; and Leo Treitler, "Language and the Interpretation of Music," in *Music and Meaning*, ed. Jenefer Robinson (Ithaca: Cornell University Press, 1997), 23–56.
5. George Brimley, "Thackeray's Esmond," *Spectator* 25 (6 Nov. 1852), 1067.
6. Hugh Blair, *Lectures on Rhetoric and Belles Lettres*, 2 vols. (London: Strachan, Cadell, and Creech, 1783), I:476.

7. Many stylistic virtue terms are gendered, doubtlessly owing to the classical context in which they arose. Consequently, stylistic terms such as "masculine" and "muscular" have received considerable attention for their role in shaping concepts of gender and sexuality. My interest in how these terms were applied to literary technique does not undermine this research, but rather draws attention to a neglected dimension of their meaning. For more on "manliness" as a social and institutional ethos in the nineteenth century, see Stefan Collini, *Public Moralists: Political Thought and Intellectual Life in Britain 1850–1930* (Oxford: Clarendon Press, 1991), chap. 5; for its manifestations in literary form, see Herbert Sussman, *Victorian Masculinities: Manhood and Masculine Poetics in Early Victorian Literature and Art* (Cambridge: Cambridge University Press, 1995); for the relationship between gender, *virtus*, and homosexual communities, see Linda Dowling, *Hellenism and Homosexuality in Victorian Oxford* (Ithaca: Cornell University Press, 1994), 1–31; for masculinity and manliness as social performance, see James Eli Adams, *Dandies and Desert Saints* (Ithaca: Cornell University Press, 1995), 1–19; for "muscularity" as a physical, political, and spiritual ideal, see essays in Donald E. Hall, ed., *Muscular Christianity: Embodying the Victorian Age* (Cambridge: Cambridge University Press, 1994); for masculinity as a sexually valorized term in relation to "effeminacy," particularly with respect to the fleshly controversy, see Thaïs Morgan, "Reimagining Masculinity in Victorian Criticism: Swinburne and Pater," *Victorian Studies* 36.3 (Spring 1993), 315–32, and "Victorian Effeminacies," in *Victorian Sexual Dissidence*, ed. Richard Dellamora (Chicago: University of Chicago Press, 1999), 109–26. The literature on classical manliness is voluminous. For a succinct overview of the relationship between rhetorical terms and gender, see Joy Connolly, "Virile Tongues: Rhetoric and Masculinity," in *A Companion to Roman Rhetoric*, ed. William Dominik and John Hall (London: Blackwell, 2007), 83–97.
8. John Morley, "Mr. Swinburne's New Poems," *Saturday Review* (4 Aug. 1866), 145.
9. Algernon Charles Swinburne, *Swinburne Replies*, ed. Clyde Kenneth Hyder (Syracuse: Syracuse University Press, 1966), 28.
10. Quintilian, *Institutio Oratoria*, trans. David A. Russell (Cambridge: Harvard University Press, 2001), 8.3.6.
11. Quintilian in full: "However (let me say this again) this Ornament must be manly, strong, and chaste. It must not favour effeminate smoothness or the false colouring of cosmetics; it must shine with health and vigour. And this is so true that, since vices and virtues in this area are particularly close neighbours, those who adopt the vices actually give them the names of the virtues" (8.3.6–7). Swinburne may also have had in mind Quintilian's use of

sanctus to describe the Doryphoros (5.12.20), widely admired in the ancient world as a sculptural paragon of manliness (another irony, given the double-sexed nature of the statue in "Hermaphroditus").

12. As shall become clear, my use of the word "autonomous" differs from one that imagines the work of art as discontinuous with politics or society (that is, as a fundamentally de-contextualized event). Instead, the word points to a conception of style that is not reducible to something outside itself.
13. The *locus classicus* of critical efforts to account for the rhetorical (or non-mimetic) aspects of realist prose remains Wayne C. Booth, *The Rhetoric of Fiction* (Chicago: University of Chicago Press, 1961). More recently, Anna Kornbluh has sought to re-conceptualize non-mimesis in spatial rather than rhetorical terms; see Anna Kornbluh, *The Order of Forms: Realism, Formalism, and Social Space* (Chicago: University of Chicago Press, 2019). For a fuller discussion of Aristotle's distinction between poetry and rhetoric as a function of mimesis, see Wilbur Samuel Howell, "Aristotle and Horace on Rhetoric and Poetics," in *Poetics, Rhetoric, and Logic: Studies in the Basic Disciplines of Criticism* (Ithaca: Cornell University Press, 1975), 49–62. Most surveys of "English" as a discipline locate the origins of formalism (European or Anglo-American) in the early twentieth century. See, for example, Terry Eagleton, *Literary Theory: An Introduction* (Oxford: Basil Blackwell, 1983), introduction and chap. 1 and Joseph North, *Literary Criticism: A Concise Political History* (Cambridge: Harvard University Press, 2017), who traces the modern origins of formalist reading practices to I.A. Richards.
14. For a succinct overview of the twentieth-century tradition that opposes "aesthetic" criticism to "historical" scholarship and contextualism (identified with disinterestedness and instrumentalism, respectively), see North, *Literary Criticism*. North's rejection of this opposition is timely, as is Rita Felski's, in *The Limits of Critique* (Chicago: University of Chicago Press, 2017). For a further discussion of disinterestedness as an ethical and aesthetic concept, see Chapter 3.
15. Caroline Levine, *The Serious Pleasures of Suspense: Victorian Realism and Narrative Doubt* (Charlottesville: University of Virginia Press, 2003), 12.
16. The Greek word *arete* (ἀρετή) presents a challenge to translators: in literary contexts, such as Aristotle's *Rhetoric* and *Poetics*, it may be variously translated as "virtue," "excellence," "strength," "merit," or even the more neutral "quality," because the ancient idea of *arete* was wide enough to encompass each of these ideas. In most cases the translation is arbitrary: for example, where the Penguin translation of the *Rhetoric* uses "virtue" (at 1404b), the 1926 edition of the Loeb Classical Library prefers "merit"; conversely, where the Penguin translation of the *Poetics* (in which Aristotle discusses stylistic *arete* at 1458a) employs "quality," the Loeb translation says "excellence." See *Art of Rhetoric*,

trans. H.C. Lawson-Tancred (London: Penguin, 1991); *Art of Rhetoric*, trans. J. H. Freese (Cambridge: Harvard University Press, 1926); *Poetics*, trans. Malcolm Heath (London: Penguin, 1996); *Poetics*, trans. Stephen Halliwell (Cambridge: Harvard University Press, 1995). Nonetheless, it became customary to designate admirable qualities of style as "virtues," in part because of Quintilian's extensive use of that term (Latin *virtutes*) with respect to stylistic properties in Book 8 of the *Institutio Oratoria*. In the context of Aristotelian ethics, the word "*arete*" is typically translated as "virtue," though "excellence" is also used; see, for example, *Nicomachean Ethics*, trans. David Ross, rev. ed. (Oxford: Oxford University Press, 1998). Unless otherwise specified, in-text references are to the Penguin editions of Aristotle's works.

17. In medieval contexts, the word "virtue" subsequently became synonymous with "power," from which we derive the common idiom "in virtue of." See "virtue, n.," *OED Online*, June 2020, Oxford University Press, www.oed.com /view/Entry/223835.
18. Brad Inwood, *Ethics after Aristotle* (Cambridge: Harvard University Press, 2014), 7.
19. For the centrality of Aristotle in the classical stylistic tradition and his influence, see Laurent Pernot, *Rhetoric in Antiquity*, trans. W.E. Higgins (Washington, DC: Catholic University of America Press, 2005), 41–44 and 58–63. Modern scholars often prefer less characterological translations of Aristotle's virtues ("appropriateness" for propriety, "correctness" for purity, and "ornament" for beauty), in order, one presumes, to minimize their moralistic connotations.
20. Thomas Hurka, "The Three Faces of Flourishing," *Social Philosophy and Policy* 16.1 (Winter 1999), 44.
21. Aristotle, *Ethics*, trans. Ross, 1742 n. 7.
22. Throughout this book, I italicize *ethos* only when indicating the rhetorical appeal to character.
23. For more on the relationship between virtue and eloquence in Quintilian, see Prentice A. Meador, Jr., "Quintilian's 'Vir Bonus'," *Western Speech* 34.3 (1970): 162–69 and Alan Brinton, "Quintilian, Plato, and the Vir Bonus," *Philosophy and Rhetoric* 16.3 (1983): 167–84.
24. Seneca the Younger, "Styles and Morals," in *Ancient Literary Criticism: The Principal Texts in New Translations*, ed. D.A. Russell and M. Winterbottom (Oxford: Clarendon Press, 1983), 363.
25. For a classic mid-twentieth-century account of the romantic-expressivist theory of style in its reductionist form, see F.L. Lucas, who argues that style "is personality clothed in words, character embodied in speech ... The fundamental thing, therefore, is *not* technique." F.L. Lucas, *Style* (London: Cassell and Company, 1955), 49. Interestingly, this referential conception of

style persisted even as intentionalist modes of criticism fell out of fashion, not least because style can still reduce to the ethos of the "dramatic *speaker*" or the "implied author" or an author's "hypothetical" intention. See, respectively, W.K. Wimsatt and M.C. Beardsley, "The Intentional Fallacy," *The Sewanee Review* 54.3 (July–Sep. 1946), 470 (original emphasis); Booth, *Rhetoric of Fiction*, 71–76; and Stephen Davies, "Authors' Intentions, Literary Interpretation, and Literary Value," *British Journal of Aesthetics* 46.3 (July 2006), 238.

26. Demetrius, *Demetrius on Style*, trans. W. Rhys Roberts (Cambridge: Cambridge University Press, 1902).
27. Scholars of classical rhetoric sometimes distinguish between stylistic "virtues," "genres," "levels," "qualities," and "types," all of which share overlapping features. In general, "virtues" refer to the particular stylistic features that, taken together, characterize a "genre" or "level," but such definitional niceties tend to be more obfuscating than helpful and have not been systematically used by either classical or modern writers.
28. Hermogenes, *Hermogenes' On Types of Style*, trans. Cecil W. Wooten (Chapel Hill: University of North Carolina Press, 1987), 6.
29. Annabel M. Patterson, *Hermogenes and the Renaissance: Seven Ideas of Style* (Princeton: Princeton University Press, 1970), 36.
30. Patterson, *Hermogenes*, 36.
31. Samuel Johnson, *Lives of the Poets*, ed. Roger Lonsdale, vol. 1 (Oxford: Clarendon Press, 2006), 230. Johnson paraphrases Quintilian, *Institutio Oratorio*, 8.Pr.20 as well as Pope's *An Essay on Criticism*, ll. 318–19 ("Expression is the *Dress* of *Thought*, and still/Appears more *decent* as more *suitable*"). Alexander Pope, *The Poetry and Prose of Alexander Pope*, ed. Aubrey Williams (London: Houghton Mifflin, 1969), 46.
32. Quoted in George A. Kennedy, "The Contributions of Rhetoric to Literary Criticism," in *The Cambridge History of Literary Criticism*, ed. H.B. Nisbet and Claude Rawson, vol. 4 (Cambridge: Cambridge University Press, 1997), 353. Guillory cites George Puttenham's *The Art of English Poesy* (1589) to provide an even earlier example of how the "concept of style slides from the *techne* of rhetoric to a more nebulous realm of psychology," to wit: "This continual course and manner of writing or speech showeth the matter and disposition of the writer's mind more than one or few words or sentences can show." Quoted in John Guillory, "Mercury's Words," 77.
33. Archibald Alison, *Essays on the Nature and Principles of Taste*, 2nd ed. (Hartford: George Goodwin, 1821), 443.
34. Adam Smith, *Lectures on Rhetoric and Belles Lettres*, The Glasgow Edition of the Works and Correspondence of Adam Smith, ed. J.C. Bryce, vol. 4 (Oxford: Oxford University Press, 1983), 35.

35. Thomas Carlyle, *Sartor Resartus*, ed. Kerry McSweeney and Peter Sabor (Oxford: Oxford University Press, 1987), 57.
36. Georges-Louis Leclerc Buffon, "Discourse on Style," in *Theories of Style in Literature*, ed. Lane Cooper (New York: Macmillan, 1923), 178. "[L]e style est l'homme même." Lane Cooper's translation was first published in 1907 and remains the most common source for English readers in the twentieth century. However, Buffon's maxim (variously translated) was well-known to Victorian audiences by at least the mid-nineteenth century, a by-product of Buffon's enormous intellectual authority during the period. For example, in 1851, a reviewer for *The British Quarterly Review* invokes Buffon's idea before attributing it: "The *art* of the style belongs less to the writer; the *genius* of the style is the man himself . . . an imitator will never have a style because, to use Buffon's own words, 'the style is the man'." "Buffon: His Life and Writings," *The British Quarterly Review* 13.25 (Feb. 1851), 152. In 1869, an essayist in *Saint Paul's*, referring to Buffon's "famous essay on style," offers a subtle variation: "the style is the author himself." James Leakey, "The Count de Buffon," *Saint Paul's* 5 (Oct. 1869), 87.
37. W.C. Brownell, *The Genius of Style* (London and New York: Scribner's, 1924), 43.
38. I discuss belletrism's influence on the Victorian period, and its relation to other strands of the "new rhetoric," more fully in Chapter 2. For useful background, see James L. Golden and Edward P.J. Corbett, introduction to *The Rhetoric of Blair, Campbell, and Whately* (New York: Holt, Rinehart and Winston, 1968), 1–22; James L. Golden et al., *The Rhetoric of Western Thought*, 8th ed. (USA: Kendall/Hunt, 2004), chap. 6–9; and Wilbur Samuel Howell, *Eighteenth-Century British Logic and Rhetoric* (Bristol: Thoemmes Press, 1999), chap. 6.
39. Matthew Arnold, "Marcus Aurelius," in *The Complete Prose Works of Matthew Arnold*, ed. R.H. Super, vol. 3 (Ann Arbor: University of Michigan Press, 1962), 139.
40. Although a topic of great interest to ancient and Renaissance philosophers, the study of style, once one of the five canons of Roman rhetoric (known as *elocutio*), had fallen into disrepute by the early eighteenth century. Under the influence of Peter Ramus, "dialectic" (which involves reason and argument) took precedence over "rhetoric" (which came to mean verbal tricks and extrinsic devices), a trend buttressed by the Royal Society's demand for clarity and simplicity in every kind of prose. For the Ramist background in England, see Wilbur Samuel Howell, *Logic and Rhetoric in England, 1500–1700* (Bristol: Thoemmes Press, 1999), chap. 4. For the rise of "plain" style in English, see classic accounts by Morris Croll, "Attic Prose," in *Style, Rhetoric, and Rhythm* (Princeton: Princeton University Press, 1966), George Williamson, *The Senecan*

Amble: A Study in Prose Form from Bacon to Collier (London: Faber and Faber, 1951), especially chap. 6–7 and 9–11, and Richard Foster Jones, "Science and English Prose Style in the Third Quarter of the Seventeenth Century," in *Seventeenth-Century Prose: Modern Essays in Criticism*, ed. Stanley E. Fish (New York: Oxford University Press, 1971), 53–89.

41. Gerald Graff describes the importance of this perspective to philology, which he associates with the rise of academic English. See Gerald Graff, *Professing Literature: An Institutional History*, 20th anniversary ed. (Chicago: University of Chicago Press, 2007), chap. 5. My own emphasis on style and rhetoric offers a contrasting (though complementary) account.
42. Tzvetan Todorov, "Structural Analysis of Narrative," *NOVEL: A Forum on Fiction* 3.1 (Autumn 1969), 72.
43. My use of the word "ethical" here is related to the projected science of human behavior, or "ethology," once entertained by J.S. Mill, insofar as both reflect the Victorian desire to establish "character" as a unifying explanatory paradigm, though on rather different grounds. For Mill's discussion of ethology, see *System of Logic: Ratiocinative and Inductive: Being a Connected View of the Principles of Evidence and the Methods of Scientific Investigation*, 8th ed., vol. 2 (London: Longmans, Green, Reader, and Dyer, 1872), bk. 6, chap. 5. For the relation of ethology to character, see Terence Ball, "The Formation of Character: Mill's 'Ethology' Reconsidered," *Polity* 33.1 (Fall 2000): 25–48. For more on the scope of "character" as a capacious Victorian signifier, see Jonathan Farina, *Everyday Words and the Character of Prose in Nineteenth-Century Britain* (Cambridge: Cambridge University Press, 2017).
44. William Archer, "Robert Louis Stevenson: His Style and His Thought," *Time* 13.11 (Nov. 1885), 581.
45. Collini, *Public Moralists: Political Thought and Intellectual Life in Britain 1850–1930* (Oxford: Clarendon Press, 1991), 100.
46. Classic accounts of Victorian literary moralism include Richard Stang, *The Theory of the Novel in England, 1850–1870* (London: Routledge and Kegan Paul, 1959), chap. 2 and David J. Skilton, *Anthony Trollope and His Contemporaries: A Study in the Theory and Conventions of Mid-Victorian Fiction* (London: Macmillan, 1972).
47. Rohan Maitzen was among the first to notice that "because we have taken Victorian critical moralizing for granted, we have not bothered to look closely at it, to find out how Victorian critics actually went about assessing the moral qualities of novels." She argues that debates about literary morality centered around a novelist's "treatment" rather than "subject." Rohan Maitzen, "'The Soul of Art': Understanding Victorian Ethical Criticism," *English Studies in Canada* 31.2–3 (2005), 154, 158–61. Jesse Rosenthal describes how moral intuitionism provided critics with forms of literary experience and

interpretation "shaped by moral concerns and yet somehow understood to be morally neutral." Jesse Rosenthal, *Good Form: The Ethical Experience of the Victorian Novel* (Princeton: Princeton University Press, 2017), 5. Sarah Allison argues that Victorian reviewers examined "fictional texts as persuasive arguments" both "through – or despite – its style," and sees style itself as a "proxy" for moral practices. Sarah Allison, *Reductive Reading: A Syntax of Victorian Moralizing* (Baltimore: Johns Hopkins University Press, 2018), 40, 15.

48. Walter Pater, *The Renaissance: Studies in Art and Poetry*, ed. Adam Phillips (Oxford: Oxford University Press, 1986), 153.
49. Oscar Wilde, *The Picture of Dorian Gray*, ed. Robert Mighall (London: Penguin, 2003), 3.
50. Walter Pater, *Appreciations, with an Essay on Style* (Evanston: Northwestern University Press, 1987), 36.
51. Oscar Wilde, *Intentions* (London: James R. Osgood, McIlvaine, and Co., 1891), 201.
52. Critics whose work engages with Victorian virtue ethics typically neglect its Aristotelian lineage. See, for example, Collini, *Public Moralists*, chap. 3; Amanda Anderson, *The Powers of Distance: Cosmopolitanism and the Cultivation of Detachment* (Princeton: Princeton University Press, 2001), chap. 1; and fleeting references to Aristotle in Andrew H. Miller, *The Burdens of Perfection: On Ethics and Reading in Nineteenth-Century British Literature* (Ithaca: Cornell University Press, 2008), 25, 55. I present detailed evidence for Aristotle's influence in Chapters 2 and 3.
53. Martha Nussbaum, *Love's Knowledge: Essays on Philosophy and Literature* (Oxford: Oxford University Press, 1990).
54. Joshua Landy, *How to Do Things with Fictions* (Oxford: Oxford University Press, 2012), 19.
55. Miller, *Burdens of Perfection*, 6.
56. Wayne C. Booth, *The Company We Keep: An Ethics of Fiction* (Berkeley: University of California Press, 1998), 10.
57. Landy, *How to Do Things*, 10.
58. See James O. Pawelski and D.J. Moores, eds., *The Eudaimonic Turn: Well-Being in Literary Studies* (Madison: Fairleigh Dickinson University Press, 2013): "Scholars across a large number of disciplines are increasingly focusing their attention on the immediate constituents of well-being, attempting to identify and investigate those aspects of the human condition widely accepted to be at the center of human flourishing" (3). Pawelski and Moores add that the eudaimonic turn is "not driven by particular ideological agendas" (26) other than to "return to the central questions of Greek ethics: How ought I to live? What should my life be like?" (17).

59. Booth, *Company*, chap. 9. Sarah Allison, who uses the term "reductive" in a somewhat different manner, could not be accused of neglecting style's "mode of signification" insofar as she pays minute attention to the meaning-making properties of syntax. But, like Booth, her ethical goal is ultimately consequentialist rather than self-reflexively aesthetic: "My contribution, finally, to a new ethics of syntax is an emphasis on the mental attitudes that the writer forces on the reader: the way that reading novels might, through recurrent patterns of language, provide formulas for perceiving, even judging, others" (*Reductive Reading*, 133).
60. Anderson, *Powers of Distance*, 6. In a subsequent work, Anderson uses the term "ethos" to refer to "thicker characterological conceptions of theoretical stances" that inform general ways of thinking and being. Amanda Anderson, *The Way We Argue Now: A Study in the Cultures of Theory* (Princeton: Princeton University Press, 2006), 3. Much of the material that Anderson drew on from Daston and Galison was subsequently collected in Daston and Galison, *Objectivity* (New York: Zone, 2007).
61. Matthew Bevis, *The Art of Eloquence: Byron, Dickens, Tennyson, Joyce* (Oxford: Oxford University Press, 2007), 8.
62. Elaine Hadley, *Living Liberalism: Practical Citizenship in Mid-Victorian Britain* (Chicago: University of Chicago Press, 2010), 9. Hadley continues: "mid-Victorian political liberalism outlines *how* one ought to think but not precisely *what* to think about" (10).
63. Christine Korsgaard, *Self-Constitution: Agency, Identity, Integrity* (New York: Oxford University Press, 2009), 47.
64. David Russell, *Tact: Aesthetic Liberalism and the Essay Form in Nineteenth-Century Britain* (Princeton: Princeton University Press, 2017), 41, 6. Critics in this tradition include Lauren Goodlad, *Victorian Liberalism and the Victorian State: Character and Governance in Liberal Society* (Baltimore: Johns Hopkins University Press, 2003); David Wayne Thomas, *Cultivating Victorians: Liberal Culture and the Aesthetic* (Philadelphia: University of Pennsylvania Press, 2004); Hadley, *Living Liberalism*; and Amanda Anderson, *The Powers of Distance* and *Bleak Liberalism* (Chicago: University of Chicago Press, 2016).
65. Farina, *Everyday Words*, xvi.
66. Russell, *Tact*, 6.
67. The distinction between substantive and formal morality maps helpfully onto the difference between what are sometimes called "substantive" and "proceduralist" approaches in political theory. As a general rule, substantive political views specify the goods that political procedures ought to attain, while procedural views specify only what decision-making protocols ought to be followed. Hence, as Amy Gutmann and Dennis Thompson note, "many procedural theories of democracy usually present themselves as second-order

theories, because they purport to be neutral among competing substantive theories." However, they add that all procedural theories contain implicit substantive principles concerning a vision of the good life. In the same way, the virtue theory of style I advocate here does not specify the pursuit of any one particular virtue, but it does maintain the normative value of style *as* virtuous. Amy Gutmann and Dennis Thompson, "Why Deliberative Democracy Is Different," in *Liberalism: Critical Concepts in Political Theory*, ed. G.W. Smith, vol. 4: The Limits of Liberalism (London: Routledge, 2002), 275.

68. Jenefer M. Robinson, "Style and Personality in the Literary Work," *The Philosophical Review* 94.2 (Apr. 1985), 228. In general, aesthetic philosophers and literary critics use the words "character" and "personality" interchangeably, as I shall do, though Peter Goldie seeks a sharper distinction, using "character" to refer to durable habits and dispositions and "personality" to more fleeting preferences and behaviors. See Peter Goldie, *On Personality* (London: Routledge, 2004).
69. Robinson, "Style and Personality," 231–34.
70. Robinson, "Style and Personality," 244. Here, we recall Wolfgang Iser's axiom that the reader will always "strive, even if unconsciously, to fit everything together in a consistent pattern," dismissing what "cannot be immediately integrated or will resist final integration." Wolfgang Iser, "The Reading Process: A Phenomenological Approach," *New Literary History* 3.2 (Winter 1972), 288, 290.
71. Nick Riggle, "Personal Style and Artistic Style," *The Philosophical Quarterly* 65.261 (Oct. 2015), 728.
72. Northrop Frye, *Anatomy of Criticism* (Princeton: Princeton University Press, 1957), 268.
73. Frye, *Anatomy*, 268.
74. Frye, *Anatomy*, 268.
75. George Levine and William Madden, eds., *The Art of Victorian Prose* (New York: Oxford University Press, 1968) and Michael D. Hurley and Marcus Waithe, eds., *Thinking through Style: Non-Fiction Prose of the Long Nineteenth Century* (Oxford: Oxford University Press, 2018).
76. Hurley and Waithe, *Thinking through Style*, 1.
77. Frye, *Anatomy*, 73–74.
78. Frye, *Anatomy*, 268.
79. Frye, *Anatomy*, 131.
80. Viktor Shklovsky, "Art as Technique," in *Critical Theory Since Plato*, ed. Hazard Adams, rev. ed. (Fort Worth: Harcourt Brace, 1992), 758–59.
81. John Crowe Ransom, "Criticism, Inc.," *The Virginia Quarterly Review* 13.4 (Autumn 1937), 602. The use of "prose" as an enemy term was partly rhetorical: Shklovsky finds many examples of defamiliarization in Tolstoy

and Ransom ends his essay by speculating that "similar considerations hold, I think, for the critique of fiction" (602). However, as Ransom admitted nearly fifteen years later, "poems have monopolized the attention of critics" and "some of them have now taken the matter under advisement" by seeking to determine "to what extent can the understanding of poetry be applied to the understanding of fiction." John Crowe Ransom, "The Understanding of Fiction," *The Kenyon Review* 12.2 (Spring 1950), 193. Incidentally, Philip Rahv decried what he called "this recent infection of the prose-sense by poetics" and rejected Ransom's desire to claim "style" (in the classical rhetorical sense) as the "essential activity" (Ransom, "Understanding," 197) of prose, a dismissal with lasting consequences. Philip Rahv, "Fiction and the Criticism of Fiction," *The Kenyon Review* 18.2 (Spring 1956), 280.

82. In structuralist poetics, style plays an important but generic role, serving to distinguish literary from non-literary uses of language. It ultimately proved less useful as a term of art for fiction than more specific concepts such as *suyzhet* (Shklovsky), foregrounding (Jakobson), or morphology (Propp), and in *S/Z* (1970), Roland Barthes failed to include style among the five major signifying codes of the novel. The dissemination of the work of Mikhail Bakhtin in the 1980s challenged this orthodoxy, though it did not return style to a central place in criticism; see Gary Saul Morson and Caryl Emerson, *Mikhail Bakhtin: Creation of a Prosaics* (Stanford: Stanford University Press, 1990).

83. For a concise overview of stylistics at the crest of its development, see Graham Hough, *Style and Stylistics* (London: Routledge and Kegan Paul, 1969). For a contemporary perspective, see Michael Burke, ed., *The Routledge Handbook of Stylistics* (London: Routledge, 2014); Peter Stockwell and Sara Whiteley, eds., *The Cambridge Handbook of Stylistics* (Cambridge: Cambridge University Press, 2014); and Michael Toolan, "Stylistics," in *A Companion to Literary Theory*, ed. David H. Richter (West Sussex: John Wiley and Sons, 2018), 60–71.

84. Stanley Fish, *Is There a Text in This Class? The Authority of Interpretive Communities* (Cambridge: Harvard University Press, 1980), 267.

85. David Lodge, *Language of Fiction: Essays in Criticism and Verbal Analysis of the English Novel* (London: Routledge and Kegan Paul, 1966), 51.

86. Michael Burke, "Stylistics: From Classical Rhetoric to Cognitive Neuroscience," in *The Routledge Handbook of Stylistics*, ed. Michael Burke (London: Routledge, 2014), 5.

87. Burke, in "Stylistics," describes the literary-critical dimensions of contemporary stylistics while also emphasizing its differences, noting that it has its own modes of analysis ("writing a stylistics paper can be a fraught and sometimes daunting endeavour," 3), institutional settings ("stylistics also has its own home, though, and that is the 'International Poetics and Linguistics Association,'" 7), and

interdisciplinary affiliations ("it is a welcome guest in many intellectual homes in many locations across disciplines such as communication studies, rhetoric, pragmatics, discourse analysis, applied linguistics, literary studies, film, television and theatre studies, museum studies and so on," 7). In a useful review essay, Sandrine Sorlin discusses the sometimes antagonistic position of stylistics vis-à-vis literary studies as evinced in the three major handbooks on stylistics that were published between 2014 and 2016. Sandrine Sorlin, "Three Major Handbooks in Three Years: Stylistics as a Mature Discipline," *Language and Literature* 25.3 (Aug. 2016), 293–99. Michael Toolan describes the more nuanced role played by objectivity and falsifiability in contemporary stylistics in "The Theory and Philosophy of Stylistics," in *The Cambridge Handbook of Stylistics*, ed. Stockwell and Whiteley, 28–31.

88. As Robert Adolph observed in 1981, "quantitative stylistics" – the form of literary linguistics then prevalent, and that remains popular today – only reveals one aspect of style, namely "its linguistic aspect," without taking into account the way those properties are "apprehended by *readers*." Adolph anticipates my own approach in claiming that because "style is more than the sum of its quantified linguistic parts, then it is the very bagginess of words like 'plain,' referring both to 'linguistic facts' and the extra-linguistic contexts of style, that make them useful." Robert Adolph, "On the Possibility of a History of Prose Style," *Style* 15.4 (Fall 1981), 437–38, 442.
89. For more on the relationship between facts and interpretations in stylistic analysis, see Jenefer M. Robinson, "Style and Significance in Art History and Art Criticism," *The Journal of Aesthetics and Art Criticism* 40.1 (Fall 1981): "it is impossible to figure out the style of a painting unless we know that it has aesthetic significance and what that significance is" (10).
90. Nicholas Dames, *The Physiology of the Novel: Reading, Neural Science, and the Form of Victorian Fiction* (Oxford: Oxford University Press, 2007), 21.
91. Benjamin Morgan, *The Outward Mind: Materialist Aesthetics in Victorian Science and Literature* (Chicago: University of Chicago Press, 2017) and Daniel Wright, *Bad Logic: Reasoning about Desire in the Victorian Novel* (Baltimore: Johns Hopkins University Press, 2018).
92. The dispute between Morris Croll and Ernest Foster Jones (now almost a hundred years old) over the nature of the seventeenth-century sentence spawned a flurry of work on early modern forms, but the terms of this debate – Ciceronian, Senecan, curt, loose, and *coupé* – are rarely applied beyond the seventeenth century. The fact that belletrists often regarded Addison's writing as a crystallization of the modern prose ideal may have reinforced the notion that the history of prose style had effectively terminated by 1800. For the Croll-Jones debate, see the essays collected in *Seventeenth Century Prose*, ed. Stanley Fish (New York: Oxford University Press, 1971).

For more on the scholarly neglect of prose history, see Adolph, "On the Possibility," and Beatrix Busse, "(New) Historical Stylistics," in *The Routledge Handbook of Stylistics*, 101–17. For an excellent examination of the relationship between formalism and historicism, and of the need for a new synthesis, see Frederic V. Bogel, *New Formalist Criticism: Theory and Practice* (Basingstoke: Palgrave, 2013), introduction and chap. 2.

93. James Sutherland, *On English Prose* (Toronto: University of Toronto Press, 1957), 84.
94. Milic, "Stylistics," 703.
95. Caroline Levine, *Forms: Whole, Rhythm, Hierarchy, Network* (Princeton: Princeton University Press, 2015), 3.
96. Levine, *Forms*, 18.
97. Carolyn Lesjak has been among the more prominent skeptics of a "new formalism" that, in her view, seeks to restore a discredited notion of textual autonomy frequently attributed to New Criticism. See Carolyn Lesjak, "Reading Dialectically," *Criticism* 55.2 (Spring 2013): 233–77. For an early and influential account of "new formalism," see Marjorie Levinson, "What Is New Formalism?" *PMLA* 122.2 (Mar. 2007): 558–69.

1 Stylistic Virtue and the Rise of Literary Formalism

1. Frederic Harrison, *Studies in Early Victorian Literature* (London, New York: Edward Arnold, 1895), 18.
2. Douglas Patey, "The Institution of Criticism in the Eighteenth Century," in *The Cambridge History of Literary Criticism*, vol. 4, 7.
3. See Hayden White, "The Suppression of Rhetoric in the Nineteenth Century," in *The Rhetoric Canon*, ed. Brenda Deen Schildgen (Detroit: Wayne State University Press, 1997), 21–32.
4. John Addington Symonds, *Essays Speculative and Suggestive*, vol. 1 (London: Chapman and Hall, 1890), 91–92, 90.
5. For more on the socio-cultural value of rhetoric in eighteenth-century Scotland, see Robert Crawford, *Devolving English Literature* (Oxford: Clarendon Press, 1992), especially chap. 1, and Paul G. Bator, "The Formation of the Regius Chair of Rhetoric and Belles Lettres at the University of Edinburgh," *Quarterly Journal of Speech* 75.1 (1989), 41–47.
6. I discuss this tradition more extensively in Chapter 3. For useful background, see Vincent M. Bevilacqua, "Adam Smith and Some Philosophical Origins of Eighteenth-Century Rhetorical Theory," *Modern Language Review* 63.3 (July 1968): 559–68; Patey, "Institutions of Criticism"; Wilbur Samuel Howell, *Eighteenth-Century British Rhetoric and Logic*, chap. 6; and James Engell, *The Creative Imagination* (Cambridge: Harvard University Press, 1981), chap. 6.

7. Howell's *Eighteenth-Century British Rhetoric and Logic* still provides the most detailed discussion of the relationship between rhetoric and logic, as well as other aspects of the eighteenth-century university curriculum. For the relationship between rhetoric and moral philosophy in Scottish universities, see Thomas P. Miller, "The Formation of College English: A Survey of the Archives of Eighteenth-Century Rhetorical Theory and Practice," *Rhetoric Society Quarterly* 20.3 (Summer 1990), 267–70 and Bator, "The Formation," 47–51.
8. Trevor Ross, *The Making of the English Literary Canon: From the Middle Ages to the Late Eighteenth Century* (Montreal: McGill-Queen's University Press, 1998), 21.
9. Patey claims that the phrase "belles lettres" first gained currency in France around the late seventeenth century ("Institutions," 19), while Howell suggests that it entered English through a 1734 translation of lectures by the French academic Charles Rollin (*Eighteenth-Century*, 529–35). Samuel Johnson's dictionary of 1755 defines "belles lettres" as "polite literature," quoting an essay from the *Tatler*. Samuel Johnson, "Belles Lettres, n.s," *A Dictionary of the English Language*, vol. 1 (London: W. Strahan, 1755), 228.
10. Scholars debate whether Smith's lectures offer a genuine theory of rhetoric. Howell, for example, argues that "Smith intended them, not as discourses on ancient and modern literature, but as discourses to expound a system of rhetoric" (*Eighteenth-Century*, 545), while William M. Purcell counters that "to describe the Lectures as Adam Smith's theory of rhetoric is a disservice to a distinguished scholar" because "a rhetorical treatise which is belletristic is different from a belletristic treatise which includes a treatment of rhetoric." William M. Purcell, "Reassessment of Adam Smith's Lectures on Rhetoric and Belles Lettres," *Communication Studies* 37:1 (1986), 52, 46. Given the instability of the concept of "rhetoric" during this period, it seems fruitless to split hairs on the matter; the important point is that Smith, as Golden and Corbett argue, "became the first Englishman to give impetus to the belletristic movement" ("Introduction," 8), using rhetoric to understand literature as a specially identified category within "belles lettres."
11. Howell, citing Wilbur Robert Scott, notes that Smith's *Lectures* were probably not delivered at the university but "at the quarters of the Philosophical Society of Edinburgh" (*Eighteenth-Century*, 543), while Bator notes the phrase "belles lettres" may not have appeared in their original title ("Formation," 55–56). See also Vincent M. Bevilacqua, "Adam Smith's Lectures on Rhetoric and Belles Lettres," *Studies in Scottish Literature* 3.1 (1965): 41–60.
12. Bevilacqua, "Philosophical Origins," 568.
13. See Bator, "Formation," 46–55 for an account of their connection. Notably, both Smith and Blair were appointed to the subcommittee on "Belles Lettres

and Criticism" of the Select Society, an Edinburgh-based gathering of academics, philosophers, and intellectuals.

14. George S. Rousseau, *Nervous Acts: Essays on Literature, Culture, and Sensibility* (Basingstoke: Palgrave Macmillan, 2004), 10.
15. Rousseau, *Nervous Acts*, 42.
16. Rousseau, *Nervous Acts*, 284 n. 41.
17. Blair first published his lectures in two volumes; in the second edition of 1785, he redistributed them over three.
18. The term originates with Samuel Taylor Coleridge; see Engell, *Creative Imagination*, 328.
19. David E. Wellbery, "The Transformation of Rhetoric," in *The Cambridge History of Literary Criticism*, ed. Marshall Brown, vol. 5 (Cambridge: Cambridge University Press, 2000), 189.
20. According to Wellbery, "The idea that art, including literary art, serves no other aim than its own self-presentation is inimical to rhetoric because rhetoric is an instrumental technique of language, its entire design is determined by the perlocutionary, most notably 'persuasion', it seeks to bring about" ("Transformation," 189).
21. James A. Berlin, *Writing Instruction in Nineteenth-Century American Colleges* (Carbondale: Southern Illinois University Press, 1984), 25; Kennedy, "Contributions of Rhetoric," 362.
22. Linda Ferreira-Buckley and S. Michael Hollaran provide an overview of Blair's "immense popularity," arguing that "it was unrivalled by any language text for a full half-century." This influence, moreover, "extended well beyond formal university and school settings." Linda Ferreira-Buckley and S. Michael Halloran, editors' introduction to *Lectures on Rhetoric and Belles Lettres*, by Hugh Blair (Carbondale: Southern Illinois University Press, 2005), xvi, xvii. For a cogent summary of Blair's influence, see also Jack M. Downs, "David Masson, Belles Lettres, and a Victorian Theory of the Novel," *Victorian Literature and Culture* 43.1 (Mar. 2015), 2–3.
23. Kennedy notes that the *Elements* "is primarily a psychological study of the emotions and their expression in all the arts" that "seems deliberately to avoid making any connections with rhetoric as it was understood at the time" ("Contributions of Rhetoric," 362). He suggests that Campbell's debt to Kames is one reason why, in contrast to Blair, Campbell "has rather little to say about literature" (362). However, Bevilacqua stresses Kames's similarities to Blair rather than his differences, noting that they equally regarded belles lettres as "united in the native powers of the mind as those powers are expressed in language" ("Philosophical Origins," 564). Indeed, the assumption that "style is a verbal manifestation of the natural powers of the mind" (561) was shared by all of the new rhetoricians, but nonetheless led to

different conceptions of style's role and significance within both rhetoric and literary criticism.

24. Lord Henry Home Kames, *Elements of Criticism*, ed. Peter Jones, 2 vols. (Indianapolis: Liberty Fund, 2005), I:14.

25. Douglas Ehninger, "Dominant Trends in English Rhetorical Thought, 1750–1800," *Southern Journal of Communication* 18.1 (1952–53): 3–12. In this seminal article, Ehninger distinguished between four "dominant trends" in late-eighteenth-century rhetoric, usefully summarized by Bruce Gronbeck: "a neoclassical rhetoric, grounded in classical ontology and epistemology, with strongly normative features; a belletristic rhetoric, anchored in the nature of language, language use, and genres of discourse, with emphases on creativity (original genius) and critical practice; a psychological-epistemological rhetoric, flowing from the British empiricists and Scottish common-sense epistemologies and featuring speculation on message-mind relationships; and an elocutionary rhetoric, arising from defects in oratorical practices of the time and allied with aural-visual sciences of communication." These trends, though by no means mutually exclusive, can nonetheless be "followed forward to alternative nineteenth-century manifestations." Bruce E. Gronbeck, "Ehninger, Douglas W. (1913–1979)," in *Encyclopedia of Rhetoric and Composition*, 204.

26. Sharon Crowley writes that "the influence of Campbell's *Philosophy of Rhetoric* on subsequent rhetorical theory was enormous. It was cited or quoted in textbook after textbook throughout the nineteenth century up to as late as 1920." Sharon Crowley, *The Methodical Memory: Invention in Current-Traditional Rhetoric* (Carbondale: Southern Illinois University Press, 1990), 175 n. 1; also quoted in Miller, "Formation," 223. Even so, Miller notes that Blair's *Lectures* went through five times as many editions as Campbell's *Philosophy* ("Formation," 227). As Kennedy writes: "The works of Kames and Campbell were widely studied, but by far the most influential late eighteenth-century contributions to rhetorical criticism were the *Lectures on Rhetoric and Belles Lettres* of Hugh Blair" ("Contributions of Rhetoric," 362).

27. George Campbell, *The Philosophy of Rhetoric*, new edition, with the author's last additions and corrections (1808; New York: Harper and Brothers, 1841; reprint, Delmar, NY: Scholars' Facsimiles and Reprints, 1992), 5.

28. For accounts of Whately's influence, which ranks just below that of Blair and Campbell, see Linda Ferreira-Buckley, "Writing Instruction in Eighteenth- and Nineteenth-Century Great Britain: Continuity and Change, Transitions and Shifts," in *A Short History of Writing Instruction: From Ancient Greece to Contemporary America*, ed. James J. Murphy, 3rd ed. (New York: Routledge: 2012), 182–84; Linda Ferreira-Buckley, "Nineteenth-Century Rhetoric," in *Encyclopedia of Rhetoric and Composition*; Berlin, "Writing Instruction,"

29–32; and Robert Connors, *Composition-Rhetoric: Backgrounds, Theory, and Pedagogy* (Pittsburgh: University of Pittsburgh Press, 1997), 219.

29. Richard Whately, *Elements of Rhetoric* (1828; Nashville: Southern Methodist Publishing House, 1861; reprint, Delmar, NY: Scholars' Facsimiles and Reprints, 1996), 21.
30. I.A. Richards, *The Philosophy of Rhetoric* (New York: Oxford University Press, 1936), 5.
31. Richards, *Philosophy of Rhetoric*, 8.
32. William M. Purcell, "Style," in *Encyclopedia of Rhetoric and Composition*, 701.
33. Ferreira-Buckley, "Nineteenth-Century Rhetoric," 468.
34. Alexander Bain, *English Composition and Rhetoric* (1866; New York: D. Appleton and Company, 1871; reprint, Delmar, NY: Scholars' Facsimiles and Reprints, 1996), 4.
35. Franklin E. Court, *Institutionalizing English Literature* (Stanford: Stanford University Press, 1992), 4.
36. Miller, "Formation," 2.
37. Ross, *Making of the English Literary Canon*, 5.
38. Ross, 5.
39. Thomas De Quincey, *Essays on Style, Rhetoric, and Language*, ed. Fred Scott (Boston: Allyn and Bacon, 1893).
40. Recent work on De Quincey – for example, by Craig Smith and Lois Peters Agnew – has noted more continuity than difference with the eighteenth-century rhetorical tradition, marking a shift away from an earlier scholarly narrative (exemplified by John Bender and David E. Wellbery) that regards "romantic rhetoric" as a contradiction in terms. See Craig R. Smith, "Constructing a Neo-Romantic Rhetorical Theory," *Western Journal of Communication* 80.2 (Mar.–Apr. 2016): 220–37; Lois Peters Agnew, *Thomas De Quincey: British Rhetoric's Romantic Turn* (Carbondale: Southern Illinois University Press, 2012); and John E. Bender and David E. Wellbery, "Rhetoricality: On the Modernist Return of Rhetoric," in *The Ends of Rhetoric: History, Theory, Practice*, ed. John Bender and David E. Wellbery (Stanford: Stanford University Press, 1990), 3–39.
41. Patey, "Institutions," 9. Similarly, Engell claims that Kames's comparison of the work of art to "an organic system" in the first pages of the *Elements* represents "a forerunner of the general Romantic ideal of organic unity found in Hazlitt, Coleridge, and so much German thought" (*Creative Imagination*, 72).
42. Patey, "Institutions," 9.
43. Blair defines genius as "that talent or aptitude which we receive from nature, for excelling in any one thing whatever" (I:41). As David Wayne Thomas puts it in his discussion of Mill's *On Liberty*, "here individuality is not an absolute

but a relative quality, with genius being 'more individual' than all the rest" (*Cultivating Victorians*, 29).

44. John Henry Newman, *The Idea of a University* (1852; London: Basil, Montagu, Pickering, 1873), 275.
45. Hayden White, "Suppression of Rhetoric," 22.
46. David Masson, "Notes and Documents: Masson's Inaugural Lecture," ed. James R.M. Irvin and G. Jack Gravlee, *Studies in Scottish Literature* 14.1 (1979), 243–44.
47. Downs notes that the first half of the lectures focus on rhetorical principles and style, the second half on the history of imaginative texts ("David Masson," 16); see also Masson, "Inaugural Lecture," 248 n. 4. Following Joanne Shattock, Sarah Allison notices a distinct shift in the 1860s as the "increasingly professionalized" critic "gradually became an arbiter of taste instead of moral appropriateness" (*Reductive Reading*, 40); another way of understanding this shift is as the assimilation of *elocutio* into all aspects of appreciation and reviewing.
48. Downs, "David Masson," 17.
49. Downs, "David Masson," 7.
50. Downs, "David Masson," 18.
51. *Episodes of Fiction, or Choice Stories from the Great Novelists* (Edinburgh: William P. Nimmo, 1870), vi; also quoted in Downs, "David Masson," 18.
52. Dames, *Physiology of the Novel*, 45.
53. Herbert Spencer, *Philosophy of Style: An Essay*, with notes by the editor (1852; New York: D. Appleton, 1884), 9.
54. Shklovsky, "Art as Technique," 751.
55. Shklovsky, "Art as Technique," 754.
56. Shklovsky, "Art as Technique," 759.
57. For further background, see Travis R. Merritt, "Taste, Opinion, and Theory in the Rise of Victorian Prose Stylism," in *The Art of Victorian Prose*, ed. Levine and Madden, 21–34 and Jason Camlot, *Style and the Nineteenth-Century British Critic: Sincere Mannerisms* (Burlington: Ashgate, 2008), chap. 6–7.
58. In an essay on Aristotle's use of the term *ethos*, S. Michael Halloran helpfully distinguishes between the "technical" study of style, which focuses on mechanics and correctness, and an ethological one that focuses on style as an expression of habitual character to be developed through imitation and practice – a dichotomy that roughly maps onto De Quincey's distinction between "mechanology" and "organology" respectively. It can be difficult to discern which concept Victorian writers have in mind when they address stylistic technique, but for those in the literary-critical tradition (such as Robert Louis Stevenson, in his essay "On Style in Literature: Some Technical Elements"), it is usually the latter. See S. Michael Halloran,

"Aristotle's Concept of Ethos, or if Not His Somebody Else's," *Rhetoric Review* 1.1 (Sept. 1982), 60.

59. T.H. Wright, "Style," *Macmillan's Magazine* 37.217 (Nov. 1877), 78.
60. W.H. Mallock, "Le Style C'est L'Homme," *The New Review* 6.35 (Apr. 1892), 443.
61. In "Concerning Style," for example, Owen Legge decries "the obtrusion of artistic self-consciousness" in the construction of sentences, writing that "the author who labours after elegance as an end . . . will betray the effort, and so fail of success." Alfred Owen Legge, "Concerning Style," *The Manchester Quarterly* 2 (1883), 58.
62. Walter Raleigh, "Style" (London: Edward Arnold, 1897; reprint, New York: Garland Publishing, Inc., 1986), 126.
63. In his history of *Philology*, James Turner calls rhetoric a "cousin" (xiv) or "partner" (xv) of philology but also emphasizes their differences. With respect to the development of literary studies in the nineteenth century, Turner writes that "philological ingredients came from both textual philology and comparative grammar," which "bestowed the elements of scholarly editing and literary history" and "a parallel study of the English language and its historical evolution" (254). Rhetoric, on the other hand, "contributed to literary study much of its critical vocabulary as well as the germ of the idea of 'criticism' in the modern literary sense (as distinct from its original meaning, the learned emendation of texts)" (254). Although Graff has demonstrated the influence of philology in establishing evaluative standards for academic critics (*Professing Literature*, chap. 5), rhetoric, as Turner suggests, was a far richer source for concepts and methods (though Earle's work demonstrates how both approaches could be used in tandem). See James Turner, *Philology: The Forgotten Origins of the Modern Humanities* (Princeton: Princeton University Press, 2014) and John Earle, *English Prose: Its Elements, History, and Usage* (London: Smith, Elder, and Co., 1890).
64. Walter Raleigh, *The English Novel: Being a Short Sketch of Its History from the Earliest Times to the Appearance of Waverley*, 5th ed. (London: John Murray, 1911), 2.
65. Henry James, "Guy de Maupassant," in *Literary Criticism: French Writers, Other European Writers, The Prefaces to the New York Edition* (New York: Library of America, 1984), 522.
66. Debora K. Shuger, "Conceptions of Style," in *The Cambridge History of Literary Criticism*, ed. George Kennedy, vol. 3 (Cambridge: Cambridge University Press, 1999), 177.
67. Robert Louis Stevenson, "On Style in Literature: Its Technical Elements," *The Contemporary Review* 47 (Apr. 1885), 552.
68. Wright, "Style," 84.

2 Stylistic Virtue between Moralism and Aestheticism

1. For accounts of this shift, and of why classics in general remained at the heart of Victorian culture, see Frank M. Turner, *The Greek Heritage in Victorian Britain* (New Haven and London: Yale University Press, 1984); Richard Jenkyns, *The Victorians and Ancient Greece* (Cambridge: Harvard University Press, 1980); Frank M. Turner, "Why the Greeks and Not the Romans in Victorian Britain?" in *Rediscovering Hellenism: The Hellenic Inheritance and the English Imagination*, ed. G.W. Clarke (Cambridge: Cambridge University Press, 1989), 61–81; Christopher Stray, *Classics Transformed: Schools, Universities, and Society in England, 1830–1960* (Oxford: Clarendon Press, 1998); Dowling, *Hellenism and Homosexuality*; Leslie Howsam et al., "What the Victorians Learned: Perspectives on Nineteenth-Century Schoolbooks," *Journal of Victorian Culture* 12.2 (2007): 262–85; and Isobel Hurst, "Victorian Literature and the Reception of Greece and Rome," *Literature Compass* 7.6 (June 2010): 484–95.
2. Turner, *Greek Heritage*, 69.
3. Turner, *Greek Heritage*, 78.
4. Thomas Hardy, *Tess of the D'Urbervilles*, ed. Tim Dolin (London: Penguin, 2003), 158.
5. Hurst, "Victorian Literature," 483 and Howsam et al., "What the Victorians Learned," 265.
6. W.H. Walsh, "The Zenith of Greats," in *The History of the University of Oxford*, ed. M.G. Brock and M.C. Curthoys, vol. 7: Nineteenth-Century Oxford, Part 2 (Oxford: Oxford University Press, 2000), 311.
7. Turner, *Greek Heritage*, 323–33.
8. For more on the Victorian reception of Aristotle and Plato, see Turner, *Greek Heritage*, chap. 8; M.R. Stopper [Jonathan Barnes], "Greek Philosophy and the Victorians," *Phronesis* 26.3 (1981): 267–85; and Adam Lee, "The Ethics of Contemplation: Pater's Reading of Aristotle," in *Pater the Classicist: Classical Scholarship, Reception, and Aestheticism*, ed. Charles Martindale, Stefano Evangelista, and Elizabeth Prettlejohn (Oxford: Oxford University Press, 2017), 309–21. Stopper convincingly argues that Jenkyns (in *The Victorians and Ancient Greece*) vastly overlooks Aristotle's importance in the period, and that even Turner "underestimates the full scope and duration of his importance" (277). Similarly, Lee claims that "there has been a mistaken tendency to believe that, with the surge of interest in Plato during the latter half of the nineteenth century, Aristotle somehow faded away" (310) when in fact "it was generally accepted at Oxford that Aristotle explicated Plato's ideas and fixed some of his terminology ... Plato thus informed the study of Aristotle, while Aristotle complemented knowledge of Plato" (311).
9. Stopper, "Greek Philosophy," 278.

10. Quoted in Turner, *Greek Heritage*, 329. Andrew Miller argues that evangelicalism was a stronger influence on Victorian perfectionism than Hellenism while acknowledging their interconnectedness. See *The Burdens of Perfection*, 19–23.
11. Frederick Oakeley, quoted in Turner, *Greek Heritage*, 332.
12. Samuel Smiles, *Character* (1871; London: John Murray, 1876), 1.
13. Carol Poster, "Pedagogy and Bibliography: Aristotle's *Rhetoric* in Nineteenth-Century England," *Rhetoric Society Quarterly* 31.2 (Spring 2001), 8.
14. Poster, "Pedagogy and Bibliography," 8. Furthermore, Russell Wyland notes in his survey of rhetorical instruction at Oxford from 1785 to 1820 that vastly more students read the *Rhetoric* of Aristotle than the Ciceronian rhetoric often presumed to have then been dominant. Russell M. Wyland, "An Archival Study of Rhetoric Texts and Teaching at the University of Oxford, 1785–1821," *Rhetorica: A Journal of the History of Rhetoric* 21.3 (Summer 2003), 183.
15. Halloran, "Aristotle's Concept of Ethos," 61.
16. Poster, "Pedagogy and Bibliography," 9.
17. Edward Meredith Cope, *An Introduction to Aristotle's Rhetoric, with Analysis Notes and Appendices* (London and Cambridge: Macmillan and Co., 1867; reprint, Hildesheim: Georg Olms Verlag, 1970), 6.
18. Carol Poster, "Whose Aristotle? Which Aristotelianism?: A Historical Prolegomenon to Thomas Farrell's *Norms of Rhetorical Culture*," *Philosophy and Rhetoric* 41.4 (2008), 376.
19. See Court, *Institutionalizing English Literature*, 9.
20. John Gillies, *A New Translation of Aristotle's Rhetoric with an Introduction and Appendix* (London and Edinburgh: Cadell and Blackwood, 1823), 6.
21. Turner, "Why the Greeks," 322. Whereas Thomas Hobbes first translated the *Rhetoric* into English in 1637 (John T. Harwood, ed., *The Rhetorics of Thomas Hobbes and Bernard Lamy* [Carbondale: Southern Illinois University Press, 1986], xi), the *Poetics* did not appear until 1789 (George Whalley, "On Translating Aristotle's *Poetics*," *University of Toronto Quarterly* 39.2 [Jan. 1970], 104 n. 1).
22. For a modern treatment of this view, see Howell, "Aristotle and Horace," 45–72.
23. John Ruskin, *Lectures on Art Delivered before the University of Oxford in Hilary Term, 1870* (New York: Maynard, 1893), 85, 87.
24. Landow, George P., *The Aesthetic and Critical Theories of John Ruskin* (Princeton: Princeton University Press, 1971), 28.
25. Harold Bloom, introduction to *Walter Pater: Modern Critical Views*, ed. Harold Bloom (New York: Chelsea, 1985), 21, 4.
26. David Craig, *John Ruskin and the Ethics of Consumption* (Charlottesville: University Press of Virginia, 2006), 36.

27. Craig, *John Ruskin*, 37.
28. Craig, *John Ruskin*, 4.
29. As Keith Hanley and Brian Maidment argue, "If his philosophical affinities are complex, unspecific and even inconsistent on occasion, his underlying thought stems from the Aristotelian-Thomist tradition." They note that Ruskin quotes approvingly of Aristotle's "definition of pleasure" in *The Poetry of Architecture*, his first major work. Keith Hanley and Brian Maidment, introduction to *Persistent Ruskin: Studies in Influence, Assimilation and Effect*, ed. Keith Hanley and Brian Maidment (London: Routledge, 2016), 5.
30. John Ruskin, *Modern Painters*, vol. 2 (London: Allen, 1903), 35.
31. Katherine Gilbert, "Ruskin's Relation to Aristotle," *Philosophical Review* 49.1 (1940), 58.
32. Gilbert, "Ruskin's Relation," 35.
33. Gilbert, "Ruskin's Relation," 43.
34. John Ruskin, *The Stones of Venice*, 3 vols. (London: Smith, 1853), II:153.
35. Though Ruskin was unlikely to have been influenced by Hegel, there are obvious parallels between Ruskin's virtue-based theophany and Hegel's notion of symbolic embodiment. For Hegel's influence in Britain, see my own discussion in Chapter 3, as well as James Bradley and Kirk Willis, who both agree that, although some figures engaged with Hegel in the 1840s and 50s, it was not until the 1860s that he penetrated mainstream thought. James Bradley, "Hegel in Britain: A Brief History of British Commentary and Attitudes (1)," Heythrop Journal 20.1 (1979), 12, and Kirk Willis, "The Introduction and Critical Reception of Hegelian Thought in Britain 1830–1900," *Victorian Studies* 32.1 (Autumn 1988), 100. For more on Hegel and aestheticism, see Jonathan Loesberg, *A Return to Aesthetics* (Stanford: Stanford University Press, 2005), 74–144.
36. The relationship between artistic intentions and aesthetic quality is a major topic in philosophical virtue aesthetics, explored most comprehensively in Tom Roberts, "Aesthetic Virtues: Traits and Faculties," *Philosophical Studies* 175.2 (Feb. 2018): 429–47.
37. Kenneth Daley, "From the Theoretic to the Practical: Ruskin, British Aestheticism, and the Relation of Art to Use," *Prose Studies* 20.2 (1997), 90.
38. Daley, "Theoretic to the Practical," 96.
39. Daley, "Theoretic to the Practical," 91.
40. For an excellent overview of the relation between moralism and aesthetic autonomy in philosophical aesthetics, see Berys Gaut, *Art, Emotion, and Ethics* (Oxford: Oxford University Press, 2007), chap. 1–4.
41. Warren D. Anderson, *Matthew Arnold and the Classical Tradition* (Ann Arbor: University of Michigan Press, 1971), 11.
42. Quoted in Anderson, *Matthew Arnold*, 126.

43. Matthew Arnold, *Culture and Anarchy*, ed. Jane Garnett (Oxford: Oxford University Press, 2006), 4.
44. Turner discusses the compatibility of Aristotle with Anglicanism in *Greek Heritage*, 325–40. Andrew Miller interprets the Victorian emulation of ethical models as a "secularized vision of spiritual perfection" in *The Burdens of Perfection*, 9.
45. Henry Sidgwick, "The Prophet of Culture," in *Culture and Anarchy*, ed. Jane Garnett (Oxford: Oxford University Press, 2006), 160.
46. Henry Sidgwick, *The Methods of Ethics* (London: Macmillan, 1874), 92.
47. The definition of virtue as "the power or operative influence inherent in a supernatural or divine being" is its oldest meaning in English and is intimately connected to its moral sense. As I discuss later in this chapter, Pater explicitly defines virtue as power. See "virtue, n.," *OED Online.*
48. In response to Sidgwick's complaint that he values sweetness and light at the expense of strength and fire, throughout the Preface Arnold emphatically repeats how Hellenism and Hebraism are complementary rather than mutually exclusive, that both are necessary for "harmonious" – that is to say, complete and symphonic – perfection.
49. Matthew Arnold, "The Function of Criticism at the Present Time," in *The Complete Prose Works*, vol. 3, 271.
50. Timothy Peltason, "Seeing Things as They Are: Literary Judgment and Disinterestedness," *Literary Imagination* 9.2 (2007), 181.
51. For more on detachment and objectivity as virtues, see Anderson, *The Powers of Distance*; Daston and Galison, *Objectivity*, 17–54; and George Levine, *Dying to Know: Scientific Epistemology and Narrative in Victorian England* (Chicago: University of Chicago Press, 2010), 1–15. For more on the ways in which sets of virtues may aggregate into a more general critical ethos (of which "Hellenism" or "criticism" may be examples), see Anderson, *The Way We Argue Now*, 134–60.
52. Matthew Arnold, "Preface to the First Edition of *Poems* (1853)," in *The Complete Prose Works of Matthew Arnold*, ed. R.H. Super, vol. 1, 3.
53. T.S. Eliot, "Arnold and Pater," *The Bookman: A Review of Books and Life* 72.1 (1930), 5.
54. Ian Fletcher, "Walter Pater," in *Walter Pater: Modern Critical Views*, ed. Harold Bloom (New York: Chelsea, 1985), 71.
55. In his review of *Appreciations*, Wilde called "Style" the least successful of the essays, and his summary of its main precepts, though meant to be complimentary, presents nothing that would have been unfamiliar to an eighteenth-century reader: "How good it is for us . . . to be reminded of the real scholarship that is essential to the perfect writer, who . . . will avoid what is mere rhetoric, or ostentatious ornament, or negligent misuse of

terms, or ineffective surplusage, and will be known by his tact of omission, by his skilful economy of means, by his selection and self-restraints, and perhaps above all by that conscious artistic structure which is the expression of mind in style." Oscar Wilde, "Mr. Pater's Last Volume," *Speaker* 1 (22 Mar. 1890), 319. In arguing for the conventionality of Pater's essay, I diverge sharply from Wolfgang Iser, *Walter Pater: The Aesthetic Moment*, trans. David Henry Wilson (Cambridge: Cambridge University Press, 1987), 46–60.

56. In a recent essay, Spencer Lee-Lenfield writes that "Pater reads into Flaubert's writing on style an entire worldview that surpasses questions of idiosyncratic procedure to become a general theory for the existence of style," though the outlines of this theory clearly predate his reading of Flaubert. Spencer Lee-Lenfield, "Translating Style: Flaubert's Influence on English Narrative Prose," *Modern Language Quarterly* 81.2 (June 2020), 211.
57. For more on Pater's use of Hegel, see William Shuter, "History as Palingenesis in Pater and Hegel," *PMLA* 86.3 (1971), 411–16; Giles Whiteley, *Aestheticism and the Philosophy of Death: Walter Pater and Post-Hegelianism* (New York: Legenda, 2010); and Benjamin Morgan, "Aesthetic Freedom: Walter Pater and the Politics of Autonomy," *ELH* 77.3 (Fall 2010), 742–49.
58. For further accounts of how Pater objectifies subjectivity, see Carolyn Williams, *Transfigured World: Walter Pater's Aesthetic Historicism* (Ithaca: Cornell University Press, 1989), 46–47 and Levine, *Dying to Know*, 244–67.
59. G.H. Lewes, *The Principles of Success in Literature*, 3rd ed. (Boston: Allyn, 1891), 90.
60. Walter Pater, *Marius the Epicurean*, ed. Michael Levy (London: Penguin, 1985), 119.
61. Adam Lee reads the Wordsworth essay as a "turning point" (311) in Pater's understanding of Aristotle because it invests "the contemplative life – as *being* above action – with higher moral value" (317, original emphasis). See Lee, "The Ethics of Contemplation," 311–19.
62. Lionel Trilling first observed the significance of this passage for Arnold in *Matthew Arnold* (1939; New York: Harcourt, 1977), 258–59.
63. Eliot, "Arnold and Pater," 3.
64. Although Pater's position naturally inclines to doctrinal relativism, he consistently appeals to dispositional virtues (such as "sincerity") as providing more objective, process-based standards of value. In the essay on "Coleridge," for example, he celebrates "the relative spirit" for "breaking through a thousand rough and brutal classifications, and giving elasticity to inflexible principles" (*Appreciations*, 103); in the same way, he objects to Coleridge's likening of the work of art to a living organism

because, while it "expresses truly the sense of a self-delighting independent life which the finished work of art gives us: it hardly figures the processes by which such work was produced" (80–81). True to relativist form, the final essay in *Appreciations* is a comparison of the classical and romantic spirits, not an adjudication between them; Pater ends by appealing to the idea of style *in general* as normatively good: "For, in truth, the legitimate contention is, not of one age or school of literary art against another, but of all successive schools alike, against the stupidity which is dead to the substance, and the vulgarity which is dead to form" (261).

65. Julia Prewitt Brown, *Cosmopolitan Criticism: Oscar Wilde's Philosophy of Art* (Charlottesville: University Press of Virginia, 1997), xvi.
66. Brown, *Cosmopolitan Criticism*, 17. For more on Wilde's classical education and influences, see Iain Ross, *Oscar Wilde and Ancient Greece* (Cambridge: Cambridge University Press, 2012), who stresses "Wilde's indebtedness to Aristotle" (8); Leanne Grech, *Oscar Wilde's Aesthetic Education: The Oxford Classical Curriculum* (New York: Palgrave Macmillan, 2019); and Stefano Evangelista, *British Aestheticism and Ancient Greece: Hellenism, Reception, Gods in Exile* (New York: Palgrave Macmillan, 2009), chap. 4.
67. As Brown notes, "the contemplative attitude (*theoria*), which was the basis of Aristotle's *Ethics* as Wilde understood it, is the means and end of self-perfection" (*Cosmopolitan Criticism*, 17).
68. Following the work of Amanda Anderson, who defines Victorian cosmopolitanism as a "reflective distance from one's original or primary cultural affiliations, a broad understanding of other cultures, and customs, and a belief in universal humanity" (*Powers of Distance*, 63), numerous critics have explored the concept's many reverberations, typically emphasizing its political or geopolitical dimensions. (Anderson claims that Wilde "introduces the term largely to argue that criticism, rather than appeals to emotions or abstract ethics, will conduce most to peace and understanding among nations and races," 150.) See, for example, Pheng Cheah and Bruce Robbins, eds., *Cosmopolitics: Thinking and Feeling beyond the Nation* (Minneapolis: University of Minnesota Press, 1998); Regenia Gagnier, *Individualism, Decadence, and Globalization: On the Relationship of Part to Whole, 1859–1920* (Basingstoke: Palgrave, 2010); and Lauren Goodlad and Julia M. Wright, "Introduction and Keywords," in "Victorian Internationalisms," ed. Lauren Goodlad and Julia M. Wright, special issue of *Romanticism and Victorianism on the Net* 48 (November 2007), doi: 10.7202/017435ar.
69. Henry James, "The Art of Fiction," in *Literary Criticism: Essays on Literature, American Writers, English Writers* (New York: Library of America, 1984), 56.
70. Oscar Wilde, *De Profundis and Other Writings*, ed. Hesketh Pearson (London: Penguin, 1986), 165.

3 Virtue Theory and the Nature of the Aesthetic

1. Three recent studies take seriously the relationship between Victorian moral philosophy and literature from perspectives other than Kantianism or utilitarianism: Andrew Miller, *The Burdens of Perfection*, which discusses "moral perfectionism" as a form of "responsiveness to exemplars" (3); Jesse Rosenthal, *Good Form*, which relates literary forms to moral intuitionism; and Benjamin Morgan, *The Outward Mind*, which reads "science-based aesthetic theories … as participating in a tradition of philosophical aesthetics despite the fact that its practitioners often avoided a philosophical idiom" (8–9). These valuable studies have done much to bolster the significance of nineteenth-century British philosophy to literary criticism and theory, correcting the tendency, apparent in Costelloe's *British Aesthetic Theory*, to focus more exclusively on the "great writers" discussed in the previous chapter. See Timothy M. Costelloe, *The British Aesthetic Tradition: From Shaftesbury to Wittgenstein* (Cambridge: Cambridge University Press, 2013), chap. 6.
2. Elizabeth Anscombe, "Modern Moral Philosophy," *Philosophy* 33 (1958): 1–19.
3. Philosophically, Mill's utilitarianism is usually opposed to Green and Bosanquet's idealism, with Grote occupying an intuitionist middle ground. However, these thinkers *were* united in their commitment to liberalism and liberal reform. The extent to which stylistic virtue reflects a "liberal" aesthetic is a question worthy of future research, but the political angle only takes us so far when we remember that Sidgwick, too, was a lifelong liberal. For more on the politics of these figures, see Thomas, *Cultivating Victorians*, 28–29; Goodlad, *Victorian Liberalism*; and Elaine Hadley, *Living Liberalism*.
4. C.D. Broad, *Five Types of Ethical Theory* (London: Routledge and Kegan Paul, 1930), 143.
5. John Rawls, foreword to *The Methods of Ethics*, by Henry Sidgwick, 7th ed. (Indianapolis: Hackett, 1981), v.
6. Alasdair MacIntyre, *A Short History of Ethics* (New York: Macmillan, 1966), 243.
7. Roger Crisp, *The Cosmos of Duty: Henry Sidgwick's* Methods of Ethics (Oxford: Oxford University Press, 2015), x.
8. Henry Sidgwick, *The Methods of Ethics*, 7th ed., xvii.
9. J.B. Schneewind, *Sidgwick's Ethics and Victorian Moral Philosophy* (Oxford: Oxford University Press, 1986), 421.
10. J.B. Schneewind, *Essays on the History of Moral Philosophy* (Oxford: Oxford University Press, 2010), 26–27.
11. Henry Sidgwick, *The Methods of Ethics* (London: Macmillan, 1874), 318–21. Unless otherwise indicated, all further in-text references are to this edition.

12. "aesthetic, n. and adj.," *OED Online*, June 2020, Oxford University Press, www.oed.com/view/Entry/3237.
13. Timothy M. Costelloe distinguishes between "aesthetics," understood as "philosophical reflection on beauty and the arts," a tradition inaugurated by eighteenth-century British philosophers under the rubric of "taste" and "criticism," and "philosophical aesthetics," which is a philosophical subdiscipline most identified with Kantian idealism. These traditions overlap with but also differ from the concept of the aesthetic that (following Sidgwick) I elaborate here. See *The British Aesthetic Tradition*, chap. 1. According to Jerome Stolnitz, "The British [in the eighteenth century] did not invent and never use the words 'aesthetic' or 'aesthetics,' but it is simply frivolous to allow this to decide who 'created' aesthetic theory. The British were the first to envision the possibility of a philosophical discipline, embracing the study of all of the arts, one which would be, moreover, autonomous, because its subject-matter is not explicable by any of the other disciplines." Jerome Stolnitz, "On the Origins of 'Aesthetic Disinterestedness,'" *The Journal of Aesthetics and Art Criticism* 20.2 (Winter 1961), 131–32.
14. For example, in his lectures on T.H. Green, Sidgwick excoriates Aristotle's analysis of liberality and magnificence, which "show very clearly how simply Aristotle is following the ethico-aesthetic – or even purely aesthetic – sentiment of admiration for certain qualities in the conduct of a Greek gentleman, and how far he is from conceiving self-devotion to a social end as essential to the notion of virtue." Henry Sidgwick, *Lectures on the Ethics of T.H. Green, Mr. Herbert Spencer, and J. Martineau* (London: Macmillan, 1902), 296.
15. Henry Sidgwick, *The Methods of Ethics*, 2nd ed. (London: Macmillan, 1877), 196. This description of "aesthetic intuitionism" comes from the second edition of *The Methods*, where it replaces the vaguer formulation of the first edition: "The question, Which of these two views [the jural or the aesthetic] is the true one? is the most important presented in this part of our inquiry into ethical method; for it is only on the latter view that we can give Ethics a scientific treatment, instead of the looser manner of exposition in which we throw together the results of criticism in any branch of the Fine Arts" (199).
16. This point, added in the second edition, was preserved all the way through the seventh.
17. Henry Sidgwick, *Miscellaneous Essays and Addresses* (London: Macmillan, 1904), 42.
18. J.S. Mill, *On Liberty and Utilitarianism* (New York: Bantam, 2003), 155.
19. Varieties of hedonism differ according to how one defines pleasure and pain, but they all imply that pleasure is the only thing that is intrinsically good. If

Mill argued that the higher pleasures were good only because they tend to produce greater happiness over the long-run, he would be consistent as a hedonist; but this does not appear to be Mill's argument, since the higher pleasures are to be valued regardless of how much pleasure they produce and/ or because they serve some non-hedonic end (such as "dignity"). Sidgwick, being a true hedonist, accepts Mill's qualitative distinctions among pleasures only "in so far as they can be resolved into distinctions of quantity" (*Methods*, 2nd ed., 109), that is, only insofar as they are consistent with empirical hedonism, the method by which the utilitarian calculates the overall balance of pleasures and pains.

20. J.S. Mill, *On Liberty and Utilitarianism* (New York: Bantam, 2003), 75.
21. George Eliot, *The Mill on the Floss*, ed. A.S. Byatt (Oxford: Oxford University Press, 2008), 498.
22. Terry Eagleton, *The Ideology of the Aesthetic* (Oxford: Blackwell, 1990), 61.
23. John Grote, *An Examination of the Utilitarian Philosophy* (Cambridge: Deighton Bell, 1870), 119.
24. John Grote, *A Treatise on the Moral Ideals* (Cambridge: Deighton Bell, 1876). Grote's use of "eudaimonics" to describe what is essentially utilitarian hedonism is a confusing departure from Aristotle's use of the word and was probably motivated by his desire to describe nineteenth-century philosophical positions through the familiar vocabulary derived from Aristotleanism. Grote further distinguishes eudaimonics, which treats happiness as an ideal science, from hedonics, which treats pleasure and pain as mere facts in the universe unconnected to human aspirations (14). Grote's use of "aretaic" is also anomalous in that he does not use it to signify "virtue for virtue's sake" but rather a love of virtue formed in concert with ideal eudaimonics, i.e. pleasure consistent with the good.
25. Grote's understanding of aretaics as combining action *with* duty departs from Aristotle's emphasis on being *rather* than doing but anticipates T.H. Green's understanding of happiness as self-realization *in accordance* with one's rational capacities, conceived, as in Kant, as a duty. This is characteristic of the post-Kantian Victorian synthesis of virtue ethics and deontology to which I refer broadly throughout this chapter as instantiating an aretaic way of thinking about moral philosophy.
26. Reginald A.P. Rogers, *A Short History of Greek Ethics* (London: Macmillan, 1921), 152.
27. The word beauty functions as something of an aesthetic catch-all in the eighteenth century, sometimes referring to any stimulus capable of producing a particular pleasurable response (especially art, nature, and the human face and figure), sometimes being distinguished from other related categories such as the picturesque and the sublime. Unless otherwise specified,

I invoke beauty in its broad meaning (that is, the meaning that would later be signified by the word "aesthetic").

28. Lord Anthony Ashley Cooper, Third Earl of Shaftesbury, *Characteristics of Men, Manners, Opinions, Times*, ed. Lawrence E. Klein (1699–1710; Cambridge: Cambridge University Press, 1999), 29.
29. Michael B. Gill, "Lord Shaftesbury [Anthony Ashley Cooper, Third Earl of Shaftesbury]," in *The Stanford Encyclopedia of Philosophy*, July 2011, https://stanford.library.sydney.edu.au/archives/sum2012/entries/shaftesbury/. In a recent revision of this article, Gill notes that some scholars dispute this characterization (see Michael B. Gill, "Lord Shaftesbury [Anthony Ashley Cooper, Third Earl of Shaftesbury]," in *The Stanford Encyclopedia of Philosophy*, Sept. 2019, https://plato.stanford.edu/entries/shaftesbury/).
30. Rogers, *Short History of Greek Ethics*, 154.
31. It is difficult to tell whether later philosophers are influenced more by Shaftesbury or Hutcheson, who followed his predecessor closely. For the purposes of virtue aesthetics, the differences between their views are far less important than the similarities.
32. David Hume, *An Enquiry Concerning the Principles of Morals* (Indianapolis: Hackett, 1983), 15.
33. Terry Eagleton may have done much to popularize this genealogy. In his influential *Literary Theory: An Introduction*, Eagleton argues that "it is mainly from this era, in the work of Kant, Hegel, Schiller, Coleridge and others, that we inherit our contemporary ideas of the 'symbol' and 'aesthetic experience', of 'aesthetic harmony' and the unique nature of the artefact" (21). Eagleton is not insensitive to the fact that variants of these ideas circulated throughout the eighteenth century, dedicating the second chapter of *Ideology of the Aesthetic* to British sentimentalist philosophers. Nonetheless, in describing this tradition (in a related essay) as "all along too aesthetic for its own good" he suggests that, just as Kant's Second Critique offers itself as a solution to Hume's *Enquiry Concerning Human Understanding*, so does the Third Critique provide a solution to the internal contradictions that bedevil sentimentalist aesthetics. Terry Eagleton, "The Ideology of the Aesthetic," *Poetics Today* 9.2 (1988), 335.
34. Harold Schweizer, "Literary Autonomy: The Growth of a Modern Concept," in *The Cambridge History of Literary Criticism*, ed. Rafey Habib, vol. 6 (Cambridge: Cambridge University Press, 2013), 231–32.
35. Ross, *Making of the English Literary Canon*, 228.
36. Ross, *Making of the English Literary Canon*, 228.
37. Wellbery, "Transformation of Rhetoric," 189.

38. Here, Shaftesbury specifically addresses mathematics, claiming that "a natural joy in the contemplation of those numbers, that harmony proportion and concord . . . is essential in the constitution and form of every particular species or order of beings" (*Characteristics*, 203).
39. David E.W. Fenner, *Art in Context: Understanding Aesthetic Value* (Athens: Swallow Press/Ohio University Press, 2008), chap. 3.
40. Rosemary Ashton, *The German Idea* (Cambridge: Cambridge University Press, 1980).
41. Quoted in Ashton, *German Idea*, 68.
42. Stephen Prickett, "England: Romantic Legacies," in *The Cambridge History of Literary Criticism*, vol. 6, 163. Schiller is also commonly cited as influential, but Lesley Sharpe notes that he was only properly discovered by readers of his *own* language in the 1850s, suggesting an even more delayed entry into Britain. See Lesley Sharpe, *Schiller's Aesthetic Essays: Two Centuries of Criticism* (Columbia: Camden House, 1995), 20–21.
43. Jonah Siegel, "Victorian Aesthetics," in *The Oxford Handbook of Victorian Literary Culture*, ed. Juliet John (Oxford: Oxford University Press, 2016), 565.
44. James Bradley, "Hegel in Britain: A Brief History of British Commentary and Attitudes (1)," Heythrop Journal 20.1 (1979), 11.
45. F.D. Maurice, *Modern Philosophy, or A Treatise of Moral and Metaphysical Philosophy from the Fourteenth Century to the French Revolution, with a Glimpse into the Nineteenth Century* (London: Griffin, Bohn, and Co., 1862). The fourth and final part of Maurice's survey was never included in the Encyclopedia, though the earlier parts' position in the second edition helped establish their claim to general knowledge. For the subtitle, see the frontispiece to the first volume of the second edition of the *Encyclopedia Metropolitana* (London: John Joseph Griffin and Co., 1849), which also reprints Coleridge's original prospectus for the work.
46. William Sweet, "British Idealist Philosophy of Religion," in *The Oxford Handbook of British Philosophy in the Nineteenth Century*, ed. W.J. Mander (Oxford: Oxford University Press, 2014), 563.
47. Turner, *Greek Heritage*, 274.
48. Quoted in Turner, "Why the Greeks," 77.
49. Schneewind, *Sidgwick's Ethics*, 63.
50. Thomas Reid, *Essays on the Intellectual Powers of Man* (Edinburgh: John Bell, 1785), 716.
51. Roger D. Gallie, *Thomas Reid: Ethics, Aesthetics, and the Anatomy of the Self* (Dordrecht: Kluwer Academic Publishers, 1998), 177.
52. Archibald Alison, *Essays on the Nature and Principles of Taste*, 2nd ed. (Hartford: George Goodwin, 1821), 443.

53. Alasdair MacIntyre makes the opposite claim, criticizing Shaftesbury and Hutcheson for assimilating ethics to aesthetics, but both objections overlook how moral and aesthetic judgments can remain distinct while being interconnected. See Alasdair MacIntyre, *A Short History of Ethics* (New York: Macmillan, 1966), 163.
54. For Alison, therefore, the distinctiveness of "emotions of taste" may inhere in a more Kantian notion of disinterestedness, for they only express the appreciation or admiration of underlying ethical qualities, as opposed to ethical judgments themselves, which call for action, justice, etc.
55. Dabney Townsend, introduction to *Eighteenth-Century British Aesthetics*, ed. Dabney Townsend (Amityville: Baywood, 1999), 30.
56. Henry Sidgwick, *Outlines of the History of Ethics for English Readers* (1886; Boston: Beacon Press, 1960), 259.
57. T.H. Irwin, "Eminent Victorians and Greek Ethics," in *Essays on Henry Sidgwick*, ed. Bart Schult (Cambridge: Cambridge University Press, 1992), 284.
58. Irwin, "Eminent Victorians," 281.
59. Irwin, "Eminent Victorians," 290.
60. Irwin, "Eminent Victorians," 282.
61. Quoted in David O. Brink, editor's introduction to *Prolegomena to Ethics*, by T.H. Green, ed. David O. Brink (Oxford: Clarendon Press, 2003), lxxix.
62. T.H. Green, *Prolegomena to Ethics*, ed. David O. Brink (Oxford: Clarendon Press, 2003), 233–34.
63. Brink, introduction, xl.
64. In the full quotation, Green explains that he has retained from Greek ethics "the conception of a free or pure morality, as resting on what we may venture to call a disinterested interest in the good; of the several virtues as so many applications of that interest to the main relations of social life; of the good itself not as anything external to the capacities virtuously exercised in its pursuit, but as their full realisation" (*Prolegomena*, 300).
65. Brink, introduction, xxxix.
66. The "form of the imagination" that matters most to Green is God, who authorizes his conception of the good; but God is not necessary to make aesthetic inferences from his work.
67. Leigh Dale, "T.H. Green and the Modern Novel: English at Oxford," *Modern Language Quarterly* 75.2 (June 2014), 245–46. With respect to style, Green's essay contains little of note, following Aristotle in seeking to gauge the novel's position in relation to drama and epic and adopting an Eliotic confidence in the novel's capacity to "bring[] man nearer to his neighbour." T.H. Green, *An Estimate of the Value and Influence of Works of Fiction in Modern Times*, ed. Fred Newton Scott (1862; Ann Arbor: The Ann Arbor Press, 1911), 69.

68. For an influential re-statement of this view, see Jacques Rancière, *The Politics of Aesthetics*, trans. Gabriel Rockhill (New York: Continuum, 2004).
69. Bernard Bosanquet, *"Science and Philosophy" and Other Essays* (London: Allen and Unwin, 1927), 384.
70. Bernard Bosanquet, *A History of Aesthetic* (1892; London: Allen and Unwin, 1922), 336.
71. John Dewey, "Review of *A History of Aesthetic*," *The Philosophical Review* 2.1 (Jan. 1893), 69.
72. According to the Scottish academic William Minto, "where we chiefly desiderate a more liberal use of examples in Mr. Bosanquet's exposition is in trying to fathom what lies behind the terms of his definition. Characteristic expressiveness, significance, symbolism, are good words, but even when supplemented by such phrases as 'deeper reality' or 'unseen reality behind the objects of common sense-perception,' they still leave us asking what deeper realities he has in his mind, and whether their character is not an essential factor in the impression of beauty." William Minto, "Bosanquet's *History of Aesthetic*," *Bookman* 3.13 (Oct. 1892), 25.
73. Bernard Bosanquet, *Three Lectures on Aesthetic* (London: Macmillan, 1915), 33.

4 Thackeray's Grace

1. From a review in *The Weekly Times* (12 Jan. 1862), quoted in Judith Law Fisher, "Historical Introduction," *The Adventures of Philip on His Way Through the World, Shewing Who Robbed Him, Who Helped Him, and Who Passed Him By*, by William Makepeace Thackeray (Ann Arbor: University of Michigan Press, 2010), 559. Law includes a generous selection of other reviews, 557–70.
2. "The Adventures of Philip," *The Spectator* 1780 (9 Aug. 1862), 885.
3. Booth, *Rhetoric of Fiction*, 135.
4. In emphasizing the early works, I share the spirit, if not the letter, of Edgar Harden's *Thackeray the Writer*: "by 1839–40 the twenty-eight-year-old author had revealed a number of characteristics that readers have come to identify as distinctively Thackerayan: his gift for mimicry; his comic wit; his acute consciousness of the artifices of ballet, painting, opera, drama, and other forms of human expression; the detailed concreteness of his narratives; his apparently instinctive use of narrative voices projected into at least partly-dramatized personas; and above all his ironical perspective on human folly – a perspective intermittently humanized by a sense of pathos." Edgar F. Harden, *Thackeray the Writer: From Journalism to Vanity Fair* (Basingstoke: Palgrave Macmillan, 1998), 87.
5. Lord David Cecil, *Early Victorian Novelists: Essays in Revaluation* (New York: Bobbs-Merrill, 1935), 100.

6. The term "pococurantism" was first used by David Masson in an influential review comparing Thackeray and Dickens, in which he claimed that Thackeray the *pococurante* "has made far fewer appearances as a controversialist or reformer" than his rival novelist. David Masson, "*Pendennis* and *Copperfield:* Thackeray and Dickens," *The North British Review* 15.29 (May 1851), 67. As Robin Gilmour argues, Thackeray's modern reception "has suffered … largely because his contemporary reputation was so identified with what was felt to be the gentlemanly tone of his narration" and by his "becoming the 'novelist as gentleman' treasured by his gentlemanly contemporaries." Robin Gilmour, *The Idea of the Gentleman in the Victorian Novel* (New York: Routledge, 1981), 37.
7. Amanpal Garcha, *From Sketch to Novel: The Development of Victorian Fiction* (Cambridge: Cambridge University Press, 2009), 83.
8. "Titmarsh's Tour through Turkeydom," *Fraser's Magazine* 33 (Jan.–June 1846), 85.
9. For those "in the know," the reference to "Visnou" may have been a sly allusion to Thackeray's Indian birth, just as Titmarsh's broken nose obliquely references Thackeray's.
10. Robert Stephen Rintoul, "Vanity Fair," *Spectator* 21 (22 July 1848), 709–10, quoted in *Thackeray: The Critical Heritage*, ed. Geoffrey Tillotson (London: Routledge, 1968), 58.
11. Rintoul, quoted in *Critical Heritage*, ed. Tillotson, 58.
12. Abraham Hayward, "Thackeray's Writings," *The Edinburgh Review* 87.175 (Jan. 1848), 50.
13. Gordon Ray, *Thackeray: The Uses of Adversity 1811–1846* (New York: McGraw-Hill, 1955) and *Thackeray: The Age of Wisdom 1847–1863* (New York: McGraw-Hill, 1958).
14. Classic works that elevate the novels include James H. Wheatley, *Patterns in Thackeray's Fiction* (Cambridge: MIT Press, 1969) and Juliet McMaster, *Thackeray: The Major Novels* (Toronto: University of Toronto Press, 1971). Garcha is the most prominent recent critic to highlight the importance of Thackeray's early work in understanding how his style developed, though the republication in 2017 of Richard Pearson's work on Thackeray's journalism, first published in 2000, reflects a broader renewal of interest. See Richard Pearson, *W.M. Thackeray and the Mediated Text: Writing for Periodicals in the Mid-Nineteenth Century* (London: Routledge, 2017).
15. See, for example, John Carey, *Thackeray: Prodigal Genius* (London: Faber, 1977), 10–21 and Brooke Allen, "Sadness Balancing Wit: Thackeray's Life and Works," *The New Criterion* (Jan. 2001), 26–27.
16. M.G. Sundell, "Thackeray Criticism: Its Fortunes and Misfortunes," *Novel* 4.3 (Fall 1972), 513.

17. These types of views recur just as frequently throughout modern criticism of Thackeray. In his introduction to the Everyman edition of *The Newcomes*, D. J. Taylor writes that "Thackeray's incidental homilies are rarely embarrassing, in the way of many minor Victorian writers, but their effect is to reinforce the impression of a writer who is not being true to himself." D.J. Taylor, introduction to *The Newcomes*, by William Makepeace Thackeray, ed. D.J. Taylor (London: Everyman, 1994), xix. In the same vein, but conversely, David Parker complains of *Barry Lyndon* that by insisting "that art ought to tell something like the truth ... Thackeray here sets his face against art." David Parker, "Thackeray's Barry Lyndon," *Ariel: A Review of International English Literature* 6.4 (1975), 79.
18. W.C. Brownell, *Victorian Prose Masters* (New York: AMC Press, 1901), 15.
19. Wolfgang Iser's argument that the narrator of *Vanity Fair* "moves even further and further away from the implied author by virtue of being an actual character in the story itself" is salutary, but perhaps owing to the excessive identification of *Vanity Fair* with Thackeray, his analysis does not extend beyond that novel. Wolfgang Iser, *The Implied Reader: Patterns of Communication in Prose Fiction from Bunyan to Beckett* (Baltimore: Johns Hopkins University Press, 1974), 103. Edgar F. Harden, in *Thackeray the Writer*, is also sensitive to the distance between Thackeray and his character-narrators, especially Pendennis (in *The Newcomes* and *Philip*) and "Mr. Roundabout" (in the Roundabout papers), as is J. Hillis Miller, who claims that "'Thackeray himself,' in fact, insofar as the reader can know him in his writing, is this need to be himself by writing himself as someone else." J. Hillis Miller, *Fiction and Repetition: Seven English Novels* (Cambridge: Harvard University Press, 1982), 74.
20. Harold Gulliver, *Thackeray's Literary Apprenticeship: A Study of the Early Newspaper and Magazine Work of William Makepeace Thackeray* (Valdosta: Southern Stationary and Printing Company, 1934), 53.
21. George Saintsbury, *Corrected Impressions: Essays on Victorian Writers* (New York: Dodd, Mead, and Co., 1895), 8.
22. Geoffrey Tillotson, *Thackeray the Novelist* (London: Methuen, 1974), 1, 54, 115.
23. Wheatley, *Patterns*, 8.
24. Judith Law Fisher, *Thackeray's Skeptical Narrative and the "Perilous Trade" of Authorship* (Burlington: Ashgate, 2002), 1.
25. As Edward White noted in 1966, "an investigation of the available bibliographies reveals an extraordinary lack of agreement about which *Fraser's* articles are actually Thackeray." Edward M. White, "Thackeray's Contributions to *Fraser's Magazine*," *Studies in Bibliography* 19 (1966), 67. More recently, Gary Simons admits that "attributions based solely on arguments of 'style' are by their very nature suspect," requiring him to

draw on the "broader basis of content, circumstances, and sometimes even cash payment records" in compiling a list of Thackeray's works. Gary Simons, "Thackeray's Articles in the *Morning Chronicle*," *Studies in Bibliography* 59.1 (2015), 253. For Clare Horrocks, it remains apparent "how little we actually know about Thackeray's contributions to *Punch* beyond his serial works." Clare Horrocks, "Digital Thackeray: Preserving the Legacy?" in *Thackeray in Time: History, Memory, and Modernity*, ed. Richard Salmon and Alice Crossley (Burlington: Ashgate, 2016), 154.

26. Gary Simons, "Thackeray's Contributions to the *Times*," *Victorian Periodicals Review* 40.4 (Winter 2007), 345.
27. Simons, "Thackeray's Contributions," 347.
28. G.W. Lewes, "Review of *Vanity Fair*," *The Athenaeum* 1085 (12 Aug. 1848), 797.
29. Anthony Trollope, *Thackeray* (New York: AMS Press, 1968), 201.
30. According to Garcha, the influence of Bakhtin on narrative studies caused the novel to be identified with "polyphony" in a way that has been detrimental to the study of style: "The Victorian novel became identified not with its author's signature manners, but rather with its capacious intermingling of *different* manners – the many voices, or 'heteroglossia,' on which Mikhail Bakhtin, writing earlier in the twentieth century, focuses" (*From Sketch to Novel*, 20). However, Garcha overlooks two possibilities that I entertain here: first, that an author's parodic imitation of other styles could itself be an individuating feature, and second, that a style may be aesthetically distinctive even in the absence of an individual "signature." It is, in fact, remarkable how little Bakhtin has influenced Thackerayan scholarship, with the most Bakhtinian of analysts, John Loofborow, writing in total ignorance of his then-untranslated works. Bakhtin himself mentions Thackeray frequently, most notably as an exemplar of the "English comic novel" that "can unite in itself parodic stylizations of generic languages, various forms of stylizations and illustrations of period-bound languages, the languages of particular generations, of social dialects and others." M.M. Bakhtin, *The Dialogic Imagination: Four Essays*, ed. Michael Holquist (Austin: University of Texas Press, 1981), 292.
31. The series was first published in *Punch* in 1847 under the title *Punch's Prize Novelists*, though in subsequent reprints the set became known as *Novels by Eminent Hands*.
32. Juliet McMaster, "*Novels by Eminent Hands:* Sincerest Flattery from the Author of *Vanity Fair*," *Dickens Studies Annual* 18 (1989), 332.
33. William Makepeace Thackeray, *The Yellowplush Correspondence, Jeames's Diary, The Great Hogarty Diamond, Etc.* (London: Macmillan, 1903), 122.

34. Yellowplush does not spell Skelton's name consistently: sometimes "Skelton," sometimes "Skeleton," sometimes "Skeliton," often using multiple variants in the same paragraph.
35. William Makepeace Thackeray, *Novels by Eminent Hands*, in *Burlesques*, by William Makepeace Thackeray (New York: John B. Alden, 1883), 63.
36. Wheatley, *Patterns*, 88.
37. Robert A. Colby, "Thackeray's Credo," *The Review of English Studies, New Series* 15.60 (Nov. 1964), 388.
38. For an excellent overview of Thackeray's targets, see Thomas McKendy, "Sources of Parody in Thackeray's *Catherine*," *Dickens Studies Annual* 23 (1994): 287–302.
39. Colby, "Thackeray's Credo," 385.
40. Colby, "Thackeray's Credo," 381, 395, 395.
41. Frederick C. Cabot, "The Two Voices in Thackeray's *Catherine*," *Nineteenth-Century Fiction* 28.4. (1974), 413.
42. Quoted in Tillotson, *The Critical Heritage*, 24.
43. A. Savkar Altinel, *Thackeray and the Problem of Realism* (Frankfurt am Main: Peter Lang, 1986), 83.
44. William Makepeace Thackeray, *Catherine: A Story*, ed. Sheldon Goldfarb (Ann Arbor: University of Michigan Press, 1999), 120.
45. Jack P. Rawlins, *Thackeray's Novels: A Fiction that Is True* (Berkeley: University of California Press, 1974), 74–75.
46. Rawlins, *Thackeray's Novels*, 75.
47. Rawlins, *Thackeray's Novels*, 76.
48. William Makepeace Thackeray, *Catherine: A Story* (London: Smith, Elder and Co., 1911), 191. All other in-text references are to the 1999 edition, previously cited.
49. In *Caught in the Act*, Joseph Litvak attends to how Victorian "theatrical energies" are both "absorbed into what one might imagine, somewhat too organically, as a narrative's flow, but also to the ways in which such energies break or complicate that kind of natural-seeming teleology" – a dynamic clearly at work in *Catherine*. Joseph Litvak, *Caught in the Act: Theatricality in the Nineteenth-Century English Novel* (Berkeley: University of California Press, 1992), xiii. David Kurnick links the "genealogy of Thackeray's narrative voice" to an "obsession with theatrical space" throughout his career in *Empty Houses: Theatrical Failure and the Novel* (Princeton: Princeton University Press, 2012), 57, 11.
50. Ray, *Uses of Adversity*, 345.
51. John Loofbourow, *Thackeray and the Form of Fiction* (Princeton: Princeton University Press, 1964), 11.
52. George Saintsbury, introduction to *The Oxford Thackeray*, vol. 6: *The Memoirs of Barry Lyndon, Esq.*, and the Miscellaneous Papers Written between 1843 and 1847 (London: Oxford University Press, 1908), ix.

53. Saintsbury, introduction, xi–xii.
54. Saintsbury, introduction, xii.
55. Ray, *Uses of Adversity*, 225.
56. William Makepeace Thackeray, "Parisian Caricatures," *London and Westminster Review* 32.2 (Apr. 1839), 295.
57. Eva Beach Touster, "The Literary Relationship of Thackeray and Fielding," *The Journal of English and German Philology* 46.4 (Oct. 1947), 390.
58. Touster, "The Literary Relationship," 384.
59. Touster, "The Literary Relationship," 390–91.
60. Parker, "Thackeray's Barry Lyndon," 79.
61. Parker, "Thackeray's Barry Lyndon," 68.
62. Parker, "Thackeray's Barry Lyndon," 78.
63. Lidmila Pantůčková, "The Relationship of W.M. Thackeray to Henry Fielding," *Sborník Prací Filosofické Fakulty Brněnské U* D.9 (1962), 104.
64. Pantůčková, "Relationship," 106.
65. Pantůčková, "Relationship," 102.
66. In *The Rhetoric of Fiction*, Wayne Booth says that Trollope fell into Thackeray's "trap," but his supporting claim that Thackeray did all he could "to make his own rejection of Barry's immorality clear" is not adequately defended. See 383.
67. Trollope, *Thackeray*, 70.
68. Booth, *Rhetoric of Fiction*, 159.
69. Henry Fielding, *The Life of Jonathan Wild the Great*, ed. Claude Rawson (Oxford: Oxford University Press, 2003), 7–8.
70. See later in this section for a discussion of G.S. Fitz-Boodle's footnotes.
71. William Makepeace Thackeray, *The Memoirs of Barry Lyndon, Esq.*, ed. Andrew Sanders (Oxford: Oxford University Press, 1990), 260.
72. Kurnick, *Empty Houses*, 31.
73. Booth, *Rhetoric of Fiction*, 320.
74. Daniel Defoe, *Roxana*, ed. John Mullan (Oxford: Oxford University Press, 1996), 252.
75. For a more detailed history of the footnotes, see Martin J. Anisman, introduction to *The Luck of Barry Lyndon: A Critical Edition*, ed. Martin J. Anisman (New York: NYU Press, 1970), 17–20. Peter L. Shillingsburg casts doubt that the 1856 revisions were actually Thackeray's, while noting that the evidence remains "equivocal," in Peter Shillingsburg's review of Anisman's edition, *The Papers of the Bibliographical Society of America*, 66.2 (1972), 220.
76. Virginia Woolf, *A Room of One's Own and Three Guineas* (Hammersmith: Harper Collins, 2014), 5.
77. In a careful review of the manuscript, John Sutherland concludes that Thackeray's revisions were minimal: "Although the novelist may have taken

pains with the historical preparation for it (though I think too much can be made of even this), *Esmond* was written, like his other novels, at the serialist's creative gallop in which the ground could only be covered once." John Sutherland, "'Henry Esmond' and the Virtues of Carelessness," *Modern Philology* 68.4 (May 1971), 354.

78. For more on *Esmond*'s prose models, see Rodney Stenning Edgecombe, "Eighteenth-Century Allusions in *Henry Esmond*," *Style* 51.1 (2017): 17–24; K.C. Phillipps, *The Language of Thackeray* (London: Andre Deutsch, 1978), chap. 7; and Loofbourow, *Thackeray*, chap. 6.
79. Theodore Martin, "Thackeray's Works," *Westminster Review* 59.116 (Apr. 1853), 384.
80. Besides being a standard form of rhetorical "beauty," unity in diversity is also a keynote of some recent Thackerayan criticism. For example, Judith Law Fisher, in *Thackeray's Skeptical Narrative*, uses "the phrase 'continuous discontinuity' to describe the experience of reading a Thackeray novel" (1), while Nicholas Dames, in *Physiology of the Novel*, describes the fiction in terms of "rhythmically punctuated oscillations" (73) that strike a balance between alternating forms of attention (including inattentiveness). Even so, the later novels remain striking for their variety: besides the contrast between the crystallization of the Thackerayan voice in *Pendennis* and the antiquated style of *Esmond*, *The Newcomes* is the putative product of a character-author, while *The Virginians* is generally regarded as the least successful of Thackeray's novels because its novelization of found letters is exaggeratedly essayistic and digressive. *Philip*, the so-called epitome of the "Thackerayan," is narrated, once again, by Pendennis, putting in doubt an overly facile identification between the author and his fictional mouthpiece.
81. Loofbourow, *Thackeray*, 5.
82. Loofbourow, *Thackeray*, 4–6.
83. William Makepeace Thackeray, "Men and Coats," *Fraser's Magazine* 24.140 (Aug. 1841), 209.
84. Johnson, *Lives of the Poets*, 230.
85. Carlyle, *Sartor Resartus*, 57. Analogies between style and dress were common in the eighteenth century. See Claude Rawson, *Satire and Sentiment, 1660–1830: Stress Points in the English Augustan Tradition* (Cambridge: Cambridge University Press, 2000), chap. 5.
86. The quotes about Thackeray's "high-bred ease" and "flexibility" come from a review of *Philip* in *The North British Review*, quoted in Judith Law Fisher, introduction to *The Adventures of Philip*, 569–70. In "Modern English Prose," Saintsbury argues that informational prose styles, which he associates with democracy, have led to the decline of a less accessible, but more beautiful and aristocratic, prose ideal. See George Saintsbury, "Modern English Prose," *Fortnightly Review* 19.110 (Feb. 1876), 248–51. Nonetheless, others have argued

that the gentlemanly ideal in the eighteenth and nineteenth centuries was socially liberal, even egalitarian in its moral outlook. Shirley Letwin quotes Coleridge's remark in the *Biographia Literaria* that "the gentlemanly character arises out of the feeling of equality acting as a habit, yet flexible to the varieties of rank, and modified without being disturbed or superseded by them." As Letwin summarizes, "the gentleman's talent for being agreeable in a variety of circumstances with a variety of people is attributed by some to the fact that he manages what may now seem to be a miracle – to treat everyone as an equal without disregarding differences of rank." Shirley Robin Letwin, *The Gentleman in Trollope: Individuality and Moral Conduct* (Cambridge: Harvard University Press, 1982), 15.

87. Hogarth describes the lines of beauty in *Analysis of Beauty* (1753); Blair defines the "line of grace" as a "waving curve, twisted round some solid body" in the *Lectures* (I:99).
88. Henry Noble Day, *Elements of the Art of Rhetoric Adapted for Use in Colleges and Academies, and for Private Study*, 3rd ed. (New York: A.S. Barnes and Co., 1853), 24.
89. Henry Noble Day, *The Science of Aesthetics; or, The Nature, Kinds, Laws, and Uses of Beauty* (New Haven: C. C. Chatfield and Co., 1872), 83.
90. In *Essays on the Nature and Principles of Taste*, Archibald Alison equates grace with "movements of the form" characterized by "self-command," or the absence of force and violence (436–37). He adds that "grace is not the result of any peculiar quality in human character, but of some general quality which may be common to all" (427).
91. William Makepeace Thackeray, *The History of Pendennis*, ed. John Sutherland (Oxford: Oxford University Press, 1999), lv.
92. Loofbourow, *Thackeray*, 7.
93. William Makepeace Thackeray, *The Newcomes*, ed. D.J. Taylor (London: Everyman, 1994), 7, 13.
94. Charles Dickens, "In Memoriam," *Cornhill Magazine* 9.50 (Feb. 1864), 130.
95. Thackeray shares his opinions on the role of the literary artist in his response to the attacks on *Pendennis* in what came to be known as the "Dignity of Literature" controversy. See William Makepeace Thackeray, "The Dignity of Literature," *Morning Chronicle* 25033 (12 Jan. 1850), 4 and Mark Cronin, "Henry Gowan, William Makepeace Thackeray, and 'The Dignity of Literature' Controversy," *Dickens Quarterly* 16.2 (June 1999): 104–15.

5 Trollope's Ease and Lucidity

1. Catherine Belsey, *Critical Practice* (London: Methuen, 1980), 2.
2. Anthony Trollope, *An Autobiography*, ed. Michael Sadleir and Frederick Page (Oxford: Oxford University Press, 1999), 144.

3. Henry James, "Anthony Trollope," in *Literary Criticism: Essays on Literature, American Writers, English Writers* (New York: Library of America, 1984), 528.
4. Ruth apRoberts, *The Moral Trollope* (Athens: Ohio University Press, 1971), 20.
5. James Kincaid, *The Novels of Anthony Trollope* (Oxford: Clarendon Press, 1977), 47.
6. Walter Kendrick, *The Novel-Machine: The Theory and Fiction of Anthony Trollope* (Baltimore: Johns Hopkins University Press, 1980), 4. Other variants of the "disappearing" style theory include C.P. Snow, *Trollope: His Life and Art* (New York: Charles Scribner's Sons, 1975); John W. Clark, *The Language and Style of Anthony Trollope* (London: Andre Deutsch, 1975); R.C. Terry, *Anthony Trollope: The Artist in Hiding* (London: Macmillan, 1977); Juliet McMaster, *Trollope's Palliser Novels: Theme and Pattern* (New York: Oxford University Press, 1978); and Robert Tracy, *Trollope's Later Novels* (Berkeley and Los Angeles: University of California Press, 1978). The role of transparency in Trollope's nineteenth-century reception is discussed by Skilton, *Anthony Trollope*, chap. 1–2.
7. Kendrick, *Novel-Machine*, 47, 84. In the words of Geoffrey and Kathleen Tillotson, Trollope's "style has no pretensions. It reveals its honesty in its preference for monosyllables. It likes plain words." Geoffrey Tillotson and Kathleen Tillotson, *Mid-Victorian Studies* (London: Athlone Press, 1965), 56. For other moralistic interpretations of Trollope's formal "honesty," see Henry James, "Anthony Trollope," 527–32 and 545 and Gerald Warner Brace, "The World of Anthony Trollope," in *The Trollope Critics*, ed. N. John Hall (London: Macmillan, 1981), 99–109. Numerous critics have studied "honesty" as a moral virtue in Trollope, most notably Letwin, *The Gentleman in Trollope*; Jane Nardin, *Trollope and Victorian Moral Philosophy* (Athens: Ohio University Press, 1996); and Amanda Anderson, who calls it a "crux virtue" (57), in *Bleak Liberalism*. For Trollope's relative lack of honesty in representing the facts of his life in *An Autobiography*, see R.H. Super, "Truth and Fiction in Trollope's Autobiography," *Nineteenth-Century Literature* 48.1 (June 1993): 74–88.
8. Kendrick sees things differently. For him, "Trollope's theory is an elaborate exercise in a very subtle rhetoric, persuading its reader that certain things are true about fiction ... And the most important of these things is that good fiction (Trollope's) is equivalent to life (all life)" (*Novel-Machine*, 62).
9. Farina, *Everyday Words*, chap. 5.
10. Wright, *Bad Logic*, 83, 79.
11. In 2010, Lauren Goodlad edited a collection of essays on Trollope, including pieces by Nicholas Dames and Carolyn Dever, whose "special motive is to explore his distinctiveness as a practitioner of form." Lauren Goodlad, "Trollopian Form: An Introduction," *Literature Compass* 7.9 (2010), 851.

In addition to Farina and Wright, other examples of more formalist work in Trollope studies include Frederik Van Dam, *Anthony Trollope's Late Style: Victorian Liberalism and Literary Form* (Edinburgh: Edinburgh University Press, 2016); the essays in Part 3 of *The Routledge Research Companion to Anthony Trollope*, ed. Deborah Denenholz Morse, Margaret Markwick, and Mark W. Turner (London: Routledge, 2017); and the cluster of "Style" essays in *The Edinburgh Companion to Anthony Trollope*, ed. Frederick Van Dam (Edinburgh: Edinburgh University Press, 2019).

12. In *The Language and Style of Anthony Trollope*, John W. Clark notes that "what may be called Trollope's normal style is remarkably uniform, from beginning to end" (18), making the selection of case studies for stylistic purposes almost arbitrary. While generic differences do affect the tone and content of Trollope's works – ranging from mock-heroism in *Barchester Towers*, to tragedy in *He Knew He Was Right*, to Thackerayan satire in *The Way We Live Now* – they do not, as I argue in the conclusion to this chapter, influence the structure of his sentences. Elsewhere, I defend the claim that *Can You Forgive Her?*, along with its immediate predecessor *The Small House at Allington*, represent the first fully realized products of Trollope's "mature imaginative method, whereby character comes to replace plot as the source of narrative energy and interest." Matthew Sussman, "Optative Form in Anthony Trollope's *The Small House at Allington*," *Nineteenth-Century Literature* 71.4 (Mar. 2017), 504. Other recent work focuses on the novel's erotic dynamics, making a strong case for the novel's importance to Trollope's *oeuvre*. See Wright, *Bad Logic*, chap. 2 and Claire Jarvis, *Exquisite Masochism: Marriage, Sex, and the Novel Form* (Baltimore: Johns Hopkins University Press, 2016), chap. 3. Here, I make a complementary case for its stylistic representativeness.
13. Kornbluh, *Order of Forms*, 51.
14. Anthony Trollope, *The Small House at Allington*, ed. Julian Thompson (London: Penguin, 1991), 574.
15. As Geoffrey Harvey notes, "Trollope knew better than most that art is artificial. Like most other writers he recognized that realism is only a convention, but unlike them he said so unequivocally." Geoffrey Harvey, *The Art of Anthony Trollope* (New York: St. Martin's Press, 1980), 5.
16. In "Trollope on the Novel," Bradford Booth draws on *Thackeray* as a complement to the theory of technique found in *An Autobiography*, though few others have paid as much attention to the work. See Bradford A. Booth, "Trollope on the Novel," in *Essays Critical and Historical* (Berkeley: University of California Press, 1950), 219–31.

17. Ease and lucidity derive from the classical virtues of correctness and clarity but reflect a nineteenth-century emphasis on rapidity of comprehension within the context of a robust reading culture. In *Thackeray*, Trollope provides the period's most fulsome definition of these widespread terms.
18. Anthony Trollope, *Can You Forgive Her?*, ed. Stephen Wall (London: Penguin, 1986), 39.
19. See, for example, Anthony Trollope, *Barchester Towers*, ed. Michael Sadleir and Frederick Page (Oxford: Oxford University Press, 1998), 252 – "Do I not myself know that I am at this moment in want of a dozen pages, and that I am sick with cudgeling my brains to find them?" – and *An Autobiography*, 118–22 and 174–76.
20. Skilton, *Anthony Trollope*, chap. 1–2, provides an account of such criticisms in the nineteenth century; for twentieth-century examples, see Brace, "The World," and Booth, "Trollope and the Novel." Other critics have sought to redeem Trollope's repetitions by recoding them as a technique of characterization and plotting; for example, Tracy, *Trollope's Later Novels*, and Helen Lucy Blythe, "Forms of Storytelling, Repetition, and Voice in Anthony Trollope's *Kept in the Dark*," in *Routledge Companion*, ed. Morse et al., 177–89. Elizabeth Epperly takes a more style-centric approach, though her book focuses on clichés, allusions, and verbal tags over other elements of diction and syntax. Elizabeth Epperly, *Patterns of Repetition in Trollope* (Washington, DC: Catholic University of America Press, 1989).
21. Ruth apRoberts, *The Moral Trollope* (Athens: Ohio University Press, 1971), 61.
22. apRoberts, *The Moral Trollope*, 32 n. 21. In seeming contrast to apRoberts, Van Dam argues that "the rejuvenation of Trollope's interest in Latin and in Cicero's works during the autumn of his life is intrinsic to the development of his late style" (*Trollope's Late Style*, 63). However, this conception of "style" is more ethical than linguistic, with Van Dam discerning Cicero's influence largely in terms of politics and theology. See chap. 5–6.
23. Anthony Trollope, *The Life of Cicero*, vol. 2 (London: Chapman and Hall, 1880), 327.
24. Cicero, *Orator*, trans. H.M. Hubbell (Cambridge: Harvard University Press, 1962), 319–79.
25. Morris Croll, *Style, Rhetoric, and Rhythm*, 219–20. Croll introduced a major topic to the study of seventeenth-century prose, namely the reaction against the Ciceronian sentence in the form of the "curt" or "loose" styles associated with the development of more naturalistic, speech-based writing. As I argue here, Croll's distinctions provide a useful starting point but they cannot be relied upon absolutely, for Trollope blends the simplicity of "Attic" styles with a Ciceronian aurality that Croll regards as its opposite. For more context, see Croll's "'Attic Prose' in the Seventeenth Century," in *Style, Rhetoric, and*

Rhythm and Gordon, *The Movement of English Prose* (Bloomington: Indiana University Press, 1966).

26. This term is usually used in reference to seventeenth-century prose, but it may be usefully applied to the writing of any era. For more on the loose sentence see Croll, *Style, Rhetoric, and Rhythm*, 219–30 and Williamson, *Senecan Amble*, 37–60. For a still-relevant account of Trollope's conversational looseness, see David Aitken, "'A Kind of Felicity': Some Notes about Trollope's Style," *Nineteenth-Century Fiction* 20.4 (Mar. 1966): 337–53.
27. In *Anatomy of Criticism*, Northrop Frye notes that "the writers most frequently called musical in the sentimental sense are usually the ones most remote from actual music," by which he means the "sense of a metronome beat" (267, 256). But "musical" has value in describing a style whose power inheres in the careful management of rhythm and euphony as opposed to the use of tropes, pictorialism, or logic. For a sympathetic use of "musical" in this way, see James Thorpe, *The Sense of Style: Reading English Prose* (Hamden, CT: Archon Press, 1987), chap. 4.
28. While Trollope emphasizes rhythm, he was not insensitive to the more phonetic aspects of euphony, as my analysis below shows. Still, he followed Cicero (and later Blair) in elevating "rhythm" over "sound" in prose style (see Blair, *Lectures*, I:316). For Victorian scientific investigations into the material bases of harmony, both aural and visual, see Morgan, *Outward Mind*, chap. 1.
29. Stephanie Shirilan, "The Forbidden Pleasures of Style: Seventeenth-Century Prose in Twentieth-Century Criticism," *Prose Studies* 34.2 (Aug. 2012), 119.
30. Cross, *Style, Rhetoric, and Rhythm*, 54.
31. William Forsyth, "Literary Style," *Fraser's Magazine* 55.327 (Mar. 1857), 252.
32. Forsyth, "Literary Style," 252. Consider too these remarks from G.H. Lewes: "The ear is only a guide to the harmony of a period, and often tempts us into the feebleness of expletives or approximative expressions for the sake of a cadence. Yet, on the other hand, if we disregard the subtle influences of harmonious arrangement, our thoughts lose much of the force which would otherwise result from their logical subordination. The easy evolution of thought in a melodious period . . . is the product of a natural gift, as rare as the gift of music, or of poetry" (*Principles*, 194).
33. This phrase was used by Lord David Cecil in an argument that Trollope had "no characteristic cadence, no typical unique use of image and epithet" (*Early Victorian Novelists*, 270) and was first rebutted by Hugh Sykes Davies, who located Trollope's "characteristic cadence" in his use of morally relevant adversatives such as "and" and "but." Ironically, the term "cadence," which for Davies is more conceptual than musical, is uniquely suited to a writer for whom the rhythmic quality of words is so

important. See Hugh Sykes Davies, "Trollope and His Style," *A Review of English Literature* 1.4 (Oct. 1960): 73–85.

34. Notably, for both Blair and Croll, rhythm and cadence are functions not of the sentence but of the period, which is, Croll explains, "not a syntactic logical unit, but on the one hand a psychological, and on the other a rhythmical unit" (*Style, Rhetoric, and Rhythm*, 325). Blair's emphasis on periods over sentences was strong enough to compel Alexander Jamieson, who reproduces much of Blair's *Lectures* in his 1818 *Grammar*, to promote the former term to his table of contents (where it does not appear in Blair) in his discussion of harmony and rhythm. See Alexander Jamieson, *A Grammar of Rhetoric and Polite Literature* (London: G. and W.B. Whittaker, 1818).
35. Davies, "Trollope and His Style," 76.
36. Roger Fowler, *Linguistics and the Novel* (London: Methuen, 1977), 103. The fact that in his later works, notably *Linguistic Criticism*, Fowler sharpened his definition of "mind style" to refer to an author's "point of view on the ideological plane" points to the increasing marginalization of the aesthetic dimension in stylistic criticism that this chapter seeks to redress. Roger Fowler, *Linguistic Criticism* (Oxford: Oxford University Press, 1986), 150.
37. Jarvis insists that the novel was "almost comically unpopular" (*Exquisite Masochism*, 58), but she overstates the case. As McMaster notes, despite some distaste for Alice Vavasor as a heroine and the tedium of her vacillations, "*Can You Forgive Her?* was popular, and sustained Trollope's reputation at its highest – his publishers paid him more for this novel than for any other in his career" (*Trollope's Palliser Novels*, 20).
38. Michael Sadleir, *Anthony Trollope: A Commentary* (Boston: Houghton Mifflin, 1927), 260.
39. Angela Thirlwell, introduction to *Nina Balatka*, by Anthony Trollope (London: Trollope Society, 1996), vi.
40. Judith Knelman, "Trollope's Experiments with Anonymity," *Victorian Periodicals Review* 14.1 (Spring 1981), 23.
41. Lucy Stebbins and Richard Stebbins, *The Trollopes: The Chronicle of a Writing Family* (London: Secker and Warburg, 1947), 237.
42. R.H. Hutton, "Nina Balatka," *Spectator* 40.23 (Mar. 1867), 329. Though the *Spectator* article was published anonymously, Trollope thought Hutton wrote it (*Autobiography*, 205), an attribution confirmed by Robert H. Tener, "R.H. Hutton: Some Attributions," *Victorian Periodicals Newsletter* 6.2 (June 1973), 22–23.
43. Louis T. Milic, "Rhetorical Choice and Stylistic Option: The Conscious and Unconscious Poles," in *Literary Style: A Symposium*, ed. Seymour Chatman (New York: Oxford University Press, 1971), 85.

44. Notably, Hutton based his attribution not on subject or setting but on Trollope's characteristic use of language. "'If it is written by Mr. Trollope,'" he wrote of his reflections while reading, "'I shall soon meet with the phrase "made his way," as applied to walking where there is no physical difficulty or embarrassment, but only a certain moral hesitation as to the end and aim of the walking in question,' and behold within a page of the point at which the silent remark was made, came the very phrase in the peculiar sense indicated" ("Nina Balatka," 329). Hutton thought he could account for at least a "dozen" of such "test-phrases."
45. Anthony Trollope, *Nina Balatka: The Story of a Maiden of Prague* (London: Trollope Society, 1996), 3.

6 Meredith's Fervidness

1. Meredith's reception has always been mixed, and during the nineteenth century he owed his fame largely to the efforts of *cognoscenti*. Even among admirers, reactions to his style varied, as the evaluative paradoxes indicate in W.E. Henley's favorable review of *The Egoist* in 1879: "Mr. Meredith is one of the worst and least attractive of great writers as well as one of the best and most fascinating . . . The better half of his genius is always suffering eclipse from the worse half . . . He is tediously amusing; he is brilliant to the point of being obscure; his helpfulness is so extravagant as to worry and confound." W.E. Henley, "Review of *The Egoist*," *The Athenaeum* 2714 (1 Nov. 1879), 555. Meredith's apologists argued that his wit and wisdom justified the style, but this view declined precipitously in the twentieth century. For example, E.M. Forster sighs that Meredith's "philosophy has not worn well" since its zenith twenty years earlier, and Virginia Woolf notes that Meredith's "fame as a talker has necessarily dimmed, and his fame as a writer seems also under a cloud." E.M. Forster, *Aspects of the Novel* (New York: Harcourt, 1927), 134 and Virginia Woolf, "The Novels of George Meredith," in *The Common Reader: Second Series* (London: Hogarth Press, 1948), 246. Both writers emphasize the prevailing impression of contrivance and artificiality (Woolf more favorably than Forster), culminating in F.R. Leavis's denigrating the novelist as a "shallow exhibitionist (his famous 'intelligence' a laboured and vulgar brilliance)." F.R. Leavis, *The Great Tradition* (1948; London: Chatto and Windus, 1960), 124.
2. John M. Robertson, "Concerning Preciosity," *Yellow Book* 13 (1897), 82, 100.
3. Letter printed in *The Art of Authorship: Literary Reminiscences, Methods of Work, and Advice to Young Beginners*, ed. George Bainton (New York: Appleton, 1891), 130.

4. George Meredith to George Pierce Baker, 27 July 1887, in *The Letters of George Meredith*, ed. Clarence Lee Cline, vol. 2 (Oxford: Oxford University Press, 1970), 876.
5. Dorothy Van Ghent, *The English Novel: Form and Function* (New York: Rinehart, 1953), 184.
6. Quoted in Tillotson, *Critical Heritage*, 145.
7. George Meredith, *The Shaving of Shagpat* (London: Chapman and Hall, 1856), vi.
8. George Eliot, *The Writings of George Eliot*, vol. 22 (Boston: Houghton and Mifflin, 1908), 336–37.
9. Edward Gosse, *Gossip in a Library* (New York: Scribner's, 1914), 268–69.
10. George Meredith, *The Shaving of Shagpat* (New York: Ballantine, 1970), 261. All further references will be to this more accessible edition.
11. August Henry Able III, *George Meredith and Thomas Love Peacock: A Study in Literary Influence* (Philadelphia: University of Pennsylvania, 1933), 29.
12. Croll describes Stoic "brevity of utterance" as one form that Attic style could take, along with "a deliberately rude, formless, negligent style" and "colloquial ease" (*Style, Rhetoric, and Rhythm*, 60). He notes that the Stoics – in contrast to Aristotle – placed brevity above clearness in their hierarchy of stylistic virtues (87), anticipating not only the *sententiae* of Bacon but also the tradition of philosophical wit. In a later essay ("The Baroque Style in Prose"), Croll assimilated brief styles within the rubric of the "baroque," now calling these styles "curt" or "pointed."
13. Quoted in *George Meredith: The Critical Heritage*, ed. Ioan Williams (London: Routledge, 2002), 500, my emphasis.
14. Quoted in Williams, *Critical Heritage*, 45.
15. Frye, *Anatomy of Criticism*, 304.
16. H.M. Cecil, "George Meredith," *The Free Review: A Monthly Magazine* (1 Aug. 1894), 399.
17. Arthur Symons, "A Note on George Meredith," *The Fortnightly Review* (Nov. 1897), 673.
18. Henry James, "The Lesson of Balzac," in *Literary Criticism: French Writers, Other European Writers, The Prefaces to the New York Edition* (New York: Library of America, 1984), 122.
19. Donald Fanger, "Meredith as Novelist," *Nineteenth-Century Fiction* 16.4 (Mar. 1962), 321.
20. Quoted in Sidney Colvin, *Memories and Notes of Persons and Places* (New York: Scribner's, 1921), 182.
21. For a more detailed analysis of the influence of dramatic speech on Meredith's style, see Matthew Sussman, "Meredith's Style," in *On Style in Victorian Fiction*, ed. Daniel Tyler (Cambridge: Cambridge University Press, 2021), 244–62.

22. Croll, *Style, Rhetoric, and Rhythm*, 230.
23. Croll, *Style, Rhetoric, and Rhythm*, 212.
24. Croll, *Style, Rhetoric, and Rhythm*, 214, 212.
25. Croll, *Style, Rhetoric, and Rhythm*, 219–22.
26. Croll, *Style, Rhetoric, and Rhythm*, 210.
27. Croll, *Style, Rhetoric, and Rhythm*, 218–19.
28. Croll, *Style, Rhetoric, and Rhythm*, 208.
29. George Meredith, *The Ordeal of Richard Feverel* (New York: Random House, 1950), 1.
30. Croll, *Style, Rhetoric, and Rhythm*, 230.
31. See *Paradise Lost*, Book X, ll. 547–73.
32. In "Meredith's Style," I argue that "epigram" in the Victorian period was synonymous with rhetorical schemes such as antithesis, while "aphorism," as the more poetic form, was more closely associated with tropes.
33. Vanessa L. Ryan, *Thinking without Thinking in the Victorian Novel* (Baltimore: Johns Hopkins University Press, 2012), 13.
34. Ryan, *Thinking*, 26.
35. George Meredith, *The Egoist*, ed. George Woodcock (London: Penguin, 1987), 35.
36. George Meredith, *The Amazing Marriage* (London: Constable and Company, 1910), 71.
37. George Meredith, *Diana of the Crossways: A Novel* (London: Constable and Company, 1910), 381.
38. John Morley, *Aphorisms*, delivered before the Edinburgh Philosophical Institution, Nov. 11, 1887 (London: Macmillan, 1887), 7, 4.
39. George Meredith, *An Essay on Comedy and the Uses of the Comic Spirit*, in *George Meredith's Essay on Comedy and Other New Quarterly Magazine Publications*, ed. Maura C. Ives (London: Associated Universities Press, 1998), 128–29. Of Molière, Meredith writes further that "he did not paint in raw realism. He seized his characters firmly for the central purpose of the play, stamped them in the idea, and by slightly raising and softening the object of study . . . generalized upon it so as to make it permanently human" (118).
40. Croll, *Style, Rhetoric, and Rhythm*, 219.
41. Ryan, *Thinking without Thinking*, 150.
42. Neil Roberts, *Meredith and the Novel* (Basingstoke: Macmillan Press, 1997), 2.
43. For a helpful overview of Meredith's attitudes toward women, and critical attitudes toward those attitudes, see Maura C. Ives, "Introduction: Meredith's *New Quarterly Magazine* Writing: Comedy, the Male Writer, and the Female Reader," in *George Meredith's Essay on Comedy and Other New Quarterly Magazine Publications*, ed. Maura C. Ives (London: Associated Universities Press, 1998), 13–43.

44. Gillian Beer was the first to pay serious attention to the symbolic significance of the narrators, seeing them as embodiments of "romance" and "realism" respectively. See Gillian Beer, *Meredith: A Change of Masks: A Study of the Novels* (London: Athlone Press, 1970), 172–80.
45. Jacob Korg, "Expressive Styles in *The Ordeal of Richard Feverel*," *Nineteenth-Century Fiction* 27.3 (Dec. 1972), 266.
46. Roberts, *Meredith and the Novel*, 3.
47. Korg, 266.
48. Roberts, 3.
49. Croll, *Style, Rhetoric, and Rhythm*, 226.
50. J. Hillis Miller, *Ariadne's Thread: Story Lines* (New Haven: Yale University Press, 1992), 115.
51. Barbara Johnson, *A World of Difference* (Baltimore: Johns Hopkins University Press, 1987), 53.
52. "catachresis," in *The Oxford Companion to English Literature*, ed. Dinah Birch (Oxford: Oxford University Press, 2009),www.oxfordreference.com/view/10.1093/acref/9780192806871.001.0001/acref-9780192806871-e-1387.
53. George Steiner, *On Difficulty and Other Essays* (Oxford: Oxford University Press, 1978), 34.
54. Paul de Man, "The Epistemology of Metaphor," *Critical Inquiry* 5.1 (Autumn 1978), 21.
55. Miller, *Ariadne's Thread*, 118.
56. Miller, *Ariadne's Thread*, 119.
57. Ultimately, however, my use of "catachresis" is less specific than Miller's. I follow Peter Goodrich in treating catachresis as "the exemplary source of linguistic novelty because it is the most extreme form of metaphor or altered use." Peter Goodrich, "catachresis," in *Routledge Encyclopedia of Narrative Theory*, ed. David Herman, Manfred Jahn, and Marie-Laure Ryan (London: Routledge, 2005), 47.
58. From the *St. James Gazette* (Nov. 1895), quoted in Williams, *Critical Heritage*, 429.
59. V.S. Pritchett, *George Meredith and English Comedy* (London: Chatto and Windus, 1970), 46.
60. Pritchett, *George Meredith*, 46.
61. Here my argument crosses paths with that of Nicholas Dames, who argues not simply that Meredith's "discontinuous" style "slows reading down" but also that it "detemporalizes it altogether, making the causally related, anticipatory momentum of novel-reading-as-usual submit to a series of disconnected flashes of insight or bafflement" (*Physiology*, 167–68). I think Dames is right that Meredith focuses our attention on "the small moment of sense making or comprehension" (168) but I am less inclined to see the

reading process, or Meredith's own account of consciousness, as essentially "fragmented" (175).

62. Richard Steele, "From My Own Apartment, October 24," *The Tatler* 85 (25 Oct. 1709).
63. "Christmas Games: Snapdragon," in *The Book of Days: A Miscellany of Popular Antiquities*, ed. Robert Chambers (London and Edinburgh: W. and R. Chambers, 1864), 738.
64. Pritchett, *George Meredith*, 46.
65. Pritchett, *George Meredith*, 46.
66. George Meredith, *Celt and Saxon* (New York: Scribner's, 1916), 207.
67. Meredith thus participates in a nineteenth-century tradition that finds its other greatest exponents in Carlyle and Emily Brontë, whose dense and knotty styles may be linked to their broadly romantic (that is, revisionary) outlooks.
68. George Meredith, *Beauchamp's Career*, ed. Margaret Harris (Oxford: Oxford University Press, 1988), 20.

Afterword: Stylistic Virtue and Literary Value

1. Booth, *Company*, 92.
2. Gaut offers the best summary of these claims as elaborated within contemporary Anglo-American aesthetics in *Art, Emotion, and Ethics*, chap. 7–9.
3. Booth, *Company*, 196.
4. Alan Donagan, *The Theory of Morality* (Chicago: University of Chicago Press, 1977), 1, quoted in Nardin, *Trollope and Victorian Moral Philosophy*, 3.
5. T.S. Eliot, "Tradition and the Individual Talent," in *The Selected Prose of T.S. Eliot*, ed. Frank Kermode (London: Faber and Faber, 1975), 37.
6. T.S. Eliot, "Religion and Literature," in *Selected Prose*, ed. John Hayward (London: Penguin, 1953), 35.
7. North, *Literary Criticism*, 22.
8. I.A. Richards, *Principles of Literary Criticism* (1924; London: Routledge and Kegan Paul, 1976), 54.
9. I.A. Richards, *Science and Poetry* (London: Kegan Paul, Trench, and Trubner, 1926), 56.
10. Frank Sibley, "Particularity, Art and Evaluation (1974)," in *Approach to Aesthetics: Collected Papers on Philosophical Aesthetics*, ed. John Benson, Betty Redfern, and Jeremy Roxbee Cox (Oxford: Oxford University Press, 2001), 88–103.
11. Sibley, "Particularity," 92.

12. Daniel Statman, "Introduction to Virtue Ethics," in *Virtue Ethics: A Critical Reader*, ed. Daniel Statman (Edinburgh: Edinburgh University Press, 1997), 14.
13. Gaut, *Art, Emotions, and Ethics*, chap. 3 provides a useful overview. For the major sources, see Noël Carroll, "Moderate Moralism," *British Journal of Aesthetics* 36.3 (July 1996): 223–38; Carroll, "Moderate Moralism versus Moderate Autonomism," *British Journal of Aesthetics* 38.4 (Oct. 1998): 419–24; Carroll, "Art and Ethical Criticism: An Overview of Recent Directions of Research," *Ethics* 110.2 (Jan. 2000): 350–87; James C. Anderson and Jeffrey T. Dean, "Moderate Autonomism," *British Journal of Aesthetics* 38.2 (Apr. 1998): 150–66; Oliver Conolly, "Ethicism and Moderate Moralism," *British Journal of Aesthetics* 40.3 (July 2000): 302–16; and Gaut, *Art, Emotion, and Ethics*, chap. 10, for his own theory of "merited response."
14. Peter Goldie, "Towards a Virtue Theory of Art," *The British Journal of Aesthetics* 47.4 (2007), 373.
15. Goldie, "Towards a Virtue Theory," 373.
16. Goldie, "Towards a Virtue Theory," 373.
17. Peter Goldie, "Virtues of Art and Human Well-Being," *Proceedings of the Aristotelian Society Supplementary Volume* 82 (2008), 181.
18. On the whole, Goldie argues that aesthetic virtues are more like Aristotle's "intellectual," or skills-based, virtues than his ethical ones, in part because we do not indict the character of a person who lacks them in the same way. See Peter Goldie, "Virtues of Art and Human Well-Being," 182–87.
19. Goldie, "Virtues of Art and Human Well-Being," 187.
20. Peter Goldie, "Virtues of Art," *Philosophy Compass* 5.10 (2010), 833.
21. Dominic McIver Lopes, "Virtues of Art: Good Taste," *Proceedings of the Aristotelian Society Supplementary Volume* 82 (2008), 203–04.
22. Lopes, "Virtues of Art," 204.
23. Alison Hills, "Moral and Aesthetic Virtue," *Proceedings of the Aristotelian Society* 118.3 (Oct. 2018), 268.
24. Hadley, *Living Liberalism*, 25.
25. Thomas, *Cultivating Victorians*, 47.
26. As Richards puts it, "all those [fundamental conditions] which we have enumerated as desirable in the recipient are also necessary in the artist. He is pre-eminently accessible to external influences and discriminating with regard to them. He is distinguished further by the freedom in which all these impressions are held in suspension and the ease with which they form new relations between themselves" (*Principles*, 139–40). Compare to Wilde: "It is a strange thing, this transference of emotion. We sicken with the same maladies as the poets, and the singer lends us his pain . . . There is no passion

that we cannot feel, no pleasure that we may not gratify, and we can choose the time of our initiation and the time of our freedom also. Life! Life! Don't let us go to life for our fulfilment or our experience. It is a thing narrowed by circumstances, incoherent in its utterance, and without that fine correspondence of form and spirit which is the only thing that can satisfy the artistic and critical temperament" (*Intentions*, 164–65). Felski's *The Limits of Critique* is in many ways an extended defense of the paradoxical freedom that arises from disciplining a narrow-minded temperament: "Reining in critique is not a matter of trying to impose a single mood upon the critic but of striving for a greater receptivity to the multifarious and many-shaded moods of texts" (12), something that can only be accomplished when we "expand our repertoire of critical moods while embracing a richer array of critical methods" (13). For Stephen Best and Sharon Marcus, the celebration of freedom *from* "the text's deceptive, ideological surface" ought to be contrasted with the freedom *to* maintain "a true openness to all the potentials made available by texts," recalling the difference between negative and positive liberty that has animated much twentieth-century liberal thought. Stephen Best and Sharon Marcus, "Surface Reading: An Introduction," *Representations* 108.1 (Fall 2009), 17, 16.

27. De Quincey, "On Murder Considered as One of the Fine Arts," *Blackwood's Edinburgh Magazine* 21.122 (Feb. 1827), 200–01.

Bibliography

Able, August Henry III. *George Meredith and Thomas Love Peacock: A Study in Literary Influence*. Philadelphia: University of Pennsylvania, 1933.

Adams, James Eli. *Dandies and Desert Saints*. Ithaca: Cornell University Press, 1995.

Adolph, Robert. "On the Possibility of a History of Prose Style." *Style* 15.4 (Fall 1981): 435–50.

"The Adventures of Philip." *The Spectator* 1780 (9 Aug. 1862): 885–86.

"aesthetic, n. and adj." *OED Online*. Oxford: Oxford University Press, July 2018. www.oed.com/view/Entry/3237.

Agnew, Lois Peters. *Thomas De Quincey: British Rhetoric's Romantic Turn*. Carbondale: Southern Illinois University Press, 2012.

Aitken, David. "'A Kind of Felicity': Some Notes about Trollope's Style." *Nineteenth-Century Fiction* 20.4 (Mar. 1966): 337–53.

Alison, Archibald. *Essays on the Nature and Principles of Taste*. 2nd ed. Hartford: George Goodwin, 1821.

Allen, Brooke. "Sadness Balancing Wit: Thackeray's Life and Works." *The New Criterion* (Jan. 2001): 19–28.

Allison, Sarah. *Reductive Reading: A Syntax of Victorian Moralizing*. Baltimore: Johns Hopkins University Press, 2018.

Altinel, A. Savkar. *Thackeray and the Problem of Realism*. Frankfurt am Main: Peter Lang, 1986.

Anderson, Amanda. *Bleak Liberalism*. Chicago: University of Chicago Press, 2016.

The Powers of Distance: Cosmopolitanism and the Cultivation of Detachment. Princeton: Princeton University Press, 2001.

The Way We Argue Now: A Study in the Cultures of Theory. Princeton: Princeton University Press, 2006.

Anderson, James C. and Jeffrey T. Dean. "Moderate Autonomism." *British Journal of Aesthetics* 38.2 (Apr. 1998): 150–66.

Anderson, Warren D. *Matthew Arnold and the Classical Tradition*. Ann Arbor: University of Michigan Press, 1971.

Anisman, Martin J. Introduction to *The Luck of Barry Lyndon: A Critical Edition*, ed. Martin J. Anisman. New York: NYU Press, 1970.

Anscombe, Elizabeth. "Modern Moral Philosophy." *Philosophy* 33 (1958): 1–19.

apRoberts, Ruth. *The Moral Trollope*. Athens: Ohio University Press, 1971.

Archer, William. "Robert Louis Stevenson: His Style and His Thought." *Time* 13.11 (Nov. 1885): 581–91.

Aristotle. *Art of Rhetoric*. Trans. J.H. Freese. Cambridge: Harvard University Press, 1926.

Art of Rhetoric. Trans. H.C. Lawson-Tancred. London: Penguin, 1991.

Nicomachean Ethics. Trans. H. Rackman. Cambridge: Harvard University Press, 1926.

Nicomachean Ethics. Trans. David Ross. Rev. ed. Oxford: Oxford University Press, 1998.

Poetics. Trans. Stephen Halliwell. Cambridge: Harvard University Press, 1995.

Poetics. Trans. Malcolm Heath. London: Penguin, 1996.

Arnold, Matthew. *Culture and Anarchy*. Ed. Jane Garnett. Oxford: Oxford University Press, 2006.

"The Function of Criticism at the Present Time." In *The Complete Prose Works of Matthew Arnold*, ed. R.H. Super, vol. 3, 258–90. Ann Arbor: University of Michigan Press, 1962.

"Marcus Aurelius." In *The Complete Prose Works of Matthew Arnold*, ed. R. H. Super, vol. 3, 133–57. Ann Arbor: University of Michigan Press, 1962.

"Preface to First Edition of *Poems* (1853)." In *The Complete Prose Works of Matthew Arnold*, ed. R.H. Super, vol. 1, 1–15. Ann Arbor: University of Michigan Press, 1960.

"The Study of Poetry." In *The Complete Prose Works of Matthew Arnold*, ed. R. H. Super, vol. 11, 161–88. Ann Arbor: University of Michigan Press, 1973.

Ashton, Rosemary. *The German Idea*. Cambridge: Cambridge University Press, 1980.

Bakhtin, M.M. *The Dialogic Imagination: Four Essays*. Ed. Michael Holquist. Austin: University of Texas Press, 1981.

Bain, Alexander. *English Composition and Rhetoric*. New York: D. Appleton and Company, 1871. Reprint, Delmar, NY: Scholars' Facsimiles and Reprints, 1996.

Bainton, George, ed. *The Art of Authorship: Literary Reminiscences, Methods of Work, and Advice to Young Beginners*. New York: Appleton, 1891.

Baldick, Chris. *The Social Mission of English Criticism: 1848–1932*. Oxford: Clarendon Press, 1983.

Ball, Terence. "The Formation of Character: Mill's 'Ethology' Reconsidered." *Polity* 33.1 (Fall 2000): 25–48.

Bator, Paul G. "The Formation of the Regius Chair of Rhetoric and Belles Lettres at the University of Edinburgh." *Quarterly Journal of Speech* 75.1 (1989): 40–64.

Beer, Gillian. *Meredith: A Change of Masks: A Study of the Novels*. London: Athlone Press, 1970.

Belsey, Catherine. *Critical Practice*. London: Methuen, 1980.

Bender, John and David E. Wellbery. "Rhetoricality: On the Modernist Return of Rhetoric." In *The Ends of Rhetoric: History, Theory, Practice*, ed. John Bender and David E. Wellbery, 3–39. Stanford: Stanford University Press, 1990.

Berlin, James A. *Writing Instruction in Nineteenth-Century American Colleges.* Carbondale: Southern Illinois University Press, 1984.

Best, Stephen and Sharon Marcus. "Surface Reading: An Introduction." *Representations* 108.1 (Fall 2009): 1–21.

Bevilacqua, Vincent M. "Adam Smith's Lectures on Rhetoric and Belles Lettres." *Studies in Scottish Literature* 3.1 (1965): 41–60.

"Adam Smith and Some Philosophical Origins of Eighteenth-Century Rhetorical Theory." *Modern Language Review* 63.3 (July 1968): 559–68.

Bevis, Matthew. *The Art of Eloquence: Byron, Dickens, Tennyson, Joyce.* Oxford: Oxford University Press, 2007.

Blair, Hugh. *Lectures on Rhetoric and Belles Lettres.* 2 vols. London: Strachan, Cadell, and Creech, 1783.

Bloom, Harold. Introduction to *Walter Pater: Modern Critical Views*, ed. Harold Bloom, 1–21. New York: Chelsea, 1985.

Blythe, Helen Lucy. "Forms of Storytelling, Repetition, and Voice in Anthony Trollope's *Kept in the Dark.*" In *The Routledge Research Companion to Anthony Trollope*, ed. Deborah Denenholz Morse, Margaret Markwick, and Mark W. Turner, 177–89. London: Routledge, 2017.

Bogel, Frederic V. *New Formalist Criticism: Theory and Practice.* Basingstoke: Palgrave, 2013.

Booth, Bradford A. "Trollope on the Novel." In *Essays Critical and Historical*, 219–31. Berkeley: University of California Press, 1950.

Booth, Wayne C. *The Company We Keep: An Ethics of Fiction.* Berkeley: University of California Press, 1998.

The Rhetoric of Fiction. Chicago: University of Chicago Press, 1961.

Bosanquet, Bernard. *A History of Aesthetic.* 1892. London: Allen and Unwin, 1922.

"Science and Philosophy" and Other Essays. London: Allen and Unwin, 1927.

Three Lectures on Aesthetic. London: Macmillan, 1915.

Brace, Gerald Warner. "The World of Anthony Trollope." In *The Trollope Critics*, ed. N. John Hall, 99–109. London: Macmillan, 1981.

Bradley, James. "Hegel in Britain: A Brief History of British Commentary and Attitudes (1)." *Heythrop Journal* 20.1 (1979): 1–24.

Brimley, George. "Thackeray's Esmond." *Spectator* 25 (6 Nov. 1852): 1066–67.

Brink, David O. Editor's Introduction to *Prolegomena to Ethics*, by T.H. Green, ed. David O. Brink, xiii-cx. Oxford: Clarendon Press, 2003.

Brinton, Alan. "Quintilian, Plato, and the Vir Bonus." *Philosophy and Rhetoric* 16.3 (1983): 167–84.

Broad, C.D. *Five Types of Ethical Theory.* London: Routledge and Kegan Paul, 1930.

Brown, Julia Prewitt. *Cosmopolitan Criticism: Oscar Wilde's Philosophy of Art.* Charlottesville: University Press of Virginia, 1997.

Brownell, W.C. *The Genius of Style.* London and New York: Scribner's, 1924.

Victorian Prose Masters. New York: AMC Press, 1901.

Buffon, Georges-Louis Leclerc. "Discourse on Style." In *Theories of Style in Literature*, ed. Lane Cooper, 162–79. New York: Macmillan, 1923.

"Buffon: His Life and Writings." *The British Quarterly Review* 13.25 (Feb. 1851): 125–59.

Burke, Michael. "Stylistics: From Classical Rhetoric to Cognitive Neuroscience." In *The Routledge Handbook of Stylistics*, ed. Michael Burke, 1–7. London: Routledge, 2014.

ed. *The Routledge Handbook of Stylistics*. London: Routledge, 2014.

Busse, Beatrix. "(New) Historical Stylistics." In *The Routledge Handbook of Stylistics*, ed. Michael Burke, 101–17. London: Routledge, 2014.

Cabot, Frederick C. "The Two Voices in Thackeray's *Catherine*." *Nineteenth-Century Fiction* 28.4. (1974): 404–16.

Camlot, Jason. *Style and the Nineteenth-Century British Critic: Sincere Mannerisms*. Burlington: Ashgate, 2008.

Campbell, George. *The Philosophy of Rhetoric*. New edition, with the author's last additions and corrections. 1808. New York: Harper and Brothers, 1841. Reprint, Delmar, NY: Scholars' Facsimiles and Reprints, 1992.

Carey, John. *Thackeray: Prodigal Genius*. London: Faber, 1977.

Carlyle, Thomas. *Sartor Resartus*. Ed. Kerry McSweeney and Peter Sabor. Oxford: Oxford University Press, 1987.

Carroll, Noël. "Art and Ethical Criticism: An Overview of Recent Directions of Research." *Ethics* 110.2 (Jan. 2000): 350–87.

"Moderate Moralism." *British Journal of Aesthetics* 36.3 (July 1996): 223–38.

"Moderate Moralism versus Moderate Autonomism." *British Journal of Aesthetics* 38.4 (Oct. 1998): 419–24.

"catachresis." In *The Oxford Companion to English Literature*, ed. Dinah Birch. Oxford: Oxford University Press, 2009. https://www.oxfordreference.com/view/10.1093/acref/9780192806871.001.0001/acref-9780192806871-e-1387.

Cheah, Pheng and Bruce Robbins, eds. *Cosmopolitics: Thinking and Feeling beyond the Nation*. Minneapolis: University of Minnesota Press, 1998.

Colby, Robert A. "Thackeray's Credo." *The Review of English Studies*, New Series 15.60 (Nov. 1964): 381–96.

Cecil, Lord David. *Early Victorian Novelists: Essays in Revaluation*. New York: Bobbs-Merrill, 1935.

Cecil, H.M. "George Meredith." *The Free Review: A Monthly Magazine* (1 Aug. 1894): 398–418.

"Christmas Games: Snapdragon." In *The Book of Days: A Miscellany of Popular Antiquities*, ed. Robert Chambers, 738–39. London and Edinburgh: W. and R. Chambers, 1864.

Cicero. *Orator*. Trans. H.M. Hubbell. Cambridge: Harvard University Press, 1962.

Clark, John W. *The Language and Style of Anthony Trollope*. London: Andre Deutsch, 1975.

Cluett, Robert. *Prose Style and Critical Reading*. New York: Teachers College Press, 1981.

Collini, Stefan. *Public Moralists: Political Thought and Intellectual Life in Britain 1850–1930*. Oxford: Clarendon Press, 1991.

Colvin, Sidney. *Memories and Notes of Persons and Places*. New York: Scribner's, 1921.

Connolly, Joy. "Virile Tongues: Rhetoric and Masculinity." In *A Companion to Roman Rhetoric*, ed. William Dominik and John Hall, 83–97. London: Blackwell, 2007.

Connolly, Oliver. "Ethicism and Moderate Moralism." *British Journal of Aesthetics* 40.3 (July 2000): 302–16.

Connors, Robert. *Composition-Rhetoric: Backgrounds, Theory, and Pedagogy*. Pittsburgh: University of Pittsburgh Press, 1997.

Cope, Edward Meredith. *An Introduction to Aristotle's Rhetoric, with Analysis Notes and Appendices*. London and Cambridge: Macmillan and Co., 1867. Reprint, Hildesheim: Georg Olms Verlag, 1970.

Costelloe, Timothy M. *The British Aesthetic Tradition: From Shaftesbury to Wittgenstein*. Cambridge: Cambridge University Press, 2013.

Court, Franklin E. *Institutionalizing English Literature*. Stanford: Stanford University Press, 1992.

Craig, David. *John Ruskin and the Ethics of Consumption*. Charlottesville: University Press of Virginia, 2006.

Crawford, Robert. *Devolving English Literature*. Oxford: Clarendon Press, 1992.

Crisp, Roger. *The Cosmos of Duty: Henry Sidgwick's Methods of Ethics*. Oxford: Oxford University Press, 2015.

Croll, Morris. *Style, Rhetoric, and Rhythm*. Ed. J. Max Patrick and Robert O. Evans. Princeton: Princeton University Press, 1966.

Cronin, Mark. "Henry Gowan, William Makepeace Thackeray, and 'The Dignity of Literature' Controversy." *Dickens Quarterly* 16.2 (June 1999): 104–15.

Crowley, Sharon. *The Methodical Memory: Invention in Current Traditional Rhetoric*. Carbondale: Southern Illinois University Press, 1990.

Dale, Leigh. "T.H. Green and the Modern Novel: English at Oxford." *Modern Language Quarterly* 75.2 (June 2014): 239–57.

Daley, Kenneth. "From the Theoretic to the Practical: Ruskin, British Aestheticism, and the Relation of Art to Use." *Prose Studies* 20.2 (1997): 90–107.

Dames, Nicholas. *The Physiology of the Novel: Reading, Neural Science, and the Form of Victorian Fiction*. Oxford: Oxford University Press, 2007.

Daston, Lorraine J. and Peter Louis Galison. *Objectivity*. New York: Zone, 2007.

Davies, Hugh Sykes. "Trollope and His Style." *A Review of English Literature* 1.4 (Oct. 1960): 73–85.

Davies, Stephen. "Authors' Intentions, Literary Interpretation, and Literary Value." *British Journal of Aesthetics* 46.3 (July 2006): 223–47.

Musical Meaning and Expression. Ithaca: Cornell University Press, 1994.

Day, Henry Noble. *Elements of the Art of Rhetoric: Adapted for Use in Colleges and Academies, and for Private Study*. 3rd ed. New York: A.S. Barnes and Co., 1853.

The Science of Aesthetics; or, The Nature, Kinds, Laws, and Uses of Beauty. New Haven: C.C. Chatfield and Co., 1872.

Defoe, Daniel. *Roxana*. Ed. John Mullan. Oxford: Oxford University Press, 1996.
De Man, Paul. "The Epistemology of Metaphor." *Critical Inquiry* 5.1 (Autumn 1978): 13–30.
Demetrius. *Demetrius on Style*. Trans. W. Rhys Roberts. Cambridge: Cambridge University Press, 1902.
Dennis, John. "Style in Literature." *Time* 13.7 (July 1885): 71–77.
De Quincey, Thomas. *Essays on Style, Rhetoric, and Language*. Ed. Fred Scott. Boston: Allyn and Bacon, 1893.
"On Murder Considered as One of the Fine Arts." *Blackwood's Edinburgh Magazine* 21.122 (Feb. 1827): 199–213.
Dewey, John. "Review of *A History of Aesthetic*." *The Philosophical Review* 2.1 (Jan. 1893): 63–69.
Dickens, Charles. "In Memoriam." *Cornhill Magazine* 9.50 (Feb. 1864): 129–32.
Dowling, Linda. *Hellenism and Homosexuality in Victorian Oxford*. Ithaca: Cornell University Press, 1994.
Downs, Jack M. "David Masson, Belles Lettres, and a Victorian Theory of the Novel." *Victorian Literature and Culture* 43.1 (Mar. 2015): 1–21.
Eagleton, Terry. *The Ideology of the Aesthetic*. Oxford: Blackwell, 1990.
"The Ideology of the Aesthetic." *Poetics Today* 9.2 (1988): 327–38.
Literary Theory: An Introduction. Oxford: Basil Blackwell, 1983.
Earle, John. *English Prose: Its Elements, History, and Usage*. London: Smith, Elder, and Co., 1890.
Edgecombe, Rodney Stenning. "Eighteenth-Century Allusions in *Henry Esmond*." *Style* 51.1 (2017): 17–24.
Ehninger, Douglas. "Dominant Trends in English Rhetorical Thought, 1750–1800." *Southern Journal of Communication* 18.1 (1952–53): 3–12.
Eliot, George. *The Mill on the Floss*. Ed. A.S. Byatt. Oxford: Oxford University Press, 2008.
The Writings of George Eliot. Vol. 22. Boston: Houghton and Mifflin, 1908.
Eliot, T.S. "Arnold and Pater." *The Bookman: A Review of Books and Life* 72.1 (1930): 1–7.
"Religion and Literature." In *Selected Prose*, ed. John Hayward, 31–42. London: Penguin, 1953.
"Tradition and the Individual Talent." In *The Selected Prose of T.S. Eliot*, ed. Frank Kermode, 37–44. London: Faber and Faber, 1975.
Encyclopedia Metropolitana. 2nd ed. Vol. 1. London: John Joseph Griffin and Co., 1849.
Engell, James. *The Creative Imagination*. Harvard: Harvard University Press, 1981.
Episodes of Fiction, or Choice Stories from the Great Novelists. Edinburgh: William P. Nimmo, 1870.
Epperly, Elizabeth. *Patterns of Repetition in Trollope*. Washington, DC: Catholic University of America Press, 1989.
Evangelista, Stefano. *British Aestheticism and Ancient Greece: Hellenism, Reception, Gods in Exile*. New York: Palgrave Macmillan, 2009.
Fanger, Donald. "Meredith as Novelist." *Nineteenth-Century Fiction* 16.4 (Mar. 1962): 317–28.

Farina, Jonathan. *Everyday Words and the Character of Prose in Nineteenth-Century Britain*. Cambridge: Cambridge University Press, 2017.
Felski, Rita. *The Limits of Critique*. Chicago: University of Chicago Press, 2017.
Fenner, David E.W. *Art in Context: Understanding Aesthetic Value*. Athens: Swallow Press/Ohio University Press, 2008.
Ferreira-Buckley, Linda. "Nineteenth-Century Rhetoric." In *Encyclopedia of Rhetoric and Composition: Communication from Ancient Times to the Information Age*, ed. Theresa Enos, 468–73. New York: Routledge, 1996.
"Writing Instruction in Eighteenth- and Nineteenth-Century Great Britain: Continuity and Change, Transitions and Shifts." In *A Short History of Writing Instruction: From Ancient Greece to Contemporary America*, ed. James J. Murphy, 3rd ed., 172–208. New York: Routledge, 2012.
Ferreira-Buckley, Linda and S. Michael Halloran. Editor's Introduction to *Lectures on Rhetoric and Belles Lettres*, by Hugh Blair, xv–liv. Carbondale: Southern Illinois University Press, 2005.
Fielding, Henry. *The Life of Jonathan Wild the Great*. Ed. Claude Rawson. Oxford: Oxford University Press, 2003.
Fish, Stanley. *Is There a Text in This Class? The Authority of Interpretive Communities*. Cambridge: Harvard University Press, 1980.
ed. *Seventeenth-Century Prose: Modern Essays in Criticism*. New York: Oxford University Press, 1971.
Fisher, Judith Law. "Historical Introduction." *The Adventures of Philip on His Way Through the World, Shewing Who Robbed Him, Who Helped Him, and Who Passed Him By*, by William Makepeace Thackeray, 535–70. Ann Arbor: University of Michigan Press, 2010.
Thackeray's Skeptical Narrative and the "Perilous Trade" of Authorship. Burlington: Ashgate, 2002.
Fletcher, Ian. "Walter Pater." In *Walter Pater: Modern Critical Views*, ed. Harold Bloom, 41–73. New York: Chelsea, 1985.
Forster, E.M. *Aspects of the Novel*. New York: Harcourt, 1927.
Forsyth, William. "Literary Style." *Fraser's Magazine* 55.327 (Mar. 1857): 249–64.
Fowler, Roger. *Linguistic Criticism*. Oxford: Oxford University Press, 1986.
Linguistics and the Novel. London: Methuen, 1977.
Frye, Northrop. *Anatomy of Criticism*. Princeton: Princeton University Press, 1957.
Gagnier, Regenia. *Individualism, Decadence, and Globalization: On the Relationship of Part to Whole, 1859–1920*. Basingstoke: Palgrave, 2010.
Gallie, Roger D. *Thomas Reid: Ethics, Aesthetics, and the Anatomy of the Self*. Dordrecht: Kluwer Academic Publishers, 1998.
Garcha, Amanpal. *From Sketch to Novel: The Development of Victorian Fiction*. Cambridge: Cambridge University Press, 2009.
Gaut, Berys. *Art, Emotion, and Ethics*. Oxford: Oxford University Press, 2007.
Gibbs, Raymond W. Jr. *The Poetics of Mind: Figurative Thought, Language, and Understanding*. Cambridge: Cambridge University Press, 1994.
Gilbert, Katherine. "Ruskin's Relation to Aristotle." *Philosophical Review* 49.1 (1940): 52–62.

Gill, Michael B. "Lord Shaftesbury [Anthony Ashley Cooper, Third Earl of Shaftesbury]." *The Stanford Encyclopedia of Philosophy*, July 2011, http://plato.stanford.edu/archives/fall2008/entries/shaftesbury/.

"Lord Shaftesbury [Anthony Ashley Cooper, Third Earl of Shaftesbury]." *The Stanford Encyclopedia of Philosophy*, Sept. 2019, https://plato.stanford.edu/entries/shaftesbury/.

Gillies, John. *A New Translation of Aristotle's Rhetoric with an Introduction and Appendix, Explaining Its Relation to His Exact Philosophy, and Vindicating that Philosophy, by Proofs that All Departures from It Have Been Deviations into Error.* London and Edinburgh: Cadell and Blackwood, 1823.

Gilmour, Robin. *The Idea of the Gentleman in the Victorian Novel.* New York: Routledge, 1981.

Golden, James L., Goodwin F. Berquest, William E. Coleman, and J. Michael Sproule. *The Rhetoric of Western Thought.* 8th ed. USA: Kendall/Hunt, 2004.

Golden, James L., and Edward P.J. Corbett. Introduction to *The Rhetoric of Blair, Campbell, and Whately*, 1–22. New York: Holt, Rinehart and Winston, 1968.

Goldie, Peter. *On Personality.* London: Routledge, 2004.

"Towards a Virtue Theory of Art." *The British Journal of Aesthetics* 47.4 (2007): 372–87.

"Virtues of Art." *Philosophy Compass* 5.10 (2010): 830–39.

"Virtues of Art and Human Well-Being." *Proceedings of the Aristotelian Society Supplementary Volume* 82 (2008): 179–95.

Goodlad, Lauren. "Trollopian Form: An Introduction." *Literature Compass* 7.9 (2010): 851–54.

Victorian Liberalism and the Victorian State: Character and Governance in Liberal Society. Baltimore: Johns Hopkins University Press, 2003.

Goodlad, Lauren and Julia M. Wright. "Introduction and Keywords." In "Victorian Internationalisms," ed. Lauren Goodlad and Julia M. Wright. Special issue, *Romanticism and Victorianism on the Net* 48 (Nov. 2007), doi 10.7202/017435ar.

Goodrich, Peter. "catachresis." In *Routledge Encyclopedia of Narrative Theory*, ed. David Herman, Manfred Jahn, and Marie-Laure Ryan, 47. London: Routledge, 2005.

Gordon, Ian A. *The Movement of English Prose.* Bloomington: Indiana University Press, 1966.

Gosse, Edward. *Gossip in a Library.* New York: Scribner's, 1914.

Graff, Gerald. *Professing Literature: An Institutional History.* Twentieth Anniversary Ed. Chicago: University of Chicago Press, 2007.

Grech, Leanne. *Oscar Wilde's Aesthetic Education: The Oxford Classical Curriculum.* New York: Palgrave Macmillan, 2019.

Green, T.H. *An Estimate of the Value and Influence of Works of Fiction in Modern Times.* 1862. Ed. Fred Newton Scott. Ann Arbor: The Ann Arbor Press, 1911.

Prolegomena to Ethics. Ed. David O. Brink. Oxford: Clarendon Press, 2003.

Gronbeck, Bruce E. "Ehninger, Douglas W. (1913–1979)." In *Encyclopedia of Rhetoric and Composition: Communication from Ancient Times to the Information Age*, ed. Theresa Enos, 204. New York: Routledge, 1996.

Grote, John. *An Examination of the Utilitarian Philosophy*. Cambridge: Deighton Bell, 1870.

A Treatise on the Moral Ideals. Cambridge: Deighton Bell, 1876.

Guillory, John. "Mercury's Words: The End of Rhetoric and the Beginning of Prose." *Representations* 138.1 (Spring 2017): 59–86.

Gulliver, Harold. *Thackeray's Literary Apprenticeship: A Study of the Early Newspaper and Magazine Work of William Makepeace Thackeray*. Valdosta: Southern Stationary and Printing Company, 1934.

Gutmann, Amy and Dennis Thompson. "Why Deliberative Democracy Is Different." In *Liberalism: Critical Concepts in Political Theory*, ed. G. W. Smith, vol. 4: The Limits of Liberalism, 274–93. London: Routledge, 2002.

Hadley, Elaine. *Living Liberalism: Practical Citizenship in Mid-Victorian Britain*. Chicago: University of Chicago Press, 2010.

Hall, Donald E. *Muscular Christianity: Embodying the Victorian Age*. Cambridge: Cambridge University Press, 1994.

Halloran, S. Michael. "Aristotle's Concept of Ethos, or if Not His Somebody Else's." *Rhetoric Review* 1.1 (Sept. 1982): 58–63.

Hanley, Keith and Brian Maidment. Introduction to *Persistent Ruskin: Studies in Influence, Assimilation and Effect*, ed. Keith Hanley and Brian Maidment, 1–14. London: Routledge, 2016.

Harden, Edgar F. *Thackeray the Writer: From Journalism to Vanity Fair*. Basingstoke: Palgrave Macmillan, 1998.

Hardy, Thomas. *Tess of the D'Urbervilles*. Ed. Tim Dolin. London: Penguin, 2003.

Harrison, Frederic. *Studies in Early Victorian Literature*. London: Edward Arnold, 1895.

Harvey, Geoffrey. *The Art of Anthony Trollope*. New York: St. Martin's Press, 1980.

Harwood, John T., ed. *The Rhetorics of Thomas Hobbes and Bernard Lamy*. Carbondale: Southern Illinois University Press, 1986.

Hayward, Abraham. "Thackeray's Writings." *The Edinburgh Review* 87.175 (Jan. 1848): 46–67.

Henley, W.E. "Review of *The Egoist*." *The Athenaeum* 2714 (1 Nov. 1879): 555–56.

Hermogenes. *Hermogenes' On Types of Style*. Trans. Cecil W. Wooten. Chapel Hill: University of North Carolina Press, 1987.

Hills, Alison. "Moral and Aesthetic Virtue." *Proceedings of the Aristotelian Society* 118.3 (Oct. 2018): 255–74.

Horrocks, Clare. "Digital Thackeray: Preserving the Legacy?" In *Thackeray in Time: History, Memory, and Modernity*, ed. Richard Salmon and Alice Crossley, 152–68. Burlington: Ashgate, 2016.

Hough, Graham. *Style and Stylistics*. London: Routledge and Kegan Paul, 1969.

Howell, Wilbur Samuel. "Aristotle and Horace on Rhetoric and Poetics." In *Poetics, Rhetoric, and Logic: Studies in the Basic Disciplines of Criticism*, 45–72. Ithaca: Cornell University Press, 1975.

Eighteenth-Century British Rhetoric and Logic. Bristol: Thoemmes Press, 1999.
Logic and Rhetoric in England, 1500–1700. Bristol: Thoemmes Press, 1999.
Howsam, Leslie, Christopher Stray, Alice Jenkins, James A. Secord, and Anna Vaninskaya. "What the Victorians Learned: Perspectives on Nineteenth-Century Schoolbooks." *Journal of Victorian Culture* 12.2 (2007): 262–85.
Hume, David. *An Enquiry Concerning the Principles of Morals*. Indianapolis: Hackett, 1983.
Hurka, Thomas. "The Three Faces of Flourishing." *Social Philosophy and Policy* 16.1 (Winter 1999): 44–71.
Hurley, Michael D. and Marcus Waithe. *Thinking through Style: Non-Fiction Prose of the Long Nineteenth Century*. Oxford: Oxford University Press, 2018.
Hurst, Isobel. "Victorian Literature and the Reception of Greece and Rome." *Literature Compass* 7.6 (June 2010): 484–95.
Hutton, R.H. "Nina Balatka." *Spectator* 40.23 (Mar. 1867): 329–30.
Inwood, Brad. *Ethics after Aristotle*. Cambridge: Harvard University Press, 2014.
Irwin, T.H. "Eminent Victorians and Greek Ethics." In *Essays on Henry Sidgwick*, ed. Bart Schultz, 279–310. Cambridge: Cambridge University Press, 1992.
Iser, Wolfgang. *The Implied Reader: Patterns of Communication in Prose Fiction from Bunyan to Beckett*. Baltimore: Johns Hopkins University Press, 1974.
"The Reading Process: A Phenomenological Approach." *New Literary History* 3.2 (Winter 1972): 279–99.
Walter Pater: The Aesthetic Moment. Trans. David Henry Wilson. Cambridge: Cambridge University Press, 1987.
Ives, Maura C. "Introduction: Meredith's *New Quarterly Magazine* Writing: Comedy, the Male Writer, and the Female Reader." In *Meredith's Essay on Comedy and Other New Quarterly Magazine Publications*, ed. Maura C. Ives, 13–43. London: Associated Universities Press, 1998.
James, Henry. "Anthony Trollope." In *Literary Criticism: Essays on Literature, American Writers, English Writers*, 1330–54. New York: Library of America, 1984.
"The Art of Fiction." In *Literary Criticism: Essays on Literature, American Writers, English Writers*, 44–65. New York: Library of America, 1984.
"Guy de Maupassant." In *Literary Criticism: French Writers, Other European Writers, The Prefaces to the New York Edition*, 521–49. New York: Library of America, 1984.
"The Lesson of Balzac." In *Literary Criticism: French Writers, Other European Writers, The Prefaces to the New York Edition*, 115–39. New York: Library of America, 1984.
Jamieson, Alexander. *A Grammar of Rhetoric and Polite Literature*. London: G. and W.B. Whittaker, 1818.
Jarvis, Claire. *Exquisite Masochism: Marriage, Sex, and the Novel Form*. Baltimore: Johns Hopkins University Press, 2016.
Jenkyns, Richard. *The Victorians and Ancient Greece*. Cambridge: Harvard University Press, 1980.

Johnson, Barbara. *A World of Difference*. Baltimore: Johns Hopkins University Press, 1987.

Johnson, Samuel. "Belles Lettres, n.s." *A Dictionary of the English Language*. Vol. 1. London: W. Strahan, 1755.

Lives of the Poets. Ed. Roger Lonsdale. Vol. 1. Oxford: Clarendon Press, 2006.

Jones, Richard Foster. "Science and English Prose Style in the Third Quarter of the Seventeenth Century." In *Seventeenth-Century Prose: Modern Essays in Criticism*, ed. Stanley E. Fish, 53–89. New York: Oxford University Press, 1971.

Kames, Lord Henry Home. *Elements of Criticism*. Ed. Peter Jones. 2 vols. Indianapolis: Liberty Fund, 2005.

Kendrick, Walter. *The Novel-Machine: The Theory and Fiction of Anthony Trollope*. Baltimore: Johns Hopkins University Press, 1980.

Kennedy, George A. "The Contributions of Rhetoric to Literary Criticism." In *The Cambridge History of Literary Criticism*, ed. H.B. Nisbet and Claude Rawson, vol. 4, 349–64. Cambridge: Cambridge University Press, 1997.

Kincaid, James. *The Novels of Anthony Trollope*. Oxford: Clarendon Press, 1977.

Knelman, Judith. "Trollope's Experiments with Anonymity." *Victorian Periodicals Review* 14.1 (Spring 1981): 21–24.

Korg, Jacob. "Expressive Styles in *The Ordeal of Richard Feverel*." *Nineteenth-Century Fiction* 27.3 (Dec. 1972): 253–67.

Kornbluh, Anna. *The Order of Forms: Realism, Formalism, and Social Space*. Chicago: University of Chicago Press, 2019.

Korsgaard, Christine. *Self-Constitution: Agency, Identity, Integrity*. New York: Oxford University Press, 2009.

Kurnick, David. *Empty Houses: Theatrical Failure and the Novel*. Princeton: Princeton University Press, 2012.

Landow, George P. *The Aesthetic and Critical Theories of John Ruskin*. Princeton: Princeton University Press, 1971.

Landy, Joshua. *How to Do Things with Fictions*. Oxford: Oxford University Press, 2012.

Leakey, James. "The Count de Buffon." *Saint Paul's* 5 (Oct. 1869): 81–97.

Leavis, F.R. *The Great Tradition*. 1948. London: Chatto and Windus, 1960.

Lee, Adam. "The Ethics of Contemplation: Pater's Reading of Aristotle." In *Pater the Classicist: Classical Scholarship, Reception, and Aestheticism*, ed. Charles Martindale, Stefano Evangelista, and Elizabeth Prettlejohn, 309–21. Oxford: Oxford University Press, 2017.

Lee-Lenfield, Spencer. "Translating Style: Flaubert's Influence on English Narrative Prose." *Modern Language Quarterly* 81.2 (June 2020): 193–217.

Legge, Alfred Owen. "Concerning Style." *The Manchester Quarterly* 2 (1883): 37–63.

Lesjak, Carolyn. "Reading Dialectically." *Criticism* 55.2 (Spring 2013): 233–77.

Letwin, Shirley Robin. *The Gentleman in Trollope: Individuality and Moral Conduct*. Cambridge: Harvard University Press, 1982.

Levine, Caroline. *Forms: Whole, Rhythm, Hierarchy, Network*. Princeton: Princeton University Press, 2015.

The Serious Pleasures of Suspense: Victorian Realism and Narrative Doubt. Charlottesville: University of Virginia Press, 2003.

Levine, George. *Dying to Know: Scientific Epistemology and Narrative in Victorian England*. Chicago: University of Chicago Press, 2010.

Levine, George and William Madden, eds. *The Art of Victorian Prose*. New York: Oxford University Press, 1968.

Levinson, Marjorie. "What Is New Formalism?" *PMLA* 122.2 (Mar. 2007): 558–69.

Lewes, G.H. *The Principles of Success in Literature*. 3rd ed. Boston: Allyn, 1891.

"Review of *Vanity Fair*." *The Athenaeum* 1085 (12 Aug. 1848): 794–97.

Litvak, Joseph. *Caught in the Act: Theatricality in the Nineteenth-Century English Novel*. Berkeley: University of California Press, 1992.

Lodge, David. *Language of Fiction: Essays in Criticism and Verbal Analysis of the English Novel*. London: Routledge and Kegan Paul, 1966.

Loesberg, Jonathan. *A Return to Aesthetics*. Stanford: Stanford University Press, 2005.

Loofbourow, John. *Thackeray and the Form of Fiction*. Princeton: Princeton University Press, 1964.

Lopes, Dominic McIver. "Virtues of Art: Good Taste." *Proceedings of the Aristotelian Society Supplementary Volume* 82 (2008): 197–211.

Lucas, F.L. *Style*. London: Cassell and Company, 1955.

MacIntyre, Alasdair. *A Short History of Ethics*. New York: Macmillan, 1966.

Maitzen, Rohan. "'The Soul of Art': Understanding Victorian Ethical Criticism." *English Studies in Canada* 31.2–3 (2005): 151–85.

Mallock, W.H. "Le Style C'est L'Homme." *The New Review* 6.35 (Apr. 1892): 441–54.

Martin, Theodore. "Thackeray's Works." *Westminster Review* 59.116 (1853): 363–88.

Masson, David. *British Novelists and Their Styles*. London: Macmillan, 1859.

"Notes and Documents: Masson's Inaugural Lecture." Ed. James R.M. Irvin and G. Jack Gravlee. *Studies in Scottish Literature* 14.1 (1979): 239–49.

"*Pendennis* and *Copperfield:* Thackeray and Dickens." *The North British Review* 15.29 (May 1851): 57–89.

Maurice, F.D. *Modern Philosophy, or A Treatise of Moral and Metaphysical Philosophy from the Fourteenth Century to the French Revolution, with a Glimpse into the Nineteenth Century*. London: Griffin, Bohn, and Co., 1862.

McKendy, Thomas. "Sources of Parody in Thackeray's *Catherine*." *Dickens Studies Annual* 23 (1994): 287–302.

McMaster, Juliet. "*Novels by Eminent Hands:* Sincerest Flattery from the Author of *Vanity Fair*." *Dickens Studies Annual* 18 (1989): 309–36.

Thackeray: The Major Novels. Toronto: University of Toronto Press, 1971.

Trollope's Palliser Novels: Theme and Pattern. New York: Oxford University Press, 1978.

Meador, Prentice A., Jr. "Quintilian's 'Vir Bonus.'" *Western Speech* 34.3 (1970): 162–69.

Meredith, George. *The Amazing Marriage*. London: Constable and Company, 1910.

Beauchamp's Career. Ed. Margaret Harris. Oxford: Oxford University Press, 1988.

Celt and Saxon. New York: Scribner's, 1916.

Diana of the Crossways: A Novel. London: Constable and Company, 1910.

The Egoist. Ed. George Woodcock. London: Penguin, 1987.

An Essay on Comedy and the Uses of the Comic Spirit. In *Meredith's Essay on Comedy and Other New Quarterly Magazine Publications*, ed. Maura C. Ives, 114–45. London: Associated Universities Press, 1998.

The Letters of George Meredith. Ed. Clarence Lee Cline. Vol 2. Oxford: Oxford University Press, 1970.

The Ordeal of Richard Feverel. New York: Random House, 1950.

The Shaving of Shagpat. London: Chapman and Hall, 1856.

The Shaving of Shagpat. New York: Ballantine, 1970.

Merritt, Travis R. "Taste, Opinion, and Theory in the Rise of Victorian Prose Stylism." In *The Art of Victorian Prose*, ed. George Levine and William Madden, 3–38. New York: Oxford University Press, 1968.

Milic, Louis T. "Rhetorical Choice and Stylistic Option: The Conscious and Unconscious Poles." In *Literary Style: A Symposium*, ed. Seymour Chatman, 77–94. New York: Oxford University Press, 1971.

"Stylistics." In *Encyclopedia of Rhetoric and Composition: Communication from Ancient Times to the Information Age*, ed. Theresa Enos, 703–08. New York: Routledge, 1996.

Mill, J.S. *On Liberty and Utilitarianism*. New York: Bantam, 2003.

System of Logic: Ratiocinative and Inductive: Being a Connected View of the Principles of Evidence and the Methods of Scientific Investigation. 8th ed. Vol. 2. London: Longmans, Green, Reader, and Dyer, 1872.

Miller, Andrew H. *The Burdens of Perfection: On Ethics and Reading in Nineteenth-Century British Literature*. Ithaca: Cornell University Press, 2008.

Miller, J. Hillis. *Ariadne's Thread: Story Lines*. New Haven: Yale University Press, 1992.

Fiction and Repetition: Seven English Novels. Cambridge: Harvard University Press, 1982.

Miller, Thomas P. *The Formation of College English: Rhetoric and Belles Lettres in the British Cultural Provinces*. Pittsburgh: University of Pittsburgh Press, 1997.

"The Formation of College English: A Survey of the Archives of Eighteenth-Century Rhetorical Theory and Practice." *Rhetoric Society Quarterly* 20.3 (Summer 1990): 261–86.

Minto, William. "Bosanquet's *History of Aesthetic*." *Bookman* 3.13 (Oct. 1892): 24–25.

Morgan, Benjamin. "Aesthetic Freedom: Walter Pater and the Politics of Autonomy." *ELH* 77.3 (Fall 2010): 731–56.

The Outward Mind: Materialist Aesthetics in Victorian Science and Literature. Chicago: University of Chicago Press, 2017.

Morgan, Thaïs. "Reimagining Masculinity in Victorian Criticism: Swinburne and Pater." *Victorian Studies* 36.3 (Spring 1993): 315–32.

"Victorian Effeminacies." In *Victorian Sexual Dissidence*, ed. Richard Dellamora, 109–26. Chicago: University of Chicago Press, 1999.

Morley, John. *Aphorisms*. Delivered before the Edinburgh Philosophical Institution Nov. 11, 1887. London: Macmillan, 1887.

"Mr. Swinburne's New Poems." *Saturday Review* (4 Aug. 1866): 145–47.

Morse, Deborah Denenholz, Margaret Markwick, and Mark W. Turner, eds. *The Routledge Research Companion to Anthony Trollope*. London: Routledge, 2017.

Morson, Gary Saul and Caryl Emerson. *Mikhail Bakhtin: Creation of a Prosaics*. Stanford: Stanford University Press, 1990.

Nardin, Jane. *Trollope and Victorian Moral Philosophy*. Athens: Ohio University Press, 1996.

Newman, John Henry. *The Idea of a University, Defined and Illustrated*. 3rd ed. London: Basil, Montagu, Pickering, 1873.

North, Joseph. *Literary Criticism: A Concise Political History*. Cambridge: Harvard University Press, 2017.

Nussbaum, Martha. *Love's Knowledge: Essays on Philosophy and Literature*. Oxford: Oxford University Press, 1990.

Ohmann, Richard M. "Prolegomena to the Analysis of Prose Style." In *Style in Prose Fiction*, ed. Harold C. Martin, 1–24. New York: Columbia University Press, 1958.

Pantůčková, Lidmila. "The Relationship of W.M. Thackeray to Henry Fielding." *Sborník Prací Filosofické Fakulty Brněnské U* D.9 (1962): 99–114.

Parker, David. "Thackeray's Barry Lyndon." *Ariel: A Review of International English Literature* 6.4 (1975): 68–80.

Pater, Walter. *Appreciations, with an Essay on Style*. Evanston: Northwestern University Press, 1987.

Marius the Epicurean. Ed. Michael Levy. London: Penguin, 1985.

The Renaissance: Studies in Art and Poetry. Ed. Adam Phillips. Oxford: Oxford University Press, 1986.

Patey, Douglas Lane. "The Eighteenth Century Invents the Canon." *Modern Language Studies* 18.1 (Winter 1988): 17–37.

"The Institution of Criticism in the Eighteenth Century." In *The Cambridge History of Literary Criticism*, ed. H.B. Nisbet and Claude Rawson, vol. 4, 3–31. Cambridge: Cambridge University Press, 1997.

Patterson, Annabel M. *Hermogenes and the Renaissance: Seven Ideas of Style*. Princeton: Princeton University Press, 1970.

Pawelski, James O. and D.J. Moores, eds. *The Eudaimonic Turn: Well-Being in Literary Studies*. Madison: Fairleigh Dickinson University Press, 2013.

Pearson, Richard. *W.M. Thackeray and the Mediated Text: Writing for Periodicals in the Mid-Nineteenth Century*. London: Routledge, 2017.

Peltason, Timothy. "Seeing Things as They Are: Literary Judgment and Disinterestedness." *Literary Imagination* 9.2 (2007): 177–94.

Pernot, Laurent. *Rhetoric in Antiquity*. Trans. W.E. Higgins. Washington, DC: Catholic University of America Press, 2005.

Phillipps, K.C. *The Language of Thackeray*. London: Andre Deutsch, 1978.

Pope, Alexander. *The Poetry and Prose of Alexander Pope*. Ed. Aubrey Williams. London: Houghton Mifflin, 1969.

Poster, Carol. "Pedagogy and Bibliography: Aristotle's *Rhetoric* in Nineteenth-Century England." *Rhetoric Society Quarterly* 31.2 (Spring 2001): 5–35.

"Whose Aristotle? Which Aristotelianism?: A Historical Prolegomenon to Thomas Farrell's *Norms of Rhetorical Culture*." *Philosophy and Rhetoric* 41.4 (2008): 375–97.

Prickett, Stephen. "England: Romantic Legacies." In *The Cambridge History of Literary Criticism*, ed. M.A.R Habib, vol. 6, 154–71. Cambridge: Cambridge University Press, 2013.

Pritchett, V.S. *George Meredith and English Comedy*. London: Chatto and Windus, 1970.

Purcell, William M. "A Reassessment of Adam Smith's Lectures on Rhetoric and Belles Lettres." *Communication Studies* 37:1 (1986): 45–54.

"Style." In *Encyclopedia of Rhetoric and Composition: Communication from Ancient Times to the Information Age*, ed. Theresa Enos, 698–702. New York: Routledge, 1996.

Quintilian. *Institutio Oratoria*. Trans. David A. Russell. Cambridge: Harvard University Press, 2001.

Rahv, Philip. "Fiction and the Criticism of Fiction." *The Kenyon Review* 18.2 (Spring 1956): 276–99.

Raleigh, Walter. *The English Novel: Being a Short Sketch of Its History from the Earliest Times to the Appearance of Waverley*. 5th ed. London: John Murray, 1911.

"*Style*." London: Edward Arnold, 1897. Reprint, New York: Garland Publishing, 1986.

Rancière, Jacques. *The Politics of Aesthetics*. Trans. Gabriel Rockhill. New York: Continuum, 2004.

Ransom, John Crowe. "Criticism, Inc." *The Virginia Quarterly Review* 13.4 (Autumn 1937): 586–602.

"The Understanding of Fiction." *The Kenyon Review* 12.2 (Spring 1950): 189–218.

Rawlins, Jack P. *Thackeray's Novels: A Fiction that Is True*. Berkeley: University of California Press, 1974.

Rawls, John. Foreword to *The Methods of Ethic*, by Henry Sidgwick. 7th ed. Indianapolis: Hackett, 1981.

Rawson, Claude. *Satire and Sentiment, 1660–1830: Stress Points in the English Augustan Tradition*. Cambridge: Cambridge University Press, 2000.

Ray, Gordon. *Thackeray: The Age of Wisdom 1847–1863*. New York: McGraw-Hill, 1958.

Thackeray: The Uses of Adversity 1811–1846. New York: McGraw-Hill, 1955.
Reid, Thomas. *Essays on the Intellectual Powers of Man*. Edinburgh: John Bell, 1785.
Richards, I.A. *The Philosophy of Rhetoric*. New York: Oxford University Press, 1936.
Principles of Literary Criticism. 1924. London: Routledge and Kegan Paul, 1976.
Science and Poetry. London: Kegan Paul, Trench, and Trubner, 1926.
Riggle, Nick. "Personal Style and Artistic Style." *The Philosophical Quarterly* 65.261 (Oct. 2015): 711–31.
Roberts, Neil. *Meredith and the Novel*. Basingstoke: Macmillan Press, 1997.
Roberts, Tom. "Aesthetic Virtues: Traits and Faculties." *Philosophical Studies* 175.2 (Feb. 2018): 429–47.
Robertson, John M. "Concerning Preciosity." *Yellow Book* 13 (1897): 79–106.
Robinson, Jenefer M. "Style and Personality in the Literary Work." *The Philosophical Review* 94.2 (Apr. 1985): 227–47.
"Style and Significance in Art History and Art Criticism." *The Journal of Aesthetics and Art Criticism* 40.1 (Fall 1981): 5–14.
Rogers, Reginald A.P. *A Short History of Greek Ethics*. London: Macmillan, 1921.
Rosenthal, Jesse. *Good Form: The Ethical Experience of the Victorian Novel*. Princeton: Princeton University Press, 2017.
Ross, Iain. *Oscar Wilde and Ancient Greece*. Cambridge: Cambridge University Press, 2012.
Ross, Trevor. *The Making of the English Literary Canon: From the Middle Ages to the Late Eighteenth Century*. Montreal: McGill-Queen's University Press, 1998.
Rousseau, George S. *Nervous Acts: Essays on Literature, Culture, and Sensibility*. Basingstoke: Palgrave Macmillan, 2004.
Ruskin, John. *Lectures on Art Delivered before the University of Oxford in Hilary Term, 1870*. New York: Maynard, 1893.
Modern Painters. Vol. 2. London: Allen, 1903.
The Stones of Venice. 3 vols. London: Smith, 1853.
Russell, David. *Tact: Aesthetic Liberalism and the Essay Form in Nineteenth-Century Britain*. Princeton: Princeton University Press, 2017.
Ryan, Vanessa L. *Thinking without Thinking in the Victorian Novel*. Baltimore: Johns Hopkins University Press, 2012.
Sadleir, Michael. *Anthony Trollope: A Commentary*. Boston: Houghton Mifflin, 1927.
Saintsbury, George. *Corrected Impressions: Essays on Victorian Writers*. New York: Dodd, Mead, and Co., 1895.
Introduction to *The Oxford Thackeray*. Vol. 6: *The Memoirs of Barry Lyndon, Esq*., and the Miscellaneous Papers Written between 1843 and 1847, ix-xxii. London: Oxford University Press, 1908.
"Modern English Prose." *Fortnightly Review* 19.110 (Feb. 1876): 243–59.
Schneewind, J.B. *Essays on the History of Moral Philosophy*. Oxford: Oxford University Press, 2010.
Sidgwick's Ethics and Victorian Moral Philosophy. Oxford: Oxford University Press, 1986.

Schweizer, Harold. "Literary Autonomy: The Growth of a Modern Concept." In *The Cambridge History of Literary Criticism*, ed. Rafey Habib, vol. 6, 231–50. Cambridge: Cambridge University Press, 2013.

Scott, William Robert. *Adam Smith as Student and Professor*. Glasgow: Jackson, 1937.

Seneca the Younger. "Styles and Morals." In *Ancient Literary Criticism: The Principal Texts in New Translations*, ed. D.A. Russell and M. Winterbottom, 362–67. Oxford: Clarendon Press, 1983.

Shaftesbury, Anthony Ashley Cooper (Third Earl of). *Characteristics of Men, Manners, Opinions, Times*. Ed. Lawrence E. Klein. Cambridge: Cambridge University Press, 1999.

Sharpe, Lesley. *Schiller's Aesthetic Essays: Two Centuries of Criticism*. Columbia: Camden House, 1995.

Shillingsburg, Peter L. Review of *The Luck of Barry Lyndon: A Critical Edition*, by William Makepeace Thackeray, ed. Martin J. Anisman. *The Papers of the Bibliographical Society of America* 66.2 (1972): 219–23.

Shirilan, Stephanie. "The Forbidden Pleasures of Style: Seventeenth-Century Prose in Twentieth-Century Criticism." *Prose Studies* 34.2 (Aug. 2012): 115–28.

Shklovsky, Viktor. "Art as Technique." In *Critical Theory Since Plato*, ed. Hazard Adams, rev. ed., 750–59. Fort Worth: Harcourt Brace, 1992.

Shuger, Debora K. "Conceptions of Style." In *The Cambridge History of Literary Criticism*, ed. George Kennedy, vol. 3, 176–86. Cambridge: Cambridge University Press, 1999.

Shuter, William. "History as Palingenesis in Pater and Hegel." *PMLA* 86.3 (1971): 411–21.

Sibley, Frank. "Making Music Our Own." In *The Interpretation of Music: Philosophical Essays*, ed. Michael Krausz, 165–76. Oxford: Oxford University Press, 1993.

"Particularity, Art and Evaluation." In *Approach to Aesthetics: Collected Papers on Philosophical Aesthetics*, ed. John Benson, Betty Redfern, and Jeremy Roxbee Cox, 88–103. Oxford: Oxford University Press, 2001.

Sidgwick, Henry. *Lectures on the Ethics of T.H. Green, Mr. Herbert Spencer, and J. Martineau*. London: Macmillan, 1902.

The Methods of Ethics. London: Macmillan, 1874.

The Methods of Ethics. 2nd ed. London: Macmillan, 1877.

The Methods of Ethics. 7th ed. Foreword by John Rawls. Indianapolis: Hackett, 1981.

Miscellaneous Essays and Addresses. London: Macmillan, 1904.

Outlines of the History of Ethics for English Readers. 1886. Boston: Beacon Press, 1960.

"The Prophet of Culture." In *Culture and Anarchy*, by Matthew Arnold, ed. Jane Garnett, 157–72. Oxford: Oxford University Press, 2006.

Siegel, Jonah. "Victorian Aesthetics." In *The Oxford Handbook of Victorian Literary Culture*, ed. Juliet John, 561–79. Oxford: Oxford University Press, 2016.

Simons, Gary. "Thackeray's Articles in the *Morning Chronicle.*" *Studies in Bibliography* 59.1 (2015): 249–68.

"Thackeray's Contributions to the *Times.*" *Victorian Periodicals Review* 40.4 (Winter 2007): 332–54.

Skilton, David J. *Anthony Trollope and His Contemporaries: A Study in the Theory and Conventions of Mid-Victorian Fiction*. London: Macmillan, 1972.

Smiles, Samuel. *Character*. London: John Murray, 1876.

Smith, Adam. *Lectures on Rhetoric and Belles Lettres*. The Glasgow Edition of the Works and Correspondence of Adam Smith, ed. J.C. Bryce, vol. 4. Oxford: Oxford University Press, 1983.

Smith, Craig R. "Constructing a Neo-Romantic Rhetorical Theory." *Western Journal of Communication* 80.2 (Mar.–Apr. 2016): 220–37.

Snow, C.P. *Trollope: His Life and Art*. New York: Charles Scribner's Sons, 1975.

Sorlin, Sandrine. "Three Major Handbooks in Three Years: Stylistics as a Mature Discipline." *Language and Literature* 25.3 (Aug. 2016): 286–301.

Spencer, Herbert. *Philosophy of Style: An Essay*. With notes by the editor. New York: D. Appleton, 1884.

Stang, Richard. *The Theory of the Novel in England, 1850–1870*. London: Routledge and Kegan Paul, 1959.

Statman, Daniel. "Introduction to Virtue Ethics." In *Virtue Ethics: A Critical Reader*, ed. Daniel Statman, 1–41. Edinburgh: Edinburgh University Press, 1997.

Stebbins, Lucy and Richard Stebbins. *The Trollopes: The Chronicle of a Writing Family*. London: Secker and Warburg, 1947.

Steele, Richard. "From My Own Apartment, October 24." *The Tatler* 85 (25 Oct. 1709).

Steiner, George. *On Difficulty and Other Essays*. Oxford: Oxford University Press, 1978.

Stevenson, Robert Louis. "On Style in Literature: Its Technical Elements." *The Contemporary Review* 47 (Apr. 1885): 548–61.

Stockwell, Peter and Sara Whiteley, eds. *The Cambridge Handbook of Stylistics*. Cambridge: Cambridge University Press, 2014.

Stolnitz, Jerome. "On the Origins of 'Aesthetic Disinterestedness.'" *The Journal of Aesthetics and Art Criticism* 20.2 (Winter 1961): 131–43.

Stopper, M.R. [Jonathan Barnes]. "Greek Philosophy and the Victorians." *Phronesis* 26.3 (1981): 267–85.

Stray, Christopher. *Classics Transformed: Schools, Universities, and Society in England, 1830–1960*. Oxford: Clarendon Press, 1998.

"style, n." *OED Online*. Oxford: Oxford University Press, June 2020. www.oed.com/view/Entry/192315.

Sundell, M.G. "Thackeray Criticism: Its Fortunes and Misfortunes." *Novel* 4.3 (Fall 1972): 513–21.

Super, R.H. "Truth and Fiction in Trollope's Autobiography." *Nineteenth-Century Literature* 48.1 (June 1993): 74–88.

Sussman, Herbert. *Victorian Masculinities: Manhood and Masculine Poetics in Early Victorian Literature and Art*. Cambridge: Cambridge University Press, 1995.

Sussman, Matthew. "Meredith's Style." In *On Style in Victorian Fiction*, ed. Daniel Tyler, 244–62. Cambridge: Cambridge University Press, 2021.

"Optative Form in Anthony Trollope's *The Small House at Allington.*" *Nineteenth-Century Literature* 71.4 (Mar. 2017): 485–515.

Sutherland, James. *On English Prose*. Toronto: University of Toronto Press, 1957.

Sutherland, John. "'Henry Esmond' and the Virtues of Carelessness." *Modern Philology* 68.4 (May 1971): 345–54.

Sweet, William. "British Idealist Philosophy of Religion." In *The Oxford Handbook of British Philosophy in the Nineteenth Century*, ed. W.J. Mander, 560–86. Oxford: Oxford University Press, 2014.

Swinburne, Algernon Charles. *Swinburne Replies*. Ed. Clyde Kenneth Hyder. Syracuse: Syracuse University Press, 1966.

Symonds, John Addington. *Essays Speculative and Suggestive*. Vol. 1. London: Chapman and Hall, 1890.

Symons, Arthur. "A Note on George Meredith." *The Fortnightly Review* (Nov. 1897): 673–78.

Taylor, D.J. Introduction to *The Newcomes*, by William Makepeace Thackeray, ed. D.J. Taylor, xviii–xxix. London: Everyman, 1994.

Tener, Robert H. "R.H. Hutton: Some Attributions." *Victorian Periodicals Newsletter* 6.2 (June 1973): 1–65.

Terry, R.C. *Anthony Trollope: The Artist in Hiding*. London: Macmillan, 1977.

Thackeray, William Makepeace. *Catherine: A Story*. London: Smith, Elder and Co., 1911.

Catherine: A Story. Ed. Sheldon Goldfarb. Ann Arbor: University of Michigan Press, 1999.

"The Dignity of Literature." *Morning Chronicle* 25033 (12 Jan. 1850): 4.

The History of Pendennis. Ed. John Sutherland. Oxford: Oxford University Press, 1999.

The Memoirs of Barry Lyndon, Esq. Ed. Andrew Sanders. Oxford: Oxford University Press, 1990.

"Men and Coats." *Fraser's Magazine* 24.140 (Aug. 1841): 208–217.

The Newcomes. Ed. D.J. Taylor. London: Everyman, 1994.

Novels by Eminent Hands. In *Burlesques*. New York: John B. Alden, 1883.

"Parisian Caricatures." *London and Westminster Review* 32.2 (Apr. 1839): 282–305.

The Yellowplush Correspondence, Jeames's Diary, The Great Hogarty Diamond, Etc. London: Macmillan, 1903.

Thirlwell, Angela. Introduction to *Nina Balatka*, by Anthony Trollope, v–xiii. London: Trollope Society, 1996.

Thomas, David Wayne. *Cultivating Victorians: Liberal Culture and the Aesthetic*. Philadelphia: University of Pennsylvania Press, 2004.

Thorpe, James. *The Sense of Style: Reading English Prose*. Hamden, CT: Archon Press, 1987.

Tillotson, Geoffrey. *Thackeray the Novelist*. London: Methuen, 1974.

ed. *Thackeray: The Critical Heritage*. London: Routledge, 1968.

Tillotson, Geoffrey and Kathleen Tillotson. *Mid-Victorian Studies*. London: Athlone Press, 1965.

"Titmarsh's Tour through Turkeydom." *Fraser's Magazine* 33 (Jan.–June 1846): 85–96.

Todorov, Tzvetan. "Structural Analysis of Narrative." *NOVEL: A Forum on Fiction* 3.1 (Autumn 1969): 70–76.

Toolan, Michael. "Stylistics." In *A Companion to Literary Theory*, ed. David H. Richter, 60–71. West Sussex: John Wiley and Sons, 2018.

"The Theory and Philosophy of Stylistics." In *The Cambridge Handbook of Stylistics*, ed. Peter Stockwell and Sara Whiteley, 13–31. Cambridge: Cambridge University Press, 2014.

Touster, Eva Beach. "The Literary Relationship of Thackeray and Fielding." *The Journal of English and German Philology* 46.4 (Oct. 1947): 383–94.

Townsend, Dabney. "Introduction: Aesthetics in the Eighteenth Century." In *Eighteenth-Century British Aesthetics*, ed. Dabney Townsend, 1–31. Amityville: Baywood, 1999.

Tracy, Robert. *Trollope's Later Novels*. Berkeley and Los Angeles: University of California Press, 1978.

Treitler, Leo. "Language and the Interpretation of Music." In *Music and Meaning*, ed. Jenefer Robinson, 23–56. Ithaca: Cornell University Press, 1997.

Trilling, Lionel. *Matthew Arnold*. 1939. New York: Harcourt, 1977.

Trollope, Anthony. *An Autobiography*. Ed. Michael Sadleir and Frederick Page. Oxford: Oxford University Press, 1999.

Barchester Towers. Ed. Michael Sadleir and Frederick Page. Oxford: Oxford University Press, 1998.

Can You Forgive Her? Ed. Stephen Wall. London: Penguin, 1986.

The Life of Cicero. Vol. 2. London: Chapman and Hall, 1880.

Nina Balatka: The Story of a Maiden of Prague. Ed. Angela Thirlwell. London: Trollope Society, 1996.

The Small House at Allington. Ed. Julian Thompson. London: Penguin, 1991.

Thackeray. New York: AMS Press, 1968.

Turner, Frank M. *The Greek Heritage in Victorian Britain*. New Haven and London: Yale University Press, 1984.

"Why the Greeks and Not the Romans in Victorian Britain?" In *Rediscovering Hellenism: The Hellenic Inheritance and the English Imagination*, ed. G. W. Clarke, 61–81. Cambridge: Cambridge University Press, 1989.

Turner, James. *Philology: The Forgotten Origins of the Modern Humanities*. Princeton: Princeton University Press, 2014.

Van Dam, Frederik. *Anthony Trollope's Late Style: Victorian Liberalism and Literary Form*. Edinburgh: Edinburgh University Press, 2016.

ed. *Edinburgh Companion to Anthony Trollope*. Edinburgh: Edinburgh University Press, 2019.

Van Ghent, Dorothy. *The English Novel: Form and Function*. New York: Rinehart, 1953.

"virtue, n." *OED Online*. Oxford: Oxford University Press, June 2020. www.oed.com/view/Entry/223835.

Walsh, W.H. "The Zenith of Greats." In *The History of the University of Oxford*, ed. M.G. Brock and M.C. Curthoys, vol. 7: Nineteenth-Century Oxford, Part 2, 311–27. Oxford: Oxford University Press, 2000.

Wellbery, David E. "The Transformation of Rhetoric." In *The Cambridge History of Literary Criticism*, ed. Marshall Brown, vol. 5, 185–202. Cambridge: Cambridge University Press, 2000.

Whalley, George. "On Translating Aristotle's *Poetics*." *University of Toronto Quarterly* 39.2 (Jan. 1970): 77–106.

Whately, Richard. *Elements of Rhetoric*. 1828. Nashville: Southern Methodist Publishing House, 1861. Reprint, Delmar, NY: Scholars' Facsimiles and Reprints, 1996.

Wheatley, James H. *Patterns in Thackeray's Fiction*. Cambridge: MIT Press, 1969.

White, Edward M. "Thackeray's Contributions to *Fraser's Magazine*." *Studies in Bibliography* 19 (1966): 67–84.

White, Hayden. "The Suppression of Rhetoric in the Nineteenth Century." In *The Rhetoric Canon*, ed. Brenda Deen Schildgen, 21–32. Detroit: Wayne State University Press, 1997.

Whiteley, Giles. *Aestheticism and the Philosophy of Death: Walter Pater and Post-Hegelianism*. New York: Legenda, 2010.

Wilde, Oscar. *De Profundis and Other Writings*. Ed. Hesketh Pearson. London: Penguin, 1986.

Intentions. London: James R. Osgood, McIlvaine, and Co., 1891.

"Mr. Pater's Last Volume." *Speaker* 1 (22 Mar. 1890): 319–20.

The Picture of Dorian Gray. Ed. Robert Mighall. London: Penguin, 2000.

Williams, Carolyn. *Transfigured World: Walter Pater's Aesthetic Historicism*. Ithaca: Cornell University Press, 1989.

Williams, Ioan. *George Meredith: The Critical Heritage*. London: Routledge, 2002.

Williamson, George. *The Senecan Amble: A Study in Prose Form from Bacon to Collier*. London: Faber and Faber, 1951.

Willis, Kirk. "The Introduction and Critical Reception of Hegelian Thought in Britain 1830–1900." *Victorian Studies* 32.1 (Autumn 1988): 85–111.

Wimsatt, W.K. and M.C. Beardsley "The Intentional Fallacy." *The Sewanee Review* 54.3 (July–Sep. 1946): 468–88.

Woolf, Virginia. "The Novels of George Meredith." In *The Common Reader: Second Series*, 226–36. London: Hogarth Press, 1948.

A Room of One's Own and Three Guineas. Hammersmith: Harper Collins, 2014.

Wright, Daniel. *Bad Logic: Reasoning about Desire in the Victorian Novel*. Baltimore: Johns Hopkins University Press, 2018.

Wright, T.H. "Style." *T.H. Macmillan's Magazine* 37.217 (Nov. 1877): 78–84.

Wyland, Russell M. "An Archival Study of Rhetoric Texts and Teaching at the University of Oxford, 1785–1821." *Rhetorica: A Journal of the History of Rhetoric* 21.3 (Summer 2003): 175–95.

Index

Page numbers for illustrations are given in *italics*.

CAMBRIDGE STUDIES IN NINETEENTH-CENTURY LITERATURE AND CULTURE

Titles published

1. *The Sickroom in Victorian Fiction: The Art of Being Ill* Miriam Bailin, *Washington University*
2. *Muscular Christianity: Embodying the Victorian Age* edited by Donald E. Hall, *California State University, Northridge*
3. *Victorian Masculinities: Manhood and Masculine Poetics in Early Victorian Literature and Art* Herbert Sussman, *Northeastern University, Boston*
4. *Byron and the Victorians* Andrew Elfenbein, *University of Minnesota*
5. *Literature in the Marketplace: Nineteenth-Century British Publishing and the Circulation of Books* edited by John O. Jordan, *University of California, Santa Cruz* and Robert L. Patten, *Rice University, Houston*
6. *Victorian Photography, Painting and Poetry* Lindsay Smith, *University of Sussex*
7. *Charlotte Brontë and Victorian Psychology* Sally Shuttleworth, *University of Sheffield*
8. *The Gothic Body: Sexuality, Materialism and Degeneration at the Fin de Siècle* Kelly Hurley, *University of Colorado at Boulder*
9. *Rereading Walter Pater* William F. Shuter, *Eastern Michigan University*
10. *Remaking Queen Victoria* edited by Margaret Homans, *Yale University* and Adrienne Munich, *State University of New York, Stony Brook*
11. *Disease, Desire, and the Body in Victorian Women's Popular Novels* Pamela K. Gilbert, *University of Florida*
12. *Realism, Representation, and the Arts in Nineteenth-Century Literature* Alison Byerly, *Middlebury College, Vermont*
13. *Literary Culture and the Pacific* Vanessa Smith, *University of Sydney*
14. *Professional Domesticity in the Victorian Novel Women, Work and Home* Monica F. Cohen
15. *Victorian Renovations of the Novel: Narrative Annexes and the Boundaries of Representation* Suzanne Keen, *Washington and Lee University, Virginia*
16. *Actresses on the Victorian Stage: Feminine Performance and the Galatea Myth* Gail Marshall, *University of Leeds*
17. *Death and the Mother from Dickens to Freud: Victorian Fiction and the Anxiety of Origin* Carolyn Dever, *Vanderbilt University, Tennessee*
18. *Ancestry and Narrative in Nineteenth-Century British Literature: Blood Relations from Edgeworth to Hardy* Sophie Gilmartin, *Royal Holloway, University of London*

19. *Dickens, Novel Reading, and the Victorian Popular Theatre* Deborah Vlock
20. *After Dickens: Reading, Adaptation and Performance* John Glavin, *Georgetown University, Washington DC*
21. *Victorian Women Writers and the Woman Question* edited by Nicola Diane Thompson, *Kingston University, London*
22. *Rhythm and Will in Victorian Poetry* Matthew Campbell, *University of Sheffield*
23. *Gender, Race, and the Writing of Empire: Public Discourse and the Boer War* Paula M. Krebs, *Wheaton College, Massachusetts*
24. *Ruskin's God* Michael Wheeler, *University of Southampton*
25. *Dickens and the Daughter of the House* Hilary M. Schor, *University of Southern California*
26. *Detective Fiction and the Rise of Forensic Science* Ronald R. Thomas, *Trinity College, Hartford, Connecticut*
27. *Testimony and Advocacy in Victorian Law, Literature, and Theology* Jan-Melissa Schramm, *Trinity Hall, Cambridge*
28. *Victorian Writing about Risk: Imagining a Safe England in a Dangerous World* Elaine Freedgood, *University of Pennsylvania*
29. *Physiognomy and the Meaning of Expression in Nineteenth-Century Culture* Lucy Hartley, *University of Southampton*
30. *The Victorian Parlour: A Cultural Study* Thad Logan, *Rice University, Houston*
31. *Aestheticism and Sexual Parody 1840–1940* Dennis Denisoff, *Ryerson University, Toronto*
32. *Literature, Technology and Magical Thinking, 1880–1920* Pamela Thurschwell, *University College London*
33. *Fairies in Nineteenth-Century Art and Literature* Nicola Bown, *Birkbeck, University of London*
34. *George Eliot and the British Empire* Nancy Henry, *The State University of New York, Binghamton*
35. *Women's Poetry and Religion in Victorian England: Jewish Identity and Christian Culture* Cynthia Scheinberg, *Mills College, California*
36. *Victorian Literature and the Anorexic Body* Anna Krugovoy Silver, *Mercer University, Georgia*
37. *Eavesdropping in the Novel from Austen to Proust* Ann Gaylin, *Yale University*
38. *Missionary Writing and Empire, 1800–1860* Anna Johnston, *University of Tasmania*
39. *London and the Culture of Homosexuality, 1885–1914* Matt Cook, *Keele University*
40. *Fiction, Famine, and the Rise of Economics in Victorian Britain and Ireland* Gordon Bigelow, *Rhodes College, Tennessee*
41. *Gender and the Victorian Periodical* Hilary Fraser, *Birkbeck, University of London* Judith Johnston and Stephanie Green, *University of Western Australia*
42. *The Victorian Supernatural* edited by Nicola Bown, *Birkbeck College, London* Carolyn Burdett, *London Metropolitan University* and Pamela Thurschwell, *University College London*

43. *The Indian Mutiny and the British Imagination* Gautam Chakravarty, *University of Delhi*
44 *The Revolution in Popular Literature: Print, Politics and the People* Ian Haywood, *Roehampton University of Surrey*
45. *Science in the Nineteenth-Century Periodical: Reading the Magazine of Nature* Geoffrey Cantor, *University of Leeds* Gowan Dawson, *University of Leicester* Graeme Gooday, *University of Leeds* Richard Noakes, *University of Cambridge* Sally Shuttleworth, *University of Sheffield* and Jonathan R. Topham, *University of Leeds*
46. *Literature and Medicine in Nineteenth-Century Britain from Mary Shelley to George Eliot* Janis McLarren Caldwell, *Wake Forest University*
47. *The Child Writer from Austen to Woolf* edited by Christine Alexander, *University of New South Wales* and Juliet McMaster, *University of Alberta*
48. *From Dickens to Dracula: Gothic, Economics, and Victorian Fiction* Gail Turley Houston, *University of New Mexico*
49. *Voice and the Victorian Storyteller* Ivan Kreilkamp, *University of Indiana*
50. *Charles Darwin and Victorian Visual Culture* Jonathan Smith, *University of Michigan-Dearborn*
51. *Catholicism, Sexual Deviance, and Victorian Gothic Culture* Patrick R. O'Malley, *Georgetown University*
52. *Epic and Empire in Nineteenth-Century Britain* Simon Dentith, *University of Gloucestershire*
53. *Victorian Honeymoons: Journeys to the Conjugal* Helena Michie, *Rice University*
54. *The Jewess in Nineteenth-Century British Literary Culture* Nadia Valman, *University of Southampton*
55. *Ireland, India and Nationalism in Nineteenth-Century Literature* Julia Wright, *Dalhousie University*
56. *Dickens and the Popular Radical Imagination* Sally Ledger, *Birkbeck, University of London*
57. *Darwin, Literature and Victorian Respectability* Gowan Dawson, *University of Leicester*
58. *"Michael Field": Poetry, Aestheticism and the Fin de Siècle* Marion Thain, *University of Birmingham*
59. *Colonies, Cults and Evolution: Literature, Science and Culture in Nineteenth-Century Writing* David Amigoni, *Keele University*
60. *Realism, Photography and Nineteenth-Century Fiction* Daniel A. Novak, *Lousiana State University*
61. *Caribbean Culture and British Fiction in the Atlantic World, 1780–1870* Tim Watson, *University of Miami*
62. *The Poetry of Chartism: Aesthetics, Politics, History* Michael Sanders, *University of Manchester*
63. *Literature and Dance in Nineteenth-Century Britain: Jane Austen to the New Woman* Cheryl Wilson, *Indiana University*
64. *Shakespeare and Victorian Women* Gail Marshall, *Oxford Brookes University*

65. *The Tragi-Comedy of Victorian Fatherhood* Valerie Sanders, *University of Hull*
66. *Darwin and the Memory of the Human: Evolution, Savages, and South America* Cannon Schmitt, *University of Toronto*
67. *From Sketch to Novel: The Development of Victorian Fiction* Amanpal Garcha, *Ohio State University*
68. *The Crimean War and the British Imagination* Stefanie Markovits, *Yale University*
69. *Shock, Memory and the Unconscious in Victorian Fiction* Jill L. Matus, *University of Toronto*
70. *Sensation and Modernity in the 1860s* Nicholas Daly, *University College Dublin*
71. *Ghost-Seers, Detectives, and Spiritualists: Theories of Vision in Victorian Literature and Science* Srdjan Smajić, *Furman University*
72. *Satire in an Age of Realism* Aaron Matz, *Scripps College, California*
73. *Thinking About Other People in Nineteenth-Century British Writing* Adela Pinch, *University of Michigan*
74. *Tuberculosis and the Victorian Literary Imagination* Katherine Byrne, *University of Ulster, Coleraine*
75. *Urban Realism and the Cosmopolitan Imagination in the Nineteenth Century: Visible City, Invisible World* Tanya Agathocleous, *Hunter College, City University of New York*
76. *Women, Literature, and the Domesticated Landscape: England's Disciples of Flora, 1780–1870* Judith W. Page, *University of Florida* Elise L. Smith, *Millsaps College, Mississippi*
77. *Time and the Moment in Victorian Literature and Society* Sue Zemka, *University of Colorado*
78. *Popular Fiction and Brain Science in the Late Nineteenth Century* Anne Stiles, *Washington State University*
79. *Picturing Reform in Victorian Britain* Janice Carlisle, *Yale University*
80. *Atonement and Self-Sacrifice in Nineteenth-Century Narrative* Jan-Melissa Schramm, *University of Cambridge*
81. *The Silver Fork Novel: Fashionable Fiction in the Age of Reform* Edward Copeland, *Pomona College, California*
82. *Oscar Wilde and Ancient Greece* Iain Ross, *Colchester Royal Grammar School*
83. *The Poetry of Victorian Scientists: Style, Science and Nonsense* Daniel Brown, *University of Southampton*
84. *Moral Authority, Men of Science, and the Victorian Novel* Anne DeWitt, *Princeton Writing Program*
85. *China and the Victorian Imagination: Empires Entwined* Ross G. Forman, *University of Warwick*
86. *Dickens's Style* edited by Daniel Tyler, *University of Oxford*
87. *The Formation of the Victorian Literary Profession* Richard Salmon, *University of Leeds*

88. *Before George Eliot: Marian Evans and the Periodical Press* Fionnuala Dillane, *University College Dublin*
89. *The Victorian Novel and the Space of Art: Fictional Form on Display* Dehn Gilmore, *California Institute of Technology*
90. *George Eliot and Money: Economics, Ethics and Literature* Dermot Coleman, *Independent Scholar*
91. *Masculinity and the New Imperialism: Rewriting Manhood in British Popular Literature, 1870–1914* Bradley Deane, *University of Minnesota*
92. *Evolution and Victorian Culture* edited by Bernard Lightman, *York University, Toronto* and Bennett Zon, *University of Durham*
93. *Victorian Literature, Energy, and the Ecological Imagination* Allen MacDuffie, *University of Texas, Austin*
94. *Popular Literature, Authorship and the Occult in Late Victorian Britain* Andrew McCann, *Dartmouth College, New Hampshire*
95. *Women Writing Art History in the Nineteenth Century: Looking Like a Woman* Hilary Fraser Birkbeck, *University of London*
96. *Relics of Death in Victorian Literature and Culture* Deborah Lutz, *Long Island University, C. W. Post Campus*
97. *The Demographic Imagination and the Nineteenth-Century City: Paris, London, New York* Nicholas Daly, *University College Dublin*
98. *Dickens and the Business of Death* Claire Wood, *University of York*
99. *Translation as Transformation in Victorian Poetry* Annmarie Drury, *Queens College, City University of New York*
100. *The Bigamy Plot: Sensation and Convention in the Victorian Novel* Maia McAleavey, *Boston College, Massachusetts*
101. *English Fiction and the Evolution of Language, 1850–1914* Will Abberley, *University of Oxford*
102. *The Racial Hand in the Victorian Imagination* Aviva Briefel, *Bowdoin College, Maine*
103. *Evolution and Imagination in Victorian Children's Literature* Jessica Straley, *University of Utah*
104. *Writing Arctic Disaster: Authorship and Exploration* Adriana Craciun, *University of California, Riverside*
105. *Science, Fiction, and the Fin-de-Siècle Periodical Press* Will Tattersdill, *University of Birmingham*
106. *Democratising Beauty in Nineteenth-Century Britain: Art and the Politics of Public Life* Lucy Hartley, *University of Michigan*
107. *Everyday Words and the Character of Prose in Nineteenth-Century Britain* Jonathan Farina, *Seton Hall University, New Jersey*
108. *Gerard Manley Hopkins and the Poetry of Religious Experience* Martin Dubois, *Newcastle University*
109. *Blindness and Writing: From Wordsworth to Gissing* Heather Tilley, *Birkbeck College, University of London*
110. *An Underground History of Early Victorian Fiction: Chartism, Radical Print Culture, and the Social Problem Novel* Gregory Vargo, *New York University*

111. *Automatism and Creative Acts in the Age of New Psychology* Linda M. Austin, *Oklahoma State University*
112. *Idleness and Aesthetic Consciousness, 1815–1900* Richard Adelman, *University of Sussex*
113. *Poetry, Media, and the Material Body: Autopoetics in Nineteenth-Century Britain* Ashley Miller, *Albion College, Michigan*
114. *Malaria and Victorian Fictions of Empire* Jessica Howell, *Texas A&M University*
115. *The Brontës and the Idea of the Human: Science, Ethics, and the Victorian Imagination* edited by Alexandra Lewis, *University of Aberdeen*
116. *The Political Lives of Victorian Animals: Liberal Creatures in Literature and Culture* Anna Feuerstein, *University of Hawai'i-Manoa*
117. *The Divine in the Commonplace: Recent Natural Histories and the Novel in Britain* Amy King, *St John's University, New York*
118. *Plagiarizing the Victorian Novel: Imitation, Parody, Aftertext* Adam Abraham, *Virginia Commonwealth University*
119. *Literature, Print Culture, and Media Technologies, 1880–1900: Many Inventions* Richard Menke, *University of Georgia*
120. *Aging, Duration, and the English Novel: Growing Old from Dickens to Woolf* Jacob Jewusiak, *Newcastle University*
121. *Autobiography, Sensation, and the Commodification of Identity in Victorian Narrative: Life upon the Exchange* Sean Grass, *Rochester Institute of Technology*
122. *Settler Colonialism in Victorian Literature: Economics and Political Identity in the Networks of Empire* Phillip Steer, *Massey University, Auckland*
123. *Mimicry and Display in Victorian Literary Culture: Nature, Science and the Nineteenth-Century Imagination* Will Abberley, *University of Sussex*
124. *Victorian Women and Wayward Reading: Crises of Identification* Marisa Palacios Knox, *University of Texas Rio Grande Valley*
125. *The Victorian Cult of Shakespeare: Bardology in the Nineteenth Century* Charles LaPorte, *University of Washington*
126. *Children's Literature and the Rise of "Mind Cure": Positive Thinking and Pseudo-Science at the Fin de Siècle* Anne Stiles, *Saint Louis University, Missouri*
127. *Virtual Play and the Victorian Novel: The Ethics and Aesthetics of Fictional Experience* Timothy Gao, *Nanyang Technological University*
128. *Colonial Law in India and the Victorian Imagination* Leila Neti, *Occidental College, Los Angeles*
129. *Convalescence in the Nineteenth-Century Novel: The Afterlife of Victorian Illness* Hosanna Krienke, *University of Wyoming*
130. *Stylistic Virtue and Victorian Fiction: Form, Ethics, and the Novel* Matthew Sussman, *The University of Sydney*

Milton Keynes UK
Ingram Content Group UK Ltd.
UKHW020843130824
446880UK00009B/91

9 781108 96590